Eleanor Roosevelt's

BOOK OF
COMMON SENSE
ETIQUETTE

New York

THE MACMILLAN COMPANY

MACMILLAN NEW YORK, LONDON

W

Chapter 3 was originally published in REDBOOK

© ELEANOR ROOSEVELT 1962

Second Printing 1962

THE MACMILLAN COMPANY, NEW YORK
COLLIER-MACMILLAN CANADA, LTD., GALT, ONTARIO
DIVISIONS OF THE CROWELL-COLLIER PUBLISHING COMPANY
PRINTED IN THE UNITED STATES OF AMERICA
LIBRARY OF CONGRESS CATALOG CARD NUMBER: 62–19687
Designed by Andor Braun

To Mr. Robert O. Ballou I want to extend my warm thanks and deepest appreciation as without his careful research and writing this book would never have been written. Both of us wanted to help people, particularly young people, and I hope that the book conveys the sensitive feeling which Mr. Ballou put into it. The greatest reward that can perhaps come to both of us is that some people may find some difficult moments made easier

Eleanor Roosevelt

CONTENTS

Introduction

I HAVE UNDERTAKEN the writing of this book because I believe that a code of social conduct should emphasize somewhat more important matters than those which have often dominated the codes of former days.

Etiquette, from my point of view, is not just a matter of knowing how a lunch or dinner should be served, or what the "proper" behavior is in this or that situation. There are many correct ways of behaving in almost any situation, and many proper ways of doing those things for which there are precise rules in formal etiquette books. But the basis of all good human behavior is kindness. If you really act toward people in your home and out of it with kindness you will never go far wrong.

Yet the formal rules have, and always have had, a signal usefulness, and are worthy of respectful attention. Fortunately they are less stringent than they once were. Yet even though we have renounced some of them we ought not to belittle the impulse that brought them into being, for it is the very essence of man's desire to achieve self-respect and dignity.

In many cases not only kindness but morality and law are combined in our rules of etiquette. One of the best examples of this that I know is in the rules for proper driving Traffic laws, common decency, kindness, and etiquette almost always coincide when you are at the wheel of an automobile. So it is also in other matters.

Two of the most important advantages of knowing the conventional rules of behavior, it seems to me, are these· that knowledge of them gives the shy person a feeling of assurance, confidence, and ease when meeting, entertaining, or being entertained by others, and that the rules are always there and sometimes become useful shields against difficult situations. Many a rule of strict convention has been quite properly ignored under some circumstances by the finest young people (and older ones, too, for that matter). But there are times when one is glad to be able to fall back on the old dictates of the social arbiters and so escape a situation that might be embarrassing or even harmful.

I hope that this book will help to give a sense of confidence to young people who want to be friendly and hospitable whether living in the United States or visiting in other countries. At home the problems are perhaps slightly easier to meet, though it may take a little courage to realize that good manners demand that you behave in a natural way, that unless they are based in sincere goodwill they are meaningless, that when you invite people into your home your greatest courtesy is to give them the warmth of your friendliness rather than elaborate entertainment which is beyond your means, and that you are not worried if your ways are different from those of others, so long as there is no pretension and only kindliness in what you offer.

If you are abroad you have a greater responsibility. No matter where you go or how you go there you cannot escape your role as an ambassador for democracy, the political and spiritual philosophy of your country.

Democracy is a way of life, and ours is a representative Republic evolved by the people. It means living, without resort to violence, under the law established by the people. It means the willingness to abide by a majority decision. Its basis is a belief in the value of each individual. We who are democrats believe that, regardless of race, creed, or color, every human being has within him a spark of the divine, and this is what makes the individual so important that the government is his servant, in contrast to the Communist belief that individuals matter little; that they are of value simply as they serve the state.

When we are representatives of our beliefs in foreign lands it is all the more important that we show consideration and understanding of the customs and the beliefs of the people among whom we live, for to do otherwise is to negate the very principles of the democratic way of life.

I hope that you will find in this book the answer to any question of etiquette, however unexpected or unusual. I urge you to learn to know the rules of social usage and to follow them when to do so constitutes kindness. If ever you find yourself in a situation in which following a formal rule would be manifestly unkind, forget it, and be kind instead.

Eleanor Roosevelt

NEW YORK, APRIL, 1962.

I

GUIDES
FROM THE PAST

1

Manners of Other Days

ETIQUETTE IS A FRENCH WORD WHICH MEANS SIMPLY "ticket" or "label." During the reign of Louis XIV (1643–1715) the functions at the French Court were so elaborate that it became necessary to give every visitor a ticket (*une étiquette*) on which were listed the formalities he was expected to observe. Thus, his behavior, if correct, was "according to the ticket." It is in this sense that we have taken the word into English and it has come to mean a code of conduct or behavior that is considered socially correct.

But long before the French Court in all its complexity adopted this device, in fact long before Western civilization came into being, ancient philosophers were concerned with man's conduct in relation to his fellows. No people have ever paid closer attention to the matter of formal courtesy than the ancient Chinese. The *Li Ki*, compiled by Confucius over twenty-five hundred years ago, says, "Of all the methods for the ordering of man, there is none more urgent than the use of ceremonies." Yet Confucius, who was a stickler for the proprieties of social custom, cautioned against letting behavior become too elaborate "In this matter of rituals and ceremonies," he wrote, "rather than be extravagant, be simple."

There are numerous other examples from the Chinese, many of which are so solidly founded in common sense that they apply today For example, Chuang Tse (fifth century B C.) said simply: "If you are always offending others by your superiority, you will come to grief. Trying to make the customs of Chu succeed in Lu is like pushing a boat on land." To Chuang Tse society was "an agreement between a certain number of families and individuals to abide by certain customs."

The ancient sacred books of the Hindus and Buddhists also contain many excellent rules for behavior, some of which sound so modern that they might appear in one of today's etiquette columns. One of these cautions us against picking our teeth, blowing our noses loudly, yawning without covering our mouths, and biting our nails

I was told as a child that it was discourteous to eat everything on my plate when I was a guest To do so was an indication of greediness and implied that the hostess had not provided enough to eat. Indian children were told the same thing nearly two thousand years ago, for one of the *Puranas* cautions "Nor should a man eat so as nothing will be left of his meal."

My grandmother came to believe, however, that food was needed in the world and we who had an abundance should not waste it. Then I was cautioned never to take more on my plate than I could eat!

Some of the ancients showed a sophistication and understanding of tact that is quite astonishing. The *Mahabharata*, of India, composed between 200 B C. and A.D. 200, contains a rule which sounds as though it might have been written by the cynical eighteenth century writer Samuel Johnson: "Whoever desires to succeed in this world must be prepared to make deep bows, swear love and friendship, speak humbly and pretend to shed and wipe away tears."

It is particularly interesting to me that so many of these rules for good manners are recorded in the sacred books of the world's great religions. The authors seemed to feel that not only cleanliness but also courtesy are next to godliness and that what we now think of as "etiquette" is part of the religious life Many of the tenets in all the codes of behavior in the West have their origins in the Old and New Testaments of the Judeo-Christian tradition, in the teachings of the great rabbis, and in the words of the fathers of the Christian Church.

Though many of our guides to proper behavior come from ancient religious thought, we have inherited others from the early royal courts where manners were based on reverence to a sovereign and where knights were the standard-bearers of courtesy.

Today, a gentleman raises his hat to a lady because it is the accepted way of showing respect. Originally when a king's crown was the symbol of supreme authority and other head covering denoted the rank and power of the wearer, every man was expected to uncover his head in the presence of a higher rank and men of equal rank bared their heads in each other's presence. During the Middle Ages this courtesy was extended to women. As democratic principles spread and tended to level rank and privilege, the custom became gradually confined to meetings with women.

In the days when armed men approached each other warily, they extended a bared hand to demonstrate that no violence was contemplated. Today, the extended hand and the handclasp denote simply friendship.

Today, it is customary under certain circumstances to honor a visiting dignitary with a salute of guns. This, like the bare hand, originally promised a friendly reception. The guns, once fired, could no longer threaten the visitor.

In the early days of Puritan New England, codes of manners were part of an overall religious way of life and our stern Puritan forebears enforced these rules with the same vigor that they enforced religious obligations. Scandalmongering, cursing, name calling, and even jeering at others were offenses punishable by flogging, ducking, or being placed in the stocks.

Manuals of etiquette were widely circulated in America during the seventeenth and eighteenth centuries. Most came from England and were frequently adapted from Lord Chesterfield's advice to his son. These were bitterly denounced by many of the Puritans who felt that religion was the basis of all good conduct. Yet many of Chesterfield's admonitions, along with their urbanity, contained a common-sense wisdom and made an impact on the American consciousness that is still reflected in contemporary books of etiquette.

Take the tone of the company that you are in. . . . Do as you would be done by is the surest method that I know of pleasing. Advice is seldom welcome, and those who want it the most always like it the least. . . . Speak of the moderns without contempt and of the ancients without idolatry. . . . Wear your learning like your watch, in a private pocket; and do not pull it out and strike it merely to show that you have one.

Some of the greatest figures of American history found the subject of etiquette important enough to offer opinions. Among these were George Washington and Benjamin Franklin. "Reprehend not the imperfections of others," wrote Washington, "for that belongs to Parents, Masters and Superiors. . . . Contradict not at every turn what others say. . . . Spit not in the fire." He listed one hundred and ten precepts in all, ending with a statement that summed up the moral tone of his time: "Labour to keep alive in your breast that little spark of celestial fire called conscience."

Benjamin Franklin in *Poor Richard's Almanac* expressed his views equally succinctly and with wit "Love your neighbor, yet don't pull down your hedges. . . . Keep your eyes wide open before marriage, half shut afterwards. . . . None but the well-bred man knows how to confess a fault or acknowledge himself in error. . . . Fish and visitors stink in three days."

During the nineteenth century American etiquette books increased rapidly in numbers. Arthur M. Schlesinger reports that during the early decades of the century there was an average of over three new books on manners issued every year, many of them by well known and respected writers of the day.*

Among those who wrote on the subject were Harriet Beecher Stowe and Ralph Waldo Emerson. Neither actually wrote a manual of etiquette, but both commented on the fundamental principles of good manners; Mrs. Stowe in two chapters of a book on housekeeping, which she wrote in collaboration with her sister, and Emerson in two essays, on "Manners" and "Behavior."

Mrs. Stowe seemed to feel that a strict adherence to the principles of religious life was the proper road to good manners and behavior. But she also became quite specific about details, cautioning children to be silent at table "unless they be addressed by others," and urging everyone to avoid "all disgusting and personal habits such as fingering the hair, obtrusively using a toothpick or carrying one in the mouth after the needful use of it, cleaning the nails in the presence

* *Learning How to Behave· A Historical Study of American Etiquette Books,* by Arthur M. Schlesinger. New York, The Macmillan Company, 1947.

of others, picking the nose, snuffing instead of using a handkerchief, or . . . lifting up the boots or shoes as some men do to tend them on the knee."

Mrs. Stowe also gave her views on general table manners, drinking (she frowned on it), and other particulars of contemporary social conduct.

Emerson, of course, was less concerned with the outward manifestations of the social graces and more with the personal character of man and the underlying philosophical forces that are at the root of social intercourse.

Manners [Emerson wrote] aim to facilitate life, to get rid of impediments, and bring the man pure to energize. They aid our dealings and conversation, as a railway aids travel, by getting rid of all avoidable obstructions in the road, and leaving nothing to be conquered but pure space. These forms very soon become fixed, and a fine sense of propriety is cultivated with more heed, that it becomes a badge of social distinction.

His specific admonitions are few but noteworthy:

Let us not be too much acquainted. . . . Absence of heat and haste indicate fine qualities. . . . A gentleman makes no noise. a lady is serene— The first point of courtesy must always be truth. . . . I could better eat with one who did not respect the truth or the laws, than with a sloven and unpresentable person. . . . Society will pardon much to genius and special gifts, but being in its nature a convention, it loves what is conventional, or what belongs to coming together. That makes the good and bad of manners, what helps or hinders fellowship. . . . The favorites of society are what it calls whole souls, and able men, and of more spirit than wit, who have no uncomfortable egotism, but who exactly fill the hour and the company, contented and contenting, at a marriage or funeral, a ball or a jury, a water party or a shooting match.

Following the Civil War the preoccupation of Americans with etiquette seemed to increase. The rapid growth of huge personal fortunes was building a new social class in the United States, what one writer called "the sham aristocracy," founded on wealth The manners of the hereditary leisure class of Europe were aped, and many who had not yet made their fortunes yearned for the day when accumulated wealth might allow them to be "gentlemen" and their wives "ladies."

Popular magazines devoted a great deal of space to questions of etiquette, and Beatrice Fairfax and Dorothy Dix in the daily newspaper columns gave advice to the lovelorn and authoritative rulings on etiquette.

The story of whiskers and beards is an interesting example of the way fashions and customs change. From 1865 to 1885 when Grover Cleveland entered the White House every president of the United States was bearded and bewhiskered. Before the end of the smooth-shaven Cleveland's first term, however, a social arbiter announced that the beard was out of fashion. Many a fashionable young man ruefully watched his proudly grown adornment fall under the barber's razor.

As late as the turn of the century, smoking in the presence of ladies was considered improper, it was thought by many that even smoking by men was regrettable. President McKinley felt so strongly about his obligation to set a good example for the youth of the nation that he refused to be photographed with a cigar in his mouth. The social arbiters, ever alert, pointed out that no lady would be seen with a man who was smoking. When the public learned that Alice Roosevelt, President Theodore Roosevelt's oldest daughter, occasionally smoked a cigarette, a gasp of pained astonishment was audible throughout the nation.

World War I and the period that followed it brought a new sense of independence, especially to younger people, and the etiquette experts faced the dilemma of choosing between conduct which had been declared proper in the past and the actual behavior of their contemporaries, most of whom were "nice" people. New etiquette books poured into the market (sixty-eight of them appeared from 1918 to 1929, according to Schlesinger), but in many matters there was a considerable gulf between theory and practice While the experts struggled to bridge the gulf, their readers were often confused because of the rapid changes and the inconsistencies with which they were faced.

But the American middle class, more prosperous than ever before in history, raised the banner of freedom and self-expression and proceeded quite merrily to make its own rules.

No longer was a lady instructed on how to lift her skirt when she crossed the street. Skirts became so short that the problem was academic. No longer did a gentleman hesitate to smoke a cigarette in front of a lady. Indeed, he was no gentleman if he didn't offer one to his lady companion before lighting up himself. If he favored pipe or cigar, he might casually ask, "Do you mind?" before proceeding. The waltz, considered a dance of "loose character" only a few decades before, had given way to faster tempos, and far more intimate dance styles were developed with a minimum of head shaking and finger wagging.

Several influences tended to free us further from the ritual codes of behavior and to spread new concepts of manners during the years between the end of World War I and today. More and more jobs were filled by women, and the working wife became commonplace rather than an exception. With her achievement of greater economic freedom, a woman expected and took freedom in other matters, including the right to adapt the laws of social usage to her own situation. Women began to regulate their behavior more by common sense and by goodwill.

The far-flung distribution of our young men during and following World War II made it advisable for the United States Government to issue a series of guides for servicemen assigned to foreign countries describing the customs, and cautioning them to have respect for other people's manners and behavior. The realization that others had social customs that differed greatly from our own inevitably led to the conclusion that no social code was universally sacrosanct and implied that this was true for groups within our own country as well.

During these years the new profession of Public Relations made its impact on business and industry. Businessmen were learning all over again that special courtesy paid. There was and is, as might be expected, a certain degree of hypocrisy about the new business courtesy, yet it was founded on realism and practical common sense. Greater consideration for the point of view of associates and customers made for better working relations (and larger profits) than formal obsequiousness or curtness. So business was influenced by and made its own contribution to the times.

Though the circumstances of life shift rapidly and the acknowledged leaders and arbiters have changed the rules of behavior throughout the ages of man, the fundamental basis of good behavior in kindness and consideration for others has never changed. Whatever the usefulness of any set of social rules, they represent, as Arthur Schlesinger says, "one aspect of the common man's struggle to achieve a larger degree of dignity and self-respect."*

* *Op. cit.*

II

THE FAMILY AT HOME

2

The Family of Two

Throughout the ages rules for social behavior have evidenced man's desire to live graciously and in harmony with his fellows. As time passes details of the codes change—sometimes because of changing circumstances, sometimes because, having come into being heaven knows how, they have proved themselves to be silly and useless. But the basic principles of kindness, consideration, behaving so that you are making life easier and pleasanter for others, rather than more difficult, remain the same.

If you may imagine a time and a place in which a number of households are supplied by water from a not very good pump that needs priming every time it is used, it will be easy to see how a rule of behavior may have been adopted which dictates that everyone who uses the pump should leave beside it a can filled with water for the next person to use as a primer. It would be a good and useful rule, and anyone who ignored it would rightly earn the censure of the rest of the community. But if one of the householders moves into a modern house equipped with running water, and because of the good rule that had been followed before, insists that everyone leave a can full of water beside the faucet, the custom becomes simply a useless bit of nonsense. Anyone of normal intelligence would abandon it on leaving the community in which it had been dictated by circumstance. But if it was a hot water faucet used by several people and the hot water supply was limited, the person devoted to correct behavior would not use the water wastefully, leaving only cold water for the one who came after him.

A rather unusual situation arose once when I was staying in a palace in Nepal occupied for the moment by our Point IV man who had not as yet had time really to settle down. There was a bathroom with a tap and a basin. The toilet was still of the original Nepalese design—a hole in the concrete floor with a place to indicate where your feet should go. Outside the basin stood one tall metal jug of hot water. No water as yet came out of the faucets, and I realized that one little jug of hot water was probably all that I could count on with which to wash that night, and that I had better use it sparingly since it might be all I could count on next morning. And—question of questions—who else used that bathroom, and how much water should I use on the chance that someone else was going to use it also?

I scrubbed with care and with a minimum of water, and left the jug half full. To my joy the next morning it was still half full, but of course cold. However, that seemed a very minor difficulty, and I thanked my hosts warmly for having provided me with a jug of water all to myself.

Etiquette, properly understood, is after all merely a way by which each of us may adjust to society as gracefully as possible. We all belong to several communities—the family, the neighborhood, the village or city in which we live, the state, the nation, and the community of nations. And within these there are others—the church, our children's schools and the parents of their schoolmates, our social and professional societies, and clubs (if we belong to any), our business and professional groups, our political parties—the list could be long indeed if it were made in logical detail. As we conduct ourselves in any one of these communities, so do we condition our conduct in all of them.

The smallest and most important of these (with perhaps one exception) is the family.

YOUR CLOSEST COMPANION

The exception? Though it may seem a bit whimsical to say so, it is for each of us himself. As John Donne said, "No man is an island." Yet each of us is in fact a small world within larger worlds, all related and interdependent. Unless we are able to find a relatively satisfactory adjustment within ourselves, so that we may look into the mirror with composure and close our eyes at night in reasonable peace, unless we make of ourselves persons whom we like, with whom, when occasion demands, we can live pleasantly in solitude, we are poorly equipped for social life in any community. The man or woman who snaps at others, becomes known for rudeness, neglects little courtesies, goes about wrapped in a mantle of gloom with which he inevitably covers others as well as himself is, as often as not, really only expressing dissatisfaction with himself. Because he cannot live happily and at ease with his inner consciousness, he projects his unhappiness and does his best to afflict others with it. If he could only so reconstitute himself that he respected the one with whom he must live every hour of the day and night, no matter where he is, if he could only learn to treat himself with genuine courtesy and consideration, these graces would become almost automatic in his contacts with others.

I am not advocating a self-centered, egotistical existence, a program of looking out for Number One without regard for others, but actually quite the contrary—a self-consciousness in the highest sense of the term, a realization of potential personal dignity that is a treasure in any society. Your attitude toward the human race as a whole must include your concept of yourself, for you are a human being. As you are dependent on others, so others depend on you. Your respect or scorn for yourself inevitably is reflected in your behavior with others. The one who is neat and orderly in his own affairs, indulges in harmless pleasures that give him satisfaction, takes reasonable and intelligent care of his health, rests when fatigued, refuses to become angry at himself when he has done a stupid thing, arranges his life efficiently so that he minimizes wasted time and effort, can amuse himself in leisure hours when he is alone, learns how to be honest to others by being honest with himself, not only will find the basic rules of courtesy to others natural and simple, but will also render perhaps the greatest of all courtesies to those with whom he has daily contact—that of being the kind of human being with whom it is a privilege to associate.

How do you become the kind of human being with whom it is a privilege to associate? I have found that the secret lies in a willingness to listen to other people and in drawing from them through their experiences, through their conflicts and confusions, something that adds to your own understanding of human beings in general. Perhaps also the secret lies in not being afraid to live yourself—in giving, even if sometimes you may get hurt. Too many of us stay walled up because we are afraid of being hurt. We are afraid to care too much, for fear that the other person does not care at all.

The best example I can remember in my life of someone who lived courageously and fully and gave a great deal to others of warmth and love and affection, regardless of how much it would be returned, was my aunt, Mrs. Cowles. For many years before she died she was completely deaf, completely crippled by arthritis, and yet she was so well worth knowing that every young person in the family longed to be with her and have the rare opportunity of talking alone with "Auntie Bye." She never lacked interest in those she talked with and there was an accumulation of understanding and knowledge of human beings that meant not an uncritical listener but an understanding one.

Drawing out people and getting their confidence and their experience is an art in itself and one well worth cultivating, for it will enrich you as a person so that you will be well worth knowing.

FORMAL ETIQUETTE AND HOMELY COMFORT

I remember having read somewhere that a man should treat his wife as he would the queen, and a woman her husband as if he were king. Interpreted literally such touch-me-not formality would obviously drive both wife and husband out of the home at the earliest opportunity to find elsewhere the true companionship that every human being needs. Yet underlying this romantic and grandiose advice there is a basis of wise truth. If a man or a woman cannot render at least as great loyalty, respect, and genuine courtesy to wife or husband as to a king or queen, he is indeed very badly married or incapable of taking his part in any successful human relationship, and especially deficient in the qualities that can make for that most important of all relationships, marriage.

There are times and circumstances in human relationships when formality and even a respectful aloofness are essential to proper behavior. There are families in which it is customary for everyone to dress formally for dinner, though the family is dining alone It is a good thing for them to do, if this is their custom and they find values in it. But a home should be a place of comfort, a refuge, a haven to which a man may return from work and children from school with eagerness and joy, and a family a unit of genuine companionship. Formal rules of etiquette, which should be adopted as means of smoothing the paths of human understanding, bringing people closer together, and making the daily functioning of living an easier and better thing, often tend to do the opposite, by erecting walls between people, complicating life, and making what should be easy and comfortable, difficult and painful.

Nowhere is this more true than in the home. Nowhere is the ancient Chinese principle of suiting your action to the time, the place, the immediate circumstances, and your age more applicable than here. If your home is not a place in which you can do many things without impropriety which you could not do elsewhere, it is not a home. If a tired man glories in relaxation at the end of a day, putting his unshod feet on an ottoman before his easy chair as he reads or talks with his family, if he comes to the dinner table clean and combed, but without jacket or tie, if having seated his wife at the table, he leans over in an impulse of affection and kisses her (as he surely would not do in a restaurant or as a guest in another's house), he is indulging in no impropriety. Rather he is paying his wife, by implication, the gracious compliment of demonstrating the ease and comfort of their companionship and his joyous appreciation of the home they have made together, but in which she has had the larger part.

Yet the basic rules that underlie all gracious social behavior, the rules of respect, kindness, consideration, tolerance, thoughtfulness, courtesy, grace, are nowhere more important than here. The intimacy and sometimes crowded environment of home life is not a temporary condition, such as that of an overcrowded room at a cocktail party It is that with which each member of a family must live every day and every night for years. It is impossible to conceive of a family in which adjustments are not necessary on the part of every member. When they are made graciously and with the courtesy and consideration which a well mannered person would show to his most respected hostess or guest, family life may become a joy and an inspiration to everyone who partakes of it, when these conditions do not exist, what should be order becomes chaos, what should be a joyful refuge becomes a prison. Happy is the man or woman who can look back with warm nostalgia and gratitude to the years spent under the parental roof, and forward to a return to the home of his adult years after a day or more away from it.

And there is an additional reason for especial care in the everyday contacts one has with his family. The home is the natural and by far the most important training ground in behavior for children. When I see children ill at ease in gatherings of their contemporaries, when I see them being aggressively rude, probably in self-defense against their own feelings of inferiority, or even adults who are acting like ill-mannered children, I am always sorry for them. In nine cases out of ten I am sure that they have come from homes in which the basic rules of courtesy and consideration were ignored.

I think that one of the nicest compliments paid to a husband by his wife, and one of the finest tributes to a good marriage was spoken to me by a woman who had been married to the same man for more than twenty years. "You see," she said simply, in ending the story of how they had worked out a potentially awkward situation in their relationship, "my husband and I are friends." In all things let the wife, as well as the husband, work toward the growth of friendship out of love and companionship.

THE INTIMATE PARTNERSHIP

A marriage is a partnership in which success and happiness are achieved by joint decisions and joint actions. Conversation and general attitudes should reflect this. Whether in the presence of the other partner or not, it is discourteous for either husband or wife to report such a decision or action in the first person singular. When you hear a married man or woman saying, "*I* have decided to send *my* son away to school next year," or "*I* am going to have *my* living room decorated this fall," you may expect to find something less than the perfect companionship which marriage should provide in the living room that is to be redecorated. Also do not be surprised to discover other rudenesses in the speaker and in the children of that marriage.

Courteous wives and husbands listen to each other's stories with interest, even though they are not being told for the first time. One who humiliates a marriage partner when in a group of other people, by saying, "Oh, I've heard that one a dozen times," is disregarding proper behavior as surely as he or she would be in interrupting a public speaker, or talking during a symphony concert.

I remember well my husband's campaign for the Vice-Presidency. I went on one leg of the trip He was speaking ten or twelve times a day—in a square near the railroad station, or from the back of the train; and once or twice a day in halls in the larger cities

As the days went by, both the newspapermen and I knew nearly every one of his speeches by heart I always sat on the platform behind him while he spoke, and as all eyes were glued on me as well as on the speaker, I had to look at least as though I had never heard anything that he said before.

As he would make his way out, women would crowd in behind him and murmur, "Isn't he handsome?" "Isn't he nice?" And the newspapermen who were with me were very wicked and would whisper, "Do you mind their open admiration?" and "How did you like Speech Number Two this morning?"

As more and more women go into politics, more and more men will have to learn that a speech is new to its audience, if not to the speaker and his entourage!

One of the most unlovely aspects of married life in many homes is the occasional atmosphere of hostility and constant quarreling that makes a husband and wife, at least when the spats are in progress, seem like enemies Often, if it is an established pattern within the home, it is carried abroad and embarrasses all who are exposed to it. More than once I have wanted to walk out of a group in which a married couple dominated the scene by hurling petty offensive remarks at each other, and have refrained only out of courtesy to my hostess. Sometimes the quarreling couple attempt to make it all sound like a joke, it is the lowest form of humor in the world—indeed it is not humor. There is nothing remotely amusing about it. Don't do it—for your own sakes, for your children's sakes, and for the sake of all with whom you come into contact. If you have differences, talk them out in a reasonable and friendly manner and in the privacy of your own rooms, with no one else present, not even your children or servants.

THE GOOD WIFE

Perhaps I shall be forgiven if I go back to one of the good old books for a description of a successful wife which is as valid as it was when it was written over two thousand years ago. Of such a one the Book of Proverbs in the Old Testament says.

Her price is far above rubies. The heart of her husband does safely trust in her. . . . She will do him good and not evil all the days of her life . . . She riseth while it is yet night, and giveth meat to her household. . . . She girdeth her loins with strength, and strengtheneth her arms. . . . She stretcheth out her hand to the poor, yea, she reacheth forth her hands to the needy . . . Her husband is known in the gates, when he sitteth among the elders of the land. . . . Strength and honour are her clothing, and she shall rejoice in time to come She openeth her mouth with wisdom, and in her tongue is the law of kindness She looketh well to the ways of her household, and eateth not the bread of idleness Her children arise up, and call her blessed, her husband also, and he praiseth her.

The successful wife is many women, lover, housekeeper, mother (not only to her children, but in many ways to her husband as well), a listening ear, a sympathetic voice, a tender and comforting hand, a first-aid nurse, a stimulant to cheerfulness on gloomy days, a gracious hostess, and frequently one who shares with her husband the task of earning the family livelihood I often have thought that less is expected of the president of a great corporation than of an American wife. Little wonder that she sometimes loses her temper with her husband and her children, or that the crown of her beautiful manners, which she is supposed to wear at all times, sometimes slips and rides slightly askew.

The sensitive husband, and even children whose relationship to their parents is a sound and secure one, will understand this, and forgive her even before forgiveness is asked The things which they cannot understand, the things that leave resentment and often bitterness are habitual nagging, habitual slovenliness, neglect of her duties as a wife and a mother, habitual rudeness in addressing the other members of the family, indifference when loving tenderness is expected, and a general pattern of conduct that seems to intimate that she is living in her house for herself alone and that all other members of the family are there by sufferance and are no concern of hers. The woman who feels that she has "captured" her husband, that he is therefore her property, to be exploited and given only such privileges in her home as she doles out to him, has learned as little of the technique of living as had the medieval husband whose wife was his chattel.

Far up toward the top—perhaps the first—of the items on the list of rules for the successful wife should be personal and household neatness and cleanliness. It is perhaps a little fatuous and not particularly pertinent to remind her how, in that shining world of the newly in love, she used to take especial care with her toilet and dress on the evening when she was going to see the man who was to become her husband, for it should not be necessary to distinguish between the codes of conduct which regulate behavior in different stages of any relationship. People are always people, and the ways to smooth social intercourse do not change materially with circumstances.

Yet women too often forget this, and one who at eighteen or twenty made her suitor say, "I could eat her with a spoon," may at forty make her husband turn his eyes away from her at the breakfast table in order not to have to look at her dishevelled hair and shabby negligee and possibly be reminded that under it is a soiled nightgown or slip.

Similarly if the man who remembers how neat and clean was the house in which his sweetheart lived when he came to call for her, returns home at night to chaos and dirt, neither he nor those of his friends who know the situation can regard this marriage as a success Nor will the children of such a home go forth to meet the world with the assurance and grace that should be every child's heritage.

A number of years ago a popular magazine printed a questionnaire asking its readers to list the principal reasons for marital failure in what, according to their opinions, was the order of their importance. A large majority of the more than one hundred thousand who replied listed slovenliness on the part of the wife—a lack of personal and household cleanliness and neatness—as the most common cause of divorce

And so the good wife will consider neatness, cleanliness, and order among the most important articles in her code of behavior, and her children shall call her blessed, and her husband praise her, which are very pleasant things for any wife.

I think I might mention here that a wife who becomes too efficient may sometimes have to remind both her husband and her children that the miracles of management she accomplishes are really not miracles and don't just happen without effort on anybody's part.

Because of my husband's illness it fell to my lot to do most of the managing of the everyday arrangements of life, and quite without knowing it my husband and the children took it for granted that things always happened without any difficulty and that their lives were always arranged in the way they wished them to be.

This was brought home to me very effectively when my husband decided to have a picnic for visiting royalty at the cottage he had built on a hill some two miles back from his mother's house in which we lived. He did not tell me that there would be no water turned on in the cottage at the time we were to have the picnic for the royal couple. When I arrived with my helpers to set out tables and lay out the food in what was still an empty house, I found that if I was going to have any water I would have to get it quickly from somewhere else. Fortunately it was early enough so that I could send a car to a farm at the foot of the hill and get milk cans filled with water and up to the house before the stream of cars and guests started to arrive. In the meantime my youngest son John, who had been married only a few weeks, came over and found us all busily arranging the food on the tables.

He looked at me in astonishment and said, "Why Mother, I thought you did not have to do any work for these parties. I thought they just happened!"

When an attitude such as this is discovered, it is well for a wife, no matter how well mannered she is, to give her family a little rude awakening!

Every sensible girl, during that delightful time when the man she loves is calling on her, taking her out, and with her exploring the future in excited expectation, is particularly careful with her dress. The most sensible wives continue to be so after marriage. But many become careless, partly perhaps because their husbands lag in their attention, and partly because they feel, if only unconsciously, that it is no longer necessary to make an impression on any man

Regardless of the reasons, if they do tend to give too little attention to neatness and attractiveness in their dress they are making a
mistake. Even though a husband may seem to be quite unaware of
what his wife is wearing, her appearance will impress him and will
honor or disparage the marriage relationship, whether he is alone
with her in their home or they are out together. In the latter case a
wife should always remember that her dress will reflect credit or discredit on her husband. Many a woman who understands that a man
must pay attention to his own clothes as a part of maintaining his
business or professional standing fails to take into account the fact
that through her appearance she also has it in her power to help or
hinder him.

If she devotes herself entirely to her household, husband, and
children, the problems connected with arranging her life will be
somewhat simpler than are those of a woman who (whether from
economic expediency or from her own desire to be active outside the
home) shares with her husband the task of earning the family living.
In either case her home, husband, and children will be her primary
concern, and she will conduct herself in her relations with them
not perhaps as though her husband were a king and her children
princes and princesses, but as a well mannered lady would with a
gentleman and with children who are expected to grow into gentlemen and ladies.

She will manage to have her husband's well prepared breakfast
on the table, and to greet him with neat hair and neat dress and a
pleasant smile by the time he has finished shaving. If she has to get
up fifteen minutes earlier than she would otherwise in order to
manage this she will do so as a matter of course.

She will study his preferences in food, and within reason cater to
them as she would to those of her most honored guests.

When he comes home at night she will welcome him with as
carefully if less formally arranged table, orderly house, and personal
neatness as she would the most welcome guest, but with an inner
and intimate warmth that is reserved for him alone.

One of the happiest and most successful marriages I have ever
known is now fifty years old. Husband and wife are devoted to, and
proud of, each other. The husband once said to me, "In all the years
I have known my wife, both before and since our marriage, she has
always given me what I would call the perfect welcome, whether I

have called her on the phone, met her at a restaurant for lunch, or when I have come home at night. And this is true even when she has had the kind of day that every mother and housewife has sometimes— the day when everything seems to go wrong, when problems seem almost too many to be solved. If the problems are there she talks to me about them, but later. Even though there may be unshed tears in her eyes, a joyous welcome shines through them as she greets me. She always makes me feel as though our coming together were some- thing very special, and as though I were the most important person in her world. I think that this is the greatest treasure a wife can give her husband. It is a blessing of priceless worth which makes me sorry for other men who are less fortunate. She has always been the same way with our children, and I'm sure that this has been one of the most important elements in their development into men and women of whom we are proud, and who are liked and respected wherever they are."

Every girl seems to have born in her the knowledge that in order to get on well with men, she must be a good listener. The girl who cannot sit beside a man at a party and listen with attention and sym- pathetic understanding to him while he talks of his home life, school, work, and ambitions not only will seem rude, but also will be un- popular. Too often a wife, beset with the cares of a household and motherhood, and sometimes too conscious of the fact that her hus- band is a fallible human being instead of the demigod she thought him when she fell in love with him, will forget this.

The courteous wife does not. She knows that for a man a woman is a natural sounding board, a sympathetic listener, a motherlike comforter, and at times a counselor. Her words may be few in such circumstances, but when she speaks "she openeth her mouth with wisdom; and in her tongue is the law of kindness." Every successful wife has at some time or other made a tentative suggestion to her husband which he has rejected, only some time later to have him mention it as a fine idea of his own which he is going to carry out. And in such situations she has praised him, and kept her peace about its true source. This is a good wifeliness. It is also good manners.

The well behaved wife will be frank with her husband, though she will keep some things to herself. The wise wife does not expect perfection, or an arrangement in which all the details of a shared life are as she would have them in an ideal situation. She adjusts herself quietly and without complaint to those matters that are of much less importance than they may have seemed in her imagination before marriage.

If there are any to which she finds she cannot adjust in this way, if she finds herself smouldering in silent resentment and disappointment, which can build up into serious barriers between her husband and herself, she will talk them over with him frankly and reasonably, and if he is ready to do his part he will change his habits, or they will find a middle way that will be acceptable to both. And she on her part will be ready to listen with understanding and cooperation to any similar explanations from him of her habits that may mar the closeness of their easy and comfortable companionship.

If, for instance, she is one who has a job outside the home, for which she must prepare each morning as her husband prepares for his, and if they have no full-time servants, she has every right to expect him to help her make the early morning rush to get away a cooperative enterprise. It is true that managing the household is primarily a wife's responsibility and that earning the family living is traditionally the obligation of the husband, yet more and more in contemporary American life the latter task is being shared by the wife. Neither a woman nor a man can do everything, and under such circumstances it is not unreasonable to expect a man to be helpful in the matter of the household chores. If the husband does not himself realize this and volunteer his help, and the wife finds that her double burden is tending to make a shrew of her, she will show her husband a greater courtesy by talking it over with him and explaining the situation reasonably than by letting silent resentment build up within her.

Surely a smooth program can be worked out. If they have to get up a little earlier than they would if the wife stayed at home, that is no great hardship. Perhaps the wife will prepare the breakfast while the husband is making his toilet and dressing. After breakfast perhaps he will do the dishes and make the bed or beds while she makes her toilet and dresses, so that they may both come back to a neat and orderly home. Thus they may leave the house together for the day's work in relaxed friendliness Surely fifteen minutes of dishwashing and bedmaking in each working day is a small contribution for any husband to make to a smooth and happy marriage.

The wife generally makes the social arrangements for the family, issuing invitations, and accepting or rejecting those of others, though she will consult her husband in both cases, unless there is some reason why she cannot, or knows beforehand that the arrangement which she plans to make is the one which he would like Usually she also writes thank you notes for gifts sent to both of them, or to the hostess who has entertained them over a weekend

The wife who is fortunate enough to have a husband who offers her the small courtesies which a gentleman customarily shows a lady should accept them graciously, and with cooperation. If it is your husband's custom to light your cigarette, his gracious gesture demands from you the courtesy of showing that you expect it as a matter of course. If you begin to light it yourself, while he is reaching for a match, you are offering him what, in a small way, is a rejection. Yet in such matters as this, there is a middle way Do not expect unreasonable small attentions from him. If he is across the room from you when you put a cigarette in your mouth, light it yourself, and if he starts to rise, simply say, "Thank you, Jim, but don't bother." Here, as in all things, the guiding principle is consideration. It is considerate and good manners to accept your husband's courtesies and show that you appreciate them, it is not to expect him to wait on you hand and foot.

THE COURTEOUS HUSBAND

The good husband, like the wife, is committed to courteous behavior twenty-four hours a day. He rises in the morning aware that he is not alone, but one member of a most precious small community in which he must take his place before he faces the outside world and his working associates. If he is addicted to before-coffee grouches he hides them, and works on himself to overcome them. Or perhaps he slips out to the kitchen and puts the coffeepot on even before he has dressed (if his wife has not preceded him) so that he may have a cup of black coffee as a bracer before sitting down at the breakfast table.

If it is a wedding anniversary or his wife's birthday his first act in the morning is to remember it, and mention it suitably.

Breakfast can be one of the pleasantest meals of the day if both husband and wife make it so. The husband can make especially apt contributions to this pleasantness and sense of well-being. As the wife will plan to have breakfast on the table by the time he is ready for it, he will not dawdle over his toilet, but will come to the table when she is ready for him. Under ordinary circumstances he will draw her chair back for her and seat her. Though this may not always be practical in the split-second timing that frequently accompanies the morning getaway, if he remembers little courtesies such as this when it is possible to render them, his wife will be aware of the intent, and know the warm glow that comes to a lady from the tributes of a gentleman.

If the coffee is unusually good on a lucky morning, the eggs and bacon done to a turn, the toast just brown enough, neither underdone nor burned, the good husband will mention it with praise, and give his wife a little extra fillip with which to start the day.

He will come promptly to his meals when they are ready and his wife summons him. He will not precede the event by shouting, "When do we eat?" He will not criticize the food she serves, though if, before the adjustment which comes only with time in marriage, she habitually puts before him specific foods toward which he has an unconquerable aversion, he will tell her so in a frank and friendly manner and with probably a candid admission that it is foolishness on his part, and the good wife will omit them from their joint menu. If they are things of which she is particularly fond herself she will plan to prepare them when she is eating alone.

The wife and husband who have nothing to talk about unless they constantly make conversation are indeed unfortunately married. Yet sometimes a little effort will go a long way to overcome a tendency to taciturnity, as it does in more formal assemblages. The considerate husband will do his part in this. The one who sits through breakfast with the propped up newspaper between his wife and himself, and speaks not nor invites being spoken to is being rude, and is also endangering his marriage

I am not sure which of the three possible newspaper-at-breakfast situations is the worst—that in which the husband is barricaded behind a newspaper while his wife eats in silence, that of a wife who has appropriated the paper before he can get it and is devouring it before he takes it away with him, or when each hides behind a part of the paper and feels a way around it by instinct to the bacon and eggs and toast.

Surely any one of these situations is an unnecessary awkwardness. Let the husband postpone his reading of the paper until he is on the train, subway, or bus, and the wife hers until her husband has left for the day. To be sure this requires two papers, but that is not beyond the means of the average family, and certainly better than allowing the paper to intrude on the pleasant and important business of eating breakfast together.

I know one family in which there used to be a bit of surface tension on Sundays because both the husband and the wife are avid crossword puzzle fans. Whoever got the puzzle first, of course, ruined it for the other One Sunday morning, after both had been out late the night before and were feeling a little the worse for it, what had been before hidden annoyance flared up in angry words from the husband. He apologized almost instantly, but a rift had been made in the weekend harmony. And then he took steps to see that it wouldn't happen again The next Sunday morning two copies of the paper were delivered, hers and his, and now each can work out his puzzle from first to last, with an occasional friendly question flung across the room after one of them has spent several minutes trying to think of a four-letter word which means "liliaceous plant," or one in seven letters which means "draw."

Some women do not mind having side dishes used as ashtrays To others it is an abomination—especially if the ashes are mixed with residues of food. In any case no well mannered guest will use the dishes of his hostess so, and habits are strong A husband will do well, if it is his custom to smoke a cigarette after a meal, to use an ashtray at home as he would elsewhere

And there is a custom more common in Europe than in America of thanking a hostess for a meal after it has been eaten. It is a gracious thing, and might well be followed by a husband after he has eaten one of his wife's good meals.

The considerate husband will tread a careful middle line between overcriticizing his wife's clothes and seeming to be completely indifferent to them. To err in the one direction is to be a boor and a bully, for a husband to seem not to care how his wife looks is to give the impression that she is really of little importance to him, an old shoe that is comfortable, but nothing to be proud of.

The truth is, of course, that there is a danger of being unaware of those persons and things nearest and most accustomed to us. It is not necessarily true that familiarity breeds contempt, but it does tend to make the familiar something that is taken for granted. It is a rare man who can tell you offhand the numbers on the registration plate of his automobile, the color of his wife's eyes, or what she wore the last time they went out together.

I think that this very phenomenon, which is widespread, frequently discourages women and makes them careless in their dress. Many a wife finds little incentive to make herself look her best when she knows that her escort, who happens to be her husband, is not going to know whether she is wearing a Mother Hubbard or a Patou model. Since it is not necessary to impress him, and he would not be impressed anyway, why bother?

Her attitude is wrong, of course, but so is that of the husband who has made it possible One of the nicest compliments a man can pay his wife is to notice what she is wearing, to praise it when it is particularly becoming, and by quiet and intelligent suggestion to let her know that she is not making the most of her natural attractiveness when she becomes careless about her dress, or chooses the wrong hat. A wife should bear in mind that a husband is often an excellent critic.

Of course he must back this up by seeing that her clothing allowance and his are in fair proportion. It is taken for granted that a business or professional man must dress with a certain amount of care in order always to look presentable. But this does not mean that he is justified in spending all the money that the family can afford for clothing on himself. It is always possible to find a middle way, and in any budget there must be room for a wife's reasonable expenditures for clothes. The husband will pay her a greater compliment by seeing that she dresses with care, even though this may sometimes involve adverse criticism, than by ignoring her dress.

The courteous husband who finds that he is to be detained at his office and so will arrive late for dinner, or perhaps must eat dinner elsewhere than at home, will let his wife know as early in the day as it is possible to do so. One of the harshest of petty irritations for a harassed wife is to have a fine dinner ready for her husband only to receive a phone call from him, at about the time she expects to hear his key in the door, saying that he will not be there to eat it.

He will not bring business associates or others home to a meal without having given his wife previous warning in plenty of time to allow her to prepare for them, and without having asked her if it is convenient for her to have him do so. Indeed it is questionable whether the home is the place to entertain business associates, unless they are also friends in the best sense of the word and an invitation to them may be regarded as any social invitation When a man uses his home, wife, and children as media in public relations, there is an element of discourtesy both to the family and to the business associate involved.

No gentleman will talk over intimate details of his relationship with his wife, with his friends and acquaintances, and this includes quarrels (if any) and disagreements which he has with her. Nor does he talk to others about any of her activities which may, by any standard, be considered her private affairs.

At meals, when there are no guests, the husband will serve his wife first, his daughters second, his sons third, and himself last. If there are guests he will serve them (beginning of course with the women) first, then his wife, then his children (if they are at the table), and himself last.

When he is introducing her to a close friend, or speaking of her to one, he calls her by her first name, if to a stranger he calls her "my wife."

The considerate guest, spending a weekend in another's house, does not leave his toilet articles lying in messy disarray about the bathroom, his outer clothing on chairs in the living room, or other personal possessions in disorder about the room in which he sleeps. Courtesy to his hostess decrees otherwise The rule of courtesy to his wife decrees the same behavior in his own home.

And of course there are a host of little things which every well mannered man would remember when with other women, and too often forgets when he is with his wife—opening doors for her, and letting her precede him through them, seeing her into the car and closing the door after her before he goes around to the driver's side and gets into it himself, allowing her privacy, seeing that she is seated before he seats himself, *asking* her if she will do this and that for him (sew on a button, make a phone call during the day while he is at the office, take his suit to the cleaner) instead of telling her to

If at all times the husband manages somehow to convey to his wife the impression that she is both his hostess and his guest, as well as his friend, loved one, companion, and partner in life, he will not go far wrong in his behavior to her

3

The Expanding Family

THE WORLD OF CHILDHOOD, FILLED WITH WONDER, QUES-
tioning, and experimentation, all of which are parts of the
difficult task of growing up, is a region for which most adults have
no map, since memory is short and many of the most important details of one's own childhood are forgotten. The surest guides for the
adult to this mysterious world are love, kindness, patience, a deep
desire to understand, and courtesy. At the center of this complex
world is the heart of the individual child, his passions, his secret
desires, his sensitiveness to criticism, his need to join the region in-
habited by adults, yet retain his own individuality, and his passionate hunger to love and be loved.

An adult far too often forgets that children are persons. Perhaps
this is a more common failing in parents than it is in others, for no
child ever lived who was not at times annoying. Yet adults are annoying also, and the well adjusted man or woman takes annoyances from
them in stride and does not, because of them, become ill-mannered.

Parents owe to their children at least as much in the way of
courtesy as they do to their contemporaries. Unless this truth is

realized and acted upon, the peace of the home is shattered, and children grow up ill equipped for the social adjustments which they must make with the world at large.

"Please" and "thank you" should be as commonly used by parents when speaking to their children, as with others. If a parent finds that he has wrongly accused his child or otherwise been unjust to him, an apology should be given as naturally as to any adult.

One of the fiercest and most insistent needs of the child is for identification, to be known as himself, a being distinct from all others He must have the satisfaction of feeling that he has a place in the total scheme of things which is not filled by any other.

When I was a child it was not uncommon to find, written in the front of a friend's school books, some such inscription as this: "Sadie Miller, New York City, New York County, New York State, the United States of America, the World, the Universe." Thus was an identity pinpointed against the cosmic background.

I have told elsewhere* the story of the little boy who came to me at one of the picnics which I give every summer for disadvantaged children at Hyde Park. He had been there before and I remembered his face, but when he asked me his name I could not recall it and told him so. After he had told me and run off to play he came back three times during the afternoon to ask me his name. Each time I was able to tell him, and finally satisfied, he said, "Now maybe you won't forget."

The story has a profound significance for all parents. Though they are unlikely to forget the names of their own children, they all too often forget to pay the little tributes to individuality which is the due of each—praising the drawing of the one who likes to draw pictures, paying attention to the song which one has learned to sing at school and repeats gladly at home, listening with attention and respect to the fantasies of the imaginative one, and never, never, laughing in ridicule at a small son or daughter (or a large one, for that matter). Laughing with your children at a joke, even when it is on one of you, is among the most wholesome experiences of life. No sense of humor is more filled with joyousness and delicate nuances than that of a sensitive, intelligent, extrovert child. Every time you share it with him you strengthen the bonds of your companionship, enhance your understanding of each other, and make

* *You Learn by Living.* New York, Harper & Brothers, 1960.

the fierce young sense of individual worth wholesomely sturdier. But for a child there is no wound deeper than that made by belittling laughter, and no wall more impenetrable than that built by habitual ridicule

Such rules of behavior as this you would follow as a matter of course with your adult friends. They are even more important in your contacts with your children. Adults, when a relationship with one friend deteriorates, may find companionship elsewhere; the child who faces an opaque and impassable wall between his parents and himself is alone in a shattered world.

CRITICISMS AND PUNISHMENTS

Of course the parent-child relationship is a very special one, complicated by the parent's responsibility to correct, and sometimes punish, the child. But this in no way negates the rule of courtesy. Correction, constructive criticism, and even punishment may be administered without rudeness The bent of the natural, healthy child who feels secure in the knowledge of his parents' love is toward goodness, the kind of behavior that will win praise and approval. When sheer animal spirits, the overwhelming temptation to fulfill a desire by breaking a rule, or simply an off-color mood such as every child and every adult sometimes knows results in making mistakes or outright naughtiness, the child knows that he deserves correction, censure, or punishment. He counts on his parents to help him back to the path of good behavior Not to give him that help is a greater discourtesy to him than administering a well deserved and, if necessary, stern punishment

But the correction, the censure, the punishment, if administered by a wise parent, will not be accompanied by belittlement of the child as a person, or insulting expressions of disgust and disrespect, or threats that the parent will not love the child if he behaves thus. Nor will it be excessive, simply because the parent has to work off his own annoyance or anger by taking it out on the child. And when the episode is over, let it be over and forgotten by both of you, as you would a difference that had been resolved between you and an adult friend.

Correction of an error, or censure when the child has been at fault, should be administered frankly and without minimizing its necessity But usually (as would be customary with an adult in a similar case) the procedure may be accompanied by praise of some other aspect of the child's personality or general behavior which will uphold his respect for himself, and imply that the misbehavior is inconsistent with the fine person which he is essentially. Sometimes, in setting right a mild mistake, the correction may be made without seeming to be a correction at all.

One of the most delightful examples of this I have ever encountered is in a letter which William James, the psychologist and philosopher, wrote in answer to one from his eight-year-old daughter. In her letter the child had obviously chosen two spellings for a word, both of them wrong. James's comment set a classic example of perfection for parents in meeting such a situation He wrote " 'Orphly' and 'ofly' are good ways to spell awfully, too "* By spelling the word correctly he had given her the desired instruction in spelling, yet he had done it with no belittlement and even made it sound like praise Five years later, when the same girl was thirteen and in a school away from home, she apparently wrote him a letter in a deeply depressed mood, filled with self-pity. In answering it her father wrote: ". . . you have been trying to do the manly thing under difficult circumstances, but one learns only gradually to do the *best* thing." Then, after several pages of wise advice about ways to overcome depressions, he adds, "I have no doubt you are doing as well as you know how, darling little Peg, but we have to learn everything, and I also have no doubt that you'll manage it better and better . . "†

Nor was the method, born of his kindly, affectionate nature and his never failing gentleness, used only with children William James was one of the keenest of literary critics for his brother Henry, the novelist. When the latter sent him a copy of *The Tragic Muse*, James wrote him a long letter, opening it with honest praise. It was, he wrote, "a most original, wonderful, delightful, and admirable production . . . the people and setting most easily and naturally English . . . it leaves a good taste in the mouth, everyone in it is human and good." Then the criticism, gently stated· "The only

* *The Letters of William James*, edited by his son Henry James. Boston, Atlantic Monthly Press, 1920, Vol II, p. 26
† *Ibid*, Vol II, pp 130–132

thing I positively find to object to is the length of the chapter on Mr Nash's portrait " Also, "I wish you had managed to bring in a little more business with Julia toward the end "

One of the most significant elements in these letters from William James is the fact that in delivering criticism to his young daughter and to his adult brother, his method was essentially the same He was treating each as a human being who, in all that mattered, was his peer No other attitude is more important in a relationship between parents and children, in spite of the duty of the parent to instruct, correct, and in some cases discipline the child

"In the disciplined home, the children have no rights," says A. S. Neill, headmaster of the Summerhill School in England "In the spoiled home they have all the rights. In the proper home, children and adults have equal rights "*

INTERFERENCE AND OVERPROTECTION

If, in a friend's house, your host were attempting to repair an electric light connection or a dripping faucet, and you took the work out of his hands saying, "Let me do it," he would quite rightly consider you rude So are you showing rudeness and a lack of wisdom in your relationship with your child, if you overdo the matter of helping him solve his problems. Who has not heard a disgruntled child say, "I want to do it my own self," or seen a very little one angrily knock down the house which a doting parent has built with his blocks? Wait until the child asks for help, or until he is facing a serious problem which he quite obviously cannot solve for himself.

Similarly know that you cannot possibly protect your child from every danger which he will encounter through life, and do not overdo the matter of keeping him from the small dangers that always surround him. To do so is to weaken his own capacity for protecting himself and is likely to fill him with unwarranted fears that may hamper him through life.

I remember a day at the country home of a friend when, in a high wind, the eight-year-old son of my host climbed to the top of a tall ash tree, and there, clinging to a small limb, shouted with delight as the tree swayed back and forth in the wind

* A S Neill, *Summerhill, A Radical Approach to Child Rearing* New York, Hart Publishing Co , 1961

"Aren't you afraid he will fall?" I asked the father.

The man smiled a little wanly.

"My heart is just back of my teeth," he said grimly. "It scares me to death every time he does a thing like that But I try not to let him see it The important thing is that he isn't scared When I was a child my mother would almost faint when I got more than two feet above the ground If I were to climb to the roof of the barn, or into a tree, and she saw me, she would go white and say, 'Come down very carefully and slowly,' and stand watching me until I was on the ground again I have been no good on a ladder or anywhere that is more than eight or ten feet above the ground ever since I can't even stand comfortably by the rail of an ocean liner. In a hotel room that is above the second floor I find it difficult to sleep if my bed is anywhere near a window

"I hope that the boy never falls, of course, but if he does the chances are that he will do no more than break an arm or a leg. Either of those can be mended. I doubt if what was done to me by my mother's fear ever can "

He was a wise father.

TEACHING THE CHILD MANNERS

It is obviously your duty to teach your children manners in their contacts with you and with others. In this your example will be more effective than any number of precepts. If parents are always courteous to each other and to their children, the children will eventually absorb courtesy.

Certain things are probably never taught in words to youngsters in a family. For instance, the automatic habit of standing when an older person or a woman enters a room. I do not remember hearing anyone ever told in my family that he should do this, but all the older people around did it and it became automatic.

Many things in good manners become an unnoticed part of one's existence. Today it is almost a forgotten thing for youngsters to stand in school when their teacher enters the room, and yet this should be automatic and should lead to an unconscious show of respect which would perhaps seep down into many other situations that arise

But absorption of good manners from example does not happen

all at once. Kindly, courteous instruction is also necessary, and here, as in all things, extreme patience. It is unrealistic and futile to expect from a three- or five-year-old the kind of manners you would take for granted in a gracious adult. The child who in a roomful of guests becomes suddenly aggressive and begins to show off with loud talking and other demands for attention is not being consciously rude. He is simply obeying the demands of an individual identity seeking recognition The same child may be quiet and well behaved in the company of a single understanding friend, or surrounded only by his family.

Under such circumstances the wise parent will not make a scene and humiliate the child by severe correction before guests. Rather he will separate the child from the guests, to the advantage of both.

Yet the child needs to become gradually accustomed to meeting adults, and should never be given the belittling feeling that he is unfit to meet his parents' friends.

One family that I know with a five-year-old daughter has solved the problem nicely. When guests are invited for the evening, the parents ask them to come in time to say good night to the daughter. After fifteen minutes or so, which both the little girl and the guests enjoy, the child is trotted off to bed.

The theory that children should be seen and not heard has as little validity today as the belief that the earth is flat. How can a child learn to communicate under an imposition of silence, or how can a parent learn to know his child or be enriched by the innate beauty and originality that so often issue from the mind of childhood if the child is not encouraged to speak freely?

But whereas in the everyday environment of home life, when the family is alone with one another, the give and take of group conversation falls into a natural pattern, a change takes place when there are guests. Within the family, if a child interrupts another, or one of the parents, he may be told, "It's Jackie's turn now," or "Father's." If the parents pay considerate attention to the children, the latter will learn that each member of the family is entitled to the same attention, and the sense of fair play which is deeply embedded in the normal, secure child will dictate proper behavior.

But the presence of strangers stimulates self-consciousness and tends to undermine the sense of security which is founded on routine. Frequently the child tries to compensate by aggressiveness.

Then a quiet separation of guests and child is the most courteous act to both.

In some homes where the family is large, it is the custom for children to eat at a separate table so long as they are young This is sometimes a good plan because it does not cut them off from the family completely, but if there are guests it is very difficult to have little children at the table and teach them to eat properly. Once they are old enough, I think the more they can be at the table with their family the better it is, first because they feel that they are part of the whole family, and second because they absorb certain things from their elders without needing to be taught

The best example of this I have ever seen was Princess Juliana (now Queen Juliana) and her children when the latter were quite small, say five or six years old. The children always had breakfast with the family. Even Queen Wilhelmina made it her habit to breakfast very often with her daughter and Prince Bernhard and the children. At the end of the meal the youngsters were never expected to stay once they had finished. The older one would slide down from her chair and stand by the younger one, helping her untie her bib. Then they would come to my chair, when they were staying with me, and ask to be excused. When at home they would of course go around to their mother's chair, and ask to be excused. They were permitted to come to the table when there were guests for lunch or dinner only when they were considerably older. I think that this was done largely out of consideration for the guests, but perhaps it was also an incentive to the children to learn good manners quickly so that they would be taken into the family circle more and more often

In the family the child who reaches high-chair age should, if it is possible, join the family at breakfast so that the mother can teach him how to eat. This is a time when the mother must be beside her young daughter or son as companion and helper. Other meals will be eaten alone—perhaps with the mother, but rarely with other members of the family—because a very small child's hours will not coincide with those of the family meals.

If there are guests who also have children, and the dining room is large enough, it is sometimes pleasant and probably more fun for the children to seat all the children who are old enough at one table, and the adults at another. In doing this you would actually only be following one of the basic rules of the courteous hostess to adult guests—that of seating compatible persons near one another.

How does one teach a child table manners? First of all by example. In all things the behavior of the parents is the most effective instructor. Yet precept is necessary too. The more gently and patiently it may be administered, the more it may appear to be fascinating learning rather than censure, the more successful it will be. Every child likes to eat with his hands. In the early high-chair stage it is futile and likely to set up a long-lasting rebellion to attempt to make him use a spoon. Fingers were not only made before forks, they are also used before by every normal human being. Gently and gradually, as the mother feeds the child (who has so much to learn about many things), preferably with his own baby spoon, and finally puts the small spoon into the child's own hands, he will learn—only to abandon his newfound learning again and again. Why should bread be eaten with the fingers, as adults do it, and not the fascinating mashed potatoes, which feel so soft and warm to the touch? Why must two different methods be used to bring a cookie and a piece of cake or pie to the mouth? What is an arm for, if it is not to reach across the table and seize a bit of food to carry to a hungry mouth? Who is going to remember to place a used utensil on the plate instead of on the nearest open expanse of table? If one has something to say, something pressing hard for expression, what more natural than to shout it out whether someone else is speaking or not?

These and many other tendencies, which in the adult are rightly considered discourteous, must be corrected when the child exhibits them. The correction must be done with patience and gentleness, if there is to be success. And it must be done over and over, even after the young person has successfully traversed the difficult path of adolescence. Reasons should be given for the corrections "It's pleasanter not to get your fingers all messy and soil your dress and other things with them. Why not use the fork or spoon?" "If you reach for food that way you are likely to upset your glass of milk. Ask your father, and he will pass it to you," etc. But do not expect too much too soon. And do not commit a greater rudeness than his, both to the child and to the others at the table, by shouting angrily at him when he has committed some quite understandable infringement of good table manners. And above all teach your children that while the home is a place for relaxed informality in many things, his table manners should be essentially the same there as they would be in the most august assemblage at a restaurant or at a dinner in the home of someone else. The basic rule of consideration on which all good social behavior rests does not change with time, place, and circumstances.

Among the rules that have fluctuated in different times and places are those connected with eating what is put on the plate. In many homes in the past it has been (and doubtless still is in some) a rule that a child must eat everything which has been served him. At the same time many have been taught that when they are guests, they must always leave a little on their plates so that they may not seem to be greedy. (I was amazed when I learned recently that this rule is in one of the Hindu Puranas, written some 2,000 years ago!) Both rules carried out to a literal extreme are silly.

No child should be allowed to be too choosy in his food. The habit is as often as not a method of gaining attention, and will be less likely to become established if his parents in all things give him the normal attention that is every child's due. But if he is allowed to demand special foods habitually at home, and reject others, he will probably become one of those nuisances who, as a guest, will look with disgust at his plate and, if he does not say loudly, "I don't like broccoli," shove it disdainfully and ostentatiously aside with his fork.

Sometimes a child's rejection of food is soundly based, and should be met with respect as a problem which you must help him to solve. Perhaps he has a genuine dislike for a certain food. If you demand that he "choke it down" he may do just that, with a physical nausea and emotional resentment that not only are bad for his young digestion, but may well establish an unconquerable resentment to the food for the rest of his life.

A friend of mine, as a child, was forced every Sunday to eat a large helping of steamed pudding smothered in marmalade. Even now he cannot bear to put marmalade on a piece of toast at breakfast.

A more pitiful story was told me recently of a man who actually was nauseated by the sight of peanuts. Born in Poland near the Russian border, and of Jewish parents, he had lived through pogroms in which most of his family had been killed. For two days he lay hidden in a hollow log in the forest beside a path along which he could hear the Cossacks' horses. Half starved he finally emerged, and began to look for food In a wrecked and abandoned store he found a large sackful of peanuts and gorged himself on them, later becoming violently ill.

Physically he survived the experience, and in America has made a fine life for himself. But his aversion to peanuts is understandably unconquerable.

If instead of insisting that a child eat food he doesn't like, you prepare it differently and give him a little of it without direct comment to him, you may solve the problem smoothly. Or perhaps you can stimulate his curiosity and desire to experiment by saying to your husband, "Aren't these young carrots good, now that I have learned to fix them with butter and orange juice?" or "I'm delighted with that recipe for fixing string beans with cheese. It makes them taste like a different vegetable." If you don't make an issue of it, but use a little tact as you would with an adult, the situation may right itself without difficulty.

Sometimes, perhaps because of a mild stomach upset, the child simply isn't hungry. In such cases do not force food on him, any more than you would on an adult guest Quietly remove it, consider the meal over, and let that be an end of the matter Hunger will return and the child will eat normally again

No child of tender age should be expected to sit through protracted conversation among adults after a meal is over. But he should be taught the graciousness of asking to be excused If the family is alone he should ask one or both of his parents, saying simply, "Will you please excuse me?" or "May I be excused?" If there are adult guests he should ask both his parents and the guests. It is one of the earliest and most common situations encountered by most children in which this courtesy is required, and learning it in this way will stand them in good stead as other situations present themselves '

The matter of children listening in on adult conversations presents some special problems. If a child happens to come into the room just as his parents are discussing something which it is best for him not to hear, the wise parent will make no special circumstance of the matter, but simply drop the subject, in the middle of a sentence if necessary. If the child becomes curious and insists on knowing what the conversation was about, the parent may say simply,

"It is something we were talking over in confidence, dear," explaining in the first instance what a "confidence" is Every child must be taught to respect the confidences of his friends, and those which others hold, and there is no age too young at which to begin this instruction. Secrets are a child's delight, and an adult confidence is after all a secret. But in order to make the instruction meaningful, a parent must respect his child's confidences and not pry into the "secrets" which he shares with his contemporaries

Conversations should never be carried on before children by spelling out words in order to make them unintelligible Every child instinctively resents it, for it is as discourteous as is speaking in a foreign language before an adult in order to conceal what you say. It is therefore also bad child training.

Another bad habit which many parents fall into is that of constantly using the first person plural "we" instead of the second person singular "you" "Are we feeling well this morning?" "Are we going to eat all of our oatmeal?" It would be a very stupid child who would not soon notice that this was a form of address quite different from that used by adults to one another, and thus feel somehow belittled by it Also it is not good training in the use of the English language When you mean "you," say "you." When you mean "we," say "we."

And the more you can legitimately use "we," thus including the child in the planning and decisions made by the family, the better "Shall we all go to the country this weekend?" is a better question than "Shall Mommy and Daddy take you to the country this weekend?" When it is possible and wise to ask the child to participate in the business of making decisions that affect the entire family, it is fine to do so. It increases his wholesome sense of importance and speeds the process of growing up It is also a lesson in courtesy. But save the use of "we" for occasions when you mean "we"

Every child should be taught respect for his elders not in such a way as to make him hypocritically unable to see anything wrong in those older than himself, but simply as one of the graces of life, a courtesy that youth in the abstract pays to age He should learn to say not simply "yes" and "no," but to add "Mother," "Father," "Mr. Smith," or "Sir" to the monosyllable He should learn, if seated, to rise when older persons enter the room, and not to sit down again until they are seated

A male child should be taught quite early to render to his small sister or girl playmate the little courtesies—seeing that she is seated before him, allowing her to precede him through doors, picking up things which she has dropped, etc —which he will be expected to show ladies when he is an adult Here, as in all matters of training children in gracious behavior, the most effective element will be the example which the father sets in his treatment of the mother

Children must, of course, be taught respect for the property of others. The soundest base for this instruction is the respect which the parents show for the children's property The father or mother who gives a child's dog away, or sends one of his most treasured, though possibly shabby toys off as a contribution to some charity drive—or to the garbage can—without first consulting the child about it, ought not to be surprised to find a son or daughter treating the property of others in the same cavalier fashion.

The realization of individual property ownership comes with difficulty to most children, and patience is needed to make them understand it. All living creatures are acquisitive. Dogs will fight over a bone; birds will try to push one another away from a choice worm or the rim of a bird feeder. The individual's instinct to gratify his own desire or satisfy his own need is a strong one. When a child first begins to understand that ownership is possible, the concept applies only to himself He thinks of *his* toy, *his* food, *his* piece of candy. It is a pleasant ego-gratifying realization, and it is only natural that he should try to increase it by adding other objects to his possessions

Instilling respect for others' rights to the same gratifications takes patience and understanding Name-calling and storming at him is not the way to success. If he has his father's silver cigarette case or gold cuff links hidden away with his collection of pretty stones, he is not a thief, but simply obeying one of the most natural instincts of mankind.

Here where bad manners may, if not corrected, become something more serious, he must be educated to understand that everyone feels about his property as the child himself does, and the examples set by his parents, both in regard to things that belong to him and those that belong to each other pointed out to him, are influential teachers. But if these are not good examples, a verbal lesson is very likely to misfire.

He must also be taught to respect privacy, to knock on closed doors before entering, not to stand about listening to his parents' or brothers' and sisters' phone calls (or for that matter, to those of other people if you have a party-line telephone), not to read other people's letters, or to peek through keyholes. But instruction in these matters will fall on deaf ears and perhaps bring a wry smile to the child's lips, if the respect you ask him to accord to others is not accorded to him.

Children should, by all means, be taught habits of neatness and cleanliness, and be made to realize that it is rude to others to leave toys and clothing scattered about in the home which the whole family shares, or to come to the table with dirty hands or face and uncombed hair. Yet it is almost as easy to overdo this as it is to neglect it. Parents who insist that a child keep spotless at play have short memories for the joys of mud pies, sandboxes, tree climbing, and the healthy games which children enjoy even though (and perhaps a little because) they become somewhat messy, and a poor understanding of the wholesome physical and mental development of the young.

TELEVISION AND RADIO

Every home in which there is a television set or even a radio, and one or more children has a combination that presents a classic contemporary problem in behavior. A part of the problem is concerned with a proper allocation of the child's time, the formation of good habits and the conditioning of the young mind, and affects manners only peripherally. Yet it is impossible to dissociate any human activity, whether of a child or of an adult, and the habits that are formed by it, from his behavior in association with other human beings. The child who habitually evades his responsibility to studies, or such duties as he has in his own home, in order to watch television is forming habits that will make it easier for him to evade his obligations to others, including those of courtesy.

There is a word that, in the past, was often (perhaps too often) used in training children, and that, for many, has seemed to slip

out of the English language. But I know no real substitute for it
It is a little word of four letters with a profound significance. It is
still a good word, a useful word, which should be made familiar to
every child—somehow in such a way that it will retain its freshness
and excitement, rather than become the label for a boring concept
which the child rejects impatiently. *Duty.* Fulfilled, it gives a child a
sense of accomplishment, increases his self-respect, sets his mind at
rest, and frees him for fun uncomplicated by a nagging sense of
guilt. These, the rewarding aftermaths, and the avoidance of unpleasant self-censure are the elements that should be stressed in
teaching a child the importance of duty or, if you dislike the word as
much as many people do, of being a responsible human being.

Training a child to proper use of the television and radio is not
an easy task. There the instrument stands It is so simple to turn it
on and escape the pressure of a bad conscience. Yet if only he can be
made to see that he will enjoy it and all else connected with his daily
life if he regards its use as a privilege to enjoy only under proper
conditions, you will have done him a service that will stand him in
good stead not only in relation to television and radio, but also in all
contacts which he has with other human beings, with his obligations,
and with that self within the self who is the constant companion
and judge of each of us.

If he is a schoolchild with homework, he should learn to do
his homework first in the evening, and watch television later—if
there is still the opportunity to do so before bedtime. This rule might
be varied in consideration of a favorite program that is on between
the time he returns from school and dinner, though the time might
be better spent in some physical activity, after the school day's
inaction. Every human being needs a break between one extended
period of sedentary concentration and another. But the child who
is allowed to rush from the dinner table to the television set, saying,
"I'll do my homework later," is being encouraged in bad habits and
a lowering of his sense of responsibility.

The television set should be regarded as something for the whole
family to enjoy. No one member of it should be permitted to
monopolize it for his favorite programs, thus robbing the others of the
opportunity to see theirs. If the child finishes his homework and finds
that his parents or, for that matter, one of his brothers or sisters
is watching a program other than the one he wants to see, he must be

taught to wait until it is finished, and not interrupt it with a demand to have his own program. If he misses his program entirely as a result of his courteous behavior, he should learn to take the disappointment graciously.

If he has a guest and they decide to spend some of their time together watching television, his guest's choice, rather than his, should determine what program they will watch.

If he has brothers and/or sisters and their favorite programs vary, he must learn to work out with them a schedule by which each may see some of their favorites without interfering with those of the others. The principle of adjustment, of give and take, of sharing fairly with others is one of the most important of all rules of community living, and if the child learns to follow it in his earliest years, partly through his television habits, it will serve him well in many contacts throughout his life.

He must learn to keep the sound turned down to the lowest volume at which he can hear it, so that it will not disturb others in the house or in the neighborhood.

He should be taught to turn it off when his parents have guests and when he is reading or studying, rather than to keep it going simply as a background noise from which he derives no real entertainment.

THE BABY SITTER

The baby sitter has become an indispensable part of the American family scene, and the use of one necessitates certain rules of conduct on the parents' part, both toward the children and toward the sitter.

It is unfair and discourteous to your children and to the one who has been called in to be with them while you are out, not to tell the children about it and to be present when they meet one another for the first time. To have a stranger come in after the children have been put to bed and are asleep, and then to slip away without the youngsters knowing that you are going is rude, may instill a fear of abandonment in childish minds, and is likely to cause trouble for the sitter in case the children wake.

There are specific courtesies which you owe to the sitter. The rate of payment should be definitely agreed on beforehand Both the sitter and the children should be given a clear understanding of the routine for the evening, and the children told that they must obey the one who has been called in, in the parents' place, as they would their own parents. Leave a phone number where you can be reached in an emergency during the evening. Say definitely when you will be back, and if you are going to be delayed more than a few minutes beyond the stated time, phone and say so. And if you arrange a snack to be eaten during the evening, and tell the baby sitter that it is for her or for him, you will have rendered a very pleasant courtesy and built a bit of good will in one who is really an important part of your family life.

HUMOR AND PLAY

All-embracing family humor that is genuine, whole-souled, and never vindictive, and games which the whole family, children and adults, can play together are among the strongest influences toward family solidarity and understanding, and often furnish opportunities for the parents to further the training of the children in social behavior. Often a wise parent may find it possible to solve a temporary problem in behavior with a child by seeing an element of humor in the situation, and gently, without ridicule, making the child see it too. And sometimes even a very young child will be able to turn a situation that is marked by excessive annoyance or anger on the part of the parent back into normal pleasant channels by the same method—if the parent-child relationship is right.

I remember having once seen an overwrought mother suddenly flare up in anger at her three-year-old boy, and the child listening calmly for a moment to her tirade, and then, as she paused to catch her breath, quietly, and with twinkling eyes misquoting an admonition which she had often delivered to him. When he said, "Don't lose your temperature, Mommy," the tension of the moment was released in laughter, the two were reunited in the affectionate companionship that was basic to their relationship, and both mother and child had received a lesson in behavior—in this case from the child himself.

There are many games that are grand fun for both adults and

children of every age. Further, they provide one of the best of all opportunities for lessons in fair play, courtesy, and give and take to be inculcated. Many an adult's happiest memories of childhood center about the fun which he and his parents and brothers and sisters had together.

I still remember how in my grandmother's home at Tivoli, Columbia County, New York, I played "tag" and "I spy" with my aunts and their friends around the old porch where you could look through the windows and catch a glimpse of someone on the other side, and any number of games which a lonely little girl (as I was) would never have played if the adults had not been willing to join in. As I grew older we played many of the word games, and even charades which were hilarious at times and brought joy to a child's heart, especially if she was allowed to dress up.

One of the things which I remember most vividly is that on Sunday evenings we all gathered around the piano and sang hymns That is a tradition which I wish (if I had been a good enough musician) I could have preserved in my own family, for I remember that it was one of the things I enjoyed deeply as a little girl.

The wise parent can often adapt a game to the understanding and abilities of the younger children. I remember an occasion in which this was done most skillfully by an English mother. She, her ten-year-old son, and I were playing "I spy."

In case you don't know how to play it, it goes like this Each player in turn says, "I spy with my little eye, something that begins with—," mentioning a letter of the alphabet which is the first letter of the word spelling the object. Then the other players guess in turn what it is. When it has been guessed the play passes to the one who has successfully identified it.

We were going along at a great rate, all three of us having a wonderful time, when the three-year-old daughter entered the room At once the mother asked her to join the game, but because the child had not yet learned to spell, changed it to one in which the object was identified by color, instead of by name. The key statement then became, "I spy with my little eye, something that is blue," or "red," or "white," or "has no color at all," and the game went merrily on.

But several important things had been accomplished besides having fun. The family had remained a unit, with no member of it having been left out, a child had been spared the pain of feeling inferior, and a ten-year-old boy had been given an excellent lesson in adjusting his activities to the ability of one who had not attained the same stage of development as he had—a situation which he would meet again and again, in one form or another, throughout his life, and must, if he were to conduct his social relations graciously, learn to manage with courtesy and consideration.

THE STEPCHILD AND THE ADOPTED CHILD

Throughout this discussion I have so far considered only the most usual situation, that in which the husband and wife are the natural parents of all the children There are two situations which present somewhat special circumstances that call for the same kind of unusually careful handling and understanding which a wise and considerate adult would give to complicated adult relationships These are the ones that arise when there are step- or adopted children.

One of the most serious hazards which every child faces in growing up is the danger that through some awkwardness in his relationship with his parents and other members of the family, his contemporaries outside the home, his schoolteachers, or others, he may lose the sense of security that is essential to healthy intellectual, spiritual, and even physical growth. In the relationship of a parent with either a stepchild or a child who has been adopted, the danger of this is increased.

This is perhaps especially true in a second marriage following the divorce of one of the parents Any change in the regular pattern of family life is upsetting to a child and may seem to him to be a menace. When the change is so radical as that which occurs in divorce, in the obvious destruction of unity between parents, and in robbing him of one of them, the danger may become acute. If the break in the family has resulted from the death of one parent, the blow to the child is no less real, but is probably less complicated. Though he is not able to understand death (who does, really?), he learns quickly that it is a final thing His mother or father is irretrievably gone—not simply somewhere else in the world when he should be at home, making up an essential part of the family. Nor is there involved the frightening and unsettling conflict between the two most important persons in his life, and the necessity to "take sides " (See also Chapter 22, "Separation, Divorce, and Second Marriage.")

In either case any second marriage that involves children should be preceded by a period in which the prospective stepparent should exert every effort to make friends with the child or children involved, so that even before the marriage takes place he may come to seem almost a part of the family, a friend whom the child or children will welcome when the marriage occurs as a permanent addition to the home. (The child, of course, will consider the original group as "his" family Only later will he be able to include in that designation the addition that has come about through the second marriage)

If it is necessary to delay the marriage while this process of acclimatization is taking place, the delay is a small price to pay for the rich rewards which it may achieve. I would almost go so far as to say that if the attempt to establish a friendly, companionable relationship between the prospective stepparent and the children of the first marriage fails, it would be better to abandon the marriage entirely than to risk the dubious prospect of a happy marriage against the opposition of the children This is perhaps a generality that might not be sound in special circumstances. But the principle behind it is sound And the process which I have recommended may be much simpler than it seems at first.

The heart of a child is warm with welcome for anyone who approaches him with affection, consideration, and respect. If overtures of friendship are made long before the child knows that a marriage is contemplated, and the acquaintance between child and adult proceeds successfully, it is likely that no resistance will be met at any time. It is the intrusion of a stranger into the family which the child resents, the acquisition of permanent closeness of a friend, the child will recognize as a gain.

And of course the child should be told of the marriage beforehand, should be allowed to participate in the planning for it and in the ceremony itself In some circles it is considered improper for the children of a first marriage that has been terminated by divorce to attend a second wedding. This seems to me to be the height of discourtesy, also cruel, and an invitation to disaster in the second marriage. What a terrible beginning for a new family venture, which at its best must present special problems, to have one or more members of the family excluded from the ceremony that launches it! It is perhaps as well, under these circumstances, to have a quiet wedding ceremony, with only members of the two families and close friends present, rather than an elaborate wedding; but simple or formal, by all means include any children who are about to become members of the new family.

If there are children by the second marriage, the situation again becomes somewhat special. Every child who is old enough to talk and understand words should be told beforehand when he is about to have a new baby brother or sister. He should be told in such a way that it will seem to him the joyous miracle that it is, so that he may come automatically to look forward to the event with eagerness and joy. And after the child or children arrive it is obvious that nothing should ever make a dividing line between the children of the first marriage and those of the second. When any man and any woman marry, parts of two families join to become one. When the part of one family consists of a child or children by an earlier marriage, the situation is enlarged, but should not be materially changed The important thing is the establishment of solidarity in the newly made family group.

The special problems in family behavior brought about by the adoption of a child in many ways resemble those created by step-children, though for the child himself it may be a somewhat more complicated one. The son or daughter who becomes a stepchild to one of the parents of a second marriage has always the feeling of security furnished by the established parent who is party to the marriage. To the adopted child the entire terrain of the new home is terra incognita, the group which he has joined there, strangers all, and at some time he is bound to feel that he has been rejected by his natural parents.

If he is adopted at an extremely early age his questioning, doubts, fears, and sense of inferiority (unless unusual wisdom and care on the part of his parents by adoption have been able to avert them) will come later, when through his contacts outside the home, he will learn that his family situation is different from that of most children, and when perhaps some cruel and misinformed youngster (or for that matter, an older person) will impute inferiority to him because of his adoption.

But if he is an older child, and especially if he is one of those most unfortunate of all children (it seems to me) who has been farmed out to several foster parents who are paid by the state or city, his precious sense of security has probably already been badly shattered, and the new parents must tread a wary path indeed, and summon up all the wisdom and patience and kindness and understanding which they possess or may acquire in order to turn potential catastrophe into success. Every detail in their plan to meet their responsibility should be arranged with this end in view

How is the addition to the family made known to the world? When a child is born within the family itself it is customary, of course, to send formal announcements to friends far and wide. Is the same custom followed when a child is adopted? In many cases, yes, but I am not sure that it is always wise, or kind to the child, for the time will come when this detail in his history should be considered strictly his own affair to be divulged to those whom he wishes to tell, and not to others He will inevitably learn (along with many other sad and disillusioning facts about the fallible human race) that, unjust and irrational as it is, in the minds of many people adoption still carries with it an implication of shame and inferiority—or at the very least of departure from the usual life pattern, something that marks him as "different" and therefore, by the illogic of mankind, open to suspicion. The prejudice against adopted children, which still exists among some people (born doubtless of the implication of birth out of wedlock, extreme poverty of the natural parents, or their dissoluteness, or any of the many reasons which make adoptions possible), is one of the most stupid and cruel of all cruel and stupid prejudices against people for circumstances that are not within their control, and that usually do not, per se, actually confer inferior qualities upon them. But it does exist, and the child should be given every possible safeguard against it.

Because of this it seems to me that the kindest and most courteous and intelligent thing for parents to do when they have made the child of someone else their own is to let it be known informally to family, close friends, and (if they live anywhere save in the atmosphere of privacy and anonymity which is one of the blessings of a large city) to the near neighbors, from whom the news could scarcely be kept in any event. If later, after the child has become an established part of the family, they should move to another location, there is no reason why they should tell anyone there at all, the knowledge has now become peculiarly the property of the child

himself (who of course must be told) to share with others or not, as
he likes.

There is an old and good formula for telling the child himself
about it, which is honest, sound, and kind. "When most people have
babies they have to take what they get, but we *picked* you. We looked
for the loveliest baby we could find, and you were it."

Years ago I read the story of an adopted child in a family of other
children, with whom this formula was so successful that one day he
came to his mother, and said, "I'd like to do something especially
nice for Tommy and Jane to make it up to them. They're so nice!"
Surprised, the mother asked, "Make what up to them, dear?" The
child answered seriously, "Because they weren't picked." The story
of his adoption had actually created in him a sense of superiority,
and with it, an innate realization of *noblesse oblige!*

The father of another adopted boy has told me the story of one
of the most moving moments in his life. He and his wife had told
their son of his adoption, using the time-tried formula. Several
years later, when the boy was about ten, the father brought him a
fine baseball mitt which he loved on sight.

In his gay and enthusiastic thanks the lad said, "This is the best,
no the second-best—it's the third-best present you have ever given
me!"

"What were the other two?" the father asked. "The first-best,"
the boy answered, still gay and smiling, "was when you took me, the
second was my bike, and this is the third."

"What was the first?" the father asked, a little incredulously, for
since the child had been told years before, the matter had rarely
been mentioned between them.

"When you took me, Stupid!" the boy answered.

"But that was a present for your mother and me," the father
answered.

Then the boy's gay smile gave way to seriousness, and his eyes
darkened with emotion and certitude. "Pop," he said, "no matter
what happens to me ever, that will always be the best present I have
ever had."

Must the adopted child be told? It seems to me that from every
point of view the answer is yes. In the complex task of child-raising
one often longs for greater wisdom than any of us has. But there are
two essentials. One is that the child may always be sure of his

parents' love and their supporting championship of him. (If Shakespeare had been writing of parent-child relationships, he could have said nothing wiser about it than that which he put into the Duke's mouth in *Measure for Measure:* "Love talks with better knowledge, and knowledge with dearer love.") The other is that parents never willfully hold back from a child any knowledge of himself.

I know of one case in which the parents of an adopted child, who were farmers, persistently lied to her about it. Whether she had heard a whisper of the truth from outside the family or had simply become obsessed with the idea that she had been adopted, as many children who have not been do, I do not know. Early in her childhood she had asked her parents about it, and they had denied it. For several years she returned to the subject, but each time was told that she was imagining it, that she was not an adopted child. When in her early adolescence she learned beyond doubt that she had been adopted, her parents' refusal to tell her the truth must have confirmed in her the conviction that to be adopted was one of the most shameful things in the world. Unable to face her shame and the fact that her parents had lied to her about something so important as this, and beset by the emotional storms of adolescence, the child rejected the entire fabric of a life that had become too painful for her to bear and killed herself.

Surely this was an exceptional case, but many an adopted child has suffered less cataclysmic traumas from similar mistakes.

It is unrealistic to believe that any adopted child can go through life without at some time or another learning of his adoption, or that however well he is told and however fine his relationship with his foster parents may be, it will not cause any ripple of emotional complications for him. There is only one sure way to minimize his potential confusion in the matter, and that is to let him know the truth as early as he is able to understand it, and by the way he is told, and by the love, respect, and consideration which his parents show him make it quite obvious to him that no possible shame incurs to him because of the situation, and that an adopted child is in no way, because of that, inferior to any other.

Yet in spite of the greatest of care and wisdom there will almost inevitably be times when the child is worried about his special status in the world. Every child at some time or other feels that a parent is being unfair, overharsh, or unreasonable. In a usual family relationship that has been soundly established, a child will take this sort of thing in stride. His capacity for forgiveness is almost infinite. But it is not unnatural that in such a situation the adopted child may think, "If I were her own she wouldn't treat me this way." Indeed many a child who has not been adopted may believe that he has been for a similar reason.

This situation, and that which may arise if the growing child overhears slighting remarks outside the home, or even the *sotto voce* statement of someone to another, "He's an adopted child, you know," intimating that because of this he is an outsider, someone not quite normal, and perhaps inferior, are hazards against which the foster parent must always be on guard.

How? It is a difficult question to answer. First of all by making sure, chiefly by the parental attitude itself, that no such implication has any validity within the family, by giving the child the surest of all bulwarks against the complicated uncertainties of living—the constant assurance of love and respect And perhaps by a special attention to the needs and wholesome desires of the adopted child, by special care not to become unjustifiably angry or annoyed at him, by being ready at all times to face any special emotional problems which may arise in him because of his adoption. The fine line between spoiling him and withholding from him the emotional support which he may need in even greater measure than other children may be a difficult one to find, but it must be sought. If an error is made in either direction, perhaps it is better to make it on the side of a bit of spoiling than on that of neglect

4

The Family of Three Generations

ANOTHER SPECIAL SITUATION FACES THOSE WHO, FOR some reason or other, have taken an elderly parent of either husband or wife into the immediate household. It is a situation which (with some exceptions) every wise elderly parent will reject as an arrangement if it is possible. This, of course, is especially true if there is marked friction between the parent and either his own child or the son- or daughter-in-law. Such friction may be based on character defects in one or the other, or simply on temperamental incompatibilities that are often very difficult to dispel.

In such cases the solution will of course depend upon many factors: the amount of money available, the nature of the aging parent (some old people would much prefer to live by themselves, even without the care that to others may seem minimally essential, or in a good home for the elderly, than with the children), and the depth of incompatibility. If your resources, or those of your parent, or a combination of the two make it possible to arrange some adequate living accommodation outside your home, you may be doing him, as well as your own family, a greater service by making such an arrangement than by insisting upon having him live with you

There is a sixteenth-century poem, "The Passionate Pilgrim" (usually considered anonymous, though sometimes attributed to William Shakespeare), which says in part.

> Crabbed age and youth cannot live together,
> Youth is full of pleasance, age is full of care;
> Youth like summer morn, age like winter weather.

Like all generalities the poem states a half truth, or less, in every line Old age is a relative term, its effects on individuals vary as much as do those of youth. I know one mother of ninety-two living with her retired widower son of sixty-seven The son at sixty-seven (which in his case is old age) is, to be sure, a bit crabbed and full of care. The mother, who has already passed the age to which none but a small minority of the human race ever attain, is full of pleasance, always gay and welcoming to visitors with shining eyes and a bright smile, always ready to take an automobile ride with a friend. She is an inspiration and a blessing to all who are privileged by her friendship. She has even proved that "crabbed age and youth" can live together by making the youthfulness of her spirit overcome, in most cases, the crabbedness of the aged son with whom she lives.

Yet there is enough truth in the poem to make it advisable for all other solutions to be considered before establishing a family of three generations, unless the circumstances are especially favorable, or a joint living arrangement is unavoidable. In that case, the well behaved husband and wife and their children will follow the same rules of courtesy and kindness and consideration which guide them in their relationship with one another.

LIVING ARRANGEMENTS

But the situation itself calls for special planning and special living arrangements, so that not only the rights of the older generation will be taken into account, but those of the two succeeding generations as well.

Separate quarters are a minimum necessity for the older person.

At least one room is essential—a room that is near enough to those occupied by the other members of the family so that they will be available quickly in case of need, yet that will furnish privacy. In this room the occupant should have complete autonomy, arranging it at will, receiving friends there, conducting all the details of life which are more comfortably and satisfactorily arranged in solitude. If it is possible to have at least minimum cooking arrangements there for the preparation of breakfasts, snacks, or tea, so much the better. Today this can be managed very simply by an electric frying pan, electric coffee percolator, electric teakettle, electric toaster, and an electric broiler, a few dishes, and a little table silver.

If it is economically possible to arrange for more room, so much the better. A son and daughter-in-law of whom I know have built onto their house a small wing containing a living room, bedroom, kitchenette, and bath. A communicating door opens into the family living room, and the wing has its own outside door A bell system, which rings in both the kitchen and the bedroom of the main house, has buttons at the bedside, in the living room, and in the bath of the wing, so that the occupant can ring for help in case she needs it. In the four years that the arrangement has prevailed the bell has never been used Here an eighty-year-old mother lives in contentment, and (partly because of her present peace of mind) is a joy to her children and grandchildren. She gets her own breakfast—not because she is not welcome at the family breakfast table, or because she likes to sleep late, but because, an early riser all her life, her day begins at six, while her son and daughter-in-law rise habitually at seven-thirty. She has her own telephone—not an extension to that in the main house, but a private line. She cares for her own small apartment, keeping it clean, neat, and inviting, and entertains her own friends. Sometimes her son and daughter-in-law are asked in when she entertains—sometimes not, and vice versa. She manages her own finances with an income that is enough for essentials—and a little fun. She is still active in church work and has a large list of correspondents among relatives and friends.

She is a happy woman, and her son and daughter-in-law consider her presence a blessing rather than an unfortunate responsibility.

This solution in which there is a fine combination of autonomy in essential things, yet nearness in case of need, and a companionship which all three generations prize is impossible in many cases, but the principle behind it sets a pattern that may be approached within the limits imposed by financial and other circumstances.

THE QUESTION OF AUTHORITY

It is obviously essential that a husband and wife must run their own household and raise their children without interference. The wise grandparent knows this and does not interfere If the grandparent who comes into the home is troublesome in this respect, it becomes a problem that must be met frankly with understanding and courtesy, but also with firmness A frank and full discussion of the matter should establish autonomy without resentment on either side.

A good approach is to assume that when a mother-in-law begins to tell a housewife how to cook vegetables the way her son likes them and how to dress to please him, or begins to give orders to the children, she is trying to be helpful, her desire to help is appreciated, but that the housewife must be allowed to do things her own way, just as she intends to allow her mother-in-law to follow her way in matters that concern her private life.

Certainly it is far more courteous to the older one, and kinder to the other members of your family, to establish an understanding than to let resentment smoulder unexpressed, and confuse the children by secretly countermanding orders that have been given by their grandparent.

I remember a one-act play, entitled, "Joint Owners in Spain," which used to be given by amateur groups years ago, in which an elderly woman who for years had enjoyed her room alone in an old people's home had to share it with a newcomer for whom there was room nowhere else. The original tenant of the room, when she learned this, drew a chalk line on the floor down the middle of the room between the two beds, and explained to the newcomer that this divided their two "houses." "When you want to come to see me," she said, "you rap on the footboard of my bed, and when I want to come to see you, I'll rap on yours."

On the face of it an absurd arrangement in an environment as intimate as this, but it worked. In the warmth of this mutual respect for privacy the two became firm friends and comforting companions.

THE VIRTUES OF BUSYNESS

Yet along with this firm understanding that privacy and independence on both sides are essential in the three-generation family, just as in the case of the adopted child the "adopted" parent must be made to feel welcome and important. It is not exploitation but kindness and courtesy to allow the older person to share such of the household chores as is practical.

If the older person is a woman and she takes it upon herself to wash the breakfast dishes regularly, or even for all three meals, by all means let her do so, and show your appreciation by now and then pointing out how it permits you to do things for which you would not otherwise find the time. If he is a man, and you are fortunate enough to have a small garden, and he is happy gardening, leave it in his charge and see how he blossoms among his flowers and vegetables!

The greatest tragedy of old age is the tendency for the old to feel unneeded, unwanted, and of no use to anyone; the secret of happiness in the declining years is to remain interested in life, as active as possible, useful to others, busy, and forward looking.

I know one marvelous woman of eighty-four, living on an income just large enough to meet her modest needs and leave a little left over each year. She is one of the most interesting conversationalists I know, alert, physically spry within the limits imposed by arthritis, of which she never complains, and a joy to all who know her. I have never once heard her talk of the past, in the self-pitying, nostalgic tones that so often afflict the elderly. She has a small country place, and each year she plans what she will do next year with the money she can spare—build a retaining wall along the edge of a slope in her garden, against which she can plant gay shrubs and flowers, build a garden house, extend the lawn—and each year she carries out her plans. Two or three years ago she had a hundred tiny pine trees planted in a vacant space behind her house. I am sure that in her mind's eye she sees them now as forest giants, though she will never see them so in reality. The secret of her happiness is that she still lives in the future. No one could possibly be sorry for her because she is old, indeed the adjective would never occur to anyone who knows her well.

This is the sort of thing which, in some way or another, must be encouraged in the old by those who are younger—not by constant harping on it, not by pontifical lectures, but by encouraging every tendency toward it which is apparent in the older one, by talking over plans for the future and inviting participation, by treating the one who is older as though he were an adult who is respected, wanted, and useful, not as one in a second childhood.

ARGUING IS BETTER THAN INDIFFERENCE

Julietta K. Arthur, in *How to Help Older People*, tells of a grandmother who expressed her frustration in a letter to a newspaper.

"I can't understand," she wrote, "the attitude of the current generation which my own generation produced. It's not disrespect. It's not scorn. Rather it's utter indifference and disregard." She had been able-bodied and keen of mind when her husband died, leaving her a widow with a small income insufficient for her full support. When she had proposed to her son that she find any one of a number of jobs which she could have done well, he protested, saying that it would make people think that he was negligent. Instead, he proposed that she live with him and his wife. Finally, to please him, she consented, and was given a small room at the top of the house, from which she descends to eat meals with the family. One of her complaints, interestingly enough, was that no one ever argued with her, or criticized her for anything No one ever consulted her about anything. She was not allowed by her daughter-in-law to do any of the household work. Essentially she was ignored. "I am prepared to be tolerated for the rest of my life," she added. "My children and my children's children endure me, but they don't enjoy me."

OVERPROTECTION

Obviously in this case there have been two mistakes—both of which may be classified as having been born of bad manners. The first was made when the son urged his mother to come and share the home of himself and his wife—not really out of regard for her, but because he was afraid of what people would say if he didn't—a self-centered, ill-mannered, and inexcusable reason for inviting anyone to your home. The second was in his treatment of her after she had accepted his invitation. He was not even a good host, to say nothing of being a bad son. It is a justifiable assumption that he was also rude to his wife, his children, his friends, and his business associates—save perhaps his superiors upon whom he depended for advancement.

There is a rather nice clause in the Constitution and By-Laws adopted on October 28, 1858, by the Association for the Relief of Aged and Indigent Women, of Portland, Maine.

They [the inmates] will . . . endeavor, by a quiet, gentle, and lady-like deportment, to infuse an air of cheerfulness and good feeling throughout the house, and by acts of kindness and forbearance, to gain the esteem, and promote the comfort and happiness of each other.

I doubt that a similar clause would be phrased quite that way today, though essentially it is sound A certain amount of quiet is fine—especially, I suppose, for older people—and cheerfulness, kindness, forbearance, and good feeling are always worth seeking to achieve. But it is well recognized today that the most important element in any association with the elderly is helping them to remain active mentally, and physically within the limits of their strength, helping them, in short, to stay in the stream of life—feeling needed and useful and wanted, looking forward rather than backward, paying little or no attention to the fact that they are nearer to the end of life than its beginning.

Many studies have been made in recent years of healthy and unhealthy old age, and the importance of these factors is being emphasized more and more. Such studies reveal amazing examples of men and women in their eighties and nineties, some of whom are still functioning in their chosen lifework, some of whom have retired from that, only to plunge into some less exacting but still stimulating activity, some of whom have relaxed into inactivity, simply waiting to die, and thereby enduring a half-death for years until they pass from the nonentity of senility to that of death. A number of old persons questioned as to the factors that had made it possible for them to stay well and active over so long a period of years have given such answers as these: "Being with people. I've never been one to crawl off and be by myself." "Working hard. I don't intend to stop before I die." "Not worrying. I figure that I can't remake the world, and that if I just keep at it and do the best I can, things usually turn out all right." "Taking some outdoor exercise every day of my life that I'm not in bed—and there haven't been many when I have been."

These are the things that are important in the mental and physical health of the old. These are the things which younger persons, who accept the responsibility of having their parents in their homes, should encourage.

Almost every retired person has long-standing desires to do something which he has not been able to do in a busy life. Try to find out what it is. Encourage him, if it is at all possible, to take it up in the later years when responsibilities have been passed on to a younger generation and, under ideal conditions, the aging mind should be free to choose. There are countless things which the aged can do well— and sometimes better than can younger people. The son or daughter should find out by tactful questioning what these elderly ambitions are, and see to it, to the best of his or her ability, that they are satisfied. Such activities will prolong their parent's life and give it meaning.

Yet even the business of trying to keep an elderly person alive, when it is carried to the extent of overprotection, may defeat its own purpose.

A friend has told me a delightful story of his mother who, at seventy, decided that she would like to go to California to spend the winter with another son who lived there. Since she had suffered from a faulty heart for some years, the son insisted that she talk the matter over with the family doctor before a decision was made.

One evening when he returned from work his mother told him that she had seen the doctor, who had approved, and that she had set the date for her departure. Wanting to make sure that all was well, the son himself called on the doctor.

This was in the day when overland railroad tickets were issued in long strips, with subdivisions, each of which covered a part of the journey.

"Your mother," the doctor said, "sat down in the chair and opened her purse. She took out a ticket as long as your arm, and said, 'Doctor, this is my ticket to California. It cost me over three hundred dollars, and you know that I am not wealthy. I don't believe that the railroad would take it back. May I go to California?' I told her she could."

The son asked him what the trip would do to her.

"It may kill her," he said soberly. "Your mother has a bad heart and she will have to go across some mountains at rather high altitudes to get there. It probably won't, for she has an amazing natural vitality, but if it does I assure you it will be a very easy death. She has lived a full and wonderful life. Don't dim the last years of it by treating her as though she were a child who had to be kept in on a rainy day. Let her go to California. And don't send anyone with her to take care of her. This is her party. Let her have her fun."

"Well, she went to California," the son went on, "and outwalked my brother on climbs in the neighborhood hills. My brother lives in a college town. After Mother had been there for a couple of weeks, he noticed that she left quietly every Tuesday and Thursday just after lunch, apparently to take a walk. She would be gone about an hour and a half and then come back, excited and pleased with herself, but never saying where she had been. Finally, he followed her without letting her see him, and saw her enter one of the halls on the university campus. She had enrolled as a special student and was taking a course in French—something she had always wanted to do and had never been able to before.

"Her heart? Well she lived to be ninety, and finally died of terminal pneumonia, after having broken her hip in a fall. The more I think of it, the more I feel sure that the doctor was right—and would still have been right if she had died in her sleep as the train was going over the Rockies. As a young wife she had borne two children after the doctor had warned her that another might kill her. As an oldster she went as blithely about the business of living as she had when a girl. Spiritually speaking, Mother knew how to 'live it up.' "

Those oldsters who don't much bother to think of how old they are, are the fortunate ones, and if those whose responsibility it is to care for them encourage them in this attitude they will do them the greatest courtesy and render them the greatest service possible. As the wise parent does not talk down to his children, constantly reminding them that they are children and thus inferior, the adept son and daughter-in-law, or daughter and son-in-law, into whose home a parent has come to live will not say and do those things that will constantly emphasize the fact that he or she is out of the running, will not overprotect him, will not, in short, push him aside.

A difficult situation may also arise when an elderly parent has money enough to live alone (in fact may be much better off financially than the younger people), but is lonely and would like to share the lives of the younger people in every way humanly possible, and tries to bring it about by using the power of money, that is, by offering in effect to subsidize the young people and give them greater opportunity. Whether the young people live under a maternal or a paternal roof, this power can be exercised, for a father can be as dominating as a mother can.

It is much better, I think, in such cases where there is no financial problem, for separate lives to be worked out. If a good relationship can be established in this way, the parent will probably be more naturally included in the lives of the young people than if there has been anything remotely resembling compulsion to make them all remain one family group.

Any situation that makes members of a younger generation feel responsible for aging parents is not a simple one, but it is one that can be managed with consideration, kindness, understanding, cooperation on both sides, and obedience to the ordinary rules of courtesy applicable to all human relationships, so that each generation may be an asset to the other rather than a liability.

5

Servants in the Home

PERHAPS NOTHING HAS CHANGED MORE RADICALLY DURING the present century than has the servant situation. The elaborate staff of cook, parlor maid, personal maid, footman, coachman (later chauffeur), butler, gardener, nurse or governess, and laundress has, save in a small number of households, passed into memory. So has the old-time "hired girl" who used to be, in more modest homes, the woman-of-all-work.

Today, in the vast majority of homes the housewife herself copes, sometimes with the help of daughters and even sons, with perhaps a once-a-week cleaning woman, and a baby sitter where there is occasion to use one.

The change, of course, has come about through several circumstances. The justified increase in wages for household help has made full-time servants economically impractical for many families. The maid who, even twenty-five years ago, was content to have a full-time job and live in at $20 a month now expects $250 a month. Fewer and fewer young women are willing to accept domestic service as a means of earning a livelihood More and more are fitting themselves for office jobs or careers in other vocations.

The character of housework also has changed and become simpler because of the constantly increasing number of labor-saving appliances available. The electric dishwasher, the automatic washing machine and dryer (or the laundromat around the corner), the vacuum cleaner, thermostatically controlled ovens and electric frying pans, household freezers, and the electric iron have taken much of the drudgery out of housework Even the electric blanket, which eliminates several ordinary blankets or comforters in winter, makes bed-making quicker and simpler

But for many the once-a-week cleaning woman is still a godsend (if you can get one!) Some households still include a full-time maid, and a very few still have a complement of servants And whether your staff is one part-time servant or several full-time, you have definite obligations of courtesy and fair dealing to discharge.

HIRING

Be sure that you enter into your relationship with any servant, with a full and frank understanding of all the pertinent facts connected with the employment. Know, before interviewing her or him, what the standard wage in your area is for the work you require, and do not try to save money by skimping If you do, and your offer is accepted, you may be sure that you are hiring an incompetent (regardless of what the references say) or that, at the very least, you have hired a temporary servant The demand for good maids, cleaning women, cooks, and other household help is such today that no self-respecting person will accept a position at less than the going rate, unless as a temporary makeshift.

Meet the applicant with the respect and courtesy which you would accord any newly-made acquaintance. You enhance, rather than diminish, your standing by addressing a prospective servant as "Miss," "Mrs.," or "Mr." when you meet each other for the first time. If you are elderly and the applicant very young, you may call her by her first name, just as you would any young person to whom you are introduced The question of what names you habitually call full-time servants will be discussed later. Do not forget, as you interview your applicant, that there is a practical consideration involved, as well as the matter of simple courtesy. Though you will ask most of the questions, you as well as the applicant are being interviewed. First impressions are very powerful, and how you first appear to one who is going to enter your household may be highly important in your later relationship.

Talk frankly and honestly with the applicant about the work involved, what you will expect, and the applicant's qualifications. Be sure that you mention everything which you will expect her or him to do It is not courteous, it is not fair, and it is not conducive to good relations, to talk vaguely and in general terms only of the duties involved, and then, after the servant has been installed, ask for onerous services that were not even hinted at in the original interview.

Have a clear understanding as to the wages that are to be paid, and when they will be paid—whether by the day, week, or month—and about days off and vacations. For the woman who comes in one or two days a week and has to travel by bus, streetcar, or subway to get to your house, be sure to mention that you will pay her transportation both ways, and never forget to do so This is the invariable custom in some places, is optional in others, and perhaps in some is not considered necessary at all. But remember that the part-time worker loses a great deal of time for which the full-time worker is paid, that time is consumed by the trips to and from your house, and that the smallest gesture you can make in recognition of this is to pay carfare. If you cannot afford it, you cannot afford the help you are hiring.

If you are employing a full-time servant, and if you have children, it will be wise to have them meet one another before hiring. If the servant's duties especially involve care of the children this becomes mandatory. Children and dogs seem to have an inbuilt mechanism for appraising people, and almost instinctively know whether they will get on well together. If you sense an automatic antagonism in either the children or the applicant, it will be kinder both to the children and the prospective servant to look elsewhere rather than to risk future trouble. You would not, if you are a good hostess, invite to the same party two persons whom you knew were deeply antagonistic to each other. Do not create the same situation between your children and a servant. Some personalities simply will not mix.

VACATIONS

Every full-time servant today expects a two weeks' vacation with pay each year, and must be given it A regular part-time worker, such as a once-a-week cleaning woman, may not expect one. Yet if she is a faithful worker, who has been with you a year or more, it is a gracious, kindly, and fair thing to see that she has her vacation and to pay for it. And from a purely practical point of view it probably will prove a good investment from which you will receive returns in a little extra dusting, a little extra attention to the dark corners, and perhaps a bit of overtime when she finds that her work isn't quite finished, as a careful housewife would have it, in the usual time. In most human relations one usually gets back about what one puts into them—or a little more.

YOU ARE A HOSTESS AS WELL AS AN EMPLOYER

If I seem to overstress the words "guest" and "hostess" it is because it seems to me that everyone who enters your house, whether as a friend or acquaintance, a relative who is going to stay an indefinite length of time, or a paid servant, is to a certain extent essentially a guest. I do not mean to say that your relationship to all of them is identical, but merely that you owe to your servant not only a strict fulfillment of the monetary and other obligations which you have assumed when you made your arrangement with her (as you will expect her to fulfill the obligations to which she has agreed), but also basic courtesies which you would show anyone who is under your roof. This rule does not of course extend to such things as having your servant eat at table with you, sit down in the living room with you when you are entertaining friends, or go to the theater with you, or accompany you when you call on friends. But it does mean that you issue instructions as courteous requests, with "please," rather than as curt and aloof orders, that you say "thank you," that you listen with sympathy and understanding to personal problems that involve service, and be cooperative in granting privileges which emergencies make necessary.

It also means that you give a full-time servant, who lives in, decent and comfortable quarters. You would not give an invited guest a bed with a broken spring and a lumpy mattress in a room in which there are insufficient or uncomfortable chairs, no clothes closet, and a dresser made out of orange crates. No more should you do so to your maid.

Before she comes you should see that the room that is to be hers is as cheerful as you can make it—with pleasant curtains, at least one comfortable easy chair with a good reading light, a bedside table and, certainly in this day and age, a radio or television set.

The room should be as neat and clean and welcoming (even though it may not be as large or elaborately furnished) as one which you had prepared for a cherished friend If she does not keep it that way after she comes, you have probably made a mistake in hiring her.

This room should be her castle. You will no more enter it without knocking, when she is in it, than you would if it had been assigned to a guest.

Nor will you in other ways intrude on her privacy. Her mail, her telephone calls, those with whom she spends her days or evenings off are her own affair.

CONSIDERATION

The fact that you have engaged someone to serve you, and that you pay her for the service, does not in any way relieve you from the responsibility to use ordinary consideration in your relationship with her.

Though you will of course expect from her the general services which you engaged her to perform, and specific services within the general category of services agreed upon, you will not expect special and additional tasks unless in an emergency, and as an acknowledged favor to you.

In general you will ask your servant to do specific things rather than order her to do them. Requests and instructions have a much different and more pleasing tone than direct orders. Saying, "Will you have a rib roast for tomorrow's dinner, when the Smiths will be here? And please remember that Mr. Smith likes his rare," will serve you better, promote better relations with your cook, and be more conducive to nourishing your own sense of proper conduct than, "Have a roast for tomorrow and see that you cook it rare."

You would not take advantage of a friend by continually and unnecessarily asking favors of him, yet in an emergency you would not hesitate to ask for his help. This also should be your attitude toward your servants. If it has been expressly understood when you have hired a maid or a cook that she will have no responsibility for the children, and that when you are leaving for the evening a baby sitter would be provided, you will arrange with a baby sitter as a matter of course. But if on an evening when you are about to go out your baby sitter phones to say that she cannot possibly come because of some emergency, and you cannot get another, it is perfectly in order for you to ask the maid or cook whether she is planning to go out that night, and if she is not, to say, "Will you, as a special favor, keep your eye on the children?" explaining the reason for the request. But remember that you *are* asking a favor, not demanding something that is your due, and express proper gratitude if the favor is granted.

If you have engaged a general maid or housekeeper who, among other duties, cares for your room, do not feel that because of her you have no responsibility for neatness, and do not treat her as though her sole responsibility were to act as a personal maid for you. Hanging your own clothes in the closet, leaving your dresser reasonably neat, drawing your own bath—these are your responsibilities, and any servant who has general household duties would be justified in resenting you if you expected her to assume them.

If you have a cook and, on her days off, prepare your own meals, do not leave the used cooking utensils and dishes for her to wash. Leave the kitchen as neat as you expect to find it when she has left it.

You and your servants are engaged in a joint enterprise. Each of you has responsibilities that must be carried out with mutual respect and consideration. One of yours is to assume authority and furnish direction. But it is equally important that, in doing so, you remember constantly that you are dealing with human beings who, like yourself, respond unfavorably to impatience, lack of a sense of proportion, injustice, and ordinary bad manners. If you and your household staff cannot be friends you are part of an unsuccessful relationship with them.

THE SERVANTS AND THE CHILDREN

᪥ If you have servants and children, the children should be trained as carefully in their behavior toward the servants as in any other regard. Rudeness to servants from children must be dealt with promptly and firmly. Make your children understand that discourtesy to one in your employ is as culpable as rudeness to you or to anyone else.

Indeed from one point of view such rudeness is worse than that to a parent, for a mother or father is in a position to take the child to task for it, while, traditionally at least, a servant is not. Actually I am not sure that the tradition is a completely sound guide for all instances. Certainly the rearing of a child is not the function of a maid or a cook, and no well trained servant will attempt to assume it. A servant should not give one of your children orders, nor should a child give orders to a servant. Yet if a trusted member of your household staff takes a child to task in a reasonable and sensible manner for some outrageous bit of impudence, I, for one, would not censure the servant. If it is done well, I think that thanks, rather than reproof, are called for.

WHAT TO CALL THE SERVANT

᪥ As I have said earlier the courteous employer will always address an applicant for a job by his or her last name, preceded by Mrs , Miss, or Mr., during the employment interview. After the servant has been hired and becomes a part of the household, customs of naming vary. There are two methods of deciding what names you will use. One is that of consulting formal practice in various places and following it The other is by looking at it from a human point of view and taking into consideration the amount of personal warmth you feel for each other, and your desire and that of the servant.

In formal usage maids are called by their first names, though in England their last names are frequently used, without Mrs. or Miss. Sometimes they are called by fictitious first names which their employers, for some reason or other, like better than their real names. Housekeepers and cooks are usually called by their surnames pre-

ceded by Mrs. or Miss, butlers and housemen by their surnames
without Mr., chauffeurs either by their first names or by their surnames. Sometimes butlers, like maids, are called by surnames chosen
by their employers, which have no relation to their actual names

But why should one follow rigid rules in this human relationship, and customs that would not be thought of in other associations
in which no employment of one by another occurred? No dignity
will be lost if you call your maid Miss or Mrs Jones, while you feel
on last-name terms with her, nor will your cook find that you are
belittling her if after you have become friends you call her by her
first name. As to manufacturing names for any of your staff, because,
for instance, you may feel that "Mignon" is a more elegant name
for a maid than "Jane" or "Mary," it is, even if to a very small extent, robbing a human being of one of the most precious of all possessions—individual identity. Don't do it. Every member of your
household staff is a human being The success of all human relationships depends upon their humanness.

THE SERVANTS' DRESS

How your servants should dress is today largely a matter of
your taste and theirs The rigid conventions that used to dictate
exactly what sort of uniform each member of the household staff
should wear, have largely passed away with the changes that have
made the old-time full complement of servants very rare indeed Yet
for those to whom the matter is of contemporary pertinence, here
are some specifications for conventional servants' uniforms. For
others they may have historical interest.

The Butler

For morning wear: a double-breasted sack suit in solid color
blue, black, or Oxford, a white shirt with detached stiff, fold-over
collar, black four-in-hand tie, plain black socks, and black oxfords.
In the summer he may wear a soft shirt and collar with four-in-hand,
a single-breasted gray or black suit, or a white linen or duck jacket,
and in the evening a wing collar and white tie instead of the soft
shirt and soft collar.

The Valet

This highly personal servant, who for the gentleman corresponds to his wife's lady's maid, usually wears a dark blue or black double-breasted business suit, with white shirt and semistiff or soft collar, and black four-in-hand tie

The Chauffeur

The customary dress of the chauffeur has changed somewhat in this generation, because he usually has duties in addition to those of driving the car and keeping it in order. He may double as butler, houseman, or gardener. He is usually dressed in a quiet oxford gray or black double-breasted suit, with a white shirt, semisoft collar, black four-in-hand tie, black shoes and socks, black gloves, and stiff-visored cap. In summer his suit may be a quiet whipcord.

The Lady's Maid

Generally wears dark clothes of her own, which may be changed to light in the summer In the afternoon she may wear a uniform that often has white collars and cuffs; in the evening she wears black silk or taffeta, sometimes with a black bibless apron.

The Waitress, Parlormaid, and Housemaid

Plain cotton dresses with short sleeves and plain white collars are customary Aprons usually have high bibs The waitress, when serving a formal dinner, changes to a long-sleeved and high-necked dress of black silk or taffeta with white collar and cuffs.

It is customary for the employer to pay for all uniforms worn by the maids of the house, and very often for the white coats which any menservants may be required to wear.

The Housekeeper, the Companion, and the Social Secretary

Do not have uniforms but wear their own clothes which are carefully chosen by them to be in unobtrusive good taste. If the companion or social secretary joins her mistress in entertaining, she will of course dress formally when her mistress does.

6

The Family Entertains

HOME ENTERTAINING MAY RANGE IN CHARACTER FROM the casual conversation and cup of tea which mark the informal dropping in of a friend on an afternoon, to the most formal of dinners attended by as many guests as may comfortably be welcomed in your dining and living rooms. Details of dress and service will vary; the basic rules of courtesy and adaptation to the pleasure of your guests will remain the same.

THE AFTERNOON TEA

The casual tea may be one of the most informal and pleasantly friendly things in the world, yet it has well established rules of its own. It is an affair at which old friends see one another and frequently make new acquaintances. Women may come to it from shopping or from home in informal afternoon dress. If men are invited they may come straight from their offices in business dress. There is an air of "just dropping in" about it which is relaxed and restful.

Invitations may be issued in any way you like. Today the telephone call has replaced the written invitation to many things, and is usual in the case of informal afternoon gatherings. It is quite correct to phone your friends and say, "Will you come to tea next Tuesday afternoon at four? That's the third." It's best always to mention the date as well as the day of the week so that there may be no misunderstanding It is equally acceptable, if you happen to run into a friend on the street or elsewhere, to issue a spoken invitation face to face. It is quite all right, of course, if you wish to write a note; and if you do, make it a very informal one. "Dear Helen, Will you have a cup of tea with us next Tuesday, the third, at four? John's fiancée is in town. She's a darling, and I want you to meet her. Best, Jane "

Be sure to say "tea" if you mean tea, and "cocktails" if you mean cocktails. It is discouraging to a nondrinker to be invited to what he believes will be a tea party and, on arrival, finds everyone drinking alcoholic beverages and no tea made.

The small tea is usually served intimately in the living room, with the hostess pouring, from an uncovered tray placed on a low table at the side of her chair.

Arranged on the tray will be the teapot, sometimes covered with a cozy, which of course is removed when the tea is poured, a small teakettle of hot water, preferably over a spirit lamp or small electric hot plate, a bowl of lump or granulated sugar, sugar tongs, if lump sugar is used, small pitcher of milk (which is much better in tea than cream, but if you want to be unusually courteous have a small pitcher of cream also, and ask your guests which, if either, they prefer), a plate of sliced lemons, and a lemon pick. On the table beside the tray there should be a stack of tea plates, with a small napkin between every two of them, so that plate and napkin may be picked up together, and (either here or on a nearby table) the cakes, buttered bread or sandwiches which are to be served.

When pouring, the hostess will ask each guest how she likes her tea, whether with milk (or cream), lemon, sugar, or plain, and whether strong or weak, and will of course serve it as directed. The tea connoisseur, especially if he knows that his hostess serves unusually good tea, will usually take it with nothing added.

The guests sit where they choose. If the room is large, and the hostess can provide enough small tables, she will place them so that one is near every chair, or at least in reach of every two chairs, in order to help the guests avoid the awkward situations in which they feel that they need three hands.

If there is a maid, she will bring the tea into the room, but she will not serve it. This is a ritual reserved to the hostess—one of the intimacies which gives this kind of gathering its special charm.

The small sandwiches, split, toasted and buttered English muffins and marmalade, *petits fours*, or similar small tidbits are passed. The English custom of serving thinly sliced, buttered brown bread or date and nut bread with tea is a pleasant one.

Often one of the guests, who is an old friend of the hostess (a man if there is one present), will volunteer to take the tea and the food around the room; or, failing this, the guests themselves, who are beyond the reach of the hostess, will usually come forward one by one to take their cups as they are ready and help themselves to the food.

Though a tea party is a tea party and not a cocktail party, and the hostess is correct in assuming that those who have accepted her invitation have come to drink tea and not alcoholic beverages, the courteous hostess whose guest declines tea will ask if he would like something else, and be prepared to offer a cocktail or whiskey and soda if that is his choice. More guests who want this sort of stimulus will drink a cup of tea, and will then seek stronger refreshment.

Afternoon teas have a relaxed informality, mixed with almost ritualistic tradition that provides an atmosphere unlike that of any other entertaining. They are admirable affairs at which to introduce a new neighbor, a relative on an extended visit, a fiancée of a son or fiancé of a daughter, or a visiting dignitary to other members of the community. They may also be merely pleasant get-togethers for old friends.

The small and intimate tea is perhaps the pleasantest of all. But regardless of the number of persons whom you invite, it is a part of your obligation of courtesy to see that everyone in the room is introduced to everyone else, as they enter. Even though most of your guests know one another, it does no harm to say, "Frank, of course you know Mary and Bob. This is Mr. Seymour, Mr. Frank Collins You know Constance," and so on until everyone in the room has been mentioned. It is a courtesy to Mr. Seymour, the one among your guests who may know no one.

THE COCKTAIL PARTY

Like the afternoon tea the cocktail party is usually an informal affair, though its atmosphere has little in common with that of the tea. While the afternoon tea is often completely a feminine affair, the cocktail party is almost always mixed. At a tea the hostess is the prime one in charge of ceremonies, and usually the only one At the cocktail party given by a married couple, host and hostess usually share the duties of hospitality; the hostess mingling informally with the guests and seeing that they are comfortable and have conversational companions, and noting whether they are supplied with refreshments, while the host takes charge of the drinks

Invitations

Cocktail invitations today are usually issued by phone, though they may also be sent in an informal note or simply on a visiting card (if you use one—many perfectly nice people don't even bother to have them made nowadays), with a mere announcement written in ink, "Cocktails at home, five to seven, Thursday the fourth." And if you want to sound especially cordial, add something like "Do come." If the invitation is to an intimate friend, cross out the name formally engraved on the card and sign it with your first name. If it is to one who may not be sure of your address, be sure to add it.

The Time

The time is usually from five to seven, but do not expect all your guests to arrive promptly at five or to be gone by seven It is quite acceptable for a guest to arrive at any time up to half an hour before the time when the party is supposed to end (and seldom does), and to leave when he likes. A cocktail party is a "drop in" affair.

The Appurtenances

You will need more glasses than you have guests (three glasses for each guest is a good safe number), for the glassware gets misplaced in the general mingling and moving about that inevitably takes place, but they need not be expensive glasses.

You should be prepared to mix one or two kinds of cocktails and offer your guests sherry, Scotch, rye, bourbon, vodka, brandy, and rum in tall or short glasses

Before your guests arrive see that there are plenty of ashtrays scattered about the room, and coasters on the small tables. Provide one or two brands of cigarettes, in the original packages, cigarette boxes, or other receptacles, and matches

The Food

Whatever you prepare to serve with the cocktails should be something that may be eaten with the fingers as it is, or provided with toothpicks by which to handle it Plates are not served with cocktails, though small napkins are. If you have enough linen, fine. If not, good, small paper napkins are acceptable Food may be hot, cold, or both, and not sweet Cold foods are placed on a table where the guests may help themselves Hot foods must of course be brought from the kitchen as ready and passed to the guests.

Serving

If there is a maid in the house she will serve the drinks and bring in and pass the hot food, if any (This is one of the several ways in which a cocktail party differs from an afternoon tea) If not, the hostess or host will serve them, often with the help of a friendly guest.

Nonalcoholic Drinks

If any of your guests says, "No thank you," to an alcoholic drink, it is courteous to accept him at his word and offer him a nonalcoholic drink instead If he asks for a glass of plain ice water, see that he is given that as quickly as possible without argument. There is nothing more discourteous than to urge liquor persistently on someone who has declined it, or counting his request for a glass of water a jest, neglecting to give it to him. Perhaps he simply doesn't like alcoholic drinks Perhaps he has a faulty digestion that is plagued by any alcohol Perhaps he is an alcoholic who has made his hard fight against a terrible enemy and won it. His reasons for refusing are his own affair Seeing that he gets what he asks for is the duty of his host or hostess.

The Excessive Drinker

The guest who does not know when to stop drinking, and so becomes noisy and troublesome, creates a problem which every host and hostess may encounter It is a difficult one Hospitality makes it impossible to refuse him a drink, even after he has already had far too much Yet he should, if possible, be prevented from making the party unpleasant for other guests

The wise host or hostess will not invite one who is known to give way habitually to this disagreeable tendency. But once the disturbance has taken place in their home, the hosts are not in a position to throw its author out

If the offender has a friend or wife at the party who sees and understands the difficulty, this good samaritan will sometimes cope with the problem by suggesting firmly to the other that it is time to go home, and taking him there. Or this is even a procedure which the hostess herself may suggest to the sober friend or wife.

Another way of handling the situation, when the possibility of it can be foreseen, is to keep the drinks in the kitchen, replenishing your guest's glasses from there, and when the troublesome one begins to be really troublesome, simply not offer anyone any more to drink. Those who are sensitive and perceptive will understand why you have adopted this course and will not be offended.

Leave-Taking

As the guests leave, the host and hostess will see them to the door and bid them good-by. Guests should not be pressed to stay. Prolonged leave-takings and arguments as to whether it is or is not time to go are as awkward as a total absence of cordial welcome.

THE INFORMAL DINNER

Serving dinner to friends in your home should be a joy, rather than something which you have worked so hard to arrange that you have no energy left with which to be a pleasant hostess and companion. The elaboration of planning for such an event should be in accord with your facilities, the time at your disposal, and what help you will have, rather than dictated by the desire to make an impression by the bounty of your table and the intricacies of the food that has been prepared. Hospitality is compounded of both tangible and intangible factors, but a warm outgoing friendship, the desire to see your friends and give them the opportunity to enjoy one another in your house, the wish to make them comfortable and happy on whatever scale is possible within your circumstances are far more important elements in entertaining than the most elaborate dinner can possibly be.

Selecting Your Guests

The number of guests you will invite at one time will depend on several things the size of your dining room and living room, whether you have servants or not, whether you or any of those whom you intend to invite definitely dislike (as some people do) being one of a large group and, most important of all, how many people you can bring together at one time who will be compatible with one another and capable of having a pleasant time.

The good hostess tries to avoid inviting a guest who notoriously talks constantly and so monopolizes the party, though this is a rule that has exceptions Sometimes one invites friends to meet and listen to a guest who has just made an interesting trip, or has done something else of great interest, so that the others may hear about it. It would be a disappointment to everyone under such circumstances if the guest of honor did not monopolize the conversation.

Nor would one consciously invite to the same party two persons known to dislike each other intensely. If you ever find yourself inadvertently host or hostess to two such feudists the best thing to do is to ignore the fact.

I remember one day at the White House having Hendrik van Loon on one side of me, and Alexander Woollcott on the other I had no idea at the time that they hated each other cordially. But I did know that both were accustomed to monopolizing the conversation, so I tried to make the whole table listen first to one and then to the other. How successful I was I have never known, but at least they did not have an open clash during the meal!

Confine the list of your invited guests for any dinner to a group of people who, you have every reason to believe, will enjoy one another.

The Invitations

As for almost any affair today, save the most formal dinner, a wedding, or a formal reception, invitations may quite properly be extended by telephone. They should be given, of course, by the hostess, unless there is some especial reason why it is more convenient for her husband to phone. In the latter case he will always issue the invitation on behalf of his wife, saying, "Helen has asked me to call you. We would like you and your wife to come to dinner at seven-thirty next Thursday night, the fourth." If there is any possibility of a question in the mind of the expected guest tell him that formal dress is not required

An informal note may be written, of course, in which case the hostess always writes it.

Planning the Meal

The menu for the informal dinner, and the way it is served, will depend upon several factors. whether the hostess works outside her home, and so must squeeze her own preparations into an hour between coming home from work and the arrival of her guests, or has the whole day at home to prepare for the event; whether she has servants; whether her husband likes to carve at the table, and, of course, any known preferences or dislikes of the guests for certain foods. The good hostess will give her guests the best and most tastefully served dinner that she can within the limits imposed by time and other considerations, but she will not prepare a meal that is ostentatiously more elaborate than her day-to-day living standards, or that has required so much time and effort on her part that she is a nervous wreck when her guests arrive.

The informal dinner for friends may, but need not, start with a soup, or fruit or seafood cocktail. The prime requisites are meat, fowl, or fish, potatoes or rice (rice is often served with fowl, or with Armenian, Turkish, Chinese or other Asian meal courses), one or two vegetables, a salad, a dessert, and coffee. If there are children among the guests who do not yet drink coffee, the offer of a glass of milk will frequently bring a grateful acceptance from the parents. In fact, in this case milk may well be served with the meal.

Table Settings

Table settings may be varied. The thing to remember is that every guest has an implement of each sort which he will need for the food which you are serving, placed in the way that will make it most convenient for him to use it.

If the dinner is to be served from the kitchen by a maid, or the hostess, the dinner plate is placed directly in front of the guest's chair. A service plate is sometimes used, which is replaced by the dinner plate after the first course is eaten, but this is an unnecessary grace note in informal dinners and is one of the little added bits of work which may safely be dispensed with by the busy servantless housewife.

If a first course is served, such as soup or seafood cocktail, it is usually put on the table before the guests are summoned, the soup dish, cup, or cocktail glass resting on the dinner plate. In this case the folded napkin is placed to the left of the dinner plate and the forks. If no such course is served, the napkin is usually placed on the dinner plate.

For a simple, informal dinner the general arrangement is somewhat as follows: dinner plate in center, and silver arranged to left and right of it in the order in which it will be used, the soup spoon (if soup is to be served) on the outside to the right, the meat knife between the soup spoon and the plate, the meat fork to the left of the plate, the salad fork (which may be omitted if it is the custom to serve the salad directly on the dinner plate, which is more and more usual at informal dinners for friends) between the meat fork and the plate. The bread and butter plate is at the left and slightly forward, with the butter knife lying on it parallel to the edge of the table and with the handle inward, the dessert spoon may be put in front of the plate, with the handle to the guest's right. The water glass is placed to the right and forward, the wine glass (if wine is to be served) to the right of the water glass.

In front of the dinner plate are placed cigarettes in a container, and there should be at least one ash tray for every two guests. If neither cigarettes nor ash trays are present, the considerate guest will not smoke at the table. If any of the men are known to prefer a cigar to a cigarette, the host will provide himself with cigars and offer them after the meal is finished Among well known friends, if the hostess knows that one of the men smokes a pipe, and knows also that none of her guests object to it, she will invite him to smoke his pipe after the dessert.

Serving

If the dinner includes a roast or a fowl, especially if there is no maid, the host carves at the table and serves both meat and vegetables. This adds a pleasant note of hospitality similar to that created by the hostess pouring at an afternoon tea. Thus he may consult his guests' preferences as to the cuts he offers them, and be instantly ready to replenish their plates. Also it is a pleasant thing for hungry guests, coming to the table, to see it laden with attractively arranged food ready to be eaten, and even after the main part of the meal has been consumed, to see the havoc they have wrought!

In this case the plates may be stacked before the host, to be filled one by one, and passed by the guests to those for whom they are intended. The host will serve the women guests first, beginning with the eldest, or any other who for one reason or another it is desired to honor especially, his wife next, the male guests next, and himself last He will indicate the person to whom each plate is intended by his remarks as he serves, "Mrs. Martin, would you like white or dark meat?" "Nellie, I know you like your beef well done," etc.

If there is a maid to serve, she will take the plates from the host as he fills them, and take each to the guest for whom it is intended. If she does not know the names of all of them, the host will indicate as he hands the plate to her the person to whom to take it She will set the plate down from the left of the guest. If service plates have been used she will remove them.

If the food is not served at the table, and there is a maid, she will bring it in on serving dishes and offer it from the left, first to the lady seated at the host's right, which is traditionally the place of honor, then to the other ladies, then to the hostess, then to the man at the hostess's right, then to the other men, and last to the host

The meat will be brought in on a platter, sliced if it is a roast, with a selection of rare and well-done pieces so that the guest may take his choice, and with light and dark meat if it is a fowl There will be a serving fork and spoon on the platter with which the guest may help himself to the pieces of his choice. The vegetables will be brought in one at a time in vegetable dishes, also with large spoon and fork, or if it is a small dinner, sometimes two may be brought at once on one dish. If salad is to be eaten on the dinner plate with the main course, it will be brought immediately after the vegetables; if it is to be served as a separate course, the dinner plates will be removed and replaced with salad plates, and the salad then brought in, in the salad bowl, with the salad set of fork and spoon, and passed as the vegetables have been. Or it may be put on the salad plates in the kitchen and brought in to serve individually. But in the servantless household the salad bowl is usually put on the table and passed from hand to hand by the guests who serve themselves. The hostess whose meal planning requires her to jump up from the table several times during a meal and leave her guests in order to serve them diminishes one of the chief factors of hospitality—the presence of her cordial and hospitable self.

Coffee may be served either at the table or in the living room. If it is served in the living room the hostess pours it, and the host passes it, whether there is or is not a maid in the house.

"COME IN FOR COFFEE"

In the typically small contemporary home the hostess may sometimes wish that she had room at her dinner table to ask more than she may accommodate. In that case she may find a way out of her dilemma by asking an extra couple or couples in for coffee after dinner. The situation is especially understandable if those who are to be asked to dinner consist of couples who, by nature of their relationship, are not to be separated. In that case the hostess may quite properly phone others and ask them to come in after dinner for coffee.

The coffee will then be served in the living room, and perhaps liqueurs or even drinks with it, in recognition of the fact that the couple or couples invited to come late are entitled to the best of the evening remaining

THE BUFFET SUPPER

Another method of coping with more persons than the table will seat comfortably is the buffet supper served in the living room, the dining room, the kitchen, or even on the terrace or lawn. In this case two things are necessary: 1] to keep the menu simple, confining it to dishes that may be easily and gracefully served under circumstances that are, at the best, informal; and 2] to arrange the chairs for your guests so that, if possible, each will have a place on which to set things that cannot be conveniently held in the lap. The food may be served on plates in the kitchen and brought in ready to hand to the guests, or they may serve themselves from the platters at the buffet table. This last is the more popular method, since it allows the guest almost complete freedom of choice. In fact some guests prefer it even to the more formal dinner table, where the host gives them either too much or too little. At this type of dinner, if the buffet has been laid out in the dining room or in the living room, the hostess gives the sign by approaching the guest of honor, or the guest who is not a close friend, and accompanies her to the table where she begins to serve her. The others will follow suit.

There is a variation of the buffet dinner which sometimes is very successful. Little tables may be set in the living room and dining room so that each guest, after he has had his plate filled at the buffet table, may return to find silver, salt and pepper at his place. This is sometimes very pleasant if you don't have one table large enough for everyone whom you have invited to sit together.

7

Living Alone and "Sharing"

To THOSE OF US WHO ARE MARRIED AND LIVING IN THAT normal and companionable security, the problems peculiar to adult unmarried life may seem remote or faintly unpleasant or even attractive, but in fact they affect a far larger proportion of our population than most of us realize.

Actually almost one-third of the men and women in the United States between the ages of eighteen and seventy-five (about 34,000,000 of a total of about 105,000,000 in 1950) have never been married, are married but living apart from husband or wife, or are legally separated, divorced, or are widowed. Of these about 14,000,000 have never been married, about 2,500,000 have been married and divorced, about 10,000,000 are widowed, and about 7,500,000 are married but separated.

Not all of these are living alone. Some live with parents, some with children, some share their homes with others who are similarly without family attachments, and some have arrangements for board and room which make them practically parts of other families; but there are a large number indeed who come back to their apartments or little houses in the evening (if indeed they have left them during the day) to no greeting save that which may be given by a caged bird, a cat, or an affectionate dog, to a lonely supper and an evening and night spent in solitude. Some are young, and some old. Some are eagerly looking forward to a marriage already arranged, some hopefully to a possible remarriage, some have given up hope and have settled down to make the best of what remains. Some are living alone because they prefer to do so.

TO LIVE ALONE OR TO SHARE?

Whether you live alone is a decision that may be difficult. What you decide will probably depend on several factors: whether you are a young man, a young woman, or an elderly person of either sex (the problem of the elderly parent is discussed in Chapter 4, "The Family of Three Generations"); whether you prefer the almost inevitable loneliness of living alone to the difficulties of adjustment that accompany sharing an apartment with even a close friend, whether, if you are a young woman, you feel you will be able to cope with the problem of predatory males who may attempt to take advantage of your unchaperoned status; your financial position (generally speaking a better apartment for two can obviously be rented for less than twice as much as one for single occupancy), and to some extent whether you live in a village or a large city.

There are some persons who have so many inner resources that they never know the agonies of loneliness experienced by those who are emotionally dependent upon others, who are so vigorous that they are constantly active, finding interesting occupations outside as well as inside their homes, and companionship with friends and associates, and who are ingenious and sensible enough to manage their lives in such a way that they seldom, if ever, encounter problems from those of the opposite sex who try to take advantage of their solitary status.

Whether you are a man or a woman you probably have a choice. If you are living in a large city, you may select (if you are a woman) to live in one of the girl's "clubs," or (if a man) in a Y.M.C.A. or Y.M.H.A., or, if you can afford it, in a club. For a young woman this plan, of course, provides constant chaperonage, and for both simplifies the responsibilities of tenancy, but it provides a somewhat institutionalized sort of life with little privacy, no possibility of anything that could properly be called entertaining, and for most people a bleak boredom.

Or you may share your problem with a friend by sharing an apartment. With a completely congenial sharer this plan may work very well indeed, and is one more frequently chosen by young women than by men It lessens the almost inevitable loneliness of solitary living, provides a built-in, yet flexible chaperonage, and makes it possible to share both the financing and the work of housekeeping.

Yet at its best it requires certain adjustments which some people find it difficult to make, and removes the possibility of complete solitude which you may really want unless you can find the most desirable of all companionships in a good marriage.

In that case, or if you are unable to find congenial companions or a suitable apartment in which to live cooperatively, the choice (unless you elect to live in a hotel or a club) is to live alone. With all its disadvantages, if you plan your arrangements and your way of living intelligently you may in later years look back to your period of "solitary" living as one of the happiest times of your life, and one that was much less lonely than you may have anticipated.

SHARING

Before you decide to share an apartment with one or two friends there are several things which you should consider.

First, and most important, have you a friend with whom you feel you will really enjoy living and who is in need of an arrangement such as you are planning? I think it a mistake to try to live with just anyone who happens to be willing to share with you in order to be able to carry out your plan, just as it would be to marry almost anyone merely in order to be married. Actually many of the adjustments necessary to a successful marriage are the same as those that must be made by any two people who learn happily to share the same living quarters.

Do you know enough about family living to feel that you can happily share a living room, bath, kitchen, and perhaps a bedroom with the kind of congenial give and take, and at times sacrifice of your own convenience without which harmonious living together is impossible?

Do you know your friend well enough to know that she (or he, if you are a man) is equally considerate and, as it were, "house-broken" so that you will not get "into each other's hair?"

Can you, in the locality in which you must live, find the kind of apartment which is suitable for the sort of living arrangement which you contemplate, and within the price range which the two of you can afford together?

If the answer to all of these questions is yes, you are ready to go ahead. If you feel hesitant about any of them you had better reconsider. Like a marriage, an apartment-sharing partnership is often much easier to establish than to dissolve.

Choosing an Apartment

Setting down exact specifications for the kind of apartment which would be ideal for a sharing arrangement in a large city may be futile, for today in most urban centers the apartment shortage seems permanent, and you will probably have to settle for something less than perfection. Yet if you have a standard at which to aim, and keep looking until you find something that fulfills most of your specifications, you will obviously do better than if you sign a lease quickly simply because you think that you have found a bargain, or you like the view from the living-room window, or are delighted because the place is air-conditioned.

Cost

Since you will share the rent with another person, together you obviously will be able to pay a higher rent than you would be if you were to live alone. And if you rent and manage carefully you should be able to keep the rent and maintenance bill of each of you somewhat below what it would be if each of you lived alone.

A sound old rule for budgeting dictated that a month's rent should cost no more than a week's salary. With contemporary rents at an all-time high in such cities as New York there are many who find themselves forced to spend more than this proportion of their income for rent, yet it is still a good rule if you can manage to be guided by it Obviously then, if two share an apartment, the amount that may be spent for rent is theoretically doubled. But whereas someone on a salary of $90 a week might be unable to find a suitable apartment for $90 a month, two, each earning $90 a week, almost certainly would be able to find a suitable place for less than $180 a month, even in apartment-hungry New York.

Generally speaking, the rule of paying no more than a week's salary for a month's rent is one that should be strictly followed in a sharing arrangement between two persons both of whom are on salaried jobs. And indeed it should be interpreted so as not to place an unwarranted burden on the one who is earning the lesser salary. For instance, if you are earning $90 a week, and the one with whom you are going to share is earning only $75 a week, your maximum rent should be $150 a month, so that your companion, paying half, would not be spending more than a week's salary on rent. If then you want unobtrusively to contribute little extras to your joint living conveniences and pleasures, the cost of which your companion will not be asked to share, it would be a gracious thing to do, so long as you can do it inconspicuously and without offense.

Location

If you are two men planning to share, the location, so long as it is convenient and pleasant, is a less important consideration than it may be for women. A young woman, whether sharing or living alone, should seek an apartment on a well lighted and well tenanted street not too far from public transportation. I say this, not because I think that long walks are to be avoided by either men or women—indeed almost all of us, in this day of traveling on wheels, walk too little—but because I am aware of the taxi bills that are incurred in self-defense by young women who live on poorly lighted, lonely streets and are justifiably afraid to walk alone the last block or two to their apartments late at night.

Whether, socially speaking, the address is "good" or not does not matter in the least (so long as it is not so "bad" as automatically to put an undesirable label on any young woman who lives there), but whether you can go to and from it alone at night with a reasonable sense of security matters a great deal. Indeed there may be advantages to living in a building that houses on its first floor, or has next door to it, a delicatessen or drugstore that stays open late at night. Such a store not only will assure you of a lighted area close to the entrance of your apartment at night, but also, if you deal with and make friends with the proprietor, may be a place where parcels can be left for you if they are delivered while you are away at work.

I hold no brief for doormen as such. Certainly for the average apartment dweller they constitute an unnecessary luxury that simply adds to the cost of operating the building and thus to the rent. Yet if there is one in the apartment which you are considering, or an all night elevator man, or someone who sits at a desk in the lobby, you will know that you will never, late at night, have to enter the lobby of your apartment to find an unwanted intruder waiting in the shadows, and that if parcels are delivered to you while you are away they will not go back to the post office or the store from which they came.

These are matters to be taken into consideration when you select an apartment. Actually thousands of young women have lived for years in walkup apartments without elevator men, doormen, or nearby stores, and have had no unpleasant experiences as a result.

Room Arrangement

You will probably not be able to find an apartment that fulfills all the specifications of the ideal. If you find one that approaches it you will be fortunate. And so when I describe here the kind of apartment which it seems to me is best suited for two young women to share, it is in order to help you see the sort of adjustments that are necessary in sharing, and to point out how ideal room arrangements can make them easier. If you cannot find them you will at least know why you are looking for them, and probably be ingenious enough to devise substitute arrangements to accomplish the same purposes.

Sharing should provide companionship, insurance against too great loneliness, and a saving through financial cooperation. But it also should be so arranged that there will be as little unwelcome impingement of one personality on another as is possible, and so that each of the sharers may be free to live her own life, to go and come as she pleases, and to entertain her friends in her home comfortably and pleasantly. In the case of two young women, one of the great advantages of sharing is that male friends may be entertained more freely without incurring the criticism and unpleasant remarks of the sort of neighbors who batten on imagined scandal.

For two young women a minimum of space for really convenient living consists of a living room, bedroom large enough for two beds and two dressers, kitchen, and bath. If by a very rare chance you are able to find a clean, well managed, old, rent-controlled building in which you can obtain a two-bedroom apartment within the price range which you can afford, you will be lucky indeed. Look also for generous closet space. You will need twice as much as you would if you were living alone.

The arrangement of the rooms should be one that will, if possible, provide at least a little privacy for both of you, and make it possible for each of you to entertain without disturbing, or being disturbed by the other. If the outside door opens into a small lobby from which you have access to living room, bedroom, and bath, and may enter any one of these without going through one of the others, the arrangement is ideal. In small modern apartments the entrance is more likely to be directly into the living room. In this case hope to find an apartment in which a short hallway, with the bath off it, leads from the living room to the bedroom. Occasionally, though rarely today, you may find a bathroom that has entrances from both the living room and the bedroom. This, too, is a satisfactory arrangement, for if you are entertaining and your companion comes in and wants to go to bed, she may go into the bathroom from the bedroom without going through the living room, yet the bath will also be available to your guest without the necessity of passing through the bedroom. If you do not find any of the above, it is better to select an apartment with the entrance to the bath through the living room rather than through the bedroom, for among modern, realistic young people, it would be much less embarrassing for one of you to go through the living room to the bath while the other was entertaining, than to make it necessary for your guest to go through the bedroom after the other had retired, or—what would probably happen in that case—forego the use of the bathroom entirely.

Apportioning Expenses

At the very outset you and your companion should agree on exactly how you are going to share the joint expenses of your establishment. Generally speaking, the fixed expenses should be shared equally. These would include rent, telephone bill (though not toll calls—these should be noted by each of you as you make them so that you will not forget to pay for those you have made when the bill arrives), gas and electric bill, Christmas gifts to mailmen and building superintendent, and perhaps household laundry (though you may find it simpler for each of you to include your bed and bathroom linen with your personal laundry and pay for it individually). Sometimes this arrangement may be varied to fit special circumstances. If, for instance, one of you (a public stenographer, writer, or artist) uses the apartment as a place of business or studio as well as a residence, you both might feel it a fairer arrangement for that one to pay more than half the rent. And if these business or professional activities involve enough outgoing phone calls to make a charge for extra calls a commonplace on the monthly phone bill, the one responsible would of course pay for them.

If it is your custom to eat most of your meals together in the apartment, and neither of you insists upon expensive luxuries which the other might feel she could not afford, the simplest arrangement is probably to share the food costs equally as you do the fixed expenses. But this arrangement may vary with circumstances. If you both have good will and fair minds and each is determined not to impose on the other the details of your arrangement will work out.

Sharing the Work

As expenses must be shared equitably, so should the day-by-day chores of housekeeping. Nothing will contribute more quickly to failure of a sharing arrangement than to have one party to it shirk her share, or to have one, who is the soul of neatness, constantly annoyed by the untidiness of the other. Each girl should take care of her bed, getting up in time in the morning to make it before leaving for work, should keep her share of closet and dresser-drawer space neat, and take no more than her share, see that she does not let her personal effects clutter the joint living room, bedroom, bath or kitchen, and cheerfully accept and carry out such share of the common housework (cooking, washing dishes, and cleaning) as the two have agreed upon.

Entertaining

Ways should be found to make it possible for each to entertain without the other. This is the sort of thing which depends more on mutual consideration and courtesy than on any hard-and-fast arrangement One does not like to dull the fine edge of spontaneity in social contacts by having them rationed and regulated by a calendar dictated regularity Better than to say, "You entertain on Tuesday evenings, and I shall on Thursday," would be to find out what the other's plans are before issuing an invitation and "fitting in." If each of you is genuinely considerate, desirous of furthering the convenience of the other, ready to lend a hand with the other's problems, and companionable yet unintrusive, the kind of cooperation necessary will not be difficult.

THREE OR MORE TOGETHER

In the above discussion I have considered only problems connected with the sharing of an apartment by two young women. Occasionally three or even more may manage a joint menage, but this seems to me to be an awkward arrangement not to be attempted save under special circumstances. Two girls *may* be able to occupy one bedroom and share a kitchen and living room harmoniously. If there are three or more, two bedrooms would seem an essential minimum, and if there is only one bath, the traffic during the rush, pre-getting-away hour in the morning would constitute a problem not conducive to domestic harmony Further, there are only seven nights in any week, and only one weekend. If each of the three of you wants at least one evening each week for entertaining alone, the difficulties of working out a program that will accommodate you all may be beyond the capacity of your ingenuity and tolerance. Still it can be done if you are all congenial and have the will to make it work, and of course the per capita expense will be reduced by your numbers.

YOUNG WOMAN ALONE

Time was when Mrs. Grundy looked askance at any young woman who occupied an apartment alone, and with marked disapproval if she ever entertained men in it. Fortunately, especially in large cities such as New York, the fact that so many fine young women do live alone and do entertain, and the triumph of common sense over the details of strict convention have made life much simpler for the young woman who prefers the freedom and privacy which she can find only in solitary living, even if she can afford only a tiny walkup apartment.

In such a place she may live today without chaperonage and without raised eyebrows by any save the most captious, who don't matter. Nor will her method of living cause modern men to misunderstand why she lives thus, or be construed as an invitation for them to take advantage of her unchaperoned state—unless they are fools, and the intelligent modern young woman quickly learns techniques by which to avoid these or, if she has made a mistake in judgment, to cope with them.

Actually any girl's best chaperone is her character, her attitudes, her dignity, her capacity for a frank and open friendship with no further implications, and her ability (to use an old-fashioned term) to be a lady. The intelligent young woman today, intent on making a good life for herself, may live alone if she likes, and to a large extent may make her own conventions, so long as her rules are based on decency, consideration for others, and a determination not unnecessarily to give cause for misunderstandings.

Yet in no situation I know is it more true that conventions and the old rules of social behavior may be useful in case of need

If she is going out with a man whom she likes but does not really know well, and of whose behavior she is unsure, she may be careful to see that she is ready before the time he is to call for her, so that she may meet him at the door and step out to join him without asking him in, without being rude, for she would be but following an old convention.

If the same man brings her home from their evening late, she may, if she wishes, tell him good night at the outer door of her apartment building Again convention would make it impossible for him to feel that she had been rude.

If she has given a small party and there is one man whom she feels she cannot completely trust, there are several ways in which she may manage to see that he is not left alone with her in her apartment after the rest have gone.

If he invites himself to call on her late in the evening alone, she may suggest that they meet somewhere else without being discourteous.

In all of these situations the rules of conventional behavior may be called to save her from what might be a difficult situation, and the man who resents her following them and so does not call again is one whom she will not miss for long.

On the other hand these rules are so elastic today that she may breach practically every one of them in entertaining trusted male friends or the one who is more than friend—especially in large cities —without criticism from understanding acquaintances who know that shamelessness is not signified by opportunity, or virtue by superficial appearances. Indeed it is not at all uncommon for a young woman living alone in a large city in a bedroom, living room, kitchen and bath, to give the day bed in the living room to a well known male friend from her home town for a night, while she sleeps virginally in her bedroom It is against the weight of old rules of convention, yet anyone who knew the young woman's integrity would not give it a second thought. After all her apartment is her home, and hospitality is one of a home's most beautiful graces.

Listing Your Name and Answering Your Doorbell

If you are a young woman living alone in a large city you may save yourself unwelcome phone calls from strange males and bothersome personal calls at your apartment by omitting "Miss" and using your initials instead of your given name in the phone book and on your mailbox, thus "R. J. Curran," instead of "Miss Ruth J. Curran" This has become increasingly general practice in recent years, since by being noncommittal as to your sex, it does not suggest that you are a target for those strange, somewhat twisted men who make it a practice of phoning (often late at night) young unattached women.

If your apartment has communication to the lobby, find out who has rung your bell before pushing the button that admits him to the building If it does not have such a system, ignore the ringing of your doorbell unless you are expecting someone. Every courteous dweller in a large city knows that he should phone before calling and will do so.

Entertaining

Of course you will want to entertain in your apartment, and of course you should do so. It is the only way that you may gracefully return the hospitality of your friends, including that of men who have taken you out, since it is awkward and difficult for you as a woman to arrange entertainment outside your home for which you will pay.

The problem for the single woman of integrity living alone today is less one of interpreting the conventions literally as hard-and-fast rules than of making sure that she can avoid the unpleasant situations against which the conventions were made to protect her.

You may wish to entertain a single man who has taken you out several times, yet whom you do not feel that you know well enough to be sure that he would not misunderstand your inviting him to dinner alone with you in your apartment In this case the situation is quite simply managed by inviting another couple to join you and him at dinner, or by arranging a small evening party to which you invite him. Later, if you come to know him well enough to be sure that he will not misunderstand your invitation, and are sure that you may rely on his behavior, you may quite properly invite him to have dinner with you at your apartment before you go off for an evening together.

One of your most difficult problems as a young woman living alone may be that of the unattached male, who having been invited to your party outstays the other guests and either settles down for a long boring chat or becomes difficult. There are several ways in which you may plan insurance against this situation.

If you feel that it will be sufficient you may rely on the simple statement that you have to get up early in the morning to go to work, and you are sure that he will excuse you. This (especially if you stand up to say it) should get any young man on his feet and headed for the door.

If, however, you are not sure that this will work you may arrange beforehand for cooperation from a friend or friends.

You may ask a couple to your party who are prepared to sit it out with the young man, not leaving until he has done so. This, of course, has its dangers and may result in a very late evening indeed.

Or you may ask one of your friends who is a young woman to spend the night with you on the daybed in the living room, and let the man know very casually during the evening what the arrangement is, so that he will learn early that his hope of having some time alone with you after the others have gone is futile.

Or you may yourself arrange to spend the night with a friend, and if your troublesome guest is still there after the others have left, may at once tell him so and ask him if he will take you to her apartment, where you need not ask him in. (If you find, after all, that he leaves with the others you may, if you like, phone her after he has gone, tell her that all is well, and sleep at home.)

A variation of the above is to arrange to have a friend phone you at some predetermined time—say 11·30—to tell you that she is not feeling well, and to ask if you won't come and spend the night with her. If the troublesome guest has left by then you may tell your friend so and thank her. If not, you have a perfect reason for getting rid of him.

Actually while these are all possible and justified stratagems none of them should be necessary for the intelligent young woman. Your own character and your judgment of the men whom you are willing to invite to your apartment should be sufficient to ensure you against unpleasant incidents. I am firmly convinced that no man who has even average decency makes, or at least persists in, unwelcome approaches to a woman. If the woman has not, in any of the thousand subtle ways which women have, invited attentions beyond those of sensible friendship, and does not respond to his attentions, most men will not offer them or, having done so, will take their cue and desist.

As to the late stayer, the really courteous and thoughtful young man, who has been invited as one of a group to the apartment of a young woman living alone, is not one. He will leave when the other guests do and create no problem. And incidentally he is the one whom his hostess will happily invite again.

Furthering Acquaintance with Men

It is most natural and right that unattached persons of marriageable age, whether young men or women, should consciously seek to meet and become acquainted with others of the opposite sex who are also unattached, and hope that among them will eventually be found an ideal marriage partner. The young woman who, fearing that she may be accused of aggressiveness, holds herself completely aloof and refuses to make any such effort is to be pitied as one who is not fully participating in life.

Yet there are ways that may be followed with dignity, and ways that because of their suggestiveness or awkwardness, or both, may well lead merely to unwelcome propositions rather than to friendships or to proposals.

If you have met a man whom you like at a party given by common friends, and have become a little acquainted with him there, you may with complete propriety invite him to a party at your apartment. It will be more gracious, the first time you do this, if you also invite the friends who introduced you to him. If, after this, he does not propose another meeting, or invite you out, it will be difficult for you to further the acquaintance with him without misunderstanding, and you had better give up.

If a young man is living alone in the same apartment building as yourself, and you have met him frequently in the hall, the elevator, or on the stairs, if you frequently meet a man in the elevator of your office building and like his looks, if shopping in your neighborhood stores you now and then run into the same young man doing his shopping, and he looks like someone you would like to know—there is no reason why, one day when a glance of recognition passes between you, you should not smile and say "good morning" or "good afternoon." The old convention which dictated that the woman should always speak first has long since been abrogated, and if the man speaks first do not (if you like his looks) freeze up as though you had been insulted, but respond to his greeting. Yet there are many men who, because of the old convention or simply because they are shy, will not speak to a woman to whom they have not been introduced, yet would welcome your greeting if you offered it.

Out of such chance meetings and greetings as these sound friendships and even closer relationships often spring. And there is no reason why anywhere in the world, at any time, between any two people, sound, good friendship, waiting for acceptance, should not be apparent.

There are other ways in which you may meet marriageable young men, of course. You may join groups with interests similar to your own and meet compatible friends of both sexes there, though this plan will likely be futile unless your interest in the subject, as well as meeting others, is real. At a large party you may quite properly introduce yourself and talk to anyone there, even if your host or hostess has neglected to introduce you. Actually, if you see a young man sitting alone in a corner, neglected by the hostess and other guests, you have a measure of responsibility as a good guest to approach him and change his status from that of loneliness to that of companionship. Your married friends may give a hand by inviting you to their house and at the same time inviting an unattached male for you to meet.

MAN LIVING ALONE

The problems faced by a man living alone in an apartment are less complex than are those of a woman, and little need be said about them. He may entertain as may a woman, and perhaps with even greater freedom, since for some unexplained reason, even in groups that might criticize a woman for entertaining a man alone in her apartment, a man who entertains a woman will receive less censure.

He should not, however, invite a young woman whom he does not know to visit him alone at his apartment late at night unless he is willing to have her reputation tarnished, nor should he urge a single woman to stay alone with him after the other guests at a party he has given have left.

He may of course use all the devices suggested above for getting acquainted with unattached women, and probably others will occur to him.

He will do well at the outset of an acquaintance with a young woman, to include other guests when he first invites her to his apartment.

If he has an elderly friend who is living alone, the older person may welcome the opportunity to be useful to a young man (or for that matter a young woman) as a tactful chaperone with sense enough to disappear at the right moment. Contrary to the beliefs of many young people, elderly people often feel freer to ignore some of the conventions than do the young.

THE FAMILY
IN THE COMMUNITY

8

The Nature of a Community

MOST OF US USE THE WORD "COMMUNITY" LOOSELY AND vaguely to mean "a place where a group of people live," a village, a city, or a neighborhood within a city, a collection of people and houses, stores, churches, moving picture theaters, streets, and parks. We too often think of such a group quite objectively, as a collection of animated human bodies and material things, a purely physical entity. But in order to understand the relationship of an individual to the community of which he is a part, and his proper behavior within it, we must look more deeply into the meaning of the word.

The Latin *communitas,* "a fellowship," originally had spiritual connotations far more important than man's increasing urge to build his house at no great distance from that of his neighbor. Ten thousand years or more ago at the end of the ice age, when the dried and warmed earth made it possible, men in groups were building their houses, gathering crops, disposing of their dead with ritualistic burials, worshiping their conception of a god or gods, instinctively fulfilling their wants as human beings in their continuous efforts to find a better way of life. They were doing these things not merely as individuals, but as cooperative groups, families, septs, tribes, villages—in short, communities. Perhaps they knew intuitively, perhaps they learned by experience, that in human association the whole is always more than the sum of its parts.

Undoubtedly among the reasons for this grouping together were the necessity to be strong in the face of enemies, and the desire to accomplish physical tasks that could not be performed by one man or family alone. Yet there was a reason deeper than this. The massive Stonehenge, which stands on Salisbury Plain in England, believed to have been built during the Bronze Age, is composed of a number of upright stone pillars some of which are twenty-two feet high and weigh tons. Bringing them to the site and putting them into place without modern mechanical equipment must have required the greatest ingenuity and the combined strength of many men. Physically it would have been impossible without group cooperation. But even more interesting is the purpose to which this cooperation was devoted. Though the exact nature and function of the structure is a mystery, it is generally agreed among archaeologists that it was the scene of religious rites—perhaps the worship of a sun god. Many men had cooperated in a gigantic labor, not for the acquisition of material rewards, not for their greater convenience or pleasure, but as an expression of aspiration and reverence. "For man was from the start, and knew it, a creature of the spirit as well as of the flesh."*

Physically a community is a collection of people and buildings. Spiritually it is a pooling of ideals, aspirations, purposes, an embodiment of the principle "one for all and all for one," a recognition of the essential fact that "no man is an island," that as an ancient Chinese saying put it, we are "one family under heaven," and that we can be a happy family only if order, brought about through adherence to certain wise rules—sometimes formalized as law, sometimes not—prevails.

When the embattled farmers stood at Lexington in 1775 and fired the shot heard 'round the world, when the British people during the Battle of Britain in World War II gave the world such a magnificent example of courage and cooperation, they were acting as a community. It may seem like a contradiction in terms to say that in both cases men (and in the Battle of Britain women) were

* H. E. L. Mellersh, *The Story of Early Man*. New York, The Viking Press, 1960.

fighting as a community in defense of the rights of the individual. But it is not. For only in an atmosphere that nurtures and encourages individual freedom, so long as it does not infringe on the rights of others, can community life flourish at its best. Only through community life can the individual personality find its fullest development, for man is by nature and necessity a gregarious creature. No individual ambition can possibly find fulfillment (certainly not if peace of mind is considered essential to it) without reconciliation with others.

The family, as I have said earlier, is the smallest and most intimate of the many communities to which each of us belongs. It is also the oldest, and the most primitive. It is reasonable to believe that there was a time in man's early history when man, woman, and children constituted a more or less isolated unit. But as the human population increased, and with it knowledge and understanding, families banded together and the units which could be called communities became larger. The wise must have come early to see that private and public interest actually coincided, and that individualism in its most ruthless meaning was incompatible with human happiness.

Mankind has traveled a long road from the cave dwelling in which a single family huddled, barricaded against the world or the first primitive communities to the United Nations, whose ideal is so to adjust differences between nations that the whole world may function as a single family. Yet we have come only a little way; the road ahead seems longer than that which we have already traversed.

And in those men and women of goodwill scattered throughout the world who are longing, and willing, to work for the day when all people shall live in peaceful cooperation and all conduct themselves as though the family were a microcosm of the world, and the world the family in macrocosm, we find a "community" somewhat different from that represented by the physical facts of the village or city. This is a community of the spirit, the true fellowship denoted by the Latin word *communitas*. It is toward the ideal of this kind of community that all physical assemblages of persons and houses should work.

Lewis Mumford, in *The Social Foundations of Post-War Building,* has discussed at some length the aims that should be expressed in community planning and legislation. Should the community work toward the bettering of physical and material conditions only, or in recognition of the deeper spiritual needs of human beings? Obviously both are necessary. But if the latter are neglected, the former are useless, and the true meaning of the community can never be realized, whether the group is a village of two or three hundred souls or the whole world of human beings.

Walt Whitman, in "Salut au Monde," expressed the true world-wide community spirit when he wrote:

> You whoever you are!
> Health to you! Good will to you all, from me and
> America sent!
> Each of us inevitable,
> Each of us limitless—each of us with his or her right
> upon the earth,
> Each of us allow'd the eternal purports of the earth,
> Each of us here as divinely as any is here.

We do not [wrote Lawrence Hyde] become concerned with community in any serious sense until we have to do with a group of people who may really be said to have committed themselves to one another, who have created and accepted a situation in which all stand or fall together. It is a question not only of sharing resources, dwelling places, and interests, but of sharing one another. Individuals enter fully into community only when they reach the point of participating in a system in which satisfaction, effort, comprehension, opportunity and reward, have become a collective instead of an individual manifestation.*

Efforts have been made at different times in history to set up more perfect communities and to live, what some of the individuals participating hoped would be, a more perfect communal life.

We have had in this country a number of such communities, one in the state of New York, the Oneida Community, concerned itself with better eugenics, and disintegrated more or less when the very strong character of the original founder was removed from the scene. This community continued to preserve many of its communal aspects for some time, and during the depression years this was manifested in the way it rallied to the local industry and all individuals helped one another in their daily lives.

In Israel the establishment of the Kibbutz was a coming together of individuals who had escaped from oppression and who wished to live together in a community, for protection and to achieve better

* Lawrence Hyde, *Spirit and Society* London, Methuen & Co., 1949.

standards of community life. This type of communal living includes some of the characteristics of socialism, but has no connection whatsoever with what one finds in Communist philosophy in Russia and China today.

In this discussion of the family and the community I have in mind, of course, the group with whom you are in immediate everyday contact—the village or suburb, if you live in one, or your city neighborhood, and the city as a whole. But in order to derive the greatest individual fulfillment from your participation in a group, you must understand that the spiritual connotation of the word "community" is of far greater importance than the physical, and that no matter how small the gathering of which you are a part, it is, in turn, a part of that larger community which embraces the world of human beings.

All proper behavior within a community is based on a realization of these two essential facts.

9

Getting Acquainted

THIS CHAPTER IS ESPECIALLY INTENDED FOR THOSE WHO
have just moved into a new community, or for those
who, having lived in one place for several years, still feel that they
are strangers, and are unhappy in their isolation. How can they get
to know their neighbors and become a part of the life of the community? What are the proper and the improper ways for them to
meet people?

On the face of it the matter may seem to be simpler in a small
village or a suburb than in a large city. Yet this is not always so.
Many small, old communities, composed largely of families who
have lived in them for several generations, have a hard shell of
conservative aloofness that may be more difficult to penetrate than
the traditional impersonal indifference of the large city. The truly
inward and spiritual aspects of the most enlightened community
may be lacking to an appalling and even frightening degree. Because
the stranger is different, because he has not the status conferred by
long residence, he may be resented and distrusted, whereas in the
large city, much of the population of which is constantly changing,

a newcomer is typically taken at face value. Indeed it is unlikely that he will be recognized as a newcomer, unless he himself announces the fact. In a large apartment building in New York City, someone who has moved in the day before, meeting someone in the same building who has lived there for years, may not even be recognized as a newcomer, nor so far as his status is concerned does it matter in the least if he is.

Yet I have found, generally speaking, whether in city or village, that the hearts of most people are essentially kind, and that anyone who wants to know others can do so, and make friends if he himself is friendly, considerate, and genuinely interested in others and their welfare. Whether in a village or a city the basic elements essential to his becoming an accepted member of the community are the same.

DOING YOUR PART

If you expect others to make the effort to know you, you will probably remain fairly lonely. Do not expect this, or wait for it to happen You must be ready not only to meet your new neighbors and fellow citizens halfway, but also to make the physical and intellectual effort necessary to learn the nature of the community into which you have moved, its customs and traditions, and to place yourself in a position that makes it easy for its members to meet you You must be ready to welcome them if you want them to welcome you In order to enter that inner, intangible community spirit, you must be eager to join in it in more than a physical sense. You must be prepared to *give* yourself, to adapt yourself to its ways, and to find ways of meeting other people without, of course, becoming pushing or intrusive.

IN THE VILLAGE OR SUBURB

Getting the Feel of the Community

One of your first tasks on moving into a new community is to "get the feel of the place." If it is a village or suburb and has a local newspaper, subscribe to it Read the local news, find out what is going on and, in so far as you are able, what the people are like—

ın addıtıon to the fact that they are human beıngs. Are they plannıng a new school? Promotıng the ıdea of a publıc playground, skatıng rink, or swimmıng pool? Is the communıty chıefly composed of people who earn theır lıvıng ın the ımmedıate neighborhood, are they commuters, or are the majorıty of homeowners retıred business-men?

Drive or walk around your new neighborhood and become visually acquainted with it so that when someone who is helping you to find an address asks, "You know where the high school is?" you do not have to answer, "No, I'm a complete stranger here." That is one of the remarks which, if you use it often and long, is likely to keep you one.

Talk to the tradesmen when you market, to the banker and the postmaster when you find yourself ın the bank or the post office, and find out as much about your new neighbors and the town they lıve ın as you can, always wıthout lettıng your questions seem in-trusıve or overınquısıtıve Make the ınterests of those who already lıve there your ınterests, so that when they meet you they wıll find you are less a stranger than they thought you were. The larger part of the task of makıng you feel at home ıs your own. Do not expect others to perform ıt for you.

The local lıbrary ıs always a good place to make contacts. You are bound to talk to the lıbrarıan about your lıkes and dıslıkes in lıterature, and as a rule other people in a small town or vıllage wıll be droppıng ın and very often joın ın the conversation. Before long you may have arranged wıth your new acquaıntances to exchange some books you have that are not ın the lıbrary

I have always found that even small vıllage lıbrarıes have ex-hıbıtıons, sometımes of local paıntıngs, sometımes of ınterestıng books borrowed from collectors near or far, sometımes of chıldren's books, and these exhıbıtıons gıve an excellent chance for openıng up acquaıntanceshıps and workıng wıth other people. There ıs no surer way of gettıng to know people well than doıng some work wıth them.

Election Day ıs also a good tıme to meet people. It really does not matter whether you are a Republıcan or a Democrat. Whatever your party, you can offer to partıcıpate on that day—drıvıng your car to brıng ın the voters, or workıng at the polls. You may find if you are workıng wıth a group that you can all lunch together somewhere. You will undoubtedly have friendly feelings for those who think as you do and who are voting the same ticket, but you may find some congenial people whose politics differ from yours, and this may lead to interesting discussions and in the end to friendship, regardless of political affiliations All along the line it is a question of how much you are willing to give of yourself.

A year ago in our particular district that is overwhelmingly Republican, the Democrats started a school for local Democratic district workers. Among the things suggested was that these workers make tours, street by street, in their particular area, asking each voter which party he belonged to and urging him, regardless of party, to register and vote in the primaries.

One of the friendliest men I know, with a very friendly young woman, called on a family who lived on a new street of our rather large and fast growing village The woman was registered, the man was not. The two visitors talked first with the woman and asked if they could count on her voting in the primary and if she needed any help in getting to the voting place. Then they turned to the man and asked him why he was not registered. His response was that nobody ever asked him to register. He said he was a Democrat all right, but he figured if they wanted his vote they should come and ask him about it. Though he had been in the village for three years nobody had ever been to see him. He was one of the people who wait for all the advances to be made by someone else, but it pointed up the fact that we can go out of the way ourselves and improve the quality of our locality by drawing other citizens into the political interests of the community.

The Letter of Introduction

If you are fortunate enough to have a friend who knows someone in your new community whom he feels you will like, let him by all means write a letter of introduction. In most cases the letter is mailed by your friend to the person to whom it is addressed, rather than taken by you to be presented. The reason for this is obvious. If you have a letter from your friend John Markham to his friend Mary Forsyth in your possession, and you phone Mary and say, "I have a letter of introduction from John Markham. May I come and see you?" courtesy demands that Mary Forsyth say, "Certainly," whether she wants to or not, and whether the time you have suggested is convenient for her. But if she has received the letter by mail, with no communication from you, she will decide when she wants to call on you and will telephone to arrange things if she is courteous.

The first requirements of courtesy will have been discharged if she calls on you, and invites you to call on her. You will of course return her call, probably within a week or two, but if, after that, Mary makes no further move to see you, you cannot in courtesy press the acquaintance. The next move is for her to make. If she does not make it, you must accept the fact that your friend has made a mistake. His well-meant effort has been futile.

There may be circumstances that make it unnecessary for you to wait for Mary Forsyth to call on you, but they constitute the exception rather than the rule. If your friend and Mary Forsyth have been in regular correspondence, for instance, if you know that he has told her in his letters that you are moving to her community, and if she has written to him saying, "Do tell your friend to phone me as soon as she gets settled," it would be quite in order for you to do exactly that and invite her to come and see you. From that point on the matter is in your hands and hers, and should take its course smoothly, unless you find that you don't like each other.

Even in that case nothing has been lost. In actual experience this often proves true. The friendships you form in a community eventually are with other people than Mary to whom you had your first introduction, but hers is valuable just the same, because in some way it gives you a start and removes that awful stigma of "stranger."

Who Calls First?

The custom of informal afternoon calls without previous announcement is seldom observed in America today, though it still is occasionally followed in suburbs and villages. And with its passing has passed too the routine calls of old inhabitants to welcome new-comers to a neighborhood.

Yet in some communities it still survives and constitutes one of the most gracious gestures of courtesy. Such calls are not made, according to custom, until the family has had time to get the house in order, settle down, and catch their breaths.

One very pleasant thing that may happen to people, particularly if they are a young couple, is finding that someone in the new community once knew the parents, grandparents, or uncles or aunts of either the wife or the husband, and if they had a happy relationship they will carry this feeling to the young people moving into the neighborhood. The young people may have no idea who they are and may have to write home to find out, but it will be a very pleasant surprise if the older people, with a gracious note, have some little welcoming token delivered to the newcomers in the first few days of "settling down."

I remember the first time my husband and I went to Albany we discovered that my husband's father and mother had known well old Mr. and Mrs Pruyn. The next generation lived in Albany, and almost on the day of our arrival some very delicious cookies which were a special Albany delicacy were left at our door with a charming note of welcome The friendship grew and strengthened with several members of the family, and when we returned to Albany at the time my husband was elected Governor and we held our first New Year's Day reception, we were pleasantly surprised to find upon our dining-room table large quantities of an old Dutch New Year's delicacy, *oly koeks*. They continued to surprise us with traditional Albany foods at times, and it was always particularly welcome. I decided that friendships that came down through generations are valuable things to foster.

There is another welcoming gesture which some unusually thoughtful people may make. If on the day when the mover has just deposited your furniture and packing cases in any open space which he finds in your new house, and left you looking in desperation at the chaos before you without knowing where to find even a clean glass for the drink of water you so badly need, a tap at the back door brings you face to face with a friendly woman bearing a large bowl of soup, or a saucepan of good stew, or slices from her dinner roast, you are probably lucky. If her motive is simply the desire to be helpful by feeding you a sample of her cooking when it would be difficult for you to cook yourself, she will do little more than introduce herself, tell you where she lives, give you her offering, invite you to call on her for any information or help, and leave you to the obvious immediacy of your problem. If, on the contrary, she settles down on a chair or packing case for a good long chat, asking you endless questions about yourself and your affairs, passing on neighborhood gossip, and warning you about Mrs. Smith and Mrs. Jones, you will probably find that you have a problem on your hands which must be dealt with adroitly if you do not want to be the subject of gossip on her next visit elsewhere. You are also in danger of having no privacy in your own home.

But in either case you will treat her with courtesy, and after you have eaten the food she has given you, you will return the receptacle in which it was brought, clean, and with thanks. You will have made one acquaintance for better or worse. Which it is to be will depend partly upon yourself, but almost entirely on your visitor.

It happens that I was very shy as a young woman and found unexpected visitors quite devastating. Because of my shyness I counted my privacy a great blessing and filled my days with numberless small duties that were rudely interrupted if someone just dropped in on me. My inclination was to be perfectly polite but rather unresponsive and cold to the kindest of visitors. I had been brought up, however, in the tradition that you were a failure if you did not meet your social obligations and not even a headache or slight illness should interfere with one. This made me polite but not really easy to know or very warm in my interest in other people, so the problem of controlling someone who was overzealous in his curiosity and his desire for intimacy was never great, but the ability to be really warm and interested in other people took me some time to acquire. It was not till I realized how selfish it was not to know about someone else, and how harmful it was to my husband's political life if I made no close relationships that I began to make an effort to meet people halfway and give a sense of warmth to my own hospitality. This is an art that you have to learn very quickly if you have to move from place to place often.

Traditionally the courtesy of the first call is reserved to the older inhabitants of the village or neighborhood. The newcomer's first call will be made only in return for earlier calls. But since, as I have said, the welcoming call has almost gone out of existence even in village and suburban communities, and is unheard of for the vast majority of city dwellers, the matter is chiefly one for academic or historical discussion.

There are circumstances under which the procedure may be reversed with no impropriety. In an emergency the newcomer who would not run next door, or phone to ask for help, would imply a lack of humanity on the part of her neighbor which would in itself be a discourtesy.

Asking for help in situations that could not be considered emergencies may also be an avenue to acquaintance. You are a stranger. There is no impropriety, when on the streets of a strange city, in asking directions from a passerby. Nor is there any in asking similar questions of a neighbor when you have moved into a new community. How do you get to Smith's Poultry Farm, whose advertisement you have read in the local paper? How do you arrange for garbage collection? Is there a willing, hardworking boy in the neighborhood who may be engaged to mow your lawn, or keep your sidewalks clear of snow in winter? Is there a bus which will take you to the next town, and if so, where does it stop?

Only the most churlish of human beings would be annoyed by having a newcomer ask such questions as these, or feel that she was taking undue advantage of propinquity, if they were asked considerately. But be sure that they are genuine questions and reflect an authentic need.

If you know the name of the neighbor of whom you wish to ask, use the telephone, introduce yourself by name and identify yourself as "Mrs. Markham who has just moved in next door," or "across the street," ask for help, and state your questions briefly and clearly. Do not attempt to prolong the conversation, but when you have the answers thank your neighbor and consider the conversation at an end, unless she wishes to prolong it. There is no impropriety in saying, just before you bid her good-by, "I do hope that you will run in some time." If she has liked the sound of your voice she probably will, unless she is one who is dedicated to the principle that only those whose families have lived in the community for several generations or have two cars in the garage are worth knowing

If you do not know her name or if your phone hasn't yet been installed, there is no reason why you should not go over—either to the back door or the front, whichever is more convenient—and follow the same procedure there. Go as you are. This is not a social call. But it is one that may break the ice.

Church

If you are a member of a church you will probably have brought with you a letter from the minister of the church you have left to the minister of the church where you have moved. This will bring you in touch not only with your new minister, but also with members of the congregation. If you are not a church member, but an occasional churchgoer with or without a denominational preference, the church of your choice in your new home will inevitably enable you to meet a group of human beings, one or two of whom at least may become close friends. Among the spiritual benefits of the church none is more cherished than the social opportunities it confers upon a new member of the congregation.

Children

If you have children of school age you have brought with you instinctive ambassadors, trained by nature to help you meet your neighbors. Children do not need introductions to one another. They approach strangers of their own kind as easily, and in much the same way, as dogs do, with curiosity, interest, a little aloofness and truculence, and a genuine need to know one another. They are as gossipy, in their way, as chambermaids, each trying to find out as much about their new acquaintances and their families as possible. They agree, disagree, sometimes fight, and shake down their friendships Then if their relations to their parents are good, they bring their friends home. Soon, when your Johnny doesn't get home in time for dinner one day, you will be calling Tommy's mother, because Johnny has brought Tommy home so many times you think it likely that he has gone home with Tommy. Or Tommy's mother will be phoning you to ask a similar question about her wanderer, or simply to say that she would like to meet you, adding, "Tommy has told me so much about you, and especially what good cookies you make."

Or you may give Johnny a party, asking him, of course, for the names of the children he would like you to ask. If he is a young child you will write your notes of invitation to the mothers of his prospective guests, and may add, "When you come to get him after the party, do plan to stay a moment." There are a hundred ways by which you, through your children's friends, may meet their parents.

Clubs and Societies

Find out whether there are some clubs or societies in your community whose interests are your own—the drama (amateur theatrical group), music, art, gardening, a historical association, a

Great Book Circle, a Women Voters' League. Find out which of them accept members through application, and which only by invitation, and do not make the mistake of applying for membership to one of the latter But there are almost surely some which you may join merely by expressing your desire to do so and paying your dues, and if you pick them carefully with your own interests in mind you will be sure to meet people whose genuine interests are your own.

Door-Bell Ringers

Increasingly the suburban or village dweller, whether a newcomer or an old-timer, finds herself answering the doorbell to face a man or woman wanting to sell something or to solicit a contribution. It may be a donation to the Heart Fund, the Red Cross, the Cancer Fund, the local firemen's ball, or any number of other causes. If you like the looks of the man or woman who comes to the door soliciting for a worthy charity, ask your caller in, instead of letting him or her wait at the door while you get your money out of your purse. A little talk may be the beginning of a friendship which you will value.

Or you may reverse the process, volunteering for such work yourself, and thus extend your potential acquaintances by the number of people in the area assigned to you.

Of course all of these things take time and call for an especial efficiency in budgeting your work and your leisure activities. Every program you make should be regulated by your sense of relative values. If it means a great deal to you to meet and make friends quickly when you move into a new community, arrange your life so that you can give the necessary effort to doing so adequately. If you like solitude better than sociability, that is another matter. But if you want to meet people you must do something about it yourself, keeping within the proprieties that should regulate your entrance into a new community.

IN THE CITY

Traditionally a large city is a place in which you may remain a stranger all your life. Yet I have often thought that the reputation of coldness and impersonality of a great metropolis is a false one.

Here you may be called on to make a greater effort yourself than in the suburb or village, but you have the advantage of a wider range in your choice of acquaintances and friends, and a far greater number of groups brought together by common interests, but essentially the same kind of creatures as you would meet elsewhere—that is, human beings.

Special Interest Groups

As to special interest groups which you may join by application, they have been formed in a place such as New York to satisfy practically every interest you can think of—camera, drama, art, music, hiking, cinema, bird watching, plane spotting, historical study, tennis, hobbies such as woodworking and stamp collecting, chess, and practically everything else. Pick your interest and find the group that shares it Some of them you will find in the classified telephone directory. An attendant at the public library will probably be able to refer you to a directory which lists others In New York City, the New School for Social Research admirably fulfills its function as a center of intellectual activity, but also, situated in the heart of an indifferent city, it has become a point of attraction for groups of the same tastes or ambitions In other cities in the United States such groups or schools can be found or formed, if your interest is genuine and sustained As in the suburb or village, people in the city are people and the desire for human companionship is strong.

Dogs. Even a dog may carry a card of introduction for you. Most people walk their dogs about the same time of day whether morning or evening, and dogs, like children, introduce themselves to one another if you give them half a chance A real dog lover will usually give her or his dog a moment in which to smell noses and wag tails with your dog By the time the four-legged strangers at one end of the leash begin to feel acquainted their owners should know that they have at least a love of dogs in common, and perhaps decide to find out what other matters make them potential friends—and an invitation (with or without dog) may follow.

When I first moved to New York from Washington after my husband's death, I was living in an apartment at 29 Washington Square West, and early in the morning and late in the evening I would walk around the square or neighboring streets with my husband's dog Fala. Soon I began to make real friends, not always other dog lovers even, because the students from the university on the other side of the square would be loitering along or sitting on the benches, and as walking a dog means frequently stopping, I began to make friends with many people whom I meet even today and who remember that we all lived or studied around Washington Square.

After I moved to Sixty-second Street I met a lady one day with her very much pampered and cared for Scotty She stopped me volubly, explaining that she and her husband had long admired my husband and that they would like above everything else to mate their little dog with Fala. All the necessary arrangements were duly made, but to our mutual regret Fala had no interest in the lady Scotty and what, I am sure, might have ripened into a very pleasant relationship ended when I moved away.

SOME DO'S AND DON'T'S

When you meet those who have lived in the community longer than you have, remember that in a sense you are undergoing inspection and are on trial. They are at least as curious about you as you are about them, and, even though unconsciously, feel that they have a prior claim on the community. This is especially true in small towns, where customs are more stable and community pride more prevalent than in the city At the outset there may be those among your neighbors who will think of you as they would an uninvited guest, not necessarily with overt hostility, yet with reservations and doubts in their minds which they will want to resolve before they welcome you without reservation.

You are somewhat in the position of an adopted child who has come into a large family, if not against the will of the other children, certainly without it. To them, even though they do not so analyze it, they have conferred a privilege on you. Let them see that you appreciate it, that you consider yourself fortunate to be there. You are the guest; be a well behaved guest, yet at the same time welcome them with the cordiality and good will that are the marks of a good hostess If you have made the preliminary effort to get properly acquainted with the physical community and its environment, you will certainly have seen some things which you admire—the new school building, the charming eighteenth century church of which the town is justly proud, the conveniently arranged shopping center, the little grove at the edge of the town which was bought by a wise village government a century ago and preserved in its wild state as a park, the school playground where you have watched eager boys playing baseball.

These are the things to talk about with praise. Remember that they *belong* to the people you are meeting. Praise them, but not so fulsomely as to make your words open to suspicion.

Forget, for the moment, the shabby, run-down, untidy group of houses and yards which you found on the other side of the tracks, the potholes in the streets there, the rudeness of the chain-store clerk, the ugly war memorial in the village square, the appalling fact that the village has no sewers and still depends upon antique cesspools and septic tanks for drainage, the unfair method of assessing water charges by the number of bathtubs in the house rather than by consumption measured by meters, the inadequate equipment of the local light and power company and the consequently frequent power failures.

Many of those whom you are meeting actually feel the same way about these things as you do, but to have you, a newcomer, voice criticism of them will almost inevitably result in their closing ranks to defend their town against the outsider. Let your adverse opinions be buried in your silence until you have become genuinely integrated within the community and may join with your progressive neighbors in trying to better the conditions that need bettering.

Do not go out of your way, at first, to tell your new friends about what a fine place you have left behind you. Answer their questions about it, of course, but avoid describing with too much enthusiasm aspects of your old environment in a way that may imply that it is superior to your new one.

I remember standing by an American tourist once before a counter at Selfridge's in London. I have forgotten what it was that she was trying to buy, but her dissatisfaction mounted as the clerk brought one after another offering to show her. Finally she said crossly, "Why at Marshall Field's in Chicago, they have twice the choice you have here!"

The clerk's British courtesy did not desert him, but I saw him stiffen, as he said, "I'm sorry, Madam Perhaps you will find what you are looking for on the third floor." I saw his relief as she marched truculently away, and realized that she, an adult, had been trying to get something which suited her in a department devoted to accessories for teen-age girls.

I quickly bought something which I really didn't want, and praised it, in an attempt to soften some of the bad impression of American manners which the clerk had received from my compatriot.

This is the kind of provincialism which keeps one from enjoying the history and beauty of other countries. I remember well the wife of one of my husband's legal advisers who accompanied us on a trip to France and England at the end of World War I. My husband was arranging to close American naval installations and the men of the party were busy much of the time, so I was delegated to show Mrs. H—— the sights of Paris. The first thing I did was to drive her up the Champs Elysées. To my surprise, she looked around and remarked· "I think our park in —— is quite as nice as this. I don't see anything remarkable about this avenue." A little later as we were driving in the Bois de Bologne she again referred to her native town in comparison to what she was seeing, and when she developed eye trouble a few days later I could not help feeling that she was cut off from sightseeing for a while because she had no ability to appreciate or enjoy anything different from her own home environment.

As much as is possible conform, at first at least, to the customs of your neighbors. If you have children, and there is a school bus for those in your neighborhood, let your children use it instead of driving them to school in your car, unless there is some special reason, such as physical incapacitation, that makes the latter obligatory

If there is a parking law or even a custom which dictates that cars shall not be parked overnight on the street in front of your house, park yours at the back of the house or in your driveway, or even in a public parking lot or garage, rather than in front of your house.

The rules that govern conversation with your new neighbors are those that should prevail wherever you are, but they are perhaps particularly important during the period when you are more or less on trial in a new community.

Try to remember their interests—even if you don't know them in detail you are on safe ground talking about the town itself, with appreciation for the things you like about it—and when you initiate a subject let it be one which they are predisposed to enjoy. Do not dwell on your personal affairs, your husband's business, the cleverness of your children, or your own exploits.

Avoid gossip as you would the plague. You may hear plenty of it. Let it go in one ear and out the other.

Avoid political and religious controversy. If you happen to be a Democrat in a predominantly Republican community, express your political convictions at the polls. After you are "settled in," if you wish to work with the Democratic minority for a Democratic candidate, by all means do so. But do not endanger your welcome at the outset by unnecessarily citing the inadequacies of Republican Presidents back to Ulysses S. Grant, and singing the praises of Woodrow Wilson, Franklin D. Roosevelt, and John F. Kennedy. By all means make a simple declaration of your political convictions if called upon to do so, but let the voluntary exhibition of any crusading enthusiasm which you feel wait a bit.

As to religion, remember the pragmatic philosophy expressed so eloquently by William James in *The Varieties of Religious Experience*, which convincingly demonstrates that the good religion for any individual is that which bears fruits in a good life, and the words of a wise Eastern religious teacher, quoted in a book I read years ago and the title of which I have forgotten: "All paths lead to God so long as they lead upwards." If asked what your church is, name it, or if you do not go to church, say so simply, without going into explanations or a defense of your own beliefs which might, by implication, seem a criticism of those who hold others.

If you know a foreign language, or have tucked away in your memory a few telling phrases in one, save your knowledge for your trip abroad or until you meet someone here who cannot speak English but does speak a language which you know. Speak English to your new English-speaking acquaintances. Parading unnecessarily a linguistic ability is a shortcut to a reputation for being "stuck up."

And even in using the English language do not try to prove at every opportunity that you have an extraordinarily large vocabulary When you have the choice between a long word of uncertain familiarity and a short one of common usage, use the latter if you want to make friends with your new neighbors.

If you keep a dog, keep him in your house or yard. Perhaps

your neighbors do not like dogs. But even if they do like them they probably will not enjoy having your pet rooting in their garbage cans, running through their flower beds, or standing in front of their guests and barking.

Similarly see that your children play in your own yard rather than your neighbors', unless by invitation they are playing there with the neighbors' children. Even then make sure that they do not outstay the welcome of the adults, which may become threadbare before that of their children.

These are just some of the examples of behavior which will smooth your way to a pleasant and harmonious absorption into your community. Though they seem to be directed to the dweller in a village or suburb, the principles behind them are equally applicable to one who moves into a new neighborhood in the city.

When I was a child, children used to be told to mind their "company manners" when guests were coming. I have never really liked the expression, for the same rules of courtesy should dictate one's behavior whether there are guests or not. And if I urge especial care in conduct when meeting new neighbors, it is not that I believe in "company manners" in the old sense of the word, but rather that I know that things that may be done and said to old, trusted, understanding friends, may be misinterpreted by people who don't know you. And every courteous person will abide, in so far as he may do so without offense to his own principles, with the customs of the community in which he finds himself. Until you know surely how the people in the community of which you are becoming a part feel and act, it is well not to be too positive about most things. Perhaps I am trying to say something akin to that which St. Paul gave as advice in his First Epistle to the Corinthians, "If meat make my brother to offend, I will eat no flesh while the world standeth." That is perhaps a little extreme, but the principle behind it is sound.

10

The Family Is Entertained

IT IS GRACIOUS TO BE A GOOD HOST OR HOSTESS, IT IS equally so to be a good guest. The road to pleasant human relationships is a two-way street, along which your guests come to you and you go to your hostess with, in either case, a pleasant sense of taking and giving pleasure, a sharing of one another, and the gratifying knowledge that whether you are entertaining or being entertained you are giving not only yourself pleasure but others as well, and thus enhancing your own Properly understood there is little, if any, basic difference between the attitude of a good hostess and that of a good guest. Entertaining at its best is a cooperative enterprise to which hostess and guests contribute, each taking an active part to see that the gathering is as harmonious and pleasant as possible The details of hostess and guest activities vary, the spirit which motivates them—that of consideration and cooperation—is the same.

Phone Call

Today the telephone has taken the place of the note or letter for many people as a means of issuing invitations for all but formal affairs. And when it is used, the call is as informal as the instrument. Your caller will probably say something like this "Won't you (or you and your husband, or you and your friend) come to tea (or cocktails or dinner) next Wednesday?" And you will answer her as informally with, "We'd love to, but I shall have to ask my husband. He may have made another engagement," or "I'm so sorry, but we can't," and probably explain the reason why.

If you have a house guest you will not ask whether you may bring him, unless you and the one who has invited you are very close friends and you know without asking that your guest will be acceptable. Instead you will simply mention your guest as the reason you must decline the invitation. If your friend then says, "But by all means bring him along, we'd love to have him," you may of course take her at her word But before making your acceptance definite you will consult your guest. Your obligation as a hostess takes precedence over that as a prospective guest. Your guest will probably say that he is delighted. Or he may feel enough at home in your house to suggest that you go along without him, leaving him to read the fascinating book that is yet unfinished, or to go to a movie he wants to see, or to write some letters. If his suggestion is an obviously sincere one, there is no reason why you should not accept it and thank him. Perhaps he would actually welcome an evening alone. In any case, after a decision has been made, you will phone your friend as early as possible and tell her that you will, or will not be there, with or without your guest. If there is the slightest question in your mind as to whether or not you are expected to wear dinner clothes, it is quite proper for you to ask, though it should not be necessary. Unless your hostess is sure that you understand that this is not a dress affair she will probably have told you.

The Formal Invitation

If you receive a formal invitation, it may be an engraved card, a letter, or even a telegram. In any case the wording will be substantially the same. "Mr. and Mrs. James Wolfe Guernsey request the pleasure of Mr. and Mrs. Scott's company at dinner on Monday, September the twelfth, at eight o'clock, 101 Milwaukee Avenue." It almost certainly will include "R.S.V.P." in the lower left-hand corner.

But whether it does or not you will of course answer it promptly, using the formal language of the invitation itself "Mr. and Mrs. James Weldon Scott accept with pleasure Mr. and Mrs. James Wolfe Guernsey's kind invitation to dinner on Monday, September the twelfth, at eight o'clock, 101 Milwaukee Avenue." Or "Mr and Mrs. James Weldon Scott regret that because of a previous engagement they will be unable to accept Mr. and Mrs. Guernsey's kind invitation for September the twelfth." If the answer is an acceptance, the date, time, and address should be included in it, as evidence that there is no confusion in the mind of the guest as to the time and the place. If it is a rejection, these details are unnecessary and should be omitted.

The invitation may or may not say "black tie." But if it is a formal invitation to dinner or for an evening dance or reception, it is understood that you will be expected to dress.

The Informal Note

If your invitation is an informal note from a friend, it is quite proper for you to accept or decline it by a similarly informal note or by a phone call.

Children

Never assume that an invitation to you and your husband includes your children. If your hostess wants them to come with you, she will say so. If she does not, and they are too young to be left alone, call your baby sitter as soon as you have accepted the invitation.

Semiformal and Formal Clothes

Rigidity in the conventions of dress has fortunately relaxed considerably in the United States during the past twenty-five years. It is symptomatic of the general relaxation in manners, and morals perhaps, of the generation that lived through World War II. Except in the case of certain wealthy families no one today would think of changing into a dinner jacket every evening for dinner.

The practice of dressing for dinner never has been as prevalent in the United States as it was in England, and possibly our fore-fathers who took up the habit were copying the English customs, as they did in so many ways. Dressing for dinner, to the British, was, I think, part of bolstering the Empire, because a man who was governing a distant outpost far from civilization would put on his evening clothes even though he was dining alone. In our country and even in England today the lack of servants, the compactness of the modern home, the tensions of modern life have all contributed to an informality in manners, which shows itself in an ignoring or even dislike of many of the old conventions of dress. Yet a decent consideration for your appearance and what is expected of you in the way of dress by your hostess and her other guests is still an essential courtesy.

"Black Tie"

If your invitation reads "black tie," it means that the man is expected to wear a dinner jacket, commonly called a "tuxedo," with black trousers without cuffs, and braid down the seams of the trouser legs. The suit is usually black, though it may be midnight blue, and in summer the jacket may be white. But if you can afford only one evening suit, by all means stick to black. The jacket may be single-breasted or double-breasted.

The waistcoat is of the same material as the coat and trousers, or of white piqué A black cummerbund may be substituted for the waistcoat. Neither waistcoat nor cummerbund is necessary with a double-breasted jacket

The old-fashioned shirt with stiff white bosom is seldom worn with a dinner jacket today, though there is no impropriety in wearing it. More usual is the white shirt with finely pleated front, worn with a wing or turn-down collar. In very hot weather a soft white shirt (never colored or striped) with soft collar may be worn.

The tie is traditionally a black silk bow regardless of which type of shirt you wear, though maroon is now sometimes worn.

Socks are customarily black silk or nylon, but if you are accustomed to wool socks, and subject to colds, by all means wear plain black wool. You will not be conspicuous. However, if like most men today you do not wear garters, and your socks have a tendency to sag about the ankles, better buy a pair to wear with your evening clothes

The conventional shoes to wear with either dinner jacket or full dress are black patent leather pumps or oxfords. But if you do not own a pair and do not feel justified in buying them for the rare occasions on which you will wear a dinner jacket, an ordinary pair of good, well-cared-for and shined black oxfords, which you can wear on other occasions, will not make you conspicuous.

Your hat may be an opera hat, a black Homburg, or even a gray felt. It is not customary to wear a derby with a dinner jacket. But since you discard your outer clothing as soon as you enter your hostess's house, it is not of vital importance.

What does the young man who does not own a dinner suit do when he receives a formal invitation or one that has on it the notation "black tie?" He has several choices. He may of course tighten his financial belt and buy one, feeling that he must do so sooner or later anyway. Or he may rent one, a procedure extremely distasteful to some men who feel that it is pretentious hypocrisy. He may courteously decline the invitation without giving any reason for doing so, or with a polite white lie about a previous engagement. Or he may frankly tell his hostess, especially if she is an understanding friend, why he is declining her invitation. In that case she may say, "Oh, that's all right. Just wear a dark suit. Jim Hanson hasn't got one either, and he'll be here." If her formality is as flexible as that, it is quite proper to appear in a dark suit—but with a white shirt and black tie (surely the young man can afford that, even if he has to buy it especially for the occasion), and black shoes. But it is more courteous to decline the invitation than to arrive without announcement in an ordinary business suit.

I remember well some amusing occurrences in the White House. Guests often arrived, particularly gentlemen, without the tie they needed or the waistcoat or even the shoes; and then the ushers were called upon to find something to replace the forgotten articles, and in some miraculous way they usually found them. I remember one night when we were having a state dinner for the President of Liberia and the President elect, both of whom were staying with us in the White House, the usher came to me in some trepidation to announce that the President elect had called his valet at Blair House where the overflow of guests and servants sometimes stayed, and had been told that no black shoes had been brought—and there he was with only his pair of brown day shoes. Everything else was perfectly correct about his evening clothes, but the ushers looked upon brown shoes at a state dinner as not quite the proper footwear, so they tried to find someone with an extra pair of proper shoes in the correct size. They could not be found, and our guest came to dinner in his brown shoes. I hope he was not embarrassed, because neither the President nor I would have ever noticed what he had on his feet in the ordinary course of events.

My husband had a great dislike of putting on a tuxedo, but a white tie and tails was really a horror to him and he would try to think up all sorts of excuses for not wearing this formal attire. However, he almost always had to, because the colored valet would look at him sternly and tell him that was the proper thing to wear, and the President of the United States did not have the courage to refuse to put it on.

"White Tie"

If the invitation reads "White Tie," or if it is a formal invitation to a ball, a very formal evening wedding, or a formal diplomatic reception, it means that the hostess expects you to wear "tails," or full evening dress. The waistcoat worn with a tail coat is always white piqué, the trousers usually have a somewhat wider braid of finer material down the seams, but it is possible, for economy's sake, to wear the trousers which you wear with your dinner jacket without impropriety. The shirt has a stiff bosom, the collar is always a wing collar, the tie is white lawn or piqué, socks black, and shoes black patent leather pumps or oxfords. A black silk topper, white buckskin gloves, a black overcoat, and a white muffler are worn.

Sometimes a considerate hostess, knowing that many men do not own a tail coat, will specify "White or black tie." In this case either a dinner jacket or full evening dress may be worn.

The Evening Dress

Considerable latitude is allowed contemporary women in the dresses they wear when accompanying their husbands at a "black tie" or "white tie" affair. The dress should be simple and dignified, of chiffon, crepe, moiré or taffeta, or cotton lace, in any becoming color or in black. The dinner dress may have long or short sleeves, or be sleeveless, and is longer than an afternoon dress, but not so long as an evening dress. Very formal evening dresses are sleeveless and may have trains. Elbow-length or longer white suede or kid gloves are usually worn, though today short gloves are allowable.

INFORMAL CLOTHES

When dining or spending the evening informally with friends the only clothing requirements are that you should be dressed neatly and with dignity in the kind of clothing which you and the group you are meeting are accustomed to wearing For a man this usually means the kind of suit he wears at the office, though he may change from a lighter to a darker one, and wear a white shirt instead of a striped or colored one, and black shoes and socks instead of tan shoes and the fancy socks he cherishes for daytime wear. Or he may not, and still be dressed properly.

A woman may follow a similar program, perhaps changing from the more restrained costume which she wears at the office, or when she is shopping, to what she might call a "party" (but not a formal) dress, and a smarter pair of shoes than the practical ones she wears during the day.

The amount of "dressing up" anyone does for informal gatherings of friends is determined by no set rules, but rather by the customs of the group. Indeed in the country it is not unusual for friends to assemble for dinner or a pleasant evening together in modified sports clothes. Naturally these would not be the clothes in which you had played tennis or golf, or gardened all day. You would appear neat and clean and fresh as if you were dressed for the most formal dinner. But if you know that you may expect your host to greet you in a tweed jacket, restrained sports shirt, slacks, and loafers, and your hostess in a similar costume, there is no reason why you should not dress in the same way. Indeed it would be in as bad taste to appear at such a dinner in a tuxedo as it would be to go to a formal church wedding dressed in Bermuda shorts and carrying a tennis racket.

The important thing is to be fresh and clean; and a word should be said here about children, because very often at informal parties children are included. I think one cannot begin too soon to teach them that they must wash or perhaps, if they have been doing something very strenuous, take a bath before dinner and change. Even though it may be the same kind of dress or suit that the boy or girl has worn all day it should be a clean one.

My mother-in-law used to tell my children that when they had been playing in the stable they must be sure to listen for the gong which she had rung before lunch or dinner so that they would have ample time to clean up; and if they rushed in at the last minute saying· "Oh, Granny, we are so sorry we did not hear the gong," or "We just did not have time to come sooner," she would answer the last excuse with the words of her aunt, Mrs. Franklin Delano: "My dears, you had all the time there was." And she always sent them upstairs to clean up before allowing them to come to table.

AT THE TABLE

Whether at the most formal banquet or the most informal dinner at the home of a friend, good table manners are essentially the same, save as they are modified in details by the manner of service, and your familiarity with your host and hostess and probably with those who sit next to you.

Seating

If there are no place cards (and there seldom are at informal dinners) wait to be seated until your hostess has told you where to sit. Even then, if you are a man, do not seat yourself until the rest have assembled and you have helped the lady at your right into her chair.

The Napkin

Spread your napkin over your knees If it is a large one, it is more convenient to leave it folded once. It seems hardly necessary to say that it should not be tucked in at the collar, unless you are an infant, yet I have never been able to see any reason why a man, if he chooses, should not tuck one corner of it into the lower part of his waistcoat or under his belt. Certainly it is less likely to slip off on to the floor if he does this, and I do not see why it should give offense to anyone.

This same procedure of tucking a napkin under one's belt if one is wearing an evening dress and one happens to be a stout lady is a good one, because otherwise either the lady or her escort will be constantly fishing under the table for the napkin that will slide constantly off the nonexistent lap!

Grace or "the Blessing"

It is unlikely that your host or hostess will "say grace" or, as it used to be referred to, "ask the blessing." It is a custom that, a generation or two ago, was widespread among devout American Christian families, but that is today followed by few. Yet there are some who still begin every meal with this simple religious rite, sometimes spoken by the father, sometimes by the mother, sometimes at different meals by different members of the family or a guest (especially if the guest happens to be a minister), sometimes silent. A similar ritual is followed in devout Jewish families.

Even if it is not customary to say grace in your home, it is courteous if you have a minister or priest or rabbi as a guest, to ask him to do so, while the others at the table bow their heads in respectful silence.

Quakers almost always have a silent grace. Sometimes the gathering holds hands during this period of silent meditation. Sometimes they just sit with their hands folded in their laps.

I have always liked this Quaker habit, except that I find myself wondering when the proper time is come to start conversation—forgetting, of course, that I am a guest and that this is not my obligation and that I should give myself up to meditation until someone else breaks the silence.

If you, as a guest, encounter grace in any form in the home of your host and hostess, you will of course join the ritual to the extent of bowing your head and maintaining silence, regardless of your own religious beliefs and practices. To do otherwise would be the height of rudeness.

Your host or hostess probably will not ask you to say grace unless she knows that you are accustomed to do so in your home. If you are asked, however, and you have never done so in your life, which is true of vast numbers today, you may find yourself in a difficult position. It need not be so, really, if you face it squarely in one of the only two ways you may with courtesy.

If you simply do not feel up to it you may say, "I'm sorry, but I have never done so, and I just don't think I could with conviction." This should cause no offense, but it certainly would cause a certain amount of embarrassment to you, your host and hostess, and the other guests.

It would be far better to bow your head and do as you have been asked to do, using the short grace that has been used in millions of families, "Our Father, we thank thee for this food. Bless it to our use and us to thy service, Amen." It is quickly said, is acceptable to Protestant, Catholic, or Jew, can offend no one, yet fulfills the obligation that has been placed on you. Even if you are the most hard-boiled of unbelievers you can bring yourself to pay this courtesy to the religious beliefs of others.

It is possible to find oneself just taken by surprise, however, and in that case remembering any grace at all is apt to be difficult. I recall being a guest in a Kentucky home one morning when I had joined Senator Barkley for a tour of an area of that state. I had come off a train and was conscious as soon as I entered the house that great preparations for breakfast were going on, and I remembered the traditions of old Southern hospitality and wondered what would be given us to eat and hoped it would not be too long before we were sitting down for breakfast.

First I had to be interviewed, however, for a small local paper by two youngsters who had quite evidently never interviewed anyone before, so I had to ask myself the questions and give the answers!

When finally we did sit down I was on the right of the host and we had with us one Quaker gentleman. Dead silence reigned around the table. When the silence became embarrassing, I looked inquiringly at my host and he said "We are waiting for you to say grace." All I could remember at that moment was the grace I had learned as a child· "For what we are about to receive may the Lord make us truly thankful," and that is what I said.

We certainly should have been thankful, for we were served the most delicious fried chicken with cream sauce, hominy grits, jelly and jam, toast, coffee with thick cream, and I don't remember what else, but I think ham was also on the menu and some other delicacies. We could hardly move when we got up from the table and I was ready to go to sleep again instead of starting off to make speeches at various schoolhouses in the neighborhoods to which we drove.

When to Start Eating

At a large formal dinner you discharge the obligation of courtesy if you wait until a number of persons near you have been served and at least one of the women has started to eat. At an informal meal at which there are only a few people, wait until all have been served and your hostess begins to eat.

Eating Soup

Thick soup served in a soup dish is eaten with the soup spoon. If you want to get the last bit of it, there is no impropriety in tipping the dish away from you in order to collect it at the edge. Indeed you are paying a subtle compliment to your hostess by thus demonstrating how good it is. Drink thin soups and bouillons served in cups, as you would tea or coffee, but if there are vegetables or noodles left in the bottom, eat them with the spoon, rather than struggle unattractively to make them slide from the cup into your mouth.

Knife and Fork

In the United States the traditional custom in eating with a knife and fork dictates that the meat is cut with the knife in the right hand, the knife is then laid down on the plate (the entire knife —never rest the blade on the plate and the handle on the table cloth), the fork then shifted from the left to the right hand, the meat impaled on the fork with the tines up, and carried thus to the mouth.

The English and Europeans generally manage it more simply, by keeping the fork in the left hand, tines down, impaling the meat with it, or pushing potatoes onto it with the knife, and carrying it, still in the left hand, to the mouth.

Today it is equally proper to do it either way in America, and once you become accustomed to the European way you will find it easier and more graceful than the way most Americans of my generation were taught to eat.

When I was a young girl in France I learned that in French families you did not change your knife and fork with each course. You placed them beside you on a little glass rack that stood beside each person's plate.

At the end of World War I my husband and I were entertained by the chief naval officer and his wife in charge of the port of Brest, where we were landing. They were kind enough to ask not only the Assistant Secretary of the Navy and his wife but all the members of the party. When we sat down at table it suddenly occurred to me that I had not warned them to hold on to their knives and forks. With horror I saw them leave their knives and forks on the plates, and when the next course arrived they had nothing with which to eat. Madame, the hostess, had to ask that the cutlery be brought back. I could have spared them the embarrassment if I had warned them of the French custom which I had seen in French homes as a schoolgirl.

If you find yourself invited to a French home just look for that little rack beside your plate and use it if it is there. Our wasteful American habits are better known now, however, and my warning may be found quite unnecessary.

Difficult Foods

Some foods simply cannot be eaten gracefully with the knife and fork. These it is quite proper to eat with the fingers.

If you are served artichokes, remove the leaves one at a time, dip the edible base into the sauce that is served with them, and after you have pulled the flavorful flesh from the base with your teeth, discard the leaf at the edge of your plate. When you have reached the center, cut the spiked top off with your knife, then divide the rest of it with the knife and eat it with the fork, after dipping it too in the sauce.

Asparagus *may* be eaten with the fingers by taking up each stalk at the base, dipping the tip in the sauce (unless it is served with the sauce already poured over it), eating it from the tip down as far as it is tender, and discarding the tough base. But a long stalk of asparagus is an awkward, dangling thing to handle, and it is almost impossible to bring it to the mouth gracefully. It is probably more attractive to cut it with the knife and eat it with the fork. Still there is no impropriety in eating it with the fingers.

Bacon, so crisp that it has a tendency to fly off the plate if cut, may be eaten with the fingers, but if it is cooked rare, and is limp, it should be eaten with knife and fork.

The legs and wings of small birds and frogs' legs are eaten with the fingers. The meat of chicken should be cut from the bones and eaten with the knife and fork, but if you are eating informally with friends and want to pick up the drumstick, second joint, or wing in your fingers to get the last good bits from them, after you have taken off what you can with your knife, do so, and use your napkin (finger bowl if there is one) afterwards.

However, you may find yourself at a dinner party where the practice of picking up chicken bones is frowned on. If there is any doubt in your mind, watch your host or hostess. If neither of them does it, restrain yourself.

Celery, pickles, olives, and radishes are always eaten with the fingers.

Corn on the cob is sometimes served with holders at each end which makes it possible to handle it without soiling the fingers. If they are not there, pick the ear up boldly in both hands, butter and salt a few rows of kernels at a time so that the melted butter will not drip, and gnaw it.

Whole apples, pears, oranges and tangerines (both of which you will first divide into sections), plums, bananas, and grapes are all eaten with the fingers. But because peach juice will stain your hostess's napkin peel your peach (start it with the fruit knife, then pull the skin off with your fingers), cut it into sections, and eat it with your fork. Grapes should be removed in small secondary bunches from the large bunch in the centerpiece (if they are so served), brought to your plate, and taken one at a time from the small bunch. Do not remove individual grapes from the centerpiece.

Simple sandwiches are eaten in the fingers. But if they are three-decker, or "club," and of course if they are covered with hot gravy, eat them just as you would any meat or chicken dish.

The simplest and neatest way to eat spaghetti is to use a fork and table or dessert spoon together. With your left hand place the bowl of your spoon on edge on your plate, so that the concave portion faces the spaghetti. With your fork in your right hand impale the spaghetti, push the end of the tines against the bowl of the spoon, and keep turning the fork until you have managed to separate the strands of the spaghetti from the mass and formed a neat ball (or the functions of right and left hands may be reversed). Then put it into your mouth. If you find this too difficult you may cut the spaghetti with your fork and eat it as you would anything else, but this is rather unsatisfactory and slow. The other method is much better and quite simple once you have mastered it. Do not try to do it by getting the ends of long strands of spaghetti into your mouth and sucking the rest in. It is unattractive and apt to be noisy, and telltale traces may remain on your chin.

Persimmons are often brought to the table with the end already cut off. If not, with the fruit resting on its flat (or stem) end, remove the top as you would that of a boiled egg (this may be done easily with the edge of the spoon), and holding the fruit with your hand, dip out the soft inside meat with your spoon, much as you would a soft-boiled egg served in the shell.

Watermelon, if served in pieces in a compote cup, is eaten with a spoon; if in a slice on a plate, with a knife and fork.

The Arbiter

If in doubt as to how you should eat any article of food, or what implement to use, watch your hostess unobtrusively and do as she does.

If you have a great deal of courage you will do as one young Russian guest who came over during the war and was my guest at luncheon in the White House did when confronted with the array of implements beside her plate which was usual in setting the White House table.

This young woman was an engaging person who had come to speak for Russian relief in this country as the wife of an American correspondent stationed in Moscow who talked to us over the air every evening during World War II. She and her husband have been living here since he was exiled by the Soviet Union and she, having acquired citizenship during the two years she was speaking here for Russian relief, could not be prevented from coming with her husband which she felt it was her duty to do in order to prove that she did not believe the accusation against him of being a spy.

She was a warm and delightful person. With one look at the array of implements around her plate, she turned to me quite naturally and said. "You will have to tell me what I use. In Russia we do not have so many things on the table!" This seemed to me a perfect solution for the difficulty, but many of us would not have the courage to speak out so simply and directly.*

Drinking

If wine is served with your meal, your host, or hostess, or a servant will doubtless fill your glass as often as you empty it. Do not overdrink. Drunkenness is always unpleasant and a discourtesy to those who are with you. If you do not drink, do not turn your glass upside down which looks like rejection of hospitality as well as of wine, or hold your hand over it. Simply say, "No, thank you, I don't drink," or "I don't care for any." If you have drunk as much as you care to, or as you think wise, simply say, "No more, thank you." If your glass is filled in spite of your protest (as it should not be) you may with complete propriety leave it untouched.

* You may have read this lady's story in a book called *Nila* by Willy Snow Ethridge.

Leaving the Table

When the meal is over fold your napkin once and lay it at the left side of your plate. Do not bunch it into a ball (which is untidy), or fold it completely (to do so might seem to intimate that your hostess plans to use it again), or throw it down in your chair. Rise, and if you are a man draw back the chair of the lady sitting next to you, and when she has stepped back, push both your chair and hers back against the table so that others will not stumble over them; if you are a lady do not be so hurried that the gentleman next to you has no opportunity to pay you this small courtesy.

SOME SIMPLE DO'S AND DON'T'S

⁂ Do not drink water or wine while your mouth is full of food, unless, by chance, you have taken a mouthful that is so hot as to be painful, and must quickly cool it with a drink of water.

Avoid staining your hostess's glasses with lipstick or a residue of greasy or sticky food on your lips. Nothing is uglier. If you are a lady be sure that excess lipstick has been well patted off before you go to the table Be sure always to wipe your lips with your napkin before drinking.

Neither monopolize the conversation nor maintain an impenetrable silence. The good conversationalist is a good listener as well as talker. Do your share of both listening and talking, but don't overdo either.

Choose pleasant impersonal subjects to talk about. A dinner table is not the place for morbidness, self-praise (Is any place?), gossip, or details of your own shop talk which will interest no one save yourself. No matter how much more you know of a subject that has been introduced into the general conversation than the other guests, do not overpower them with your specialized knowledge, unless it is perfectly clear that they really want to listen to you. Above all never let yourself become embroiled in a heated argument. You may win the argument but you may lose your chance to be invited back.

Do not stir the food on your plate to mix it up and make an unpleasant-looking mess of it. A meal should be an esthetic as well as a gustatory experience.

Do not hunch over your food as though you really wanted to eat as a dog or a cat does. Sit up straight.

Do not use your spoon to remove jam or jelly from the common dish, nor your knife to take butter from the general supply if it is so served.

Neither wolf your food, nor dawdle over it. To do the latter will keep the other guests waiting and oblige your host and hostess to dawdle over theirs, for they will feel that they ought not to stop eating until after their guests have done so.

If your hostess has placed ashtrays and cigarettes on the table, smoke, if you like, after the dessert, or after the salad if your host or hostess does.

In England or any of the old dominion countries you are never allowed to light a cigarette until after the host has proposed the toast to the King or Queen, as the case may be, so people who like to smoke have to restrain themselves.

I remember presiding at a dinner in Canada at which Harry Hopkins was the main speaker. He was a chain smoker and never stopped through an entire meal. On this occasion he had refrained until the meat came and then he lit a cigarette. The major-domo came to me immediately and said: "You will have to ask the gentleman to put out his cigarette. No smoking is allowed until the King's health has been drunk."

Smoking manners have become much less rigid everywhere during the past twenty-five years, but it still seems to me unnecessary, and to some people it is objectionable, to smoke between courses If there are no ashtrays, wait until you have left the table for your smoke. Do not use the dishes for ashtrays Do not smoke a pipe without first finding out whether it is offensive to anyone else at the table. There are some who are revolted by the odor of a pipe or a cigar.

It seems scarcely necessary to say this, yet I have been at dinners at which guests, having finished their meal, get up of their own accord and leave the table. It is of course rude to do so. Wait until your hostess rises and pushes her chair back from the table before you do so.

Do not, if you are a gentleman, push your way toward the living room without regard for others, even if you sit closest to the living room door. The ladies who are guests will go first, then the hostess, then the gentlemen guests, and the host last. Do not argue the point with him. Precede him into the living room.

It is of course likely at the end of a formal dinner that the gentlemen will stay behind in the dining room or go into the host's study or library to smoke and have their after-dinner port or brandy while they talk by themselves for a time. In this case the hostess leads the way out from the dinner, shows the ladies where they can powder their noses if they wish, and directs them into the drawing room where later the gentlemen join them. It is usually polite for every gentleman to choose a lady to whom to talk after a formal dinner, but sometimes, particularly if there are extra men at the dinner, one or two who are interested in their conversation will sit together and talk in the drawing room This is permissible unless the hostess wishes to introduce a man to special people whom she desires them to talk with, or, as sometimes happens, there is a very special guest whom she may want to make the center of conversation after the dinner. In any case, even though it is hard to have an interesting conversation come to an end between two gentlemen, they have to comply if their hostess desires them to be members of a group.

WHEN AND HOW TO LEAVE

Knowing when and how to leave your host and hostess after having been entertained in their house is in itself a fine art. The line between leaving too soon and too late is a finely drawn one. It would be impossible to make any exact rule to guide you in selecting an exact period of time which should elapse after, say, a dinner, before you should say good night. The perceptive guest must learn to sense it, and it will of course vary with different groups and different circumstances.

In Washington where protocol still demands that the most important guest leaves first, I can remember when we were a young couple there that we would see with sinking hearts that Ambassador and Mme. Jusserand were the most important guests. Everyone would have to wait until they left, and for some reason they always stayed at least an hour and a half after dinner—apparently enjoying themselves every minute of the time, for M. Jusserand was a great talker. But some of the young people present who had to be at their offices the next morning would long to have them leave after the first half hour which was the usual length of time to spend in the drawing room after dinner.

A good guest does not simply "eat and run," thereby indicating that his only reason for coming was to get a free meal. On the other hand he does not stay so long that his host and hostess begin to regret having asked him.

There may be an exception to the "eat and run" rule. If the guest, when invited, has said, "I'd love to, but I have to attend a meeting at nine o'clock that night, so I'm afraid I can't," and the hostess urges him to come anyway, saying that he may go as soon as dinner is over and she will see that he gets away in time for his meeting, it will be quite proper for him to come, and to leave immediately on eating, after having made his apologies and explanation to the rest of the guests. Or his hostess may make them for him.

Certainly after eating you will enjoy the company of your host and hostess and the other guests for a time, in whatever way your hostess has planned, bridge, listening to records, if it is the kind of a group which will enjoy that, looking at the moving pictures which your host took on his recent trip to Greece, or if you are a member of a compatible group, in what may be the pleasantest of all entertainments—good conversation

At big dinners it is inevitable that you talk primarily to your two neighbors on either side and after dinner talk to one of the ladies whom you have not sat by at dinner. But if the dinner is not too big and there can be general conversation, that is, I think, one of the most delightful ways to spend an evening, granting, of course, that the guests are interesting people who like to discuss a variety of subjects.

But when the conversation lags, when your host or hostess begins to withdraw slightly from it and one of them looks surreptitiously at a clock, or when you see that the evening is far spent, it is time to go.

If you know that your host has to get up very early in the morning in order to get to his office on time, or if your host or hostess is nursing a cold, or for any similar reason deserves special consideration, these are things to remember in choosing the time for your departure.

On the other hand, I know one married couple in their late sixties, who are accustomed to going to bed at an extremely early hour They often have in to dinner a young man and his wife in their early thirties. All four are great talkers and know the joys of an evening spent in good conversation.

Recently the older woman said to me, "You know those kids often stay until one or one-thirty in the morning. My husband and I are longing for bed before they leave. But we do enjoy them so, and it's so flattering at our age to have young people show that they like to be with us, that I drag myself to bed after they've gone with a glow of pride warming my weariness, and sleep like a top because I am happy."

So there you have it—a situation where what might seem the obviously right thing to do actually gives less pleasure than what, to anyone who did not understand, might seem inconsiderate.

Of course in this particular case the young people probably felt free to stay as long as they were enjoying themselves, because it is the privilege of old age to send guests home without being in the least impolite if the young people are overstaying the usual time and the old people are getting weary.

I have friends who feel really cheated if their guests go home early and seem to be afraid they have not enjoyed themselves. And I find that young people nearly always stay far longer than older people do, that, I am sure, is because there is so much fascination when you are young about getting to know better the people who may be new or even old friends.

There is a wise rule about eating which applies equally to when you should leave. It is, "Stop eating while you still have an appetite." Leave not too soon but while your welcome is still warm, while your hostess's protestation, "It's still early, won't you stay a bit longer?" is sincerely meant.

And when you start to leave, *leave*. Thank your host and hostess, give the rest of the guests a general good night, and go. The guest who looks at his watch, says, "I must be going," and then settles down for a nice long talk makes an unattractive spectacle of himself.

There are also people who get up and start saying good-by, then everybody else gets up and there is a general move to leave. But the first person, while standing, finds a new and fascinating bit of conversation to pursue and cannot tear himself or herself away. This keeps everybody else standing and is really a habit that should not be too frequently indulged.

THANKING YOUR HOSTESS

The informal dinner or evening with friends does not absolutely require a follow-up "thank you," but a note or phone call the following day saying what a good time you have had constitutes a friendly and gracious gesture. It also assures the hostess that you have enjoyed yourself, whereas silence can be cryptic to say the least.

11

Here and There in the Community

WHEREVER THE FAMILY GOES IN THE COMMUNITY, THEY are in contact with others. If they live in a city apartment or in a house in a closely built neighborhood, their behavior even in their own home may affect the comfort of those who live nearby. The basic rules of courtesy and consideration that apply to the conduct of a host or a guest apply equally at all times to any action that may affect others.

THE APARTMENT DWELLER

Night Noises

If you live in an apartment or even in a house built close to another, remember that walls do not prevent the passage of loud noises. If you are a night owl and love to have the radio or television on, curb your desire at night. Turn it down very low or, better still, off after ten o'clock. Do this even if you are giving a party and have the radio or television on. If you explain to your guests why you are doing it, your act and explanation may help to put a curb on some of their noisiness in other ways. If you have ever lain awake until three in the morning while a radio blared as if it were necessary for the whole city to hear it, and loud talk and laughter came through the wall from your next door neighbor, remember it Know that if you are noisy late at night your neighbor will be feeling about you as you felt about him then.

As a matter of fact you can make a nuisance of yourself at any time of the day or night by letting your house or apartment be the source of penetrating noises. Learn to keep sounds, whether those of radio and television, or talking and laughing, at a level that makes communication possible but that cannot disturb others. This is sometimes difficult when you have noisy guests, yet your own example, and your control of radio and television, and to some extent of drinking will help. One of the many objections to drunkenness at parties is that it almost always is accompanied by loud and banal noise.

Garbage and Other Clutter

Do not clutter the hallway outside your door Your rubbers and overshoes belong inside your apartment, not in the hall. If you don't want to walk over your floors with them on in wet weather, take them off at the door and carry them inside. Put a newspaper down inside your door, if you like, to place them on until they dry or you have time to clean them.

Do not leave discarded furniture, empty cartons, or other rubbish piled outside your door. If you have something bulky to get rid of, speak to the building superintendent, have him remove it from your apartment at a time when it can be taken right out of the building and disposed of, and tip him.

Learn the garbage routine and follow it in such a way that your garbage will be visible for as small a time as possible. If your superintendent collects it early in the morning before you are normally stirring, put it out the very last thing at night before you go to bed, not in the morning after he has made his regular rounds, so that he must make a special trip for it or, if he doesn't, it will stand there all day and all night. And put it out neatly in a large paper bag or a neatly tied newspaper package. If yours is a small walkup building in which tenants carry their own garbage downstairs, do so, and do it every day, not only so that it will not pile up and become objectionable in your apartment, but so that it will not be objectionable in the place to which you take it.

Meeting Your Neighbors

Do not expect the other tenants in your building to make courtesy calls on you when you have moved in This custom, which has all but disappeared in rural neighborhoods, is completely non-existent in city apartment houses And do not make such calls yourself (unless there is some special reason for them) when someone else moves into the building. In the crowded environment of city living an apartment becomes even more one's castle than a house in the country. The city dweller cherishes his scant privacy!

But if you meet one of your neighbors on the stairs or in the elevator you will of course say, "Good morning," or "Good afternoon." Such greetings as this need not wait for an introduction. If your building has a push-button elevator and you have entered it first and are followed by another tenant, you will ask what floor he or she wants and push both your button and the other.

Such little courtesies as these do not imply that you are trying, or even wish, to become more than casually acquainted with your co-tenants. If by chance a warm friendship grows from such meetings, you will both be the richer for it. If not you may still be courteous to each other.

One of the interesting phenomena of city life is that your friends are more likely to live fifty blocks away from you than in the same building. Perhaps this is a natural result of the proximity that is inevitable in apartment life. It makes people cautious. If an acquaintance who lives at a distance turns out to be a bore and a nuisance he becomes much less a problem than would the one who lives just down the hall or on the next floor in the same building. Thus it has become almost an unwritten and even unspoken rule that an apartment dweller takes care not to intrude on his co-tenants.

Courtesy to the Landlord and the Superintendent

Though your relationship to both landlord and building superintendent is a business one, this fact does not preclude your obligation to follow the rules of courtesy in your dealing with both.

Read your lease carefully before you sign it. Be sure that you are willing to abide by all of its terms If you are not, discuss clauses which you feel are unfair or to which you are not willing to agree before you sign the lease Either get them changed, reject the apartment, or decide that you will abide by them even if you don't like them. Do not sign the contract and then object later to the landlord's insistence that you keep it.

Pay your rent promptly on or before the first of each month as your lease requires you to do. If for any reason you cannot always do so, tell your landlord before the date when the rent is due and tell him when you will pay it

If little things go wrong which you or some other member of your family can fix properly and easily, fix them yourself Do not expect your landlord or the superintendent to come running to repair something which you have broken and which you are quite able to take care of without his help. But if it is of a more serious nature, call him at once and give him as much time as possible to take care of it. Do not put off something for a week and expect him to fix it an hour after you have told him about it.

Do not think of the building superintendent as your servant, remember that you are only one of several tenants in the building whom he must help to keep comfortable and happy. Treat him with the courtesy and consideration that you would accord to anyone who is helping you. If you ask him for some extraordinary service expect to pay him for it. And remember him at Christmastime If (as sometimes happens) you have come to regard him more as a friend than as merely the building superintendent, and you know his tastes, a gift of something you know he will like, and which is perhaps a bit more luxurious than he would buy for himself, will constitute a thoughtful tribute. If not, or if there is any doubt in your mind, give him money. The amount is for you to decide, and may depend somewhat upon your relationship to him and how much he does for you. Two dollars is a token Five expresses more appreciation Ten is generous under most circumstances. But do not give it to him uncovered, as you would hand a tip to a doorman. Enclose it in an envelope with a Christmas card wishing him well.

(Incidentally your mailman will probably look in your mailbox for something on the day before Christmas also. It need not be much, but a token gift of two or five dollars in an envelope with a Christmas card will show him that you wish him well and are grateful for his care in getting your mail into your box.)

THE SUBURBAN OR VILLAGE DWELLER

If you live in a single-family house, either as a renter or owner, some of the situations which face a city apartment dweller do not concern you, but the general principle of consideration for the comfort of your near neighbors and members of the community as a whole remains the same

Some Do's and Don't's

In most communities the law obliges a house owner to keep the public sidewalk in front of his house free of snow in the winter. It is a law which is not always enforced, but a rule which should be followed even without a law. Extend the practice also to the walk that leads up to your door and which the mailman, the milkman, and anyone else who calls on you must use. Not to do so is a discourtesy to all who have occasion to walk that way. Do not be swayed by the shiftless cynicism of the man who looked at the deep snow on his walk, looked with disgust at the snow shovel, and then looking at the sky said, "Let the One who put it there take it away."

Your lawn and the space around your house generally is in your neighbor's view as well as your own If you need any incentive beyond that of your own pleasure to keep it neat and uncluttered remember that you are being discourteous to others if you let it become an eyesore.

Don't be a habitual borrower. If in an emergency you do borrow a tool, an electric light bulb, a fuse plug, or a cup of flour from your neighbor, return it promptly. Neighborliness is a two-way street, the one who is always on the receiving end is discourteous and unpopular.

Chatting over the back fence can be a fine and satisfying occupation—so long as it is kept within bounds. But do not keep your neighbor, who has perhaps come out to hang the clothes or to do some little chore about the place, standing for half an hour listening to your sad tale of how unfairly the teacher graded one of your children, or how inconsiderate your husband is, or how your infected sinuses are torturing you. She has other things which she would rather be doing, yet if she is a courteous human being she will find it difficult to walk away while your chatter is going full tilt.

If you have to leave in your car early in the morning or come back in it late at night, do not slam the door or race the engine. This noise may wake your neighbor; it may even disturb a light sleeper living two or three houses away Summer, when doors and windows are open, and porch sitting can be a wonderful way to relax, is the season when you should be most alert to the peace and comfort of your neighbors, even when they are not close to you. Noise carries a long way on summer nights. Do not turn on the radio to a night baseball game or turn up the volume of the television in the game room if the windows are open. Your neighbor, especially if his principal object is to get a good night's sleep, may not *like* baseball or think your favorite comedian funny.

I suppose that this list could be extended for many pages, but these examples are enough for anybody who really wants to be a "good neighbor" rather than a nuisance. You can with a little thought add a number of personal rules based upon your own circumstances and environment. To paraphrase the Golden Rule, don't do the things which have annoyed you when your neighbors have done them.

ON THE STREET

When you are walking or driving on the public street you are in a special way a part of your community, sharing a space, so to speak, with every other member of the village or city in which you live. It is your obligation of courtesy not to abuse the privilege of its use by causing inconvenience, embarrassment, discomfort, or displeasure to any who share it with you

Though there are of course no rigid rules specifying the clothing one should wear when on a casual errand, shopping, going to the corner mailbox, or taking a walk, the considerate person does not make a spectacle of himself by going out half dressed, untidy, or in conspicuously gaudy attire If only out of consideration for the esthetic sensibilities of your neighbors, be dressed decently and neatly, no matter how informally, when you appear in public.

I remember watching with interest a group of poverty-stricken farmers gathered one Saturday afternoon in the general store of a small town in the Dust Bowl during the great depression that began in 1929. On their weekly trip to town to shop and exchange news and opinions with one another they were dressed in overalls and work shirts Many of their garments were patched and faded by numerous washings and the sun But they were all clean, obviously having been put on especially for the trip to town. So were the farmers' work-hardened hands and tanned faces, and so were those of their wives, dressed in their clean patched ginghams, gathered in little groups by themselves talking woman talk. I thought as I watched them what an example they set for some women in better economic circumstances whom I had seen in New York going to a bakery or delicatessen in the early morning with their hair in curlers, a coat thrown over their pajamas, and their bare feet in bedroom slippers.

There is an excellent word "dignity" which is very important in personal behavior. The Dust Bowl farmers whom I saw in that little store in the West, beset by extreme economic misfortune, maintained it.

The courteous person does not litter the streets. If he has a newspaper, an empty cigarette package, or anything else which he wishes to discard, he holds it until he comes to a rubbish can and deposits it there If he is in a village where there are none, he keeps the litter until he finds a place where he can make proper disposition of it. Orderliness is as desirable in the public street as it is in your living room.

Russia is a very good example—though of course since everyone is trained to live under compulsion there, it may not be so remarkable. You never see a piece of paper or a match or a cigarette stub thrown on the streets. Training is begun when children are little. I remember seeing a child of about three buy food to feed the pigeons on Red Square in Moscow, and I expected her to throw the paper bag on the pavement when she emptied it. Not at all. She took it carefully back to the woman who was selling the food. Discipline is a marvelous thing, and perhaps in our country we will succeed by learning self-discipline.

Excessive demonstrations of affection are out of place in public, though this does not mean that you must maintain an air of cold detachment with one to whom you feel close I confess that, though the rules of social usage in the past would have frowned on it, when I see a young couple obviously devoted to each other, walking together on a city street hand in hand, absorbed in each other, and chatting with animation apparently about all the little things which people in love find to talk about, I think it a very pretty sight and that they are wise and fortunate. Yet when I see a similar couple parked on a city street (sometimes in daylight) closely embraced in prolonged caresses, I am embarrassed and wish that they would reserve their so intimate love-making for a private place.

In the United States, when walking with a lady, a man walks on the outside—that is, on the side nearest the curb. This has little practical meaning today. It is a relic of the time when horses and carriages on muddy streets did a good deal of splashing, and a gentleman interposed himself between the mud and the lady whom he was escorting But as a symbol of the gentleman's function as a protector of his lady it is still a pleasant courtesy. In England and on most of the continent of Europe the man walks on the lady's left. I don't know the reason for this.

If a gentleman, walking on a narrow village path that has room only for one, or on a snow-covered sidewalk with a single path trodden through the snow, meets a lady, the gentleman will of course step aside and allow the lady to keep to the path. He will do this also for an elderly and infirm man, as, for that matter, will a young and vigorous lady.

If three or four are walking together, they will not walk abreast unless the sidewalk is quite deserted and there is no chance of inconveniencing others thus. If, walking abreast, someone else approaches, one or two members of the party will drop back and allow the others room.

In passing others, follow as nearly as possible the rules of passing that control vehicular traffic. In the United States this means keep to the right.

If you carry an umbrella on rainy days, be sure to carry it high enough so that it will not scrape the hats or faces of others.

If you meet friends by all means greet them pleasantly. But do not settle down in the middle of a crowded sidewalk for a fine long chat, thus inconveniencing other pedestrians, and possibly preventing your friend from keeping an engagement, or even from getting her shopping done in the scant period she had allowed for it before fulfilling some other obligation.

If there are traffic lights in the community in which you are walking, watch them and cross with the green signal. Do not dash across dodging the traffic. It is dangerous, in many places illegal, and always is discourteous to drivers, who after all are also human beings.

If there are no lights, obey the policeman's signals. If there is no policeman use common sense, and do not make it necessary for drivers to put on their brakes suddenly to miss hitting you.

Avoid being noisy on the street at all times, but especially at night. The group that leaves a party at two or three in the morning and starts home shouting and singing can be a prime nuisance.

Driving in the Community

When you are behind the wheel of an automobile, you are in a position that obligates you to assume special responsibilities. Here, as in few other circumstances, the rules established by courtesy, safety, and law frequently coincide. You have control of what is not only a powerful, potentially destructive force, but also of a huge bulk that may be a nuisance to your fellows if you do not see that it is not.

Do not try to beat the lights. If you have a green, yellow, red system of lights in your community, stop when the light you are approaching turns yellow. Do not edge into the crosswalk before the light turns to green, trying to get a quick start.

Remember that regardless of the letter of any law the rules of common courtesy dictate that the pedestrian *always* has the right of way. He may be crossing the street in front of you foolishly and even illegally, yet if you are approaching in a car it is your responsibility to slow down, or even stop, in order to let him get across in safety. In a car you are much more powerful than he is, and in common courtesy the stronger gives right of way to the weaker.

Park considerately, as close to the curb as you can so that you will not narrow the space available to traffic. Do not park in front of driveways (whether there is a sign forbidding it or not) or in any place that should be kept open for emergency use.

If by inadvertence you bump another car and dent a fender while parking or getting away from where you have been parked, do not simply drive off and congratulate yourself on the fact that you were not caught. If you can locate the owner of the car do so, tell him about it, and accept your responsibility. If not, leave a note tucked under his windshield wiper or attached to his steering wheel, telling him what has happened, giving your name, address, and phone number, and suggesting that he phone you.

Blow your horn only on those rare occasions when you *must* give a warning. Instead of depending on it to take care of all difficulties by telling others to get out of the way, train your foot to a close liaison with the brake. Four out of five times you can manage by braking, and thus avoid making an unpleasant noise.

At a supermarket parking lot, at the station, or for that matter anywhere, avoid parking in a position in which your car will obstruct others whose drivers may want to get out before you do, or in any place that may obstruct traffic.

Other hints for safe, courteous, and legal driving will be found in Chapter 13, "Keep to the Right."

BUSES, STREETCARS, AND SUBWAYS

One of the banes of existence for those who have to travel habitually on public transportation in a large city is the pusher—the passenger who always has to get on first and who elbows his way ahead of others in order to get to the only seat left before someone else gets it. Another is the one who gets on and stands directly in front of the entrance, making everyone else push by him in order to get to the rear where there is more room. When you board a bus, subway train, or streetcar, remember that you are only one of many who are sharing the same vehicle and play fair.

It should be unnecessary to say that a gentleman always lets a lady (whether the one he is accompanying or a stranger) precede him in entering a public vehicle. If he is one of a number of unaccompanied men, and a number of unaccompanied ladies are waiting for a bus, the ladies will all enter it before any of the gentlemen. On the other hand if he is accompanying a lady, he will step down from the bus ahead of her, in order to take her arm or hand and assist her in leaving.

One rarely sees a man rise to give his seat to a lady on a bus or streetcar or subway today. It is one of the courtesies which have for the most part fallen before the onslaught of modern rush and tension and crowding. Yet it remains as gracious a custom and as much a part of the natural response to circumstance of a true gentleman as it ever was—especially if the lady is aged or infirm. A younger man will show the same courtesy to an aged one, and a younger lady to an aged gentleman or lady.

IN A HOUSE OF WORSHIP

When you attend a church or synagogue you owe a special respect to the minister, priest, or rabbi, to the congregation, and to the special spirit of reverence which should pervade every religious service.

Your dress for church should be quiet and unobtrusive. Sports clothes should never be worn. Women should not wear low-necked or sleeveless dresses. It used to be the custom in all Christian churches for the women to keep their heads covered. It still is in Roman Catholic and Episcopalian churches. At orthodox and conservative Jewish ceremonies both men and women keep their heads covered. If you are visiting a church that is not of your faith follow its customs. This does not oblige you to enter into any ritual that you feel you cannot consistently accept as a part of your own worship. A Jew, and perhaps a Protestant, would not cross himself at a Catholic service, but such matters as kneeling or standing when the rest of the congregation does so is no more than respect for the beliefs of the others, regardless of your own.

Be on time for the service. If you are unavoidably late, slip into a rear seat of the church, making your arrival as inconspicuous as possible.

If you are a regular attendant at church you may have your own pew to which you will always go. If not, allow the usher to seat you, and follow him to the seat he chooses for you. Do not slip into another that is empty and let him walk down the aisle only to find, when he gets to the place he intended for you, that you are not with him. This is not only rude to him, but it is quite possible that you will have taken a seat regularly occupied by someone else who has not yet arrived.

Conversation, even in whispers, during church service is the height of rudeness.

AT THE THEATER

At the theater as at church it is discourteous to be late, since you inevitably disturb others who are watching the play. In many theaters, if you arrive after the curtain you will not be permitted to take your seat until the first scene is over. If you are seated and others come to occupy seats beyond yours, rise and push your seat back, if the play has not begun. If it has, it is better simply to move your legs to one side, since rising may obstruct the view of those behind you.

Evening clothes are frequently worn in the orchestra for first-night performances and may be worn at any other evening performance. It is more usual today not to dress formally for the theater, save for first nights. However, on a first night or on other nights it is completely proper either to dress or to wear ordinary street clothes at an evening performance.

If you are a woman and have worn a large hat, remove it when you are seated so that it will not obstruct the view of those behind you. If a large hat worn by a woman in the row in front of you limits your vision, it is quite proper to ask her to remove it.

If you are a man accompanying a lady to the theater and you find the play an unbearable bore, it is courteous for you to ask her if she would like to leave. Since you have taken her to the theater it is your party, and for her to suggest leaving would be rude—unless you know each other very well. Don't wait for her to do it. Ask her and abide by her decision.

Don't carry on conversations while the play is in progress, or make any loud and disturbing noises. If you have a cough, take cough drops with you to assuage it. If it is so bad that they will not keep you quiet, stay at home. This holds good also for those who come to a concert or an opera. Conversation disturbs one's neighbors, coughing does also. It is not permitted nowadays to take one's seat when late, but I do think that the conductor should pause during the first part of the program once or twice to allow the latecomers to sit down without disturbing the enjoyment of the music.

SHOPPING

Nowhere does one's innate courtesy or lack of it show up more clearly than in a store crowded with busy shoppers. The scramble for service at a bargain sale counter has become a classic symbol of rudeness The self-service arrangement of contemporary supermarkets seems to encourage carelessness. Perhaps the fact that only rarely do you meet someone you know while shopping makes people careless. But it should not. You owe as great courtesy to a stranger in a store and to salesmen and salesladies, as to your most respected friends. And you owe it to yourself to practice these courtesies, for every time you are rude to someone you have detracted from that peace of mind that can come to you only when your contacts with others are gracious

There is nothing wrong with bargain sales; but if after having gone to the store to attend one, you find that you can get nowhere near the counter on which the bargains are displayed without fighting your way rudely through a crowd of others, abandon it and buy the article you want at a slightly higher price after the sale is over

Do not snap at sales persons and make unreasonable demands of them. They are doing a difficult job often against extreme pressures and rudeness on the parts of others. If one of them seems at times to be a little short, remember that his nerves may have been badly frayed by contact with an unreasonable customer, or a series of them, and be patient.

In a supermarket keep the carriage in which you are collecting your purchases as much out of the way of others as possible. Do not let it stand in any position that makes it impossible for others to get by.

Take your place in line at the check-out counter, and wait patiently as any courteous person would in any queue. If you suddenly think of something which you have forgotten, do not leave your cart in the line while you go and get it, thus holding up others if you do not get back before the check-out clerk is ready for you Take your cart out of line, and find a new place when you get back.

If there is a "quick check" counter arranged to take care of customers with only five or six purchases, do not go to it with a full cart, even if no one else is checking out and there is a line at every other counter By doing so you will embarrass the clerk who should ask you to go to another counter but will be reluctant to do so, and may well delay for some time someone who actually has made only one or two purchases.

One of the modern devices which has brought about considerable discourtesy is the revolving display rack on which paper covered books are often shown in stores. I have often seen people standing before these twirling them, scarcely looking at the books as they pass, while others try vainly to see what titles are on display. If you are shopping at one of these, turn it only if no one else is examining the books at the same time. If others are looking at the rack, you can usually see what is on it by walking around it. If you cannot, wait until the others have left, or cooperate with them so that all can see the titles as they wish.

12

Keeping Up with the Joneses

GRACIOUS HUMAN CONTACTS ARE BASED NOT UPON A MA-
terial show that accompanies them, but on an intangible
meeting of personalities. True hospitality consists of giving the best
of yourself to your guests. The material aspects of your entertainment should consist of the best *within the proper limits of your financial position and general circumstances.* Anything beyond this is
likely to become ostentation and actually an embarrassment and
discourtesy.

If you have a neighbor who can afford to drive a very expensive
car and change it for a new model every year, and does so, his custom
has no bearing whatever on what you do about your car. If he occasionally gives you a ride to the station in his car, accept it graciously
and gratefully. If now and then you give him a similar lift in your
eight-year-old, much less expensive car, do not apologize. Your
courtesy is as great as his. You would lessen it either by making excuses for your car or by going into debt beyond the dictates of wisdom in order to provide yourself with a car as grand and expensive
as his.

If someone who can afford it takes you for lunch or dinner to a restaurant far more expensive than you could afford yourself, it should cause you no embarrassment Enjoy your meal and thank him for it But if later you invite him to a meal, courtesy does not dictate that you must match his expenditure or that the restaurant to which you take him must be as grand and fashionable as the one to which he took you. If you attempt to do so, and if he knows that your economic status does not justify your choice of such a restaurant, you will actually be showing him a discourtesy by making him feel that he must choose the least expensive items on the menu in order not to make you spend more money on him than you should. Take him to one of the best of the restaurants to which you are in the habit of going. Give him the best of yourself and of your way of living, not something false based upon your desire to seem as wealthy as he is.

If you are a woman and a number of women in your circle wear mink coats, and you have none because your family budget simply will not permit its purchase without sacrificing other more important things (deposits in the savings accounts for your children's college education, a new wing on the house to take care of an expanding family, a trip to Europe on which you and your husband have been counting since the days of your courtship), let your warm cloth coat cause you no embarrassment whatever. To pester your husband for a mink coat which you cannot afford is cruel; to flaunt one bought with money that should have been better spent is the height of bad taste.

The house in which thoughtful, sensitive people of good taste live will inevitably reflect their personalities. The décor and furnishings will be as attractive and comfortable as the housewife can make them. But this does not mean that they must cost as much as, or more than, those of other houses in the neighborhood. It used to be a commonplace for young people starting out in marriage with a limited income, to buy their furniture bit by bit, much of it at second-hand stores or sales, sometimes picking up for a song charming old pieces which they could refinish themselves, and gradually to assemble the physical accouterments of a gracious home in which their odd pieces seem to go together surprisingly well. Many sensible young people still do this, but many others, beset by radio and television promotion and the pressure of installment-buying schemes, feel far too often that they must start out with matching sets of new furniture for which they will be paying for years, and which often are inferior to some of the good old pieces that would cost less.

I know one gracious home to which friends flock gladly, knowing that when they come they will enjoy the pleasantest of hospitality and friendly companionship By chance the woman who has made the home what it is mentioned that in thirty years of marriage she and her husband had bought only four pieces of new furniture.

This woman had undoubtedly the good luck to inherit much of the furniture she really needed and the good sense to realize that good pieces, while they may not be in fashion today, will always come back and be fashionable again. Certainly the atmosphere of a home is more interesting when several generations have lived with certain pieces of furniture than any decorator's buying can create.

I once heard some people in our old home in Hyde Park say as they looked at the bedrooms: "How extraordinary that they used these old wooden beds." I longed to tell them that my mother-in-law's theory was that if furniture was good when bought, it was always good and no fads or fancies interfered.

Sometimes a wise person manages to reverse the process of "keeping up with the Joneses" in order to make another feel more at ease. I know of one very wealthy young woman who married a young doctor with no money of his own save that which came from the practice into which he had just entered. Knowing that he was sensitive about the difference between his economic status and hers, and his inability to support her in the luxury she had known as a girl, a few weeks before their marriage she quietly sold the extremely expensive car which she owned, content to ride in his five-year-old car that was in the low-price range. For weeks she searched the city and finally found a small but comfortable apartment which he could afford and in which they made their first home together. Gradually she convinced him that one of the best investments she could make was in a better office and more extensive equipment for him, and before long they had moved into a more spacious apartment. But every increase in their living expenses seemed to be the natural result of his advancement in professional success rather than something which her wealth had made possible.

True hospitality comes from the heart, and is not the product of ostentatious and expensive material surroundings You will pay true courtesy to others by giving the best of yourself and not by trying to imitate others who put on a showier front than you are able to do, or than it is in your nature to do.

IV

THE FAMILY
TRAVELS

13

Keep to the Right

COURTESY, SAFETY, LEGALITY—THESE ARE THE TRIPLETS of driving so nearly identical as to make them often indistinguishable. As it is rude to push violently through a crowd of people, so is it also in a car to weave in and out of traffic carelessly. It is also unsafe and illegal. As you do not (if you are courteous) hurry on the street in order to push in front of another approaching at right angles, a courteous and safe driver does not attempt to beat another car across a road or street intersection. If he is discourteous enough to do so he may be the cause of a serious accident, and whether he is or not he may receive a ticket for a traffic law violation. So it is with many of the rules of the road. The rules of courtesy, the legal code, and the rules of safety are more often than not the same. The measure of a good driver is the extent to which he observes all three.

Before you take a car on the road you should be sure of several things upon which your courtesy, your safety, and the legality of your driving will partly depend.

Brakes

Be sure that your brakes are working properly. Faulty brakes may cause accidents, and even if they do not they may be responsible for breaches of courtesy, such as preventing your stopping at a crossing without overrunning the pedestrian right of way, making a pedestrian jump to get out of your way because you are not able to stop quickly enough, or bumping the car ahead of you when it makes a quick stop. Even if you do not seriously injure it (and you may do that), the smallest nudge is unpleasant, and rude if it can be avoided.

If you drive a car to which you are not accustomed, try out the brakes at the beginning of your drive so that you will know what you can count on in an emergency.

Lights

If you are driving at night it is your responsibility to see that all your lights are working properly. If one of your headlights is out of order on either the high beam or the low beam or both, an approaching driver may mistake you for a motorcycle. If your left headlight happens to be out, it will not then be surprising if he sideswipes you. If both of your dim lights (low beam) are out of order so that you must drive constantly with the high beams (or brights), you will blind approaching drivers, which is both dangerous and rude. If your tail-light glasses are broken so that the tail-lights show white and become bright when you apply the brakes, they may be mistaken by a driver following you at a distance for weak headlights. Even if they are not, they will glare, and therefore obstruct his vision.

Seat Adjustment

If the driver's seat is adjustable, as it is on most modern cars, be sure that it is adjusted to suit the length of your legs, so that you can manage the pedals (or pedal, if you are driving a car with automatic shift) firmly without sliding down in your seat or being cramped up with your knees bent at an uncomfortable angle. Otherwise you may not be able to use your brakes properly in the split second that may mean the difference between safety and an accident.

Windshield, Back Window, and Mirror

Your windshield should be clean, as should your back window, and your mirror properly adjusted, so that you will have clear vision both ahead of you and behind you.

Tires

If you live in a climate that produces snow and ice in the winter, be sure that in this slippery season your tires are capable of keeping a firm grip on the road. Good snow tires for normally snowy roads are the best. For really icy roads you need chains. Never take a car on the road in snow or ice with tires from which the tread has been completely worn, leaving smooth faces that are sure to skid at the least provocation, that will not hold properly when you put on the brakes, and that will spin when you try to start on an icy spot.

These physical requirements are not only prerequisites to safety; providing yourself with them is a part of the courtesy you owe to other drivers, to pedestrians, and to anyone who rides in your car with you.

GENERAL RULES OF THE ROAD

Keep to the Right

It should be unnecessary to tell Americans that the rule of the road in America is to keep to the right. While few would ever attempt to pass an approaching car by turning to the left (though even this may happen in peculiar circumstances), the rule, which should be equally applicable in other situations, is frequently disregarded.

When driving on a multiple-lane highway, parkway, or turnpike, the rule is to stay in the lane to the extreme right, except while overtaking and passing a slowly moving car. Many of our best highways now have three lanes for traffic each way, with a sodded dividing strip between The rule on such routes is for slow-moving vehicles to keep in the extreme right lane, and for those who are traveling faster to use the other two lanes. Yet one of the most common of nuisances on such roads is the driver who firmly takes his position in the extreme left lane and stays there, driving well below the speed limit, so that any driver coming behind him must either lag along for miles or adopt the questionable, unsafe, and in many places illegal practice of passing on his right. The left-lane driver may or may not cause a serious accident. In any case he is guilty of a grave breach of the rules of courtesy.

It is also important, when making a right turn at a corner, to keep well to the right. Some drivers, apparently fearing that they may strike the curb, swing far to the left. Even if they do not strike another vehicle waiting there to cross they may well cause embarrassment to a pedestrian beginning to cross the street from the left, or cause an approaching vehicle to stop suddenly.

There are two (and so far as I know only two) exceptions to the "keep to the right" rule. One applies to overtaking and passing a vehicle going in the same direction as you are driving, the other to when you are making a left turn off a street or highway that has two or three lanes in each direction In the latter case, work your way over to the left lane using proper hand or mechanical signals, well before you get to the point of turning and stay there (in case there are traffic lights) until the light gives you the right of way, or (in case there is a traffic officer) until the officer signals you ahead, or (in case there is neither light nor officer) there is no traffic approaching from the other direction; and do not let any horn-blowing from behind move you, until you are sure that it is right for you to go ahead.

Be Alert

Once on the road it is your responsibility to be alert to every circumstance that may affect your driving so that you will not endanger, or even inconvenience others. You must be constantly aware of everything ahead of you and even on each side of the road or street, as far as you can see, and ready to anticipate any movement that may affect your driving—other cars, pedestrians, children, dogs and other animals—and of the physical facts connected with the road or street itself—sharp turns, dips, bumps, obstructions, or slippery spots on the pavement.

Study the road ahead and always look for an "out," that is, space in which to swerve in case of an emergency.

Never drive faster than you can see and think. Be prepared always to stop within the space that intervenes between you and any person or moving thing that is, or may become by the time you reach it, an obstruction. One wise driver once said to me, "I always drive as though every other driver and every pedestrian were an idiot. I grew up on a farm and used to despise chickens because they were so dumb. A chicken, you know, will start across a road when it sees something coming, then change its mind (if it has any) midway, turn, and dash back. If the thing coming is a car, the foolish creature may dash right under the wheels. I always pretend that other people on the road are chickens."

It may sound a bit hard on humanity as a whole, yet what he was saying in effect was good. He drove as though it was his sole responsibility to prevent accidents, regardless of the mistakes made by anyone else.

Keep your car moving or get it off the road. Never stop your car on a highway save for stop signs. If you have to stop, pull off onto prescribed parking areas or, if there are none, onto the verge, completely out of the traffic lane

Pedestrians

In cities where there are traffic lights or traffic policemen, pedestrians are of course supposed to cross streets only on the green light or the traffic officer's signal. Yet many of them are careless or in a hurry, and disregard the rules As the driver of a car, it is your responsibility to see that you do not injure or even inconvenience one of them, even though you have the technical right of way and he does not. Be ready to stop the moment one of them attempts to cross in front of you Your obligation to be courteous and avoid hurting him is not abrogated by his failure to fulfill his own.

You must also be aware of pedestrians walking along the streets between crossings, for often they cross without waiting to come to a crosswalk. Do not drive so close to the curb or so fast that you cannot stop quickly in case one steps off suddenly into the street.

On rainy days, when there are puddles in the street, be careful not to let your car spatter pedestrians on the sidewalk. With a puddle ahead and a pedestrian close to it, avoid the puddle if you can, or slow down so that you will not splash.

Hitchhikers

In regard to most hitchhikers the rule of hospitality should be abrogated, unfortunately. If you are in or near your own community you may pick up someone you know. In many states too frequent holdups and other unpleasantnesses have brought about the passage of laws forbidding hitchhiking and the picking up of such self-invited passengers There are of course circumstances under which the courteous driver will do so, and be within the law. In the case of a bona fide breakdown or accident any decent passing driver will pick up one of the occupants of the car and take him to the nearest place from which he can summon help.

Children

In many states signs are wisely placed near houses and playgrounds where children are likely to be met. But whether there are such signs or not, you as a driver must constantly be alert for their presence or evidence of their presence. If a ball rolls into the street from the side of a house, or even if a playful puppy romps into sight, be prepared for a child to follow it If you see children playing near the curb, be sure that you can stop in time if one of them suddenly dashes into the street.

School Buses

Most states now have laws prohibiting the passing in either direction of a school bus that has stopped. Whether there is such a law or not, do stop your car. Many a child, leaving the house at the last minute in the morning to catch the bus, will dash across the street without looking, or in the evening will do the same in an exultation of relief that the long inactive day in school is over. It is your responsibility to see that his childlike thoughtlessness does not result in injury at your hands.

Dogs

Dogs are like children. Watch for them and their sudden dashes into the street as you would for that of a child.

Bicycles

When overtaking and passing bicycles do not drive too close or scare the rider out of his wits by a loud blast from your horn.

Many bicyclists are a little wobbly, and especially likely to be so when startled. Pass slowly, giving the cyclist plenty of wobble room. If another car coming from the other direction makes this impossible at the moment, slow down and tag along behind the cyclist, as you would behind another car, until you can pass safely at a distance. A rapidly moving car leaves a wind stream behind it which can be very uncomfortable for a cyclist who is caught in it.

Your Horn

A horn is placed on your car to be used in emergencies when a warning must be given instantly, and not as a noisemaker to blare annoyingly whenever an inconsiderate driver feels like making his presence known, or wants to tell someone else to get out of the way so that he does not have to make the effort necessary to apply his brakes. Use it sparingly, and only when it is absolutely necessary or courteous to do so, and even then don't overdo it. I doubt that it is an overstatement to say that nine out of ten horn toots are completely unnecessary, and because of this annoying.

When overtaking and passing a car going in the same direction as you are, it is courteous to tap the horn once lightly as the front wheels of your car come abreast of the rear wheels of that which you are passing, in order to announce your intention. The other driver should have seen you beginning to pass, but perhaps he didn't. One little toot is enough.

If in spite of this the other driver suddenly makes a sharp left turn in an attempt to pass the car in front of him, you will of course blow your horn as a second warning, and may thus avert a bad collision.

If a pedestrian suddenly steps into the street in front of you, put on your brake hard, swerve to the left if there is room for you to do so, and blow your horn. (Also let it go at that. Even though the one on foot may have been completely in the wrong and foolish, you will help neither him nor yourself by shouting vituperations at him, and only prove that you have bad manners.)

Never blow your horn in impatience while waiting for a line ahead of you to move after a red light has changed to green, or to announce your presence when calling on someone, or simply to express high spirits. An automobile horn makes a very raucous sound —excellent for its purpose, but annoying when it is needless.

Speed

Your speed when driving should always be no more than that of the legal speed limit (indicated by road signs) in the area in which you are driving, or that which road and traffic conditions and your own alertness at the time make safe, whichever is the least. It may be quite unsafe to drive more than fifteen miles an hour on slippery or rough roads in an area in which the legal speed limit is fifty. Real emergencies provide exceptions which both the law and common sense recognize.

In traffic try to fit your own speed to the median speed of the line in which you are driving, the slowpoke who makes others constantly overtake and pass him, or lag behind, is a nuisance, the speedster is a menace.

When possible slow your speed far enough from the place where you intend to stop so that the whole proceeding will be gradual and easy. Avoid (save in emergencies) slamming on your brake hard and suddenly, thereby certainly inconveniencing and possibly injuring both your passengers and the car behind you.

On a curving road and with a car behind you wanting to pass, do not drive slowly around the curves where he cannot pass, and then, when you come to a straight stretch of road, put on a sudden burst of speed which makes it unsafe for him to do so. Some over-cautious drivers, I think, do this thoughtlessly, without realizing how annoying it is to a driver behind them, others perhaps do it consciously, getting some twisted satisfaction out of the power which they thus exercise over the other fellow. In either case it is rude.

Directional Signals

Most modern cars have mechanical directional signals—either in the form of lights or (as in some foreign cars) in the form of illuminated pointers which flop up to the right or to the left to indicate the direction of a turn.

The mechanical ones are excellent, both as safety devices and as a convenience. Properly used they eliminate the confusion as to their meaning which sometimes attaches to carelessly given hand signals. But on the other hand they have given rise to one of the most annoying little situations that may confront a driver. Most of them are arranged to cancel themselves automatically after a turn has been made, but the automatic canceling mechanism doesn't always work. In such cases a driver may signal for a right turn, make it, and drive along for miles with his signal still set. He may then, forgetting to make any signal, make a left turn, thoroughly confusing the driver behind him and possibly causing an accident.

Make sure that your signals are working properly. Always use them before making a turn and see that they are canceled after making the turn. If they are out of order, or if there are none on your car, always use hand signals—the extended left hand held out and slightly down with palm to the rear, before you are going to make a stop, the left hand held straight out and still, with the index finger pointing, when you are going to make a left turn, and the left hand out and in a continuous clockwise rotary motion when you are going to make a right turn.

Right of Way

Law, courtesy, and common sense all combine to determine whether you or the other car or person or animal has the right of way.

At a crossroads or street crossing, if there are traffic lights or a traffic policeman, you must of course obey the signal. And obey it fully and with common sense. Do not feel that you must make a jack-rabbit start as soon as the light changes to green. If another car has entered the crossing from a cross street—even though the driver may have entered after the red light has been set against him—or a belated pedestrian makes a dash for it, wait patiently.

If there is no traffic light or officer, and a car reaches the crossing on a cross street at the same time that you do, the car on the right has the right of way. Even if you are on the right and the other driver disregards this rule, do not try to insist on your rights. Let him pass and go your way peacefully without arguing You may have lost thirty seconds—a much smaller loss than that of your temper. The same rule applies in the country at a fork where two roads converge into one.

If you turn a corner on a green light and there are pedestrians crossing the street into which you are turning, also moving on the green light, they *always* have the right of way. As a matter of fact a pedestrian, even when he is in the wrong, should be given right of way.

If you should be coming downhill on a very narrow country road that has scant room for two vehicles to pass, and a large loaded truck is coming uphill, do not expect the driver to pull off the road and stop to let you pass Do so yourself in plenty of time to let him see you before it is necessary. It is no hardship for you, going downhill, to lose inertia by stopping; for him, coming uphill with a load, it may be.

If you are driving slowly and another car attempts to pass you at a difficult spot, wait until you reach a favorable spot, then drive as far to the right on the road as possible and give him a hand signal to go by.

THE CARS AHEAD OF AND BEHIND YOU

One of the most frequent faults of incautious drivers is that of following too closely behind another car It is dangerous. It is also rude, for, even if you do not have an accident as a result, it is unnerving to the driver ahead of you who knows that he cannot stop quickly without risking one. As you would avoid treading on the heels of another pedestrian in a crowd, avoid seeming to be seeking a rear-end collision with another car Keep enough distance between you and the next car so that, if the other slows down or makes a quick stop, you can stop in plenty of time to keep from hitting it. A safe rule to follow is to keep a car's length between you and the car ahead for every ten miles an hour you are driving. Thus, if you are driving forty miles an hour there should be seventy-five feet between the two cars On high-speed highways allow more space than this.

If a car behind you is pushing you too closely (and you should know when this is true by constantly paying attention to what your rear-view mirror shows you), the best thing you can do is to slow down gradually, keeping well to the right, and give him a chance to pass you (which is probably what he is trying to do). After he has done so, fall back until you have established a safe distance between his car and yours.

When you are driving at night there is an added reason for not driving too close to the car ahead of you in that, if you do, your bright lights, reflected in the rear-view mirror of the car ahead of you, may blind the driver. If there is any question in your mind about it, switch your lights to the low beam when you are following another car.

Watch not only the car ahead of you, but also the one ahead

of it If the head car slows, begin to use your brake at once, thereby giving both yourself and the driver behind you a better chance for safe deceleration or stop.

Passing

When overtaking and passing another car going in the same direction as you are going, do so cautiously and in such a way that you will avoid danger and *not* unnerve the driver of the car in front by surprising him. Do not blare your horn at him from behind, but (as I have said earlier when writing of the use of the horn) give it one gentle tap as the front wheels of your car are opposite the rear wheels of his.

Pass only (a) when the other driver is going so slowly that you may do so without exceeding the speed limit of the stretch of road on which you are driving, (b) when you are on a road which has center markings and you are on a stretch which permits it (that is, where there is no line at all painted down the center, where there is a single line of dashes, or where there is a line of dashes on your side and a solid line on the other—never pass when there is a double solid line in the middle of the road), (c) when you are on a straight road with a clear view ahead of you for more than the distance which you will need to pass.

Never pass when there is anything ahead that obscures your vision so that you cannot see whether another car is approaching from the other direction. If you are behind a large truck that blocks your view, edge carefully to the left until you can see far enough ahead in the lane that is used by cars coming toward you to be quite sure that you will have room to pass. Often a courteous truck driver in this situation will give you a signal when it is safe for you to proceed But even if he does, stay alert yourself. He may be wrong

Do not pass when you are on the upgrade of a hill which prevents your seeing what is coming up on the other side of it Wait until you have crossed the crest of it and have a clear view ahead.

When passing at night it is unnecessary to use your horn. Flicking the beams of your lights up and down with the foot switch will give warning to the driver of the car you are passing.

After you have passed, do not turn abruptly back into the right lane. The other car may have speeded up a bit, and your too abrupt return will invite a collision. Wait until you can see his left headlight in your rear-view mirror and then swing gradually back into place

Do not blindly follow a car in front of you which is passing one ahead of itself Wait until it has returned to the right lane, and then see if it is safe for you to pass

Meeting

When meeting cars from the other direction do not crowd the center line. If you and the other car both do this you may sideswipe each other. Keep well to the right.

When meeting at night be sure that you switch your lights to the low beams in plenty of time to avoid dazzling the oncoming driver. Do this whether the oncoming driver does it or not. If he does not dim his lights promptly, flick your lights up again momentarily as a reminder to him, but dim them again immediately whether he responds to your suggestion or not. Having two drivers blinded by oncoming lights is twice as unfortunate as having one, and you will only lose by "giving him a dose of his own medicine." Watch the right-hand edge of your road rather than the approaching car, the headlights of which may blind you.

Driving at Night

Obviously driving at night calls for special care. Yet with good lights on your car, and vigilance, it has also special pleasures and conveniences. For one thing you can usually tell when approaching a curve or at a crossroads whether another car is coming beyond the curve or from one of the side roads, by the gleam of its headlights. But do not trust this completely. There is always the possibility of an unlighted car, a bicycle, or even (in some parts of the country) a horse and buggy!

Manage your own lights not only with thought for your own needs but also with consideration for other drivers. As dusk comes, even though you can see the road perfectly, put your parking lights or your headlights on low beam. With them on, your car will be much more visible to the drivers of approaching cars. Do this also if you are driving in early morning twilight. Always turn your headlights on in fog. The low beam will make your car visible to approaching cars and, if your eyes respond as most people's do, will give you better visibility of the road directly ahead of you than will the high beams.

And remember the caution mentioned in the preceding section on "meeting." *Always dim your lights when a car approaches.*

The faster you drive at night the less far ahead you can see. Studies show that a night driver can see eighty feet farther ahead of him at twenty miles an hour than he can at sixty.

If you have to change a tire or make a repair on the road at night pull as far off the road to the right as you can—completely off onto the shoulder if possible—and leave your lights on. The car that stands unlighted, half on and half off the road is a menace. If you do a great deal of night driving, it might be well for you to carry with you some of the red flares used by railroads, or a flasher signal now available for automobiles, and when you have to stop on the road at night, light one and place it behind your car.

Drive as quietly as possible through villages late at night, using your horn sparingly or preferably not at all, while you are near houses in which people may be sleeping. If you have to stop in such a place do not leave your engine running, even though it may seem completely quiet to you. Sounds are sometimes increased by being confined between buildings, and what may seem a whisper to you on the street, may seem a roar to someone trying to sleep in a second-floor bedroom.

Accidents

Even the best drivers sometimes have accidents, though the better you are the less likely they become. If you do have one, do not simply speed up and try to get away before the driver of the other car can take your number. Regardless of how slight it is, stop, get out of your car, and exchange names and addresses with the other driver. Give him the name and address of your insurance company, and take the name and address of his.

If there is anyone injured in the other car and you are still mobile, get to the nearest phone as quickly as possible and call for both the police and an ambulance. Even if the injury to another is not serious, it is your responsibility if there is any injury or extensive damage to either car, to notify the police

It is well to remember as a good rule that in any accident both drivers are at fault. Even though the other fellow is technically wrong, and you are technically right, you have a certain responsibility in the matter. Drive always so as to be ready to compensate as much as possible for the bad driving of others.

Driving under the Influence of Liquor, or When Overfatigued

Don't.

If You Are a Passenger

As a passenger you have a responsibility to help the driver according to the rules of courtesy, safety, and legality.

If you are the least bit nervous, keep the matter as much to yourself as you can. The back seat driver is a thorn in the side of any man or woman at the wheel of a car. Nervousness is contagious. By showing yours, and constantly telling the driver what he ought to do instead of what he is doing, you will succeed only in making him drive less skillfully. If his driving is just too bad, resolve not to ride with him again.

If you are a young woman—or one not so young, for that matter—riding in the front seat with the man you love, keep your hands off him and his off you while he is driving Caresses are wonderful in their proper setting. In the front seat of a moving car they are both an invitation to disaster and a public exhibition of something that should be private and personal.

Never, never, under any circumstances, short of a sudden collapse on the part of the driver, touch the wheel or the brake pedal while someone else is driving

Do not continuously call the driver's attention to the beautiful view, birds, little streams, or anything else. There is one place and one place only where his attention should be—that is, on the road ahead of him.

If you are sitting in the front seat do not sit any closer to the driver than the dimensions of the seat make necessary, and be particularly careful that your legs and feet do not interfere with the movements of his.

Driving Abroad

If you take your car with you to another country, or hire one there, you will have to learn some rules that are different from those in America, and probably a different system of road signs. If it is a non-English speaking country and you are unable to learn the language thoroughly before you go, be sure at least to familiarize yourself with the meaning of the road signs if you are planning to drive there.

I do not intend here to cover all the differences in rules in all the countries in which you may travel—indeed I know only a few of them. But here are some of the highlights.

Throughout the British Isles and in most British dominions or protectorates, in Sweden, and I believe in some other countries, the rule of the road is to keep to the left instead of to the right. If you drive in one of these countries, keep your speed down and drive with special care until you are sure you have accustomed your automatic reflexes to the change. You may manage perfectly well under ordinary circumstances and then, in a suddenly presented emergency, instinctively turn to the right, causing a serious accident.

Although in the United States it is bad practice to use your horn save when absolutely necessary, in France and Italy (save in cities) the opposite is true. The habit is so strongly ingrained that others count on your giving this raucous warning whenever there is the slightest possibility that it may be needed, and not to do so may make you guilty of neglect. If you are involved in an accident and you have not blown your horn, you will be considered responsible for it.

Regulations concerning lights also vary In France, for instance, headlights must cast a yellow light rather than a white one. If you take your own car there you must have your headlights changed to conform to this rule.

Speed laws also vary in different countries In Denmark the maximum speed allowed is about thirty-seven miles an hour, which must be a great annoyance to American drivers. Yet it is your responsibility, in whatever country you are driving, to learn what the speed regulations are and obey them.

These suggestions of course concern only a few foreign rules of the road. If you are going to drive in a foreign country, familiarize yourself with its rules before you go there. Most countries have information offices and/or Travel Bureaus in the United States—at least one in New York, and some branches in other large cities. If they do not, their consulates are informed and glad to give the tourist such information as he needs. The American Automobile Association will also help you if you are a member. If you arrange your trip through a travel agency, they too will be helpful. Inform yourself before you go.

UNANNOUNCED VISITS EN ROUTE

If you are passing through a town in which a friend lives and wish to make a call, stop first at a public phone to see whether it is convenient. Do not expect to be fed or to be put up overnight unless you have been previously invited, or unless you are very close friends indeed and know that you will be welcome and that it will be quite convenient to your host and hostess Plan your visit in so far as possible so that it will take place at a time which does not suggest that you are expecting an invitation to a meal or for an overnight stay If it is to be an evening visit, register at a hotel or motel before you make your phone call.

YOU AND YOUR DOG

If a dog is a part of your family and you want to take him with you on a motor trip, by all means do so if he has been properly trained to mind his company manners and you can count on him, or if you are willing to take along a crate in which to confine him at night when you are staying at a hotel or motor court Some hotels will accept dogs as guests, and most (though not all) motor courts will * You will save yourself time and annoyance by mentioning when you make your reservation that you will be accompanied by a dog

Pack for your dog as well as for yourself and your family when you prepare for the trip. You should have with you his drinking and food dishes, a supply of the canned and/or dry food to which he is accustomed so that he does not have to add to the strain of the trip that of becoming accustomed to strange food, a can opener, and a blanket or cushion on which he may sleep. It is as rude for you to use a hotel pillow for his bed as it would be to use one in a home where you are a social weekend guest, and besides, the dog will be happier on the bed to which he is accustomed.

Do not feed the dog a large meal before starting the day's drive, or during it Train him before you leave (if it is not already his

* At the time of this writing the Gaines Dog Research Center, 250 Park Avenue, New York 17, New York, issues a forty-eight page booklet listing several hundred hotels and motor courts in America which welcome dogs as guests It will be sent to anyone upon receipt of 25 cts.

habit) to expect one satisfying meal a day—in the evening, after your day's drive is over. Then be sure to give him a good long walk half an hour or so later so that he will have no trouble remaining continent during the night

Keep him on leash when in public rooms, hallways, and elevators.

Do not take him into the dining room unless he is a guide dog serving a blind member of the family.

When he is exercising, see that he does not soil walks, lawns, or gardens

Never leave your dog alone in a hotel or motor court room unless you are quite sure that he will not bark and disturb other guests. Even if you are sure, it will be wise for you to put a "Do Not Disturb" sign on the door while you are out in case your best four-legged friend may be overzealous in guarding your property when the maid comes in to tidy your room, or turn your bed down at night

You must expect to pay for any damage done by your dog Do not try to conceal it and leave without facing your responsibility. This not only is unfair and rude to the hostelry, but also is unsporting to other dog owners, for every dog will suffer a little through the bad reputation made by one.

Be sure that your dog has an identification tag on which his name and your name and address (including the state) are stamped so that if he is lost, anyone who encounters him can put him at ease by using his name, and communicate with you.

If you take him across the United States–Canadian border in either direction you must have a health certificate and a statement from a veterinarian to the effect that he has been immunized against rabies within the preceding six months.

Tipping

Suggestions for tipping at hotels en route will be found in Chapter 16, "Tipping in America and at Sea."

14

Train, Bus, Plane, and Ship

W̶HEN YOU TRAVEL ON ANY OF THE COMMON CARRIERS you share a convenience with many other people, and your conduct should be regulated by a realization of this fact. In the family car the seating, the placing of the baggage, and other details may be simply and amicably arranged among the riders before the trip begins. On a train or bus the trip may begin with few passengers and end with a crowd, each member of which should receive your consideration if you come into contact with him On a ship or plane trip, where, generally speaking, arrangements for the whole trip are made before the trip starts, it is your responsibility to fit into those accommodations that have been provided for you.

TRAIN TRAVEL

Train travel falls into several categories. the short trip from the suburb to the city for shopping, visiting, or the theater, the daily commuting trip, the trip between the city and the country for weekend visits, and the overland trip in day coach or Pullman.

Shopping Trips

Monday morning is the time when many weekend guests to the country go back to the city. Friday evening is the time when the direction of weekend travel is reversed, and many go from the city to the country. Therefore the considerate woman who goes from a suburb to the city to shop will, so far as possible, choose Tuesday, Wednesday, Thursday, or Saturday as her shopping day so as not to add to the congestion on Monday morning or Friday evening. Of course, if there is an especially attractive sale on a Monday or Friday it provides a dilemma. But there are exceptions to every rule.

Smoking

Whether on a shopping trip, commuting, weekending, or during overland travel, neither a lady nor a gentleman smokes on a train in any save the smoking car. It is a rule that is too often forgotten, and, I'm sorry to say, more often by women than by men, perhaps because they know that male passengers and trainmen are less likely to take them to task than they are to reprove members of their own sex. It is a discourtesy that should be avoided. Tobacco smoke is extremely annoying to some people.

Seating

As a passenger on a day coach you are entitled to one seating space, not two, and certainly not four If you have baggage or parcels, see that they are stowed neatly in the luggage rack. If you are a woman, and they are too heavy for you to put up there, ask the trainman to put them up for you and to take them down when you reach your destination. If you have more baggage than the rack will accommodate, check it in the baggage car or, if there is none, ask the trainman to help you place it where it will not be in the way of others Do not pile it on the seat beside you, which may be empty when you board the train, but may be needed by a passenger who gets on at a later stop. And above all, do not turn the empty seat in front of you over and appropriate it for your belongings.

Weekend travelers to the country are among the worst offenders in this regard. I do not know why it is, but some city people, leaving the restraints of the city behind them for a weekend of freedom and relaxation in the country, leave many of their wholesome restraints behind them also—along with their general relaxation, relaxing their consideration for others.

A friend of mine has told me of a nightmarish trip he made to New York one Sunday evening on a train that carried a large party of ski enthusiasts back to the city after a weekend in the snow-covered hills of New England. Though the train was crowded many of the young people had spread their baggage, skis, boots, and poles over the seats beside them. Here and there a seat had been turned over and one person actually occupied the space intended for four. Though oncoming passengers had to walk through several cars looking for seats, none of the young people moved any of their equipment to make room for them. A number of them had been drinking heavily and kept drinking during the trip, parading up and down the aisles, singing raucously. One had a bongo drum which he kept pounding throughout the entire trip. One member of the train crew joined them and became so tipsy that he was quite incapacitated.

Two of the young men, who had been drinking a great deal, thought it amusing to climb into the luggage racks and stretch out. They did so, and no member of the train crew interfered.

The entire trip, my friend told me, was chaotic. Obviously the train crew rated severe censure, and it is to be assumed that they received it, for a long letter was written to the president of the railroad involved. But the saddest part of the story to me was the reflection which it cast upon the manners of a group of young people traveling presumably in order to engage in one of the finest and most beautiful of sports. It should have been a pleasure and a privilege to travel with them, feeling satisfaction that they had spent the weekend so wholesomely. Instead it became a nerve-racking trial—all because (with the exception of a few who refused to join the melee) they showed no sense of consideration for others and forgot their dignity in a rowdy spectacle.

Most people prefer to sit by a window, and if there is an empty seat on the train will do so. Some, however, prefer the aisle seat because of a draft from the window, too much heat—or just because. If you are one of the latter there is no reason why you should not take an aisle seat, even if the rest of the seat is empty, so long as you are prepared to rise and allow someone else to take the window seat. Conversely, if you find someone in an aisle seat with the rest of the seat empty, there is no discourtesy in your asking the one in the aisle seat whether the window seat is taken, and if the answer is no, taking it yourself.

Conversations with Fellow Passengers

Whether you start a conversation with someone sharing a seat with you on a train, or continue in one started by another, is for you to decide. I can see no earthly reason why two people who like the looks of each other and who have been accidentally thrown together on a trip should not talk to each other without formal introductions if they want to On the other hand the rules of courtesy do not demand that a lady put up with, and encourage by her refusal to discourage it, the attention of a man who is making a nuisance of himself. Or vice versa, for that matter.

Talk with your seat mate if you like, and if your conversation is welcome If you are annoyed, courteous but monosyllabic replies to questions, or none at all if they are too personal, will usually discourage the boldest of men. A book or magazine close at hand to pick up and read is often a useful ally.

The Commuter

The seasoned commuter has usually fallen into a routine that makes the daily grind of traveling to and from the city a more pleasant thing for himself and for those who travel with him

The courteous daily traveler is perhaps even more careful not to inconvenience others than the occasional train rider, for he knows how many of his fellow commuters (and perhaps himself) like to make the most of that morning and evening hour on the train as perhaps the one bit of complete inner privacy and relaxation which they have in their day, in which they may read the newspaper, perhaps catnap, or just sit quietly and see the landscape go by while sorting out mentally some of the problems of the day. The lady or gentleman on a commuters' train respects this privacy of others.

Whether it is night or morning, when he boards the train and finds there are no window seats left, he will pause before taking an aisle seat and ask the person sitting near the window whether it is taken, or perhaps say, "May I share this with you?"

He will be especially careful not to take up more than his share of the seat. If he has a briefcase or packages, he will find a place where they will not inconvenience his seat mate.

He will not sprawl, and will keep his elbows close to himself. One of the most annoying events of the daily ride to the commuter who is trying to get a fifteen-minute nap is to be just dropping off and feel himself nudged in the ribs by the elbow of the one sitting next to him.

He will not let his newspaper interfere with the other by opening it widely so that a part of it is in front of his seat mate. There is a simple technique for avoiding this It consists of folding the paper over to the back once, thus making it half its original size. As you read it you continue to fold it back in half pages, and you find that the whole is very easily managed while keeping it quite in front of yourself. Most courteous old-time commuters have adopted this habit. It is an excellent one for the younger, less seasoned ones to learn.

Special Features of Pullman Travel

In a Pullman car, whether it is a parlor car, or a car with roomettes, compartments, or drawing rooms, each passenger occupies the space which he has reserved. On a Pullman you should remember that as you are entitled to your space, so is each other passenger to his, do not encroach on the space assigned to another.

In a parlor car, do not move from the seat assigned to you to another that happens to be vacant at the moment, simply because you like the position of it better. Though there may be no one in it at the moment, the rightful occupant may be in the club car or dining car, or may enter the train at the next stop, and your presence in the seat assigned to him will be an embarrassment.

Generally speaking, conversation with anyone who happens to be sitting at the same table as you are in the dining car is not indicated, beyond asking him or her to pass salt, pepper, sugar, or cream, when necessary. Yet I have never been able to see why two people, who like the looks of each other and want to become acquainted when accidentally thrown together, should not do so if it happens naturally and without misunderstanding. I should think it likely that in the history of the human race more fine friendships have been formed which did not begin with formal introduction than those which have. Retain your sense of courtesy, fitness, and personal dignity, and let yourself make friends. But do not intrude on the privacy of another. There are many, many situations in human relations that simply cannot be regulated by hard-and-fast rules which will fit every one of them. I think that talking to other people on trains is one.

I remember a day, years ago, when I was on the boat train from

Dunkerque to Paris eating breakfast in the dining car after a channel crossing. At a table opposite me sat a shy young American couple and a lone Englishman. The Englishman was reading his paper, and gave no evidence of the fact that he knew the young people were sitting across from him. When the porter presented his bill, the young American gave him a bank note (this was in the days when the franc had much greater value than it has now), the porter gave him change, and the young man sat looking sadly at the coins in his hand

At that point the Englishman said crisply, "I beg your pardon, but wasn't that a 200 franc note you gave him?" "Yes," the young man said ruefully, "but I do not speak French and have no way to tell him" The Englishman did speak French, called the porter back, and told him in no uncertain terms that he had given the young man change for 100 francs only, and that he owed him 100 francs With a flourish the porter drew out the 100 franc note which he had ready and waiting for the expected protest; the young man thanked the Englishman, and the latter, nodding acknowledgment, went back to his paper.

I remember thinking what nice people both the Englishman and the young Americans seemed to be and how typical both the Englishman's helpfulness and his withdrawal were, and liked all three of them. But I thought, too, that it would have been nice if they had become friends as a result of their chance meeting

Traveling with Children

Children, especially very young ones, create a special situation when traveling with adults on either day coach or Pullman Whether the situation becomes an unpleasant problem will of course depend to a large extent on the relationship established between parents and children long before the journey was begun, and how well the children have learned the important lesson of consideration for others which is behind all proper social behavior.

Still, even the best-behaved little ladies and gentlemen will become restless if asked to sit for hours doing nothing but look out of a train window, no matter how enchanting the scenery may be.

If you are taking a trip of any length with a child or children, keep their regular schedule of meals, naps, and bedtime, as you would if you were at home.

Take along books or magazines for them (if they are of reading age), simple puzzles for them to solve—whatever will keep their minds and, if possible, their fingers busily and happily employed.

Do not overfeed them, and beware of too much candy, soda pop, and cake or pie. Some people are subject to travel sickness, and children, like puppies, especially so. Feed them simply.

Perhaps the best solution of all is to make those trips on which your children will accompany you by car, if you can.

Tipping

This is discussed in Chapter 16, "Tipping in America and at Sea."

BUS TRAVEL

The general rules of courtesy which apply to day coach travel apply also to the passengers on a bus, though there is a marked difference in the general atmosphere here, where everything seems slightly less formal and, if the trip is a long one, everyone on board seems to become friendly with everyone else, and conversation between passengers, and between passengers and driver, seems to be the expected order of the day.

This does not of course mean that you would be justified in pressing your conversation on anyone who shows you that it is not welcome.

Room is even more at a premium here than on a day coach, but on almost all save local buses there is storage room for baggage outside passenger quarters. If you have anything larger than a very small bag or briefcase be sure that you let the driver put it away for you so that it does not inconvenience other passengers.

PLANE TRAVEL

General rules of courtesy while traveling on an airplane are of course the same as those which prevail for train or any other travel. But there are some circumstances and customs connected with air travel different from those met elsewhere. It is well to be familiar with these in order to conduct yourself properly when confronted by them for the first time.

Reservations

Make your reservation well before the time of your trip. Be sure that you understand clearly the number of the flight, the time it leaves the airport, the time you are expected to be at the airport (usually about half an hour before the time the flight leaves), and the time the limousine leaves the city terminal to take you to the airport for your flight The charge for taking you to the airport is not included in the price of your ticket. You may, if you choose, be driven to the airport in the family car or in a taxi, in which case see that you get there by the time specified. The charge for the limousine, usually about a dollar, will in most cases be less than taxi fare.

If having made your reservation, you find that you cannot make the trip, cancel the reservation as early as you can so that if the company has a waiting list of applicants for that flight (as they sometimes do) one of them may be notified in time to make arrangements. Do not be what the airlines call a "no show"; that is, one who simply does not show up for the flight after having bought a ticket Some airlines charge a premium in such cases when returning the fare or transferring you to another flight, but whether they do or not, you may have seriously inconvenienced someone else who might have occupied the seat which you left vacant.

Luggage

Do not take more luggage with you than you need, and if you do, do not complain about the rather high excess baggage charges that will be levied. There is a limit to the amount of weight a plane can carry. The excess baggage charges are consciously set high to discourage individual passengers from taking, with their baggage, more than their share. Your baggage will be weighed at the air terminal in the city or at the airport, at whichever you check in, and you will be told if there is an excess On most lines you are permitted to take about forty pounds free, though on some reduced-rate flights the allowance is less.

Seating

On some flights there are no specific seat assignments as there are on Pullman cars. In this case your ticket entitles you to a seat, and no standing room, of course, is ever sold, but you will select your own seat from among those that are vacant when you board the plane. If, however, you choose one that has a card reading "Occupied," go on to another. The card means that someone has already chosen that seat and has left it temporarily.

The Stewardess

You will be met at the door of the plane as you enter by a stewardess, or perhaps two. Many planes carry a notice telling you the names of your stewardesses, in which case use them. Otherwise the proper form of address is "Stewardess"—not "Miss."

The job of the stewardess, for which she is well trained, is complex. She will take your overcoat (if you have one) and hat, and any other impedimenta, and check them during the flight When on taking off and landing, or in exceptionally rough weather, the flashing sign tells you to fasten your seat belt, she will check to see that all passengers have done so, and will help you to do so if you need assistance. She will serve your meals, the price of which, incidentally, is included in the price of your ticket on all but some tourist flights If you are ill you will find that she has a supply of simple, often used medicines. Some stewardesses are trained nurses. All have been given instruction in meeting the emergencies of simple illnesses and first aid If you are on a night flight, she will bring you a pillow and a blanket, and if you are fortunate enough to have an unoccupied seat next to you, she will probably remove the removable arm rest that separates your seat from that next to you so that you may stretch out more comfortably. She is one of the prime reasons why your trip is likely to be comfortable and pleasant. She is deserving of the highest respect and the most courteous treatment.

Seat Belt and Smoking

When the lighted sign forbids smoking and instructs you to fasten your seat belt, obey it promptly If you wish to smoke after the lighted sign has been turned off, that is, when the plane is in the air, do so, if you smoke cigarettes On most planes you are asked not to smoke a pipe or cigars, since they are offensive in close spaces to many people.

Tipping

See Chapter 16, "Tipping in America and at Sea."

SHIP TRAVEL

The Three Classes

On most of the large transatlantic liners you may travel First Class, Cabin, or Tourist. Which one you choose will depend, probably, on which you can afford, but it may also depend somewhat on your preference in travel conditions, degree of formality, and traveling companions. The degree of formality is greatest in First Class, less in Cabin, and least of all in Tourist

So far as basic comfort goes, accommodations in Cabin Class are little different from those in First Class The First Class cabins are a bit larger and more luxurious, and are, generally speaking, higher in the ship and forward rather than midship (as are Cabin Class cabins) or at the stern and in the depths (as are those in Tourist Class). It is possible to obtain a single cabin for one in First Class Some large liners have a few, but very few, single cabins in Cabin Class. The deck space is much larger in First than in other classes (less in Cabin, very scanty in Tourist) And there is much more formality in First Class than in either of the other two.

On any reputable line the food is excellent in all three classes There are perhaps more delicacies and a somewhat larger assortment in First Class, but the Cabin Class food is beyond reproach and, by the standards of the average person, lavish and luxurious. The Tourist Class food is adequate and good.

Fellow Passengers

It is always difficult to make generalities about people as groups, and one who does so often will frequently be in error Yet the very differences that exist in the three classes on shipboard inevitably result in a somewhat different group using each class

You will of course meet fine, interesting people, and bores in all three classes Generally speaking, the per capita wealth of the First Class passengers will exceed that of those in either of the other classes (as that of those in Cabin Class will exceed that of those in Tourist). Yet I have known people who could well afford First Class travel going Cabin Class because they preferred it, and others who have had to make sacrifices in order to be able to say that they traveled First Class—"keeping up with the Joneses."

While I have no statistics to document this statement, I think it safe to say that the average age in the three classes generally varies as does the per capita wealth—oldest in First Class, younger in Cabin, and youngest in Tourist, though this too varies and you will find people of all ages in all three classes.

As to occupations and interests, they too are represented by mixtures in all three classes. Generally speaking, high ranking statesmen and government officials, high-salaried businessmen, wealthy retired couples, successful actors and actresses, and others in the public eye (there are exceptions, of course) travel First Class. In Cabin Class you will find a preponderance of middle-class businessmen, teachers (who can afford to forego the rigors of Tourist Class), commercial travelers, writers who are not on the best-seller lists (and some who are), middle-class naturalized Americans who are making a visit to their relatives in Europe, and vacationists who love travel for its own sake and are off on a trip for which they have saved many years. In Tourist Class you will find those of all ages who cannot afford more expensive accommodation, but among them usually a large number of young people, students off to see a bit of the world before settling down to their life work, sometimes in groups on arranged tours, non-English speaking immigrants whose nostalgia has sent them back to their homeland for a visit or for the rest of their lives, and in general the kind of a melting-pot mixture that has made America the racial and nationalistic conglomerate which it is

While one can find as much basic, substantial comfort in Cabin as in First Class, this is not true of Tourist Class, which is crowded, has little deck and lounge room, and is subject to more noise and vibration from the ship's machinery than are the other two classes. It is not to be recommended for the elderly, the ill, or the complete introvert who can afford one of the other two classes. Yet if you are young, vigorous, and have a bountiful interest in and liking for other people, you may, if you choose Tourist, look back on that trip as the happiest of your life, for the atmosphere is one of complete informality, friendliness, and companionship, and you may there form friendships that will endure.

Cabins

If you are traveling alone in Cabin Class or in Tourist Class you will probably have to share your cabin with either one, two, or three strangers. They will of course be of the same sex as yourself, for the steamship line sees to that when it assigns your space to you. If you like privacy you will probably do well to ask for space in a four-berth cabin rather than in one that accommodates two. Somehow the tendency to spend more time than you wish with one of your cabin mates is less when there are four of you than when there are only two. As a matter of fact, unless you are very unfortunate you will generally find no difficulty in this regard. Others will probably be as jealous of their privacy as you are, and beyond the ordinary courtesies which you would pay to one another when thrown closely together under any circumstances, you and your cabin mate or mates will not be expected to pay any more attention to one another than you wish.

Deck Chairs

There are two things for you to see to as soon as you get on board and have had your baggage stowed in your cabin. If you wish to rent a deck chair for the voyage go to the deck steward at once and arrange the matter with him. Within the limits of the space assigned to the class in which you travel, and that which is left after others who have been there before you have reserved theirs, he will allow you to pick the location you like and help you to do so, with due regard for your preferences in the matter of sun or shade and other factors.

You are not of course obliged to rent a deck chair, with or without a cushion and a steamer rug (the cost for these is extra). But if you do not do so, deciding to spend your time walking the deck, sitting in one of the lounges or on one of the few benches (which you will probably find here and there in odd corners of the deck) or in your cabin, be fair and do not appropriate deck chairs which others have reserved for their use, simply because they happen to be vacant as you pass them on deck. In a small way this is as rude as it would be to walk into a stranger's house and make yourself at home simply because the owner is not in it at the time.

Dining Salon

After you have arranged for your deck chair, go to the dining salon where you will find one of the ship's staff seated at a table with a seating chart before him. Settle with him for the place you will occupy at meals. He too will give you some choice in the matter of where you will sit. If you are traveling with a companion or more than one, he will seat you together If you are alone he will probably ask you whether you would rather sit at a small table with one or three others, or at a large one, which may seat from six to ten. If you choose a small table for two he will try (with the limited information he has) to seat you with someone who is congenial. If you choose a larger table he will try to balance the men and women as equally as possible. Here, as in the case of choosing between a cabin for two and one for four, you will decide which will please you more. You may find that you have actually greater privacy in a group of six to ten than in a group of two.

You will also probably be asked whether you prefer eating at the first or the second sitting, and will be given the times of both. But if you have children you may be asked to take the first sitting. If you are not asked, it would be wise for you to choose it anyway, in order to get the children to bed betimes and, to put it frankly, to get them out of the way before those who like to sit long over their afterdinner coffee or brandy arrive.

Whether you are at the first or second sitting at meals, be on time. Though at any save one of the ship's officer's tables, others will probably not wait for you to arrive, tardiness is a discourtesy to them, and shows a lack of consideration for the stewards who (if you are at the first sitting) must get you out of the way in order to prepare the table for the second sitting, and (if you are at the second sitting) should be allowed to get through with those duties connected with serving the meal as quickly as possible

If you are at a table with any of the ship's officers you do not order until he appears If for any reason he cannot come to the meal he will send word to the table that he is detained, and the meal will proceed. Also at officers' tables, it is considered discourteous for any of the passengers to order until all have assembled, so if you are seated at one and do not intend to come to a meal, or are going to be late, send word by your cabin steward.

Dressing at Sea

In First Class many people dress formally for dinner, save on the first and last nights out, though it is not obligatory. In Cabin Class few people do, though if you choose to do so, you may. In Tourist it is not customary. On the Captain's night (or gala, as it is sometimes called) when there is a special menu served at dinner and special entertainment afterwards, usually with dancing, some people in Cabin Class who do not otherwise don evening dress, do so. But again, it is not obligatory.

Getting to Know Others

There is generally an informality on shipboard which makes it no breach of good manners to enter conversation with others with whom you are thrown into close contact, so long as it is done courteously and you are sure that you do not press your attention on someone who does not desire it.

Indeed it would seem rude not to say good morning to your cabin mates if you are all awake at the same time in the morning, or to those whose deck chairs are next to yours It is customary also to introduce yourself to those who share a table with you in the dining salon at the first meal you eat with them.

How far you go in acquaintance beyond these ordinary courtesies will depend on the responses you get and your general compatibility with others. But do not expect, save under exceptional circumstances, that the friendships you make on shipboard will be lasting, though they may be. Indeed some very happy marriages have resulted from chance acquaintances made on shipboard. But generally speaking, you and your shipmates have for a few days shared a separate little world that vanishes as a unit once each of you has returned to land and his own accustomed sphere.

Cabin Manners

If you are sharing a cabin with others, remember that it is a restricted space and that you must not use more than your part of it. If it is a four-berth room, you are entitled to half the space under the lower berth in the tier in which you sleep, whether yours is the upper or the lower. Here you may keep the suitcase which you have kept apart from any baggage which you have sent to the hold. But do not, if you have the lower berth, think that because of this you are entitled to all of it.

Do not let your toilet articles sprawl over the space about the washbowl. It is best, indeed, to keep them in the special kit which you probably have in your bag, save when you are using them. Be sure that you clean the washbowl after you have used it.

Wardrobe space is also limited in ship's cabins. Do not take more of it than your share, even if in order not to do so you must leave some of the clothing you would like to hang there in your bag. You may, as a result, have to send it to be pressed in a hurry the day that you land, but this is better than causing your cabin mates the inconvenience of leaving no space for them to use.

If you stay up late and find, when you come to your cabin, that one or more of your cabin mates is sleeping, get ready for bed as quietly, and with as little light as possible. The same rule, of course, applies if you rise earlier than the others in your cabin.

Lifeboat Drill

It is neither courteous nor intelligent to avoid lifeboat drill. You will be notified beforehand when it is to occur. When the warning signals are sounded, go to the deck space assigned to you promptly with your life preserver adjusted, and listen carefully to the instructions given.

Tipping

This is discussed extensively in Chapter 16, "Tipping in America and at Sea."

15

When in Rome Do as Rome Does

THERE IS IN EVERY COUNTRY AN ANTIPATHY TO THE foreigner—to his accent if he speaks the language, to his dress, but above all to his manners. In the United States, even in that most cosmopolitan city New York, it is constantly expressed by taxi drivers, pedestrians, solid Westchester house owners, clerks in the great department stores. Yet when you cross the Atlantic or Pacific or even our Southern border, when you land at an airport in Mexico City or Paris or Tokyo, you have undergone a transformation. You have become yourself a foreigner, an object of suspicion or dislike, and it behooves you to remember, once on soil outside the United States, that your behavior, your sobriety, your manners are all under special scrutiny.

You have also gained a new importance which you may not have anticipated when you waved good-by to your friends at the dock or airport. You are now an ambassador of your beloved country, and it is not inconceivable that your personal conduct may be a factor in international understanding.

It has always been true that people have been wary of anything that is strange to them, and that too often they react defensively by deriding it. I remember reading somewhere the wise words of a Chinese who responded to an American's derision of his queue by saying, "When meeting with the new, the unexpected, the strange, learn the reasons and be enlightened rather than dismiss it as stupid, and thus become both ignorant and arrogant"

Many of our errors in behavior in foreign countries arise not necessarily from arrogance, but rather from ignorance and a lack of understanding Edward T Hall, in his fascinating book, *The Silent Language*, shows that complete communication with people of a culture different from our own is impossible without a deep understanding of that culture and a modification of our approach based on this understanding

Mr Hall tells of how an American agriculturist deeply offended a farmer in Egypt by a well meant question as to how much the man expected his field to yield that year. Nonplussed by the man's anger, the farmer later made inquiries and found that the Arab had believed him to be crazy, since only God knows the future, and it is presumptuous even to talk about it.

In the United States a girl who is asked for a date at the last moment might be offended In the Middle East no one ever makes an appointment very far ahead, for "the future" is so vague that it cannot be counted on; the very word itself may connote a term of thousands of years rather than a few weeks or months

Even literally translated words may be puzzling to others whose concepts of the subject may be different from ours. We speak of doing something in a week, as though the term week were a space, the Arab way of doing it before or after a week. We "go out in the rain," the Arab goes out "under the rain."

In the United States we take it for granted that a man may call on a woman he has recently met without any consent save her own In some parts of the Arab world, where it is necessary to obtain the permission of the woman's family, a call made without such permission might actually bring about the death of the woman at the hands of her brothers, and revenge of some sort on the man

Without knowing why the custom exists we might think it silly that among the Tanala of Madagascar a widow must be formally divorced from her dead husband before she can remarry. When we understand, however, that to the Tanala death is merely a change from one status to another, in which the dead still participate in the affairs of the living, the custom becomes logical.

We and the English feel that too close physical contact with strangers is undesirable, and keep our distance when talking to others. Many continental Europeans, on the other hand, feel that it is a compliment to stand very close to another when addressing him, and will be offended if you back away.

In North America a businessman would not think of making more than one appointment for the same hour. In Latin America it is customary to make appointments with several people for the same time, and a North American, arriving promptly for an appointment, may be offended when he has to wait an hour or more beyond the set time If, however, he knows the custom, while he may not approve of it he can understand the reason for his wait and try to accept it graciously. He will at least know that he has not been singled out for rudeness.

It would of course be impossible for you when about to take a short trip abroad to become thoroughly acquainted with the customs and psychology of all the peoples you are going to visit The more that you know of them, however, the better But even more important is that you take with you an open-minded, interested, receptive, and respectful attitude, determined to learn in so far as possible the reasons for the unfamiliar customs and attitudes which you will encounter, and respect them, rather than simply to scorn them in arrogance because they are strange to you.

If you arrange your trip through a travel bureau, you will find that the bureau can be helpful in giving you pamphlets or referring you to books about the customs and manners of the countries you are planning to visit.

We are a generous people, members of a powerful and progressive nation Throughout history these three attributes—generosity, power, and progressiveness—have been mixed, for better and worse, in our relations with other countries. Never in history has any nation given and lent to other nations so lavishly as has America during the last few decades These gifts and loans have been motivated by a mixture of humanitarian generosity and considerations of self-interest, and have sometimes been complicated by conditions that have made other peoples resent us. We have come to realize in these years the truth of Shakespeare's dictum that "loan oft loseth both itself and friend."

The situation is even more delicate in Asia and Africa than it is in Europe, and especially so among the countries that have recently freed themselves from European colonialism, and where the competition for influence between Communism and Democracy is strong. Here propaganda (based upon stories of lynchings, racial discrimination, labor strikes, etc., the implications of which are always skillfully exaggerated) has been put to work with far-reaching effect. There has been added to the myths of America's imperialistic designs to dominate the world by economic power, and the soulless money-grubbing tendencies of all Americans, another myth which designates every white man as one who considers inferior everyone whose skin is not white.

Since America is considered the prime exponent of democracy, it is not surprising that Asians and Africans sometimes take every protestation of the superiority of our political philosophy with a grain of salt, and regard every white person with a certain amount of suspicion.

Thus an American traveling abroad is an ambassador not only for the United States, but also for the concept of democracy and, if he is a white American, for the entire white race. Wherever he goes, America and democracy will be thought of with a little more or a little less respect after he has departed.

BEFORE YOU GO

It is assumed that before you leave the United States you will know what countries and, probably in general, what cities you will visit. Learn a little about each of them—enough so that you will have in mind when you get there not only the places you want to see (in order to enhance your own enjoyment), but also as much as you can of the country's customs and history. In your reading, look for great men and women, great events in history, or some extraordinary charm connected with each country which merit special praise, so that, even if you cannot speak fluently the language of the country you are visiting, you will be able somehow to express appreciation of these when occasion presents itself. Honest praise sincerely given will help to breach any wall of suspicion between peoples.

Language

If you do not already speak the languages of the countries which you plan to visit, you cannot of course be expected to learn them before you go As a matter of fact in all large European cities you will find enough English and French spoken so that, even with English alone, you should have no difficulty in essential communication. If you have French as well as English you will be well equipped.

Yet there are a few words which you should learn to use in other languages out of courtesy. Surely it can be no trouble for you to learn to say "good morning," "good day," "good-by," "excuse me," "please," "thank you," "madam," and "sir" in the languages of the countries in which you expect to spend some time. You should also be able to say, with an apology, that you do not speak or understand the language of the country. Using even this much of the language is a compliment and is quickly recognized as a gesture of goodwill. Learn these terms and use them when occasion calls for their use, and you will find those to whom you speak more friendly and more eager to understand what you want to say to them and more helpful in making you understand what they are trying to say to you.

For the rest, a friendly smile, an apologetic shrug of the shoulders, pantomiming, and careful study of the pantomiming of those you meet (at which the Latin races—particularly the Italians—are especially expert and creatively imaginative) will stand you in good stead. Your earnest desire to understand and to be understood are the essentials. Given that on both sides, communication finds a way.

You should also learn the little word *pourboire* (French, literally meaning "for a drink," actually meaning "tip"), for it is used throughout Europe. In many cases the demand will be unreasonable, but it may mean that you have undertipped or forgotten to tip at all, and it should be given consideration

The English term "W.C" (water closet) is used generally throughout Europe to designate toilets, and often one toilet serves both sexes, in which case you will probably find a lock on the inside of the door. Thus if you go to one and find the door locked, do not rattle the doorknob or demand that the door be opened for you Wait, just as you would in any private home in America that you were visiting. But since in some places you will find two toilets, one for men and one for women, you should also learn the words for "ladies" and "gentlemen" in the languages of the countries you are going to visit, so that you will not make the mistake of walking into the wrong one.

Numbers are the stumbling blocks of most people seeking to learn a little of a new language. And since you will need to recognize them in order to shop intelligently, it would be well for you to learn to say, "Will you please write it?" and carry with you a small pad of paper and a pencil. You will have no difficulty recognizing the price which a shopkeeper writes down for you, if you remember that many Europeans write "7" with a bar through it thus, "7," and that the 1 may look like a seven without the bar.

Do not assume that Americans and British speak the same language simply because in both cases it is called "English." There are some words that mean one thing in America and another in England, and shades of speech that markedly differentiate both countries. If you are planning to spend much time in the British Isles, it will be well for you to learn as many of these as you can. It is not necessary—and would probably be a mistake—for you to attempt to copy the English in their pronunciation of words, where this differs from that of Americans, and certainly you would be considered ridiculous if you attempted to talk with the broad vowels and swift, clipped speech that is natural to Oxford and Cambridge undergraduates and to the second-rate British actors who attempt to imitate them. But you will enhance your welcome if you learn a few of the most important differences in the meanings of commonly used words, as understood in America and in the British Isles.

The list is far too long (and many of the differences too trivial) to attempt to make it complete here, but a few of the most interesting and commonly used words are discussed below, with an explanation of the different usages in the two countries.

A theater aisle in America is a "gangway" in England (and, incidentally, the theater is a "theatre"). A baby carriage is a "pram" and baggage is "luggage." Our word "bill," to mean paper money, becomes "note" in England, whereas what we call the check in a restaurant is a "bill" to the English. In England a store is a "shop."

A piece of candy is a "sweet," a cracker a "biscuit," whereas what we call a biscuit in America, though I know of no exact counterpart of it in England, would probably be called a "scone" or a "muffin."

If you asked a functionary at Selfridge's to direct you to the elevators he would probably understand what you meant, but would doubtless say, "The lifts, Madam, are in that direction."

What we call garters when worn by men, are "sock suspenders" in England, if worn by women, "suspenders," while what we call suspenders are "braces" to the English. "Garters" in England are simple bands of elastic for holding up high socks. We may speak freely here of a man's pants (though we also use the word trousers), in England they are always "trousers" "Pants" in England are underwear, either long or short. A man never calls his waistcoat a vest in Britain, but always a "waistcoat." To him a "vest" is what we would call an undershirt.

Rare meat is, in England, "underdone"; what here is a pitcher, there is a "jug"

Where we often use the word "gotten," which actually was good usage in England centuries ago, the English use the word "got."

An English friend some time ago told me a charming story (which may be apocryphal), about the man who, on a prolonged visit to America, had found this reversion to an Old English usage so attractive that he had adopted it in his own speech. After he had returned to London he was given two tickets to the performance of a very popular play for the evening of the day on which he was given them He immediately sent a telegram to his wife in a suburb, saying, "Have gotten tickets for tonight's performance of 'Green Pastures,'" (or whatever it was). "Meet me at the theatre." He was somewhat taken aback when his wife met him that evening bringing along eight friends

And speaking of the theater, what we call an orchestra seat is to the British a "stall." If you were to tell an English friend who was not acquainted with American usage that you had sat in the orchestra, he would think you meant that you had sat with the musicians.

What we would call a preparatory or boarding school is in England a "public school." In England a preparatory school is a boarding school for small boys preparatory to or preparing them for "public school." The nearest equivalent to our public schools are "Council" schools. If you ask an English child what "grade" he is in at school, he will look at you blankly, but will, on request, tell you what "form" he is in. However, do not try to equate this with a grade bearing the same numerical designation in America, for it won't work, and different schools have different arrangements of forms. I once asked an English boy of ten or so, who had just told me what form he was in, to explain the form system to me. He did so at great length, but when he had finished, I knew as little about it as when he had begun. I turned to his parents for help, but they merely laughed and said, "We don't understand it either," and there I let the matter rest.

It is easy enough to remember that what we call a spark plug in America is invariably a "sparking plug" in England. But it is a little confusing, unless we have been forewarned, to have a man speak of the "hood" of his car and find, after a bit of conversation at cross purposes, that he is referring to what we call the top, or for us to mention the hood, and have him learn at last that we are speaking of what he calls the "bonnet."

These are only a few of the multiple differences between English and American usage in what we like to think of as a common language.*

Learning to use the English equivalents of words to which you are accustomed in America is not among your most important tasks when visiting Great Britain. You will be understood (even though occasionally explanations may be necessary) if you use good American–English. Yet in line with the dictum, "When in Rome do as Rome does," a basic principle of good manners abroad, conforming to English speech when in England in so far as you can do so naturally, will make your communication with one of the most gracious, friendly, and hospitable people in the world smoother and easier.

Do not force it, and do not try to use English slang It is subtle, involved, and ingenious, and like slang in any country changes rapidly. Best stay away from it unless you care to run the risk of making yourself ridiculous. You have only to read some of the English detective stories in which American characters talk in what is supposed to be American idiom, to see how queer the slang of another country, misused, can sound in the ears of those who are accustomed to it.

I have written in some little detail of English speech for two reasons. One is that while a language barrier is expected between

* If you wish to pursue the matter further, a charming brief book on the subject containing an American–English dictionary of 60 pages is *American into English*, by G V. Carey. London, William Heinemann, Ltd , 1953.

Americans and the people of non-English speaking countries, we are inclined to take it for granted that there is none between us and the English. Strictly speaking that should be true, and this is the second reason for my having discussed the situation at some length. Basically England and America have a common culture, a common political and social ideal, and a common language. We are traditionally allies in war and peace. One of the greatest catastrophes that could befall the democratic world would be a rift in the ties that have bound us so closely to each other for so long

Even the antagonisms that flare up sometimes on both sides are more like those that occur within a family group than those that may bring about violent conflict between strangers. It is essential that they never become more than that, and that even these family spats be reduced and minimized as much as possible.

In that process English–English and American–English should be a bridge of genuine communication rather than a barrier between two peoples whose friendship has been and must continue to be an essential factor in human progress.

It is true that wherever you are, in England, France, Spain, Italy, or the Far East, your courtesy and good manners in oral communication and all other ways will prove the greatest service which you can render democracy. But in a sense it is especially important in England, where it should be the easiest for you to be courteous.

Your Dog

If you have a dog of whom you are very fond, you will save yourself a great deal of trouble, and the dog a great deal of nervous tension, by leaving him at home with a dog-loving friend (preferably one to whom the dog is accustomed), or in a good reliable kennel.

If you insist on taking him along, learn well before the date on which you plan to leave what the regulations are governing the entry of dogs into the countries you plan to visit. Great Britain, Ireland, and Denmark insist on quarantining a dog for six months before he is allowed into the country, Holland and Norway for two months, and Sweden for six weeks, as a protection against the possible importation of rabies. Switzerland and Austria require a certificate of health; Spain, Belgium, Holland and Portugal, a certificate of recent vaccination against rabies. Italy requires that a dog must be kept on leash and muzzled at all times.

GOING THROUGH CUSTOMS

In a sense the customs barrier of a European country which you are entering is a testing ground. You are in a minor way on trial there as an American and as an exponent of democracy. Your behavior there will add to or detract from the reputation of all Americans for courtesy, integrity, and fair play, and will make it easier or more difficult for the Americans in line behind you, or coming on the next ship or plane.

Know before you leave home what you are permitted to take free into the country to which you are going, and what not, and do not attempt to take more of any article in free than the regulations say that you may.

A good way to expedite customs examinations is to make a list before you arrive of what each piece of baggage contains, and make it an honest list. If you have included in any piece of baggage more than the amount of any article that you are permitted to take in free, list the extra amounts clearly If you present the lists to the customs examiner with a smile, your bags beside you and your keys in hand ready to open any one which he asks you to open, the chances are that he will mark your bags and wave you on with an answering smile, even though your list includes slight extras. But if you are truculent and act as though every question he asks you is an insult, you will probably be in for a thorough examination and a long delay.

In all but rare cases the customs examination is brief, courteous, and takes place in the public space set aside for this purpose. If, however, you are asked to step aside and go into an office to be questioned at greater length, and perhaps have your clothing and person examined, try not to resent it. It is just possible that you, your clothing, and your luggage resemble those described in the dossier of a smuggler or other wanted person who may be entering the country at about the time that you are.

In that case the customs officials are simply carrying out their difficult duties, and your obligation is to be courteously cooperative. If you have nothing to conceal and meet the situation with patience and consideration, you will not be delayed long, and will undoubtedly receive an apology when the examination is over.

Never tip a customs official, and above all never offer him a bribe as an inducement for a quick examination and clearance of your luggage. There are of course corrupt officials everywhere, and your bribe may work. If, however, the man to whom you offer a bribe is an honest official (as he almost certainly is) your offer will be an insult, and will probably result in his making a longer and more thorough examination of your luggage than he would otherwise, and questioning to which you would not otherwise be subjected If after his examination is over and he has marked your luggage as clear, you want to give him a package of cigarettes, as a friendly gesture, he will thank you and not take offense, but this is not expected and certainly not necessary. In dealing with customs officials in any country, remember how you would behave if and when you are called into the U.S. Internal Revenue Bureau! The same rules prevail.

TRAIN TRAVEL

By Day

In Great Britain and on the continent of Europe railroad service is excellent and reliable. There was a time when it was divided into first, second, and third classes (the last called "traveling hard," because of the stiff wooden benches on which one had to sit), but now, save in Spain and Portugal, there are only first and second classes, differing in the fares charged and to some degree in comfort

The coaches are arranged, not as in America, with a center aisle passing between rows of seats on each side, but with one aisle along one side, and with compartments opening off it, as do the compartments and drawing rooms in our modern sleeping cars. (Some of the older cars, such as those used on suburban lines in England, have compartments filling the entire width of the car, each with a door opening to the outside.) If you read English detective stories, you will recognize them immediately.

In the first-class compartments there are six seats in each compartment, in the second class, eight. In first the upholstery is somewhat more elaborate and therefore a bit more comfortable than in second. Otherwise there is little difference. If you are taking a long journey you will no doubt be more comfortable in first than in second. But second is quite adequate and is generally used by all save the wealthiest or most ostentatious Europeans.

Heating

The heating on most British and continental trains is less effective than that to which Americans are accustomed. You must expect this, and dress warmly if you are about to take a train trip in cold weather. Do not go scantily clad and constantly complain to the train crew and your traveling companions. They will, and rightly, consider such complaints bad manners.

Seating

It is best to arrive early if you wish to get a comfortable corner seat, for the trains are often crowded. You will of course share the compartment in which you sit, with several other travelers, often with as many as the compartment will hold. The first arrival in a compartment is generally considered to be entitled to the window seat facing forward, and is the arbiter of whether the window shall be open or closed. If you happen to be the lucky occupant of that seat it is courteous for you to ask the others, before you open the window or close it, whether it pleases them to have you do so. Here again the rules of courtesy are the same rules that prevail on an airline bus from the East Side Terminal in New York to La Guardia Airport. But do not be as assertive of your comfort in Spain or any other European country as you might be on the bus. Nothing to the other occupants of your compartment can be worse than your insistence as a foreigner on what you feel are your rights. Hatred can be easily infused and more easily spread.

Conversation with Strangers

Even more perhaps than when you are in America, the matter of whether you will or will not talk with your fellow passengers is a delicate one, and something which you must decide in the light of your appraisal of their attitude. The English are traditionally reserved, though it is much more usual since the two world wars (which have brought them and us more closely together), for an Englishman to start a conversation with an American on a train or in a restaurant than it was before. On the Continent you will find less hesitance.

Wherever you go you will be recognized as an American, even before you speak. Just how Europeans know, I have never been able to discover, but they always do. They are naturally curious about us, whether they are pro- or anti-American, and if one of your fellow passengers addresses a remark to you, it is the part of courtesy of course for you to answer him and, so long as he does not become objectionable, to carry the conversation into whatever areas he directs it, which will almost certainly be a discussion of America. You may be asked embarrassing questions, but it is your obligation to answer them honestly and, in so doing, to dispel any misapprehensions which he has received from other sources

In general if you are courteous and considerate you will receive courtesy and consideration. If someone is rude to you, you should be especially careful, when abroad, not to be rude yourself. If his rudeness is in response to something which you have said in his language with which you are not thoroughly familiar, it is possibly based on a misunderstanding. If there is any chance that this is true, apologize for your awkwardness and try to explain. If the other is simply going out of his way to offend you, keep your temper and get away as quickly and courteously as you can. It would not be without precedent in that case, if one of his countrymen who had seen the incident were to follow you and apologize for the bad manners of the other.

I remember seeing a friend of mine handle, in what seemed to me a perfect way, a rude taxi driver in London (a marked exception to the cheerful courtesy of his tribe). It was my friend's first day in London. He was somewhat tired and confused and had not yet become accustomed to English currency. At the end of the ride he glanced at the meter, looked puzzled, and handed the driver a ten shilling note. The driver looked at it in disgust, and snapped, "Another rich American with a ten shilling note! Do you expect me to have change?"

Instantly my friend drew the note back and reaching into his pocket, withdrew a handful of silver which he extended to the driver. "I'm sorry," he said quietly. "I have just arrived and am so unfamiliar with your currency that I was afraid I might give you an inadequate amount. If you will take the fare out of this I shall be grateful."

Somewhat surprised the driver picked up a half crown and sixpence, which was exactly what was on the meter. My friend then handed him an extra shilling, which was an extremely generous tip for the short drive, thanked him, and we went our way while the driver stared after him. I'm sure that he was a little less quick to snap at the next American who rode in his cab.

Sometimes what may seem to be rudeness is based on actual misinformation and a genuine desire to understand.

I remember the story of a friend who was being quizzed by an English boy in his first year at Oxford. The boy had apparently listened to a lot of nonsense from someone who constantly belittled America, and had a fantastic picture of American "money-grabbing" and wastefulness.

"Is it true," the boy asked, "that no one in America wears a suit of clothes more than a few months before throwing it away, and that shoes are thrown away as soon as the heels and soles are a bit worn, and that they are never resoled?"

Fortunately for the reputation of the United States, my friend was wearing a suit with a dated label on the inside pocket of the jacket which showed that it had been made six years before, and a pair of shoes which had been half-soled just before he had left New York. He lifted his feet so that the boy could see the half-soles, and showed him the label in his jacket By the time he and the young man had parted, they had become good friends and one young Englishman had a somewhat more accurate conception of the American character than he had before.

I think it a good rule when in another country in general to wait for one of your fellow passengers who is native to the country in which you are, to start a conversation if one is to be started. You cannot possibly be charged with rudeness if you answer courteously remarks that are addressed to you, whereas if you start the conversation you may be accused silently, and vocally after you have left, of being "one of those brash Americans," even though the same event might not have been remarked if you had been a countryman of the one to whom you spoke.

This rule of course does not prevent your asking for information essential to your procedure at the moment. In any country in the world a courteous "excuse me" and a request for informational help will be taken amiss only by the rudest and least understanding of people

Dining Cars

In Great Britain and on the Continent meals are served in the dining cars of trains only to those who have made reservations for them. There are two, and sometimes three sittings, and if you go to the dining car steward as soon as you get on the train and tell him which sitting you prefer, he will give you a slip entitling you to a seat at that sitting. When your sitting is announced you go to the dining car and take a seat But do not expect to go to the dining car without a ticket, as you would on an American train, and be served.

The dining car waiter is tipped as he would be in America, with ten to fifteen per cent of the amount of the check.

Sleeping Cars

The *wagon-lits* (European equivalent of our Pullman sleepers) are composed of compartments, containing one (in the luxury cars and in some others), two, or three berths. If you engage space in a multiple berth compartment, anyone else who is assigned to it will be of the same sex as yourself. The cost of an upper and a lower berth is the same, so if you have a preference, specify it, and you will probably get what you ask for.

If you are on a train that will cross an international frontier during the night, the conductor will usually ask for your passport in order to show it to the frontier officials and avoid waking you Do not argue with him, let him have it gracefully (he will return it to you in the morning), unless you wish to be wakened at an awkward hour and treated with suspicion by annoyed officials who may resent your having put them to the trouble of waking you and, in addition, be suspicious of you because you refused to cooperate.

As you leave the train after an overnight journey, tip the porter of your car about as you would in America—the equivalent of between fifty cents and a dollar. If the train is one that regularly travels between two countries, you may properly tip him in the currency of either.

HOTELS AND PENSIONS

Reservations

It is well, especially during the tourist season, to make your hotel reservations before leaving the United States, at least as far ahead as you can be sure of your itinerary, and after you arrive in Europe to keep reserving rooms ahead as you plan your later stops.

If by any chance the cancellation of a flight or other unforeseen circumstance makes you arrive a day late, and you have not canceled your reservation by wire, expect to pay for it even though you have not occupied the room. Do not argue about it. Your reservation may have prevented the hotel or *pension* from renting the room to someone else and it is only fair and courteous for you to pay for it graciously as though you had expected to.

"Bed and Breakfast," Pension, and Demi-Pension

Strangely enough the so-called "American Plan" of hotel service, or a modification of it (that is an arrangement under which your room and meals, or a part of them, are included in one overall rate), is more usual in Europe than in the United States In Europe the plan is called "pension."

In England, many hotels offer "bed and breakfast" at one inclusive rate. Other meals are extra Some hotels on the Continent have the same plan. Others offer "demi-pension," which means that your rate includes your room, breakfast, and one other meal, either lunch or dinner. On a full pension plan most hotels will give you credit for a missed lunch or dinner, if you notify them beforehand that you are going to be absent. Sometimes they will do so even if you do not notify them, but be sure to notify them if you can, as you would a hostess if you were unavoidably prevented from attending a dinner for which you had accepted an invitation.

There are also hotels in Europe run on what we here call the "European Plan" (according to which the vast majority of American hotels today operate). In these the stated rate includes only the cost of your room. All meals are extra

Not to be confused with the pension plan at hotels is the *pension* itself (*pensione* in Italy). Here also the price of your room and three meals a day are included in one overall rate (or room and two meals if you choose demi-pension). Yet the *pension* is not strictly speaking a hotel. It is more relaxed and informal in atmosphere, more like a boardinghouse and, like the latter, usually has a larger proportion of permanent or semipermanent guests. Staying at one is a little like being taken, for a time, into a large family At the best of them the food is excellent, the rooms are comfortable and clean, though not luxurious, and the cost for room and three meals is often about that for a room and breakfast at a good hotel.

Baths

Save in the de luxe establishments, few hotel rooms in England or on the continent of Europe have private baths. When you do find a hotel that has them, the rate is comparatively high, and since these rooms are in demand by tourists, it is best, if you insist on having a private bath, to make your reservation far in advance.

Arrangements for use of the non-private baths vary. In London some of the good hotels have several baths (in separate rooms from the toilets) on each floor and they are used at will and without extra charge by the guests. In many continental hotels there is an extra charge for baths, and you must make arrangements for one with the room maid. At the proper time she will draw the bath for you at the approximate temperature for which you have asked, and present you with a large bath towel. In most cases, you will be expected to furnish your own soap.

"Boots"

In English hotels, and in many on the Continent, it is the custom for guests to place their shoes outside their doors at night for the "boots" to collect, clean, and polish. There is usually no charge for this. But the guests are of course expected to see that the "boots" is recompensed. Find out, before you place your shoes outside the door of your room, whether this is the custom in the hotel in which you are staying. If you happen to come in late at night, you can usually do this simply by looking outside the doors of other rooms as you go to yours; if not, the room clerk or even the boy who takes your bag to your room will be able to tell you. If you are not sure, do not make the hall untidy by putting your shoes there. If it is the custom to do so, place them neatly as close to your door as you can, so that they will not be offensive and others will not stumble over them.

Passports

In countries that require tourists to register with the police, the clerk with whom you register in your hotel or *pension* will ask for your passport and take care of that detail for you. He will return it to you later.

TIPPING

In most European hotels and *pensions* it is the custom to add ten or fifteen per cent of your rate to the bill for service. This is distributed among the members of the hotel staff who have served you, and theoretically does away with individual tipping. Actually in many places it does not—and in common decency should not, especially in cases where you have asked for and received any extra services. Wages are low, and ten or fifteen per cent of your hotel bill in any save the most expensive hotels, divided among the staff, adds very little to the income of each of them. But before you decide what you will do about tipping be sure that you know whether a service charge is to be added to your bill, if so how much, and what the general custom is in the locality in which you are. If you are in doubt as to how much you should give, err a little on the side of generosity, but do not overtip lavishly so as to make yourself ridiculous. A fair tip, or one a little on the generous side, will leave a pleasant feeling and respect for you in the one who has received it. A too lavish one will create a secret disrespect and add to the bad reputation Americans have for trying to buy their way in everything. If ten per cent has been added to your bill, give the room maid when you are leaving (or once a week if you are making a prolonged stay) enough to bring your total service charge to about fifteen per cent (more if she has given you special service)—say the equivalent of an American dollar or a bit more for a week's stay, and the "boots" the equivalent of ten cents for each time he has cleaned your shoes. Since he works at night you probably will never see him, so leave his tip in your shoes the last night you are there, or put it in an envelope addressed to him and ask the room clerk to see that he gets it.

The following general remarks may guide you somewhat in different countries.

Great Britain

In Great Britain some hotels add a service charge of ten to fifteen per cent to your bill, others do not. Find out what the custom is in the hotel at which you are staying when you register. If a service charge is added, extra tips will not be expected save for extra service, for waiters in the dining room if you eat there (ten to fifteen per cent of your bill for each meal), for porters who handle your luggage, for the "boots," and for the maid if you make a prolonged stay.

If no service charge is added to your bill the maid should receive at least a shilling per day per person, and more if she has given you extra service. If you have stayed only one night, tip her two shillings or half a crown.

Taxi drivers, as here, are tipped from ten to fifteen per cent of the fare.

The porter who handles your luggage at the railway station should be tipped a sixpence or more for each bag.

The barmaid in a pub is not tipped, but it is customary after a few drinks to buy one for her

Austria

In Austrian hotels and restaurants ten per cent is always added to the bill for service, but it is customary to tip the concierge in a hotel or *pension* for any special service, the maid and waiter in the dining room if you have made a stay of several days. In restaurants tip about five per cent in addition to the ten per cent that is on your bill.

You will also be expected to leave a tip for the musicians in a restaurant or night club, and will find a plate waiting to receive it This should be about five to ten schillings for each guest (a schilling equals about four cents).

Denmark

A fifteen per cent service charge is added to your bill, plus 75 øre per night per person for shoe-shining. The only member of the staff who will expect an extra tip is the porter, and then only if he has rendered special service.

For meals a service charge is sometimes added to your check, sometimes not. If not, between ten and twelve per cent is proper on an average or large bill, but fifteen per cent should be given on a small one.

France

Most hotels and restaurants add a service charge of from ten to fifteen per cent to your bill. This is supposed to cover all tips. Actually most of those who serve you will expect a bit more and will not hesitate to ask for it. But if a service charge has been added to the bill you will be able to satisfy them with a small addition. If it has not been added, tip as you would elsewhere—from ten to fifteen per cent of your bill. If there is a service charge on the bill you will be expected to tip the wine waiter (about Frs. 100), and in hotels the concierge, if you have used his services.

It is also good policy to tip the hotel telephone operator when you enter the hotel. If you do not, you may find that the outgoing lines are frequently all busy when you want to make a call.

Others who will expect tips are

Taxi drivers—about fifteen per cent of the bill and not less than thirty francs.

At theaters the box office attendant who exchanges your reservation slip for tickets will expect twenty francs for each ticket, the usher at a theater or a cinema will expect fifty francs for each person in your party.

Tip the attendant in a washroom at least thirty francs, and the hat check attendant about fifty.

Porters at railway stations are customarily tipped about fifty francs for each suitcase, but expect twice that from passengers on boat trains.

Guides on sight-seeing buses expect tips of about a hundred francs, those at museums and châteaux about fifty.

(Western) Germany

Ten to fifteen per cent is added to your bill for service. Nothing in addition is expected save by the baggage porter.

Greece

A service charge of fifteen per cent is added to hotel bills, but it is customary to give a small tip to maids and other attendants in addition to this. Fifteen per cent is also added to meal checks in restaurants, but the waiter will expect you to give him about five per cent more and his helper will also expect a small tip.

Holland

Most hotels add fifteen per cent to your bill for an overnight stay, ten per cent if you stay longer. Restaurants also usually add a service charge to your check. If this is not done, tip about fifteen per cent.

Ireland

Hotel and restaurant staffs in Ireland expect about ten per cent of your bill as a tip. Sometimes it is included in your bill, sometimes not.

Italy

Most hotels, *pensiones,* and restaurants add a service charge of fifteen per cent (in Rome, eighteen per cent) as well as a required tax to your bill. However, most waiters, especially in the better restaurants, expect a tip of about five per cent from you in addition to that included in your bill. If no service charge is added, tip about fifteen per cent. In restaurants where there is music an extra charge may be added, or if not, the hat is usually passed and you will be expected to contribute fifty or a hundred lire to the musicians (100 l. = 16 cts.).

In taxis there is an additional charge for each passenger and each piece of luggage, and a flat charge of 150 lire added to the fare after 10 P.M. The driver will expect a tip of about ten per cent.

Norway

A service charge of ten to fifteen per cent is usually added to hotel bills and meal checks, but at restaurants it is customary to leave about five per cent more even if the charge is added.

Portugal

Hotels add a service charge of ten per cent to the bill, and in tourist centers a tourist tax of three per cent A service charge of ten per cent is also added to meal checks, but you are expected to leave the small change behind you for the waiter.

Spain

Hotels add a service charge of fifteen per cent, and no further tipping is expected unless special services have been rendered. Fifteen per cent is also added to meal checks, but here, as in Portugal, it is customary to give the waiter also the small change.

Sweden

A service charge of fifteen per cent is added to hotel bills. No other tips are expected save by the head porter in case special service is rendered You also pay a fixed charge to the porters who carry your luggage when you leave. Ten per cent is added to all restaurant checks, but it is customary to add up to five per cent to this for the waiter.

Switzerland

Twelve or fifteen per cent is added to your bill, depending upon the length of your stay.

Turkey

Hotels add a service charge of ten or fifteen per cent, depending upon the class.

In General

Whether you like it or not, the custom of tipping is well established throughout the world. Because of this, servants who customarily receive tips are traditionally paid low wages, and without their gratuities, would fare very badly indeed. If you are one of the few who wage a private war against the practice of tipping in the United States, by refusing to follow it or by tipping much less than is customary, leave your war behind you when you go abroad. In America you are judged only as an individual, in Europe, Americans as a whole will, to some extent, be judged by your individual conduct. Learn the tipping customs wherever you are and follow them.

Remember that in most continental cities, cinema and theater ushers expect a small tip when they seat you, though this is not true in England. Find out the custom before you attend a theater and follow it.

You will find official or nonofficial guides in many places of especial interest to tourists throughout Europe—museums, ruins, famous churches, palace grounds, and the like. Before engaging one, ask what his charge will be. In some places there are fixed charges, in others not. If there is a fixed charge and the guide has been especially helpful, pay him the charge, plus about ten per cent. If there is no fixed charge and he tells you to pay whatever you wish (as he may do), you must let your conscience and your estimate of his value guide you. Some guides are egregious frauds, some well informed, intelligent, conscientious men who will add greatly to your understanding of the places you see and your pleasure in seeing them. In general if you consider that their time is worth something like the equivalent of three dollars an hour and pay them on that scale, you will have done at least as much as they expect of you, and probably a bit more

In some places, such as the Roman Forum, you will find guards who are not, strictly speaking, guides at all. If one of them goes out of his way to point out something of especial interest when you are in his vicinity, give him a small tip—say the equivalent of twenty-five or fifty cents, and you will probably make him very happy and increase his friendliness to all Americans.

SOME MISCELLANEOUS OBSERVATIONS

"Sir" and "Madam"

Throughout Europe you will find certain forms of courtesy much more widely observed than in the United States. Here it is customary to go into a shop and ask for what we want with no personal greeting whatever to the one who waits on us. In England and on the Continent the customer who does not precede his request with a "good morning" or "good afternoon" is considered, at the very least, to be in bad temper. Here a short "yes" or "no" is not unusual, on the continent of Europe, especially in the Latin countries, not to follow the monosyllable with the equivalent of "sir" or "madam" is considered rude. It is important for you to know these equivalents and to use them.

Queueing

In some places, especially in England, you will find the custom of queueing followed with an almost religious respect for order and precedence. People queue at bus stops, at cinemas, at railroad ticket (or as they call them "booking") offices, and at stores when necessary. If you find yourself in such a situation take your place at the end of the queue and do not tread on the heels of the person in front of you. No one will try to step in front of you if there is a little space there If you find a queue blocking your way across a passage, you have only to say, "Excuse me, may I go through?" and an opening will be made for you at once.

Shopping

When shopping on the Continent, always ask for a bill to attach to your customs declaration when reentering the United States. If a storekeeper or clerk offers to make the bill for a lesser amount than you have actually paid for the articles you have bought in order to reduce the amount of your duty, say, "Thank you, but I'd rather not," and do not yourself ever suggest this. If the one of whom you request this happens to be honest, you will have caused a difficult situation and lowered by a little bit the reputation of Americans for honesty. There is also a practical reason for avoiding this practice. The U.S. Customs pay informers a percentage of penalties charged when false declarations are made. Sometimes these informers are the very persons who have sold the goods which have been declared falsely.

Cinemas

In some places on the Continent you will find that, unlike the custom in the United States, latecomers to cinemas are not permitted to stay and see the next show. Find out what the custom is, and if all patrons are required to leave the theater at the end of each show, make sure that you are on time.

Smoking at Table

Throughout Europe customs connected with smoking at table vary. In England, for instance, it is considered very bad manners at a public dinner to smoke before the "Queen's toast." Wherever you are, to be on the safe side do not smoke between courses. The best plan is to wait for the hostess or host to offer cigarettes or cigars.

The Seating of Women

On the continent of Europe, save in Scandinavia, a lady is always seated at the right of a gentleman. An exception is made when, in a theater, this would seat the lady next to the aisle. In the Scandinavian countries the lady is placed at the gentleman's left, "the heart side"

The same rules are followed when a gentleman walks with a lady.

Language Again

Do not assume, because you are in a country that speaks some language other than English that no one about you can understand what you are saying if you are speaking your own language. Making personal remarks about the people you see on the street, on buses, or in streetcars is rude, regardless of a real or imagined language barrier.

I remember a story told me by a boy who had been in service in Italy during the war. He was a good boy, well educated and with manners which would pass muster anywhere under ordinary circumstances But sometimes even the habits of a lifetime may be forgotten under stress, especially when one is away from his accustomed environment.

He and one of his friends on leave were traveling on a bus which, by chance, had only one other passenger, a beautiful young Italian woman whom both the boys admired, and about whom they began to talk to each other. I did not ask what they had said—I was afraid that he might tell me. In any case I am sure that everything they said was complimentary, sprightly, and probably a little off color. As they saw that the young woman seemed to be paying no attention and apparently did not understand what they were saying, they became bolder.

Finally the bus stopped and the woman rose to leave. As she passed them she smiled and said in perfect English, with only a slight accent, "Really you boys should learn Italian. Men say things like that rather more beautifully here," and left them speechless and chagrined

Another friend has told me of an experience of his, in which there was no possible offense, but which was amusing. In Paris he went with a friend into a little restaurant for breakfast, and in halting French asked for "œufs, jambon, croissant, et café." The waiter filled his order in silence. The next morning, having found his breakfast of the day before excellent, he went with the same friend to the same place The waiter immediately came to their table smiling, and before either had a chance to speak, asked pleasantly, "Ham and eggs this morning, gentlemen?"

You will find more people able to understand and speak English in Europe than you may have imagined. Compliment them by using their language as much as you can, but do not risk offense by saying something in English which may be unpleasant and understood by the one standing next to you.

If You Are a Woman

Among the charms that rather especially, I think, characterize wholesome young American women are independence, forthrightness, and a lack of stuffy conventionality for its own sake. We glory in our sense of freedom, in friendliness and expressions of it, in modifying styles by the dictates of our own taste, and in mixing common sense with our consideration of formal rules of behavior.

I do not for a moment believe that young American women are wantons, or that Americans as a whole are typically boors, as some Europeans who have had unhappy experiences charge, or that we take pleasure in flaunting the conventions of the countries which we visit. I do think, though, that we are often misunderstood because we tend to be thoughtless, feeling that what would not be considered an impropriety at home will, because of that, be proper wherever we are, and thus we often give false impressions based on misinterpretations.

Many such misunderstandings could be avoided if we took the pains to inform ourselves more thoroughly about the conventions of the countries which we visit, and conducted ourselves in accordance with them. This is particularly important for women traveling in the Latin countries, if they do not wish to be considered not quite ladies and to be treated accordingly.

Here are some hints that may be useful.

Dress conservatively. Bare legs, skirts which are a bit shorter than the current mode, tightly fitting sweaters may be hailed with glee and misunderstanding by the roving eyes of romantic Latin men.

Do not go alone or even with another woman and without a man into a bar and order a drink; to do so will almost certainly be interpreted as a bid for male attention

Be circumspect to the point of seeming to be unconscious of all around you when alone in a group of strangers. In America you might find yourself in a circumstance in which you could share an amusing unexpected episode with a decent-looking man you had never seen before by a look or a smile, without misunderstanding. In the Latin countries such an occurrence would almost certainly mark you as one who might be inviting more intimate attention.

Do not, if you can avoid it, go out in the evening without a male escort, or at least one or two other women with you. If you do you are almost sure to have unwelcome male attention. If you must do so, take a taxi from door to door both ways. Do not go alone to the movies. If you do you may learn that they are a happy hunting ground for romantic males.

Not many American women wear anklets, though some do without reproach. If you happen to own one, leave it at home. If you were to wear it in a Latin country it could cause a serious misunderstanding of your character in the mind of a man on the prowl.

Remember that it is good form for all Latin men to compliment women when they meet them with extravagant and romantic sounding praise. Accept it graciously and without taking offense when you are introduced to men, but don't take it seriously. Actually they are just following a Latin custom of making social gatherings more sprightly than they are in other countries, and expressing something of the special regard all Latins have for all women. A man's extravagant language under these circumstances does not mean that he has fallen in love with you at first sight.

If You Are a Man

Enter the Latin game of paying compliments to the mature women you meet, if you can do it graciously, but be careful about paying attention to unmarried women, for you may easily give the impression that your interest is more than casual, whether with honorable or dishonorable intentions.

IN THE EAST

When I traveled in the East in 1952, as a result of an invitation from Prime Minister Nehru to visit India, I came back deeply impressed by the warm-hearted welcome I had been given by peoples who had come to distrust foreigners, and especially nationals of the great powers of the West. Through bitter experience they have learned to look in the mouth gift horses in the form of aid grants. They know that they need help if they are to accomplish the reforms that are necessary to a better ordering of life for their millions, many of whom are underfed, underclothed, underhoused, frequently the wholesale victims of epidemics, and without proper educational facilities. Yet they do not want sheer charity, and they especially resent the feeling that we are offering them help believing that they are inferior and that, as a condition of our help, we wish to interfere in their affairs. With one eye on Communism and another on Democracy they are wondering under which banner they will find the greatest independence and the greatest amount of freedom.

Under such circumstances I found that an American traveling in the East had a particularly pressing obligation and was faced by an extremely delicate task. He must be meticulously careful not to give offense in small ways, even through inadvertence, and he must be always ready to answer questions honestly and intelligently, in an effort to leave those whom he meets with a little greater faith in the goodwill of America than they had before he came.

Throughout the East the tradition of hospitality is deep and strong. I remember vividly the home of a Syrian tile worker which I visited in Damascus. The home was neatly but scantly furnished. Everything spoke of dignified poverty. The man himself, when I questioned him, told me how hard it was for him to support his family, and that in order to do so even minimally he had to hold two jobs. Yet in spite of his poverty and his dissatisfaction with a world in which he of the East had so little, and we of the West had so much, he insisted upon serving me with coffee before I left.

I learned that wherever you go in the Arab world you are served coffee, very hot, very black, and very strong, that you must drink it unless you are willing to offend your host, and that as soon as you empty your cup it will be refilled—and that this process will be continued until, before setting your empty cup down on the tray, you give it a little shake, the Arab signal which says, "Thank you, I have had enough."

I learned how ever-present, and how all-pervasive, is religion to a Moslem. The ancient policy of exterminating nonbelievers has long since passed out of Mohammedanism, and Moslems have become tolerant of those who follow other religions. Yet Islam, to a Moslem, is a part of every act of his life, and one who by the least intimation seems to belittle or even ignore it, belittles the whole of Moslem life. It is a part of their hospitality, of their business, of their human relationships, and of their politics. As the Communists have made politics a religion, so in Islam has a religion become the warp and woof of political life. The Moslem will forgive your ignorance of formal details of etiquette, and inform you of them in a friendly spirit of helpfulness, he will not look kindly on anything remotely intimating derogation of his religion.

I became poignantly aware of some of the bases of anti-American feeling in India when a group of students of the university at Allahabad issued an open letter in which they charged me, and Americans in general, with intervening in affairs that were India's own domestic concern, imperialistic "scheming" in which we used "bread as a weapon of interference in internal politics of other countries," "indulging in slander and abuse of personalities and ideologies," which we do not like, "disregard even for elementary courtesy by the highest representative of Wall Street," and arrogance in trying to teach others what is good and bad.

Over the protests of Madam Pandit, who was my hostess, I talked to the students, first to a delegation of ten of them, then to a crowd in the street, and finally to a large audience in the jammed students' hall. At the first meeting I took this prepared list of sixteen penetrating questions concerning America's antagonism to Communism, self-determination, the negation of small-nation neutrality by armed help from the great powers, unemployment in the United States, American color prejudice and racial discrimination, the question of admission of Communist China to the United Nations, the position of Communists in the United States, and similar matters, and answered honestly that though much of their conception of America was based on fact, the total of it was at best a half truth and inspired by Communist propaganda, but it was my task to correct their misconceptions as much as I could, hoping that a clear picture of America would stimulate greater friendliness.

I think that, to some extent, I succeeded. At least when I thanked them at the final meeting I was warmly applauded, and left the hall with an apparent feeling of amity on both sides.

I learned that in a land where, as in India, there is such widespread and extreme poverty, ostentatious display, wastefulness, and a seeming disregard for money are in the worst of taste, and thus discourteous. I am sure that one of the secrets of Gandhi's tremendous influence over the people of India lay in the fact that he gave up a large income as a lawyer and embraced the austere life of the millions of poverty-stricken people in his country.

The greatest courtesy that can be paid to these people of the East is a willingness to understand, finding a way somehow to equate

yourself with them, and make them see that, in spite of the differences in economic circumstance which mark the East and the West,
we have respect for their ancient culture, for the wisdom of their
great men, and for their aspirations, and that our desire to help them
is dictated by much more than narrow self-interest.

The little things matter too, of course, but less, and in these
there will always be someone to instruct you as to what is the proper
procedure. At the Khyber Pass a group of Afridis tribesmen, to my
consternation, presented me with three live sheep. I was at a loss,
until my escort told me that I need only make the gesture of accepting them and thanking their donors, whereupon the sheep would
later be killed and eaten in my honor. Here, too, I was asked to
break a piece of bread off a large loaf, salt it, and eat it, in demon-
stration of the fact that I was a safe and honored guest. I learned to
make the Indian sign of friendly greeting by putting the palms of
my two hands together before me—a welcome relief for my own right
hand and a gesture that pleased those whom I met.

During the war our soldiers in the East learned to remove their
shoes before entering a Japanese home, a Moslem mosque, or a
Buddhist temple, and to sit cross-legged before squat tables at many
oriental meals, eating with oriental implements, which often were
the fingers.

These and many details like them may, and should be, learned
by the American traveling in the East. But more important than any
of them is the attitude which he takes with him, his willingness to
give of himself and of his friendliness, showing that this is the feeling of the vast majority of American people, his ability to demonstrate
that democracy is not merely an empty catchword to cover imperialistic exploitation, and that the ideal of freedom and good will to all
is deep within the heart of the American dream.

16

Tipping in America and at Sea

THE MATTER OF TIPPING IN THE UNITED STATES REQUIRES thought and care. Some people object to it on principle; others overtip, and give offense by tipping the wrong people. It is a moot point whether the custom of tipping is a good one or a bad one. The fact is that it is a universal custom, and that the wages of those whom one customarily tips are usually very low in view of their expectation of a considerable amount in gratuities. In effect there is almost an unwritten agreement to which the employer, the employee, and the public are parties. It is as though the employee agreed to work for a very low salary (in some cases actually none at all) because the public has agreed to make up the difference between it and what it should be. You have an obligation to fulfill your part of the public's responsibility. To do so properly, inform yourself as to the customs that obtain in various places and in regard to different kinds of employees, and follow them.

Those Who Expect Tips

In general, they are those who give you personal service, though employed by someone else, but there are exceptions. In the

United States you tip railroad station and train porters, waiters, doormen if they render you a service, beauty parlor attendants, barbers, bartenders, taxi drivers, page boys in hotels, telegram delivery boys (though this is not compulsory), washroom attendants in public places, and a few others.

You do not tip theater ushers, service men who repair your television set, radio, or plumbing, employees of any airline, salesmen or salesladies, or the employees of a private club, who are remembered at Christmas by the members. If you are a guest at a golf club, however, you should tip the locker-room attendant

Generally speaking you do not tip the owner of any establishment, such as the proprietor of a small restaurant, even though he may personally supervise the service and perhaps even bring you a meal himself.

You may have read elsewhere that you are not expected to tip the proprietor of a barber shop, who may usually be recognized by the fact that he presides over the first chair Men whom I have consulted about this, however, tell me that though they have heard this advice repeated over and over all their lives, in actual fact the proprietor of a small barber shop probably expects a tip just as any of his barbers does, and will appreciate it if he receives it

The rule prohibiting tipping him was doubtless based on false reasoning, something like this: you tip only your inferiors, the proprietor of a shop is, because of this, your equal, therefore you do not tip him.

This is, of course, reasoning based on a false premise. Tipping does not intimate inequality, or confer an inferior status on the person tipped It is simply a part of a world-wide system of paying certain groups of workers, thus the gratuities become a part of their wages which you, who use their services, are expected to pay To refrain from tipping the head barber is to intimate that the other barbers in the shop, whom you do tip, are inferior—an influence repugnant to the social philosophy of a democratic people.

There are others who belong in no especial category and who thus present a special problem. In approaching it you must feel your way and decide what will be most pleasing to the person concerned, with especial care not to offend. Often a decision is difficult to make.

A friend (whom I shall call William, for convenience) has told me a delightful story of such a case. He keeps a small bachelor apartment in a building that houses a Chinese laundry on the first floor.

For several years the laundryman had taken in parcels that were delivered when William was not at home. When he died the Chinese who took over the business continued the practice.

When Christmas came William was not quite sure what to do. Should he give the Chinese some money (as he always did the mailman and the building superintendent) or would this cause offense? Finally he took one of the Christmas cards which he was sending to his friends, wrote under the Christmas greetings, "and thank you for taking in my packages," put a five-dollar bill with it, put the whole into an envelope which he addressed to the laundryman, stepped into the shop, and handed it to the man. The latter beamed, thanked him, and William went out.

The next day he took some laundry in and found the Chinese ill at ease and uncommunicative. But a day or so later he found a note in his mailbox, signed by the laundryman, and asking him to come in and get his mail. When William went in the Chinese beamed at him and handed him an envelope. "New Year's card!" he said. William opened it, took out a very nice card—and five one-dollar bills! "I do not want pay," the Chinese said. "I'm glad to take your packages." They grinned, shook hands, and now were friends who understood each other somewhat better than they had before.

The schedule below is intended as a guide rather than as a set of inflexible rules Tipping customs vary in different places. Do not withhold the tip because of service which you feel is a little below standard, but only for inexcusable insolence or negligence on the part of the person serving you. On the other hand, if the service is extra good, or if you have asked for and received special attention, add a bit to the usual amount.

Doorman

Nothing on arrival at the hotel if he merely opens the cab door and summons a bellboy. If he carries heavy luggage into the hotel for you, twenty-five cents for each trip If he summons a cab for you in front of the hotel, twenty-five cents. If he must go into the street in the rain to find one for you, more, depending upon how difficult it has been for him.

Bellboy

For carrying your bag to your room, opening the windows, seeing that the heat is correct, etc, twenty-five to fifty cents if he can bring all your luggage in one trip. More if he must make two or more trips. For bringing a telegram, a paper, or a small package to your room, twenty-five cents More for larger packages.

Chambermaid

Nothing for a single night, unless she has given you some special service. For a longer stay about ten per cent of your bill. Hand it to her, or put it on the dresser when you leave.

Room Waiters

About fifteen per cent of each check. You may give it in cash or enter it on your check which you sign. Do not tip less than twenty-five cents for each person. In a very expensive hotel the waiter will expect more—perhaps forty or fifty cents per person. If you are staying in the hotel as a resident for several months and have used room service repeatedly, the head room waiter will expect to be remembered periodically with a tip of five to ten dollars every four or six months.

Valet

If the valet himself calls for and delivers your clothes, no tip is usually expected If you ask a bellboy to take your clothing to him, tip the bellboy a quarter.

Dining Room

As in a restaurant tip about fifteen per cent of your check. If you are making a long stay tip the headwaiter from three to five dollars every month in an expensive hotel, or about half of that in a medium-priced one.

Do not tip room clerks or managers. If you are a permanent resident a Christmas present is in order.

Taxi

About fifteen per cent of the bill. Never less than ten cents. Indeed in large cities today most drivers will be disappointed if you give them a minimum of less than fifteen cents. Very late at night, or when there are many people in the cab, or when you have taken a driver far out of the way where he is not likely to get a fare on the way back, increase the tip somewhat. Also do this if you have asked him to make an especially speedy trip (but do not ask him to exceed the speed limit).

IN A RESTAURANT

Doorman

No tip on arrival. Twenty-five cents if he calls a cab for you from in front of the restaurant, more if he goes into the street and finds one for you. If you have arrived in your own car and he parks it for you and gets it for you when you leave, fifty cents.

Rest Room Attendant

Fifteen or twenty-five cents if no extra service is given. More if you have been given unusual help.

Wine Steward

Ten per cent of wine bill if he serves.

Hat Check Girl

Fifteen cents in a medium-priced restaurant (even if she has placed a decoy quarter on her tray), twenty-five in an expensive one.

Bartender

Fifteen per cent of the bill.

Headwaiter

No tip necessary unless he has given special service, such as finding you an especially good table, or having reserved a table for you. Then two dollars in an average restaurant, five in a very expensive one.

At a Lunch Counter

The old custom of no tipping has passed Most lunch counter attendants now expect a tip of about ten per cent of the check, with a minimum of ten cents.

At a Cafeteria

Tipping not customary, but if you feel very generous you will make the man who clears the table happy by leaving him ten or twenty-five cents.

IN A RAILROAD STATION

Redcaps

In many stations now the fee for redcap service is fixed, usually at fifteen cents for each bag If there is no fixed charge tip at about this rate, with more if the bags are unusually heavy, or if he has had a long wait. In either of the latter events, give him a little extra even if there is a fixed fee.

Baggage Checkrooms

In most metropolitan stations there are now coin-operated checking lockers If you are going to leave your baggage less than twenty-four hours, it is quicker and more convenient to use one of these. If not, and you use the attended checkroom, pay the regular fee. No tip is necessary. If the ticket agent in a small country station where there are neither lockers nor checkroom allows you to leave your luggage in his office, you may or may not be expected to pay him. The courteous thing to do, if nothing has been said about it when you leave your bags, is to ask him when you retrieve them what you owe him, rather than simply to offer him money. If he says, "Nothing at all," simply thank him, and let it go at that.

If you check your bags to go on the train, no tip is expected by the baggage handlers.

ON A PULLMAN TRAIN

Pullman Porter

If a day trip, twenty-five or fifty cents, depending on the distance, unless he has given you extra service—then more. For an overnight trip. in a roomette, a dollar to a dollar and a half, in a drawing room, two dollars. For longer trips it is not necessary to multiply these amounts by the number of nights you travel. Two to three dollars is enough for a three-night trip in a compartment; five dollars for three nights in a drawing room. These tips of course should be increased for special service If, for instance, you are sending a child on a trip alone and ask the porter to look after him, give the porter an extra dollar.

Dining Car Attendants

Tip as you would in a first-class restaurant.

ON A PLANE

Stewardess

Do not tip. In fact never tip anyone in the uniform of the airline.

Baggage Porters

No tip is required, but the men in the baggage enclosure will not refuse a quarter, and may find your bag more quickly if you produce this gratuity when asking for it The men who carry your bags from the cab or limousine to the scales when you check in will expect a tip—about the same as redcaps in stations, that is, fifteen cents a bag.

ON SHIPBOARD

There are two classes of workers to be tipped on board a ship —those who give you regular service under all circumstances, whom you tip at the end of the voyage, and those who give you special services, whom you tip either at the time they are given or at the end of the voyage. In the latter class are bellhops, cabin waiters, bartenders and bar stewards, wine stewards, baggage room attendants if you ask them for any help, and attendants in special rooms. In the former are the cabin steward, the deck steward, the dining steward (that is, your waiter), the cabin stewardess, and the bath steward —if your cabin does not have its own bath

For the last group the proper procedure is to allocate ten per cent of the cost of your ticket to be divided among the group, about as follows:

Cabin Steward

Thirty per cent of amount allowed for tipping, ten per cent more if your room has a private bath

Deck Steward

Fifteen to twenty per cent of total tipping amount.

Dining Steward

Thirty per cent.

Bath Steward

Ten per cent of total amount, if used.

Stewardess

Ten per cent.

In addition to these the following should be tipped:

Bellhop

Fifteen to twenty-five cents each time he does something for you.

Cabin Waiter

Fifteen to twenty per cent of check at the time of service.

Bartender or Bar Steward

Fifteen to twenty per cent of bar check This may be paid each time you have service, or accumulated and paid at the end of the voyage.

Wine Steward

Ten per cent of wine bill. If wine is an occasional addition to your meal, pay him when you have it. Otherwise, pay him at the end of your voyage.

Special Attendants

If you have a child who has been left with the attendant in the playroom a great deal, or you have used the swimming pool regularly, it is courteous to give the children's room attendant and/or the bathing pool attendant from one to five dollars, but it is not essential to do so.

Never tip the purser or other ship's officers, or the ship's doctor. If you have used the doctor and he has sent you no bill, send him about what you would have expected to pay your own doctor at home.

Suggestions for tipping abroad will be found in Chapter 15.

V

SPECIAL EVENTS

17

Welcoming the New Arrival

THE BIRTH ANNOUNCEMENT

WHEN A BABY IS BORN IT IS CUSTOMARY TO SEND AN announcement of the event to friends and relatives. The card should be simple and dignified. A form that has been approved by long usage consists of a small white card about 1″ × 1¾″ with the baby's name and birth date engraved or printed on it in black, tied with pink (for a girl) or blue (for a boy) ribbon through small punch holes to the upper edge of the joint card of the parents, or the card of the mother.

There are also of course ready-printed commercial cards available with a space left in which to write the baby's name, the birth date, and sometimes other data, such as the weight. There is no reason why you shouldn't use these if you wish, so long as you choose dignified and simple cards. But avoid the elaborate ones, and especially those that are lavishly decorated. The worst of all are those that bear printed messages supposedly from the baby or the stork. The helpless infant deserves to be announced with dignity and taste. These are best reflected by using simply the names of the parents, the name of the baby, and the date of his birth.

THE GODPARENTS

Before the child is formally given its name (at a christening in most Christian families, at the *brit milah* in Jewish families if the child is a boy) friends are usually asked to serve as godparents. This practice varies somewhat in different denominations. In some churches (notably the Baptist) baptism is not administered until the child is old enough to understand its significance, and in such cases there are frequently no godparents, though sometimes they are chosen, even when, in the usual sense, there is no christening at birth.

Those who are asked to sponsor the child should be carefully chosen. They should be close friends whose interest in the child may be taken for granted. They should be of the same religious faith—not necessarily of the same denomination if Protestant, though this is desirable if the parents adhere strictly to the tenets that distinguish their church from others. But a Protestant family should select Protestant godparents, Roman Catholic, Roman Catholic, and Jewish, Jewish. The Roman Catholic Church forbids its members to act as godparents to the children of any other faith, or to select godparents of another faith for their children. Even without such a prohibition common sense would dictate choosing godparents with an understanding of, and sympathy for, the religion of the parents, for the godparents are traditionally spiritual sponsors of the child, supposedly act as an example for and a leader in his spiritual education, and assume responsibility for him, if necessary, in case of the parents' deaths. There are exceptional cases however in which this rule is not followed.

A Protestant child usually has two godmothers and one godfather if a girl, and two godfathers and one godmother if a boy (as required in the Book of Common Prayer of the Church of England), but in most denominations the number is not rigidly fixed. More may be chosen, or there may be one godparent only.

A Catholic child is expected by the Church to have one godparent, preferably of the same sex as the child, but may have one of each sex if desired.

A Jewish child of either sex may have godparents, though among orthodox Jews it is customary for only male children to have one—a godfather (or *Sandek*) who takes part in the ritual circumcision and naming of the child. If the parents wish, there may be more, though if there are, they do not have to attend the *brit milah*—the ritual circumcision and dedication of the male child to God.

Asking the Godparents to Serve

Since only close friends or relatives are ever asked to serve as godparents, any formality in the request that they serve is out of place. (A close friend, incidentally, is preferable to a relative, since one of the purposes in naming godparents is to increase the child's "family.") The request should be made immediately after the child's birth so that the godparents will have plenty of time to make arrangements for attending the christening ceremony. They may be asked by phone, telegram, or letter, but in any case the request should never be put into the language of a formal invitation. If a note, it should be something like this: "Dear Cecil Our son, Allen, was born yesterday. Will you be godfather? Best. Helen and Bill." If you are Protestants, it would be considerate, especially should your friend live at a distance, to point out that while you hope he can be present at the christening, if he cannot do so, he may be represented by a proxy, which is permitted by the Protestant Church. You should be quite sure before you ask anyone to serve in this responsible capacity that he will welcome your request, for it is difficult to refuse, and you would cause acute embarrassment if your friend felt that he must say no.

The Godparent's Gift

Traditionally the godparent gives his godchild a substantial christening present (and later remembers him at Christmas and on his birthdays). The christening present, usually of silver, should be one that may be passed on and become a family heirloom, such as a drinking cup or a silver fork and spoon. If it is a cup or something else on which there is room, it may be engraved like this:

Allen Lewis Richards
June 20, 19——
From his godfather
Cecil Graham

THE CHRISTENING AND BRIT MILAH

The Significance of Baptism

The seriousness with which devout Christians regard baptism, the sacramental rite which admits a candidate to membership in the church, is attested by the long and thoughtful discussions that have been an important part of Christian literature for nearly two thousand years, by differences of opinion as to the origin and importance of the ceremony, and by the different times and methods chosen for administering it, each seeming the essential and proper way to those who adhere to it.

But whatever the form, all orthodox Christians have throughout history attached the highest importance to the ritual and believe that, in carrying it out, they are obeying the command of Jesus Christ. Christian writers have found parallels to the ritual in the circumcision rite which dedicates a Jewish child to the service of God, and the initiation rites of the mystery religions.

Throughout the centuries there have been various interpretations of its meaning. In general these are still current in some degree throughout Christendom. It is in various conceptions one or more of the following: (1) a symbolical death and resurrection of the one baptized, through which he shares in the Resurrection of Jesus and thus is able to enter the Kingdom of God, (2) a simple symbolical purification, (3) a specific process of purification that removes the stain of original sin which, unremoved, bars even the newly born child from the Kingdom of Heaven, (4) a process of marking the soul of the baptized as the property of the Holy Trinity, (5) a process by which is conferred habitual grace and the virtues and gifts of the Holy Ghost, (6) a promise of divine grace, by which the baptized is cleansed of guilt for former sins, (7) a simple symbolic ceremony commemorative of the baptism of Jesus Christ, and signifying the dedication of the baptized to his service, and (8) a declaration of union with Christ whose spirit is enabled by this purification ceremony to enter the soul of the baptized

In most Protestant churches the doctrine of original sin has lost most of its importance, and there are probably few intelligent Protestants who believe that their infants were sinful at birth and that the sin has been removed from them by baptism, or that without baptism salvation is impossible.

The doctrine is still, however, a basic tenet of Roman Catholic dogma, in accordance with which a child who dies unbaptized is barred from the Kingdom of Heaven. We are born, according to this doctrine, in a state of spiritual death, the rite of baptism confers spiritual life, removes the stain of original sin, marks the baptized with the sign of Christ, and allows the grace of God to flow freely into his soul.

But though baptism is considered essential to salvation by Catholics, the Church holds that there are exceptional cases in which it may be achieved without the formal ritual. In cases of emergency, in which an unbaptized infant, or for that matter an adult, is known to be dying, anyone—Catholic, Protestant, or unbeliever—may administer the rite simply by pouring water over the forehead and saying, "I baptize thee in the name of the Father, and of the Son, and of the Holy Spirit." But even without this simple rite it is possible for one to receive what is known as the "baptism of desire" This means that one who longs for baptism, but for some reason has not been able to receive it, and who attempts in all ways to obey the will of God receives grace by virtue of his desire.

In the Protestant Church, baptism is regarded somewhat more simply. During the time of Paul it was instituted as a signification of a union with Christ as a prerequisite to joining the church. After the ritual the baptized could say with conviction that he now had within him the presence of Christ, the very Spirit of God. The natural man ("the old man," as Paul called him) had now given place to the spiritual man. Man had been "born again."

This is still the general significance of the ritual in Protestant practice The anointing of the head with water, or the immersion of the candidate, symbolizes purification or drowning or both, the death of the unclean, and the resurrection of the pure.

The importance of the baptismal rite varies in different denominations and in the minds of different individuals within the same denomination. Some parents, even in denominations that practice infant baptism (as most do), feel that the choice to be baptized or not to be baptized should be left to the child himself, and so do nothing about it in his infancy, waiting until he has reached an age in which he may decide whether or not he wishes to have the rite administered.

Others, especially in denominations that practice confirmation, feel that they owe it to their children to see that they are baptized in infancy, for without baptism they cannot be confirmed, and without confirmation (in some churches) they cannot partake of communion, become full members of the church, or be married within the church.

The Significance of *Brit Milah*

The Jewish rite of *brit milah*, at which the male child is circumcised, named, and dedicated to the service of God, is of course much older than that of Christian baptism and christening, for it was instituted centuries before the birth of Christianity. When on the Plains of Mamre Abram had a revelation in which he heard God say to him, "I am the Lord that brought thee out of Ur of the Chaldees, to give thee this land to inherit it," he accepted the statement as a promise. The promise was later ratified in a covenant between God and Abram by which Abram was to become the leader of a new nation chosen by God to be of universal service to mankind.

The story is told in the seventeenth chapter of Genesis, and the two significant events that took place then, both as signs of the holy covenant, are reenacted at every Jewish male child's *brit milah* today. He whose name had been Abram was given a new name by God, Abraham, which means "the father of a multitude." Father, God said to Abraham,

And ye shall circumcise the flesh of your foreskin; and it shall be a token of the covenant betwixt me and you. And he that is eight days old shall be circumcised among you. . . . And the uncircumcised man child . . . shall be cut off from his people, he hath broken my covenant.

Two things, then, are obvious (1) that the christening of a Christian child and the *brit milah* of a Jewish boy have several common significances—each attends the giving of a name to the child, in itself a matter that has a sacred significance (a Catholic child must be given the name of a saint, many Jewish male children are given the names of Old Testament patriarchs), for the Jewish child the ceremony ratifies as it were his covenant with God, for the Christian child it establishes a union with Christ; in the case of the Jewish child the uncircumcised is cut off from the benefits of his nation's covenant with God, in the case of the Christian child of some denominations he is barred from the Kingdom of Heaven if unbaptized; and (2) that both are solemn religious rituals, and an invitation to take part in either is not to be taken lightly.

The Time of the Ceremony

Among Protestant sects that practice infant baptism there is no set time for the event, but it usually occurs when the child is from two to six months old. In those denominations that withhold the rite until the child has reached an age of understanding and may himself make a confession of faith, it usually does not occur until the age of ten or later, though in special instances may be earlier.

In the Roman Catholic Church and the Church of England the child was always baptized in earlier times on the first or second Sunday after birth. Today the time is less strictly fixed, but the ceremony still takes place when the child is quite young, usually within two months of its birth.

The brit milah always takes place on the eighth day after the child's birth, as established in Genesis, unless the child is ill or weakly and judged by his doctor to be unable to undergo the strain of the ceremony.

The Place

A Protestant christening may be held either at the church or at the home of the child and his parents.

A Catholic christening must always be held in the baptistry of the church, unless the child is *in extremis*, in which case, as has been pointed out, the rite may be performed by anyone in any place.

The brit milah may take place in the home, or in the hospital in which the child is born. Many modern Jewish hospitals have a special room set aside for this purpose.

The Ceremony

Invitations, whether to a Catholic or Protestant christening, or to a Jewish *brit milah* are always informal. Relatives and friends are merely notified by a casual note or a phone call and asked to attend if possible. If there is to be a caudle (see below) afterwards, the guests and of course the clergyman are invited to attend it as a part of the invitation to the christening.

Protestant Christening

If at a church the ceremony often takes place immediately after the Sunday service, those who have been invited to attend staying on after the congregation has left. If a large number of guests have been invited a day during the week is sometimes chosen

In the past it was the custom to dress the infant to be christened somewhat elaborately in a "christening gown," long, always white, and decorated with lace and embroidery. The gown was usually handmade and often an example of exquisite needlework. After the christening the dress was put away and saved to pass on to the next generation. If you have such a dress, used by your mother or father or one of your grandparents, by all means use it, even though it may have become yellowed with age. It is a pretty symbol of continuity in family life, and the custom of passing such gowns on from generation to generation is one worth perpetuating If you have not, modern versions of christening gowns may still be bought, if you like, which are longer and more elaborate than a baby's everyday dress. If you buy one specially for this occasion you may be glad later to have it to hand on for a grandchild's christening. But if you do not wish to, any white dress which the child possesses will do. Nor is it necessary to buy special footwear for the occasion. Our conventions in such matters as these have relaxed a great deal during these post-war years. If it is summer, and you wish it so, the baby may go comfortably barefooted to this ceremony which is peculiarly his own.

Guests at a christening should wear what they customarily do for church attendance. The mother wears a light-colored dress.

The church is decorated simply, if at all, with a few palms or bright flowers. Sometimes at weekday christenings in a large church when few guests have been invited, a row of large palms is set across the width of the church just behind the pews which will hold the guests, and the lighting is arranged to illuminate the enclosed area only and to give an atmosphere of intimacy to the affair.

Whether this is done or not the guests gather in the pews nearest the font. The baby is brought to the church at the last moment (preferably after a relaxing sleep!) so that he will not become restless while he waits for his cue. As soon as the clergyman appears the mother hands the child to the attending godmother (or in some cases the godfather) who stands directly in front of the clergyman with the other godparents beside her. The godmother takes the infant's cloak and cap off, tells the clergyman the given names (the family name is not spoken) of the child, and either herself holds her godchild over the font or, more usually, hands him to the clergyman for the actual ritual of baptism, in which the clergyman speaks the child's name, sprinkles water on his head, and says, "I baptize you in the name of the Father, and of the Son, and of the Holy Ghost [or Holy Spirit]" It is a wise precaution to give the clergyman beforehand a slip of paper on which the child's given names are printed so that he will make no mistake. Strictly speaking, the christened child receives his name from the clergyman at the time of the christening, and whatever name the cleric speaks is officially his.

After the ceremony the godparent hands the child to the mother, the clergyman signs the baptismal certificate and gives it to the parents, and the baby is whisked home for the quiet which, by this time, he needs. The guests follow for the caudle if there is to be one.

A home christening (permitted in Protestant churches) is typically a more intimate affair than one held at church, and certainly more comfortable for the baby, who need not be taken from his usual routine in order to make the trip to and from the church.

The ceremony may take place in the living room, or any other room in the house which is suitable. The room may be decorated with flowers, predominantly white, simply or more profusely, as you like. The font (a silver bowl if you have one or can borrow one, but a glass or pottery bowl may be used) is placed on a high stand over which a cover (not a tablecloth) has been thrown. A room should also be provided in which the clergyman may change from his vestments (if he wears them) into his ordinary clothes after the ceremony. The ceremony itself is the same whether it takes place at home or in the church.

Brit Milah, Pidyon Ha-Ben, and the Naming of Jewish Girls

The ceremony that initiates Jewish boys into the covenant between man and God today usually takes place in the hospital in which the child is born, but may be performed at home. The *brit milah* is one of the most important of Jewish rituals. While the godfather (*sandek*) holds the child (and all the guests, in Orthodox congregations always wearing hats, rise) it is circumcised by a *mohel* —a religious official of the congregation who is especially skilled in this operation. The following blessing is then spoken by the father: "Blessed are you, Lord our God, Master of the Universe, who have made us holy with your commands, and have commanded us to bring this boy into the covenant of Abraham, our father."

Candles are then usually lighted and the child is named, often with the name of a deceased relative, which is frequently that of one of the Old Testament patriarchs

The Pidyon Ha-Ben follows later, when a male child is thirty-one days old, and only if he is the first-born, who, according to Old Testament tradition, must be dedicated to the service of God It is customary today for a *kohen* (a descendant of the priestly tribe) to take over this obligation for the child.

Jewish girls are named in the synagogue on the first Sabbath after birth, and a special blessing is pronounced on them by the rabbi.

Catholic Christening

A Catholic christening is much more elaborate than is that of a Protestant church, and a more solemn occasion The ceremony, always in the baptistry of the church, begins with the priest signing the forehead and heart with the sign of the cross, and the forehead and the organs of sense with the thumb, and putting salt ("the salt of wisdom") upon the tongue, symbolically preserving a taste for the divine. The priest then performs a ritual of exorcism three times, by which the devil is commanded to disappear, and the candidate (through his godfather if he is an infant) makes a confession of faith, reciting the creed and the Lord's Prayer, and in response to questions, renounces the devil

After the priest has anointed the child with the oil of catechumens on the breast and between the shoulders in the form of a cross, the candidate again (through his godfather) makes a declaration of faith in the holy Trinity and asks to be baptized. Then with the godparent holding the infant, the priest pours holy water over his forehead, saying (as in the Protestant church), "I baptize thee in the name of the Father, and of the Son, and of the Holy Spirit." After a further anointment the priest gives the child, now a member of the church, a white garment, admonishing him to carry it without stain or blemish to the judgment seat.

The priest then gives the child a lighted candle, says, "Go in peace, and the Lord go with you," and the ceremony is over.

NAMING THE CHILD

Choosing a name for your child should be a thoughtful process which will take several factors into account: For better or worse the child will carry throughout life the label which you have attached to him, unless in later life he wants to go through the complicated and awkward process of changing it. And by then the period during which his name may play an important part in his psychological development (his childhood) has passed. From this point of view there are good names and bad, the former an asset, the latter a distinct liability to any growing child.

If you wish to give a boy the name of his father, who is John Willis Markham, the boy will of course be "John Willis Markham, Jr." In this you would follow a common practice, but it might be well to consider the possibility of the child's later objections. Will he mind being called merely "Junior" without the rest of his name, as he inevitably will be, or "Young John" or "Little John?" There comes a time in the life of every child when he feels belittled by diminutives. If the father is himself "John Willis Markham, Jr." and you wish to give the child his full name, the name he will use is "John Willis Markham III." If you wish to name him after a grandfather whose name is not borne by the father, the child becomes "John Willis Markham II," never "Jr." (Actually there is no etymological reason for not using "Junior" in this case, for the word "junior" is simply the comparative of the Latin *juvenis*, meaning "young," and thus means merely "younger." It is used in this meaning in other connections, such as "junior member of the firm," "Junior League," etc.; but when used with a name, custom has decreed that it always means that the boy has the same full name as his father) Many parents, who wish to perpetuate the father's given name in the son, but wish to avoid any possible later embarrassment for the son, give the child his own middle name, say "John Henry Markham." Thus he may, if he wishes, later designate himself "J. Henry Markham."

A girl may be named after her mother, but seldom uses "Junior" after her name. The designation is properly reserved for males.

A Catholic child must, by Church law, be given the name of a saint, either as a first name or a middle name. Actually this presents no very great problem for the roster of saints is so large that there is a wide selection.

Give thought to the matter of harmony of sound. If your family name happens to be very long and complicated, do not saddle the helpless infant with two more names equally long and complicated.

Avoid names that may be used for either sex. If you give such a name to a boy, he will be considered a sissy by his grade school comrades, if to a girl, she will be considered overmasculine. As to giving a child of one sex a name that is customarily given only to the other, it is cruel. I know of one woman whose father was so disappointed when his firstborn was a girl instead of a boy that he insisted on naming her "John." The girl, who was told why she had been so named, grew up with a painful sense of inferiority and guilt because she had so disappointed her father, and never married, having, in her twisted emotional reaction, come to feel too masculine to make a good wife.

Names that either of themselves or in combination with the family names may be the material for puns, are also unfortunate. The girl who is called "Delicia" will be constantly embarrassed when she is in her teens by being dubbed "Delicious" by every boy who asks her for a date. Even the boy called "Anson" will undoubtedly be dubbed "Handsome," with ridicule by his fellows. As for combinations, I remember a story, considered quite naughty when I was a child, in which a woman named Helen Hunt, having found a five-dollar bill on the porch of the church, asked the minister to announce it. He did so by saying, "If anyone has lost a five-dollar bill he may go to Helen Hunt for it." You can see the possibilities!

THE CAUDLE

❧ In early days of Christian ritual the baptism was preceded by fasting, and followed by a traditional meal of milk and honey. The milk and honey were later replaced by "caudle," a mixture of wine or ale, with eggs, bread or gruel, sugar and spices.

Today the traditional caudle cup is represented by champagne or champagne punch, sherry, wine, cider, or, in houses that serve no alcoholic drinks, tea or coffee. The caudle takes place at the home after the christening (whether at church or home). If it is a morning ceremony sometimes a light buffet luncheon is served. If it is in the afternoon, the gathering takes on the atmosphere of a tea. In either case there is usually a white cake, sometimes bearing the baby's name. The gathering is friendly and joyous, but quiet. It is, after all, part of a ceremony that is essentially religious, but it is not an essential part of any christening and is as often omitted as not.

18

Debuts

THERE WAS A TIME WHEN A YOUNG AMERICAN GIRL brought up to respect and abide by the conventions of a "socially proper" family was practically hidden from the view of all but the immediate family Until she arrived at a certain age, she was virtually a social prisoner in her own home She was not allowed to attend affairs, certainly not allowed a date with a young male, and, in fact, was not permitted to attend mixed parties. In this Victorian time the day finally arrived when the young girl made her debut, and, indeed, it was a real debut, a "coming out." The affair was usually in the form of a large private ball given either in the home of the parents, or in the private rooms of one of the most fashionable hotels or restaurants. If the family could not afford the sometimes huge expenditure, then a "coming-out tea" was substituted.

Arrangements for such an affair were often put in the hands of a social specialist who engaged the facilities, obtained the orchestras, and in collaboration with the hostess arranged the guest list and sent out the invitations. The rules of etiquette and manners governing the debut were strictly adhered to and any violation was viewed with suspicion by the guests and anguish by the hostess.

During the early years of the present century these private balls gave way more and more to teas and joint presentations in which a number of families would join and the daughters of all would be presented As the old order faded away, and the more formal way of life was replaced by a modern, freer set of standards, the formal debut became less and less frequent and the mass coming-out party grew in importance.

Today, this seems to be the rule in that portion of our society where the debut counts. Usually the presentation to society consists of at least two events—inclusion in a mass debutante ball (if it can be arranged) and a private dinner party or tea, either of which constitutes the actual debut.

Mass cotillions and assemblies have spread throughout the country in the years since World War II and now take place in cities as different in size and character as New York and Texarkana, Arkansas. Over one hundred of these affairs are included on a representative though far from complete list published in 1960

In some cities only one ball is given, in larger centers such as New York, Chicago, Boston, and Philadelphia there are several, and some debutantes may come out at two or three. In addition to the ball, the private dinner or tea is an important complement, and today most young society girls want both.

In order to gain an invitation to one of the top cotillions or assemblies the mother of a prospective debutante submits an application several years before her daughter attains "coming-out" age which is usually eighteen. She gets as many letters of recommendation from persons in favor with the committee as she can.

The size of the balls varies from ten or twelve to fifty or more girls, and each girl is allowed a number of guests. Two male escorts for each girl is considered a minimum. Some of the smaller balls include a dinner for all the debutantes and their guests. Sometimes, dinner parties are held at clubs or fashionable restaurants before the balls for some of the girls who are coming out and their escorts.

At the cotillion every debutante wears a white gown with long white gloves. Each girl enters the ballroom alone and is announced as she enters. She then goes to sit in a chair behind which stands her principal escort in full dress with white gloves. After all of the girls have been announced the dancing starts.

Though the private coming-out ball is comparatively rare today, it has not gone completely out of existence. But it is seldom undertaken unless the parents of the debutante have a large enough house or are willing to underwrite the expense of engaging a large private ballroom and paying for the whole affair. In such a case, there are several forms which may be properly used for the invitations. They should be engraved in script, with the name of the person invited written in, in black ink

Mr. and Mrs. Samuel Hunter
request the pleasure of
Miss Mary Smith's
company at a dance in honor of their daughter
MISS SUSAN HUNTER
Monday the ninth of January
at ten o'clock
Two East Seventy-fifth Street

R s v.p.

Or

Mr. and Mrs Samuel Hunter
Miss Susan Hunter
request the pleasure of
Miss Mary Smith's
company on Monday the ninth of January
at ten o'clock
Two East Seventy-fifth Street

Dancing
R s.v.p.

Or

Mr. and Mrs. Samuel Hunter
request the pleasure of
Miss Mary Smith's
company at a small dance
Monday the ninth of January
at ten o'clock
Two East Seventy-fifth Street

R.s.v.p

At a private ball, the debutante may wear white or a pastel color—faint rose, pale blue, or light yellow. She stands beside the hostess (usually her mother) and receives until all of the guests have arrived. Then she may join in the dancing. The first dance is usually with her father. She goes to supper with an escort of her own choice.

Usually she will have made up a table beforehand at which she will sit with her closest friends. If she does not wish to center attention on any one young man, she may ask her brother or another close male relative to escort her.

The procedure at a debutante tea is much the same It may be given at the parents' home or at a hotel or club If it is held instead of a ball the invitations are usually engraved and may read·

Mrs. Samuel Hunter
Miss Susan Hunter
At Home
on Monday the ninth of January
from four until seven o'clock
Two East Seventy-fifth Street

Dancing
R s v p.

Whether at a tea or an evening party there is always a receiving line that consists of the debutante and her sponsor, usually her mother. The debutante may ask a few friends to receive with her, but these friends do not actually stand in the line with her. They stay in the background and act in an honorary capacity. The father or another close male relative in full dress acts as host, but does not stand in the receiving line Traditionally, the debutante carries a bouquet given by her father Other flowers, customarily sent to her by the men who have been invited, are displayed on a table behind her.

Every young man who has been invited to the party should seek a dance with the debutante, with her mother, and, as far as is possible, with the other older ladies present.

There are a number of other customs which vary locally, so that no set rules can really be given. But generally, the modern-day ball or party is relatively informal, despite the formal dress and the special protocol. Some of the more energetic dances of the day are quite permissible, and the young people present are expected to enjoy themselves in a natural fashion. For those who are contemplating a debut, the more specialized rules of etiquette applying to the particular locale should be followed.

19

Engagements

As in most of our human relations, many of the formal conventions which in the past regulated the conduct of two young people who are planning a common life have relaxed a great deal. There seems to be an increasing determination on the part of a youthful generation to manage their own lives in ways that seem best to them, often regardless of the rules by which their parents' and grandparents' lives were regulated. Perhaps, in some ways, they are wiser than their elders were. Perhaps, in seeking to achieve a greater independence, they have both gained and lost.

Here, as in all things, consideration, integrity, ordinary decency, common sense, and a long-range point of view in which the wise will understand that years of solid happiness are far more precious than any temporary freedom achieved by riding roughshod at breakneck speed over the dictates of intelligence and experience are as important as they ever were

It is obvious that in attempting to set up practical codes for the regulation of human behavior throughout the ages, human beings

have often made mistakes, sometimes because of superficial thinking or a shallow sense of values which gives greater importance to
outward show than to true consideration for others and wisdom.
Some rules that were practical and wise at one time and under one
set of circumstances become useless or even destructive of wholesome happiness in other times and under other circumstances.
What may be wrong for one person, may sometimes under exceptional circumstances be right for another. Life is not by any means
a simple matter, perhaps especially in the relations of men and
women. It is a wise and courageous person who is able to decide, in
the face of a complicated set of circumstances, what course of action will give the greatest happiness and well-being to the largest
number of persons whom his life affects, and to follow that course
regardless of formal rules of behavior which he has read or heard.
"Convention" and "what people will say" must be considered, but
ought never to be allowed to become tyrants that ruin happiness.

Yet we ought always to remember that those accepted rules of
social conduct which have survived are the result of centuries of
human experience and thought, to examine the reasons for them
(which, perhaps more often than young people think offhand, are
sound), and to consider them with a prejudice in their favor. The
wise young person will always be guided by the old saying admonishing us not to throw out the baby with the dirty bath water.

BEFORE THE ENGAGEMENT

In Chapter 27 you will find some general suggestions for
the behavior of young people in their associations with others of the
opposite sex. Here I shall write only of two young people who are
falling, or have fallen, in love with each other.

I do so with some little trepidation. I could write at great length
about what has been considered proper behavior by your parents
and grandparents, but I am quite aware that if I did so in detail
some of the young people of today would think me medieval. Yet the
aims of the old rules are sound. It is of these aims that I shall write.

On Knowing Another

Someone once said that we would be a happier people if
good health rather than disease were contagious, and if things were

so arranged that when one person fell out of love the other would automatically do the same. I agree heartily, and would add another desideratum. I am sure that the number of unhappy marriages and divorces would decrease sharply if only the so common program of falling in love first and then learning to know each other were reversed. There are often physical attractions which will sweep young people off their feet. It is well if they can delay any plans for marriage long enough to be sure that the physical attraction is not the only one that is holding them together.

Even for those who "love at first sight"—who, almost before they have learned each other's names, are whirled upward in that peculiar exaltation which only lovers know—an intelligent and conscious effort will go a long way toward establishing a sound basis for a lasting relationship.

The traditional representation of love as a blindfolded child is only a half truth. I do not intend here to enter into a long discussion of the nature of love—indeed it has many natures, and a single short definition of it is impossible I wish only to say that though the newly born love of a man and a woman for each other seems to provide both with rose-colored glasses through which each can see only the best in the other, it not only stimulates that best, but also, given and received, lays open the heart so that it may be known to the other.

St. Paul, in First Corinthians, did not define love, but he did write of its attributes with a wisdom which I think has never been surpassed

> Love suffereth long, and is kind, love envieth not, love vaunteth not itself, is not puffed up, Doth not behave itself unseemly, seeketh not her own, is not easily provoked, thinketh no evil, Rejoiceth not in iniquity, but rejoiceth in the truth, Beareth all things, believeth all things, hopeth all things, endureth all things Love never faileth.

You may say that he was writing of a kind of love different from that which springs unbidden between a young man and woman, but I am not sure that I would agree. Love has, for want of a better word, many different by-products and many different expressions, each appropriate to the special relationships and the special circumstances in which it occurs, but basically it is the same phenomenon in which an individual gains strength and stature through sharing the life of another or others. When that which passes for love—

whether between a man and a woman, a child and a parent, or friends—has not the attributes which St Paul ascribed to it, it is masquerading under a name which ought not to be given to it.

A child, asked to tell what a friend was, said, "One who knows you and likes you anyway." It is as good a definition as any, and one that would equally describe, if you substitute "love" for "like," two people who may look forward with confidence to the prospects of a successful marriage. Or perhaps one should go a little farther than that, and say that only after a man and woman know each other, and love what they have learned to know, are they ready to plan marriage.

I think that it is impossible for one human being really to know another without first knowing and being at peace with himself If you find yourself spending more and more time with one person of the opposite sex to the exclusion of others your first obligation to him, to yourself, and to all others whose lives are, or in the future are likely to be, affected by your own, is to examine yourself more deeply and more honestly than you ever have done before.

What sort of person is this one who bears your name and who is perhaps falling in love with the one of whom you are seeing so much? Why do you find it so pleasant to be with him? Are the qualities which his presence seems to bring to the forefront of your personality the things which you like most about yourself—or are some of them the things that seem to you to make you less than the person you would like to be? Are you the kind of person who would continue to put your best foot forward with him if your association became more intimate and lasted throughout the years of your life? Do you find his interests, aspirations, hopes, and dislikes in general reflected in your own? Does your interest in him and his in you make you feel proud, make you hold your head high, and feel a little taller? Or is there something about it which makes you hope that your friends and parents will not see you together? Does your ripening friendship make the finest goals you have set for yourself in life seem closer, or do you find yourself making excuses for it and him, saying to yourself, "Well, you can't have everything!" How much effort are you willing to devote to another's happiness?

I think that you must answer these, and a number of questions like them about yourself, in short, that you must know yourself as well as possible before you are able to know another with whom you are sharing more and more of your life. And since the very fact of your growing interest in each other indicates the possibility that you may one day be married, it is of the highest importance that you come to know each other as quickly as possible.

Actually the process, whether you marry each other or do not, will never be completed. That is one of the wonders and joys of any human relationship. But if you are wise you will try to advance it as far as possible before you make what will probably be the most important decision of your life—whether you and the one with whom you are spending so much of your time shall become man and wife.

Much of the exciting adventure of learning to know each other is of course automatic, so to speak. Perhaps more than anything else you will need what you instinctively seek—long hours together with no one else about to inhibit or divert the flow of communication between you—long talks and long silences, exploring together each other's interests, even such seemingly unimportant things as finding out how harmoniously you go up and down broad flights of stairs together, how well you dance together, whether you enjoy taking walks together—finding out whether you proceed together in harmonious physical, as well as mental and spiritual, rhythm.

But what you find out about each other in these all-important moments of aloneness together are only a part of what you should learn before you feel that you know each other. Meet each other's friends and families and spend some time together in both of your homes so that each of you can see the other against his own background. Discuss each other's interests and work and hopes I think that it is well also for both young people to remember that a girl is trained from her babyhood to be more adaptable than a boy. She usually watches her mother make the home a liveable place by catering to the interests of the other members of the family and quite unconsciously, absorbs the habit of adapting to the needs and the wishes of the people around her. It is well to be sure in the early days of getting to know another person that the woman really is not just trying to please, but has a deep desire to find her satisfaction in the pleasure of her companion.

And do not either of you be in too great a hurry to decide whether your joy in each other as friends is to be translated into the potentially greater happiness of marriage. It is easy to get married. It is far more difficult to rectify a matrimonial mistake by divorce and to make the adjustment that must follow it. I once heard an old man say that no one ought to marry so long as he could help it. It sounded like a cynical remark, until I asked him to explain what he meant and he told me that in his opinion the only thing that justified taking so serious and important a step as this was the conviction on the part of two people that life without each other would be unbearable. I think he was wise.

Pre-engagement Behavior

The very fact that two people have been especially attracted to each other, and that each finds more pleasure in the other's company than in that of anyone else, even though they have not become engaged to be married, inevitably influences their behavior toward each other and toward their friends and acquaintances. This is natural and not in itself to be regretted so long as the preoccupation of each with the other does not become an embarrassment to either, or something that excludes other friendships and places uncomfortable limitations on normal and wholesome activities.

It is well for young people to learn early one of the most important truths in human relations and, especially during the period that precedes an engagement, to act in its light. No human being can ever "own" another, whether in friendship, love, marriage, or parenthood. Many human relationships have been ruined and happiness far too often changed to misery by a failure to understand this. The old song "You belong to me" and such a statement as "You are mine" are quite justified euphemisms indicating a very special relationship which it is assumed precludes a similar relationship with anyone else, but they do not mean literal ownership and the right to command and limit the activities of another.

Even though two people are deeply in love, even though (with no agreement yet made) each believes that he will eventually marry the other, they should not completely monopolize each other. We may assume that they are beyond their teens and have left behind them the (to me unwise) code which dictates that two persons who are "going steady" must not go out with anyone else.

It should not be necessary for Mary to feel that she must answer another old friend's invitation to spend an evening with her by a categorical "no," simply because she is afraid that she will hurt or anger John, with whom she is in love and who is in love with her, by saying, "yes." Nor should John fly into a rage of frustration and jealousy if Mary occasionally sees another man when he is not present. And of course John should have a similar freedom.

If their love for each other does not include trust and cannot survive the companionship of others it is doubtful that it can survive the long-term test of marriage. And if they do not understand each other well enough and if each does not have enough respect for the freedom of action of the other to permit each to see other friends, their prospects of a lasting and happy marriage are slight.

On the other hand if John spends most of his time with women other than Mary, or Mary with men other than John, it is likely that they will find in these facts an indication that their dreams of each other have been dreams and nothing more.

There comes a time in every intimate relationship, as understanding deepens, when many things are taken for granted between two people. A man who has been happily married for a number of years would probably not say to his wife, "Will you go to the movies with me next Wednesday night?" but rather, "Shall we go?" He would quite properly assume that she did not have an engagement with anyone else.

But during that period when two young people have not yet even reached a decision that they will marry, neither should take the other for granted. It is courteous, it is respectful, it is considerate for the man to ask the woman for a date in exactly the same way as he would any other woman, and if for any reason at all she declines, to accept her answer graciously. She will, under these circumstances, probably feel (and rightly) that she should explain the reason for her refusal, but in any case a gentleman will not reproach her if she rejects his invitation, no matter how great his disappointment. Similarly she will invite him to her house for a meal, for a party she is planning, or just for an evening, as she would any other. If the invitation is for a meal, and she lives with her parents, she will of course issue it in her mother's name. ("Mother has asked me to invite you to dinner Tuesday evening. Will you come?") And if he cannot for any reason, she will accept his refusal as graciously as she would that of any other.

Neither will inhibit the other from seeing friends of his own sex. One who does will soon become unpopular with the friends and probably eventually with the loved one.

John will call for Mary at her home when they have a date,

unless there is some very special reason why it is impractical and because of this they arrange to meet elsewhere. He will not avoid her parents, but on the contrary, welcome every meeting with them and show them every courtesy, talking with them (if they encourage this) while he is waiting for Mary to come downstairs or out of her room. And even if Mary is ready when he arrives he will, if possible, say good evening to her parents and take time to talk with them for a moment before he and Mary leave the house, remembering that while he is in their house they are his host and hostess. If it is a special day, such as a wedding anniversary or the mother's birthday, and he knows it, he may add a gracious touch to their meeting by bringing Mary's mother flowers.

He will arrive at the house at the time that has been prearranged, and Mary will be ready, and suitably dressed for whatever event has been planned, when he gets there. The old advice to "keep a man waiting" in order to enhance his interest is a counsel of rudeness and futility.

A gentleman in love with a woman to whom he is not engaged will choose his presents for her with a certain amount of discrimination. He will not buy for her gifts that are more expensive than he can afford (thus putting on a false front in the hope of impressing her). Such presents as he does buy for her should be chosen with taste and should, generally speaking, be not too intimate. Convention decrees that he may give her flowers, books, knickknacks for her room, candy, and similar things, but not wearing apparel—especially not lingerie, stockings, or jewelry. But I am sure that today such convention is frequently disregarded by young people, and I doubt that they are any the worse because of this.

The woman will be similarly guided in making pre-engagement gifts.

A considerate and courteous woman will be sure that she does not encourage a man to spend more on her than he can afford, whether in gifts or in entertainment. It is impossible to make any set rules about this which will apply to all cases and all circumstances, for it is quite possible that some special and expensive event may mean enough to both of them to justify a seeming extravagance at the cost of foregoing for some time other entertainment that costs money. In such a case a woman might justifiably be charged with lack of cooperation and understanding if she refuses to attend it. But in general the woman should take responsibility for seeing to it that the man does not spend more on their joint pleasure than is consistent with his economic position The woman who cannot, when occasion demands it, enjoy the company of the man she loves at a relatively inexpensive movie or even a walk in the country or a city park, as much as she would at a costly theater or dance, has not reached that state of maturity in which she is capable of becoming a good wife.

She should be especially careful to regulate her ordering in a restaurant by her knowledge of her escort's income. If after a movie or theater, he suggests that they get something to eat and asks her where she would like to go, her answer should depend on what she knows he can afford. If in the early stages of their acquaintanceship she has little knowledge to guide her, she will suggest a moderately priced place. If later she finds that this sort of place is either more expensive or less expensive than is fitting to the man's economic ability she may revise her ideas If he is one who really ought not to spend more than what a hamburger and a cup of coffee will cost, then a hamburger and a cup of coffee should seem the height of her desire.

Is a woman ever justified in seeking the company of a man and finding ways to increase his interest in her? If you feel that the answer to this question is no you are condemning millions of women who since the first woman found the first man desirable, have done so skillfully. Some two thousand years ago a wise woman named Naomi told her widowed daughter-in-law Ruth how to stimulate the interest of Boaz, and the result has become one of the most beautiful of love-story classics. To say that a woman must never take the initiative in a relationship with a man is to be unrealistic and ignore both history and logic.

The relationship between any man and any woman is a good relationship or a bad relationship basically because its human elements (without regard to the additional factors of romance and sexual attraction) are good or bad. Women as well as men are human beings and their search for companionship and happiness as strong. Often the feminine instinct can sense a potential compatibility before that of a man. When she does, it is natural and good for her to take an active role in advancing an acquaintance—so long as she does it with dignity and taste and in such a way that she cannot be misunderstood.

It is difficult to lay down any precise rules for this. I have been avoiding use of the word "lady" for it is open to so many interpretations, yet I know no other word that quite fits what I mean. A lady, as I understand the meaning of the word, never forces her attentions on a man who obviously is bored or annoyed by them (as for that matter no gentleman will pay continuous attention to a lady without welcome).

A lady does not attempt to assume the primary aggressive role in a romantic relationship which by nature and convention is the prerogative of the gentleman. She invites, but she does not pursue.

She may with complete propriety, after the first meeting with a man whom she has liked, say, "I've enjoyed talking with you so much. Do phone me some time," whereas she would not take the initiative in phoning him simply to talk, as he might her.

She may with propriety invite him to a gathering of any kind at her house if she lives with her parents, but would not—certainly not in the early stages of their acquaintance—invite him to spend an evening alone with her in an apartment which she occupies alone. She may, of course, do so if she has invited others. An invitation to such a gathering will be especially apt if she has invited others whose interests she knows are similar to those of the man she particularly wants to invite.

She may occasionally, if they know each other well, ask him to attend entertainments for which she has obtained tickets. If she belongs to some organization, such as a choral society, or an amateur theatrical group, or if she has two season tickets to symphony concerts or the opera, it is quite simple for her to ask a man in whom she is interested to be her guest. But she may also occasionally ask him to go to other entertainments with her, if she knows him well. If she phones him and says simply, "I have two tickets for *My Fair Lady* for Tuesday night. Would you like to see it with me?" she is committing no impropriety. She need not explain to him, unless she wishes, whether she bought the tickets or they were given to her.

The gentleman, in this case, if he accepts her invitation, will not of course attempt to pay her for the tickets. He will, however, pay for transportation to and from the theater, and if he asks her to eat with him afterwards will pay for that part of the evening's entertainment. If he does not ask her, the lady will not suggest it, though she may properly ask him in for a cup of coffee or a snack when they reach her home.

If a woman has been asked to any sort of party and told to bring a man with her, she will quite properly ask the man of her choice.

I think perhaps the chief difference between what is proper in the way of a gentleman's invitations to a lady, and a lady's to a gentleman, lies in whether an acceptance may be reasonably expected or not. The traditionally aggressive male may properly issue an invitation to a lady even though he is not sure that she will accept it, and if she refuses it, he may do so again (though if he continues to press her in the face of persistent refusals he is in danger of becoming a boor) But a lady will be reasonably sure that a man will welcome her invitation before she issues it, since convention makes it more difficult for him to say no to her than it would be for her to say no to him.

What you, a woman, do about inviting a man to spend time with you is less important on the whole than the way you do it. If you are forthright, dignified, honest, gracious, careful not to force unwelcome attentions on a man, confine your solo invitations to unattached men, and at all times exhibit a decent reserve, letting your conduct suggest friendly interest and no more, you will be on safe ground. If you like a man, let him see that you do, with frankness, but with dignity. Coyness, the suddenly dropped eyelids, the turning of the back, the suggestive smile, the "no" that means "yes" belong in Victorian novels, not in the relationship of intelligent young men and women of the twentieth century. If you feel friendly toward a man, let your actions and your words offer him friendship as frankly and as honestly as you would if he were a woman. If he has any sense at all (and if he hasn't, the sooner you find it out the better), you will not only be more attractive to him, but you will at the outset place your relationship with him on a firm basis, as no amount of skillful evasion and pretense can make it possible for you to do.

THE PROPOSAL

Asking Father

There was a time when every father of a marriageable girl expected the young man who wanted to marry her to come to him and ask his permission to propose to her before he did so I doubt that any realistic American father today expects this. If there are any who do they are almost sure to be disappointed.

Yet the wise and courteous young man will, if his beloved's relationship with her parents is a normal one with affection and respect on both sides, show them every courtesy and give them the fullest opportunity to know him, before he asks their daughter to marry him. If they know him, if they approve of him, before they receive the announcement that he is to be their son-in-law, their adjustment to the later announcement will be an easier one, and the important relationship between him and his future parents-in-law will have gotten off to a good start.

Asking the Woman

Surely the days of the bended knee and the impassioned "Will you be mine?" have gone, if they ever existed. Indeed, I think it probable that at least as many engagements are entered into today without a conventional proposal as with one. I'm not sure just how this is managed. I suppose that before there is any agreement to marry, the two young people have avowed (even if not clearly in words) their love for each other, and perhaps the time comes when either one says "When are we going to be married?" or "After we are married we shall do thus and so," and gradually the plans are made and friends and relatives are told of their intentions. Or perhaps the man shows up one evening with an engagement ring, and slips it on the finger of the girl he wants to marry. I don't know. I suppose there are many ways in which the thing is done.

But I am old-fashioned enough to believe that every woman, at this stage of her relationship with the man she loves, wants not to be taken so completely for granted by him that he feels it unnecessary to ask her to marry him. And I think that a gentleman will show enough consideration for the feelings of the woman he loves to ask her directly and without any evasion, "Darling, will you marry me?" (in whatever words he chooses). Even though he is practically certain that the answer will be "yes," he should give her the opportunity to say "no," or to ask for a little more time to consider the matter.

The Woman's Proposal

It is traditionally the prerogative of the man to propose marriage, and only the rashest of women, save under very exceptional circumstances, will risk losing the respect of the man she would like to marry by assuming that prerogative and proposing herself. There is a very good reason for this. Because of centuries' old tradition and custom it is much more difficult for a man to say no to a woman's invitation, whether to an evening's entertainment or an attempt to spend a lifetime together, than for a woman to refuse a man. Any man accepting an invitation for this reason alone will secretly resent it, and in a marriage resulting from the unwelcome proposal of a woman the man's resentment may become an insuperable obstacle to happiness.

Yet there are circumstances in which a woman may not only be justified, but also show deep wisdom by proposing marriage to the man she loves and who, she knows, loves her. There may be some real or imagined obstacle in the man's mind—such as ill health, an obligation to support an aged parent, the fact that the woman has very much more money or a higher social position than he has, a low earning capacity which he does not expect to improve for several years, the fact that his work may often take him away from home or even make him move to a foreign country to which he is loath to ask her to come. In such a case his refraining from asking her the question which she most wants to hear may actually be evidence of his deep regard for her and his unwillingness to urge her to share a life which he thinks may make her less happy than she would be with someone else.

If the man you love is being silent about marriage for some such reason as this, if you are sure that he loves you and wants to marry you, but is refraining from asking you out of gallantry, if you have weighed all the factors which he considers barriers and, considering them of little consequence in comparison with your love for each other, are willing to accept them along with him for the rest of your life, by all means take the matter out of his hands by bringing it into the open, discussing it, and making him understand exactly how you feel about it.

Inevitably the opportunity will come one day when he is talking about his future plans or his disability, or whatever it is which is keeping him silent, and you can lead the discussion carefully to the point at which it brings out his attitude toward marriage, and then say something like, "Darling can't you see that it wouldn't make a bit of difference to a woman who loves you? When are you going to stop being silly about it and ask me to marry you?" This would still seem to leave the initiative to him, though actually you had taken it, and it would be easier for him to evade this question, or at least postpone a decision on it, if he felt that he must, than it would for him to refuse a direct proposal from you.

But as you would not issue an invitation to a man unless you felt reasonably sure that he would welcome it, you would never suggest marriage to him unless you were as sure as it was possible to be that this was what he wanted and that he had not asked you because of some obstacle that seemed greater to him than it did to you.

Telling Father

Though the old custom of requesting a father's permission to ask his daughter "for her hand" no longer obtains in America, it is still the obligation of the young engaged couple to announce their engagement to their parents before it becomes common knowledge, and for the man to have a talk with his fiancée's father, revealing frankly his financial position, and thus his ability to support his wife, his plans for the future, and his prospects, all matters that intimately affect the happiness of his future father-in-law's daughter. If, before this time, the young man has made a friend of the older one, the interview should not be difficult.

I remember a young couple who became engaged while they were in college. Johnny was a shy and sensitive young man, a little vague, a bit of a dreamer and something of a poet, whose verses appeared regularly in the college magazine. He had always been somewhat overawed by Molly's father, a successful businessman, kindly and intelligent, but with little appreciation of the arts. After Molly had promised to marry him, she suggested that they go together to have a talk with her father, but Johnny felt that he couldn't face it, and left the task to her

When she told her father simply that she and Johnny were planning to get married as soon as they were through school, he did not seem surprised.

"Johnny's a nice boy," he said quietly, "and he seems very fond of you. What does he plan to do to make a living?"

Somewhat at a loss, for the charming Johnny was as vague about the future as he was about most other things, Molly hesitated. Finally she said, "Well, he writes, you know."

Her father was silent a moment. Then he said, "He writes? That's fine. But suppose he doesn't get an answer?"

His remark was indicative of the concern which every good

father feels about his daughter's future. It is one which the man who is planning to marry her should understand and make every effort to put at rest by as frank and purposeful a discussion as possible. Every intelligent older man who has worked his way up to a position of economic stability knows how many of the finest young people have to work hard and plan carefully in order to make ends meet, and knows too that the struggle, entered into willingly and cooperatively by both of them, can help to cement their union and make a sound life-long partnership possible. Only the most foolish of fathers believes that none but an extremely wealthy young husband can make his daughter happy. But any father wants to know what to look forward to, and his prospective son-in-law's attitude as they discuss the matter will probably be of greater importance to him than the actual state of his finances at the time.

The Meaning of an Engagement

An engagement is a mutual declaration of intention and a mutual plan. Like a marriage it should never be entered into lightly or with any intention save that of permanence. I have never had any patience with those who say that engagements are made to be broken, or with young things who romp in and out of one "engagement" after another like little girls skipping rope. These are not engagements at all, but merely flirtations in depth, a sort of game of collecting scalps and accumulating a mistaken sense of self-importance through conquests, and often leave behind them heartbreak and disillusionment.

Let a man be sure that he wants to marry the woman he loves before he proposes to her, and the woman be equally sure that she wants to marry him before she says yes. Let them then proceed happily together as though their marriage within a definite future were an established fact, planning together, accumulating the material things which they will need to start housekeeping, saving their money for the important expenditures that will be inevitable after they are married, and in all ways exhibiting the fact that their days of uncertainty are over and that they are embarked as a unit on life's most exciting and potentially rewarding adventure.

Yet while this should be their intent (without which neither should be willing to enter into an engagement), it does not mean that no engagement is ever irrevocable. The alchemy of newly discovered love tends to make lovers feel that they have known each other all their lives, each feeling that there is no hidden corner in the personality of the other which is unfamiliar to him. But time often clears the vision of the most bedazzled. If during the course of the engagement, they find that they have made a mistake, if after careful consideration and discussion there seems no way to adjust to each other happily, they can fulfill their obligation to themselves, to each other, and to society only by canceling their engagement. Better a broken engagement than an unhappy period of marriage terminated by divorce. But just as the engagement should not be entered lightly, neither should it be dissolved without careful thought and efforts at adjustment on both sides. Life is far too short to waste any of it in avoidable unhappiness.

The Ring or Rings

It is a wise and considerate young man who asks his fiancée to pick out her own engagement ring. A diamond solitaire set in platinum is always in good taste, but even the smallest good diamond is expensive, and a considerate woman knowing that her future husband cannot afford a diamond of any save microscopic size may prefer a less expensive setting to either a small diamond or having her fiancé spend more than he can afford on the ring.

A simple way to arrange the matter is for the man to go to a good jeweler, tell him how much he can afford to spend, and have him lay aside a selection in that price range. He may then take his fiancée to the jeweler and ask her to make a choice. Though a solitaire diamond is the traditional engagement ring, today birthstones are frequently used. These are

JANUARY	*garnet*
FEBRUARY	*amethyst*
MARCH	*jasper, bloodstone, or aquamarine*
APRIL	*sapphire or diamond*
MAY	*agate or emerald*
JUNE	*emerald, pearl, moonstone, or alexandrite*
JULY	*onyx or ruby*
AUGUST	*carnelian, sardonyx, or peridot*
SEPTEMBER	*chrysolite or sapphire*
OCTOBER	*aquamarine, opal or tourmaline*
NOVEMBER	*topaz*
DECEMBER	*ruby, turquoise, or zircon*

If the girl's birthday is in April which indicates either of the two most expensive stones, sapphire or diamond, she may with perfect taste choose an aquamarine, an amethyst, a topaz, or transparent tourmaline, any of which is today accepted as a substitute for a diamond in an engagement ring

If the woman wishes to give her fiancé a ring, she should choose one that has a sturdy masculine air; a gold seal ring, a cat's eye sunk in plain gold, a bloodstone, a small diamond set deep in plain gold, an agate seal ring, an onyx, a carnelian, or a small sapphire set deeply in plain platinum. A garnet, zircon, a large diamond or sapphire, an opal, or a turquoise is not suitable for a man's ring, since all for some reason seem effeminate.

A woman should not buy a ring for her prospective husband without first finding out whether he likes rings. Some men have a definite aversion to wearing them.

As a matter of fact many a happy bride has never had an engagement ring, or has been given one only years after marriage when her husband could afford to buy the kind of ring he wanted to buy her earlier. And many a wise young woman, knowing that the man she is going to marry has a limited income, would rather have him spend the price of an engagement ring on furniture and other household necessities An engagement that is not marked by a ring on the third finger of the left hand is no less valid than one that is.

If there is a ring, it is customarily worn in public for the first time on the day of the announcement—if there is a formal announcement Often young people today subscribe to no formality in this matter, but simply tell their friends and relatives about it as casually as they would give them any other bit of interesting news.

Traditional Announcements

If you wish to follow the social custom in announcing your engagement write (both of you) to your relatives and closest friends a week or so before the formal announcement is made, telling them the news and asking them to keep it to themselves until the announcement is made. (Relatives, if they live nearby and wish to show a sometimes expected courtesy, will call on the prospective bride or phone her to wish her happiness, but like so many other social customs the formal call is less frequent than it once was.)

The formal announcement is made by the parents of the prospective bride. It may be done by notes (never by an engraved notice) or at an engagement party or dinner, and by sending notices to the society editors of the daily papers. If the parents are divorced, the party and the announcement are attended to by the mother, unless the bride-to-be lives with her father, in which case he does it. If she has only one surviving parent, whichever it is makes the announcement. If she is an orphan, either a near relative makes the announcement or she may herself.

At an engagement party the announcement may be made by either the girl or her mother as the guests are greeted, or if it is a dinner, by the father usually in the form of a toast to the young couple, but sometimes in a simple announcement at the end of the meal. If it is a toast everyone at the table, except the engaged couple, rises and drinks it with their eyes on the happy pair. The man is then usually expected to respond to it. But if he is one who simply can't manage a gracious speech, he may do so simply by rising, saying, "Thank you all very much," bowing to the assembled guests, and sitting down.

If an announcement is sent to the newspapers it is worded formally and simply. If both parents are living, and still married, it may be somewhat as follows "Mr. and Mrs. Lawrence Squire, of 2654 Academy Street, announce the engagement of their daughter, Lillian Eugenia to John Henry Street, son of Mr and Mrs. Malcolm Street, of Tacoma, Washington." A photograph of Lillian may be included with the announcement, but it will be used only if the family is prominent or if the paper has a considerable amount of space available on the day the announcement is printed.

When No Announcement Is Possible

It should be unnecessary to say that anyone who is married must not announce an engagement to another, even though divorce proceedings are under way and the plans for a second marriage after the divorce has been granted have been made. Under these circumstances the fact of the coming second marriage should be kept strictly the property of the two persons involved, and perhaps very close friends whose discretion may be trusted. Nor may the woman involved wear the engagement ring of the man whom she plans to marry before she has been divorced from her husband.

ENGAGEMENT BEHAVIOR

Public Demonstrations

It is to be expected that an engaged couple will show their affection for and delight in each other by special attentions and affectionate glances when they are in public, and there is no impropriety in their doing so. If, however, they overdo their exhibitions by constant fondling of each other and using fulsome endearments in their speech, they become bores and make a vulgar public display of something that should be reserved for their private moments. Affection may be demonstrated without loss of dignity.

Chaperones

The attitude toward chaperones for engaged couples, who in former days seemed so necessary to at least the appearances of propriety, varies in different localities and different groups. In some circles it is considered quite proper for two young people who have declared their intention to marry to spend days and long evenings together with no one else present, but not for them to go on an overnight journey or to spend a weekend unless they are accompanied by a married couple, an older woman, or an older relative.

The whole question seems to me a little academic today. The typical contemporary young couple will take matters pretty much into their own hands, regardless of the conventions of an earlier era, and I think on the whole that this is a good thing, and also that, by and large, modern young people are a pretty wholesome lot. Life seems to be a more rapidly passing event today than it was a generation or two ago and youth is loath to waste any precious part of the happiness which they feel is their right. Young people enjoy the companionship of older people whom they love and respect, but they do not want watchdogs set over them, and are ingenious enough to find ways to escape surveillance if they are. Chaperones have never made improper conduct impossible, and never will.

And I frequently wonder, as I look about me at people whom I know, and read the newspapers, whether we of the older generation have, as a group, managed our lives sufficiently well to be sure that we are qualified to tell younger people who are in love with each other and going to be married what is proper and what improper

conduct between them. On the whole it seems to me that if they trust
each other enough, each to commit his life into the other's keeping,
we will do well to leave such matters as where they go and with
whom they go there in their own hands.

Other Friends

Though an announced engagement like a marriage serves
notice that neither the engaged woman nor the engaged man is, generally speaking, available for invitations without the other, it should
not mean for either the end of other friendships among both sexes,
but rather, in so far as possible, a combination of two groups of
friends—hers and his. When the engaged woman gives a mixed
party she will try to invite friends of her fiancé as well as her own,
and she and he will present a united front in entertaining them as,
later, they will do in their own home.

Nor does it seem to me that any engagement precludes the possibility of either party to it ever seeing alone a friend of the other
sex, any more than marriage does today. Certainly this would not be
a frequent affair, and would happen when there was some special
reason for it. The engaged man who habitually spends a great deal
of time alone with any woman other than his fiancée, or the engaged
woman who is frequently seen accompanied by a man other than the
one she has announced that she will marry, is not behaving as a
happily betrothed person should, and is probably giving evidence
that the "engagement" will not bear fruit in marriage.

Yet no engagement (nor for that matter any marriage) should
be a prison which keeps the engaged in and all but the fiancé out.

Gifts

During an engagement the nature of the presents which the
man gives the woman, or the woman gives the man, will depend
largely on their financial status, but to some extent also on their
implications. No sensible young woman will encourage her fiancé
to buy expensive presents for her when she knows that they are
going to have difficulty furnishing their new home. Nor will she
allow him to spend money on her for things that may properly be
considered maintenance, such as paying the rent for her apartment,
buying her clothing other than occasional small accessories such as
handkerchiefs, scarves, or purses. He may however give her as much
jewelry as he can afford. But if he has limited financial resources he

will demonstrate a much greater courtesy to her by saving his money until she is ready to look for furniture and household appliances with him His ability to buy the sofa or refrigerator she wants will mean more to her in the end than a pair of earrings, no matter how carefully chosen.

The Broken Engagement

If the young people learn before the date set for the marriage that they have made a mistake and thus cancel the engagement, the woman will return the ring and any expensive presents which the man has given her. If he refuses to accept them she may keep them.

In the unfortunate event of a broken engagement, probably the least said about it the better. Yet if a public announcement has been printed in the newspapers it is only courteous to those who have read it to announce the end of it by a similar notice that should be short and factual. An accepted form is: "The engagement of Miss Lillian Eugenia Squire to Mr. John Henry Street has been broken by mutual consent."

Showers

These are discussed in Chapter 20, "Showers, Anniversaries, and Surprise Parties."

20

Showers, Anniversaries, and Surprise Parties

SHOWERS

SHOWERS ARE SOMETIMES HELD BY FRIENDS FOR A PROspective bride, usually about a month before the wedding, for a bride and groom after they have returned from their honeymoon, for a baby, either before or after its birth, for a newly arrived clergyman and his wife, for a young couple moving into a newly built home, or for any other reason that would make especially appropriate gifts welcome. Since they are specifically gift-giving affairs they are not, of course, arranged by the one who is to receive the gifts or by a member of her family.

The Bridal Shower

A few weeks before the date set for the wedding one or more showers may be arranged for the prospective bride. Most appropriately this should be a surprise party, held at the home of a friend who invites other female friends, and then asks the bride to come in casually for tea or for dinner. The one who arranges the affair will do well if she learns as much as possible beforehand of the bride's special desires, and passes on her information to those whom she invites. The shower may be a general one, or be planned to meet a specific need. There may be a linen shower, a kitchen shower, a silver shower, a china shower, or what you will. Or several, each with a particular sort of gift specified.

If the gifts should conform to a special décor which the bride is planning for her new home, the hostess should find out tactfully as much about her plans for decorations as possible. If a kitchen shower is planned, and the bride wants to have a yellow kitchen, the guests should choose gifts with this in mind. If it is a linen shower, and the bride prefers white sheets and pillow cases to pastel tints, the guests should be informed so that they may choose all white.

Invitations are always informally issued by note or telephone, and the party itself is completely casual.

One of the pleasantest of ways to arrange it is to have all the guests send their presents to the house of the hostess before the party, each containing a card bearing the name of the giver. These the hostess carefully puts out of sight with their wrappings intact. (Sometimes the hostess wraps all of them a second time, using the same gay wrappings for each, so that they present a uniform decorative effect when displayed together, but this is not necessary.) The guest of honor who is to receive the gifts arrives first in what she expects to be a simple visit to the house of her friend (if the secret has been well kept). Meanwhile the guests, or as many of them as possible, assemble at the home of another friend and all troop in together.

The hostess will have arranged the presents on a table somewhere out of sight—either in a room which is not entered until the guests have arrived, or in a corner behind a screen. Or she may have piled them on a tea cart (if they are not too bulky) or in a child's wheelbarrow or wagon, parked in the kitchen or in a bedroom.

When the guests are assembled, the screen is removed, or they all go into the room where the presents are waiting, or the gifts are brought in, in whatever conveyance has been used and the prospective bride opens them one by one, thanking the giver of each as she does so.

This of course is only one way to do it—a way that may be fun It may be equally well done by each guest bringing her present as she arrives.

The gifts may be anything appropriate to the occasion, and may be inexpensive or expensive as your purse and desire dictate. They do not ordinarily take the place of wedding gifts.

The House-Warming Shower

Sometimes shortly after the bride and groom have moved into their new home they are given a house-warming shower by their friends. Since this, like the bridal shower, is most effective as a surprise, it is best given by a friend in the friend's home. It is most successful if the friend giving the party first learns, by discreet questioning, what household items are most needed in the new home-makers' equipment or furnishings. A pleasant variation from the usual practice of each guest bringing a small gift is for all of them to pool the money which they wish to spend on presents for the couple and buy together one important addition to the home.

A Shower for the Baby

A shower given to supply the needs of an expected baby may be given by a close woman friend of the mother who will invite only other similarly close female friends. The gifts will of course be things that will be useful to the new arrival and in his care—clothing, cradle toys, bath equipment and supplies, or if you like, a check with which to start his savings account.

If the shower is given after the child's birth, both parents, and male and female friends of the mother and father may be invited.

Surprise Parties in General

A surprise party, for whatever purpose, which is really a surprise, may be a very pleasant thing so long as the element of un-expectedness does not actually constitute a rudeness and cause inconvenience and embarrassment. Many a child has been delighted on his birthday by having his father take him off for a walk or to see a movie and, on arriving home, to find his house swarming with young friends who shout "Surprise! Surprise!" In such cases, the host and hostess, who are the child's mother and father, have arranged the affair and manage it.

When, however, an adult or a married couple are to be surprised, their feelings must be taken into consideration.

Nothing can be worse from the point of view of those for whom the party is given than to have a large group descend on them without any warning whatsoever In such a case those who should be guests must bear the obligations of host and hostess This can be bad enough, but it can be even more complicated if the surprised guest has invited other friends for the evening or has planned to watch a favorite television program, or even has gone to bed early in order to make up for a series of late nights. Even if they are prepared to serve refreshments to the number of people who will arrive, nothing that I know can put more strain on the ties of friendship or indeed ordinary civility.

Another equally dangerous method of which I have heard is for a group, wanting to give a surprise party to their friends the Marshalls, to arrange with neighbors, say the Browns, to invite the Marshalls to dinner that night. While the Marshalls are thus being entertained at the Browns the party invades the Marshalls' house, and when the latter return they find their home filled with uninvited guests.

Either of these methods is, if nothing else, inconsiderate and rude, at least in my opinion. If you are going to give any kind of surprise party to a friend, arrange to invite your guest or guests to the home of one who is a part of the surprise, and let the rest come in later. Or if you wish to give a surprise birthday party to a married man or woman, take the wife or husband into your confidence. In either of these ways you will not embarrass the guest of honor by making him or her disarrange plans, or by forcing unexpected obligations of hospitality on him. Any other kind of surprise party seems to me especially inconsiderate when it is given to aged people.

Wedding Anniversaries

It is a pleasant custom to congratulate close friends on their wedding anniversaries. This may be done by note, by word of mouth, by sending a gift, or by a party to which other close friends are invited who may or may not bring gifts.

If you give a gift it may be anything which you would enjoy giving the one for whom it is intended, and which you feel they will enjoy receiving Or it may conform in its substance with the material for which each wedding anniversary is named. Or for the earlier anniversaries, when the traditional present would be of little value, you may give that and something in addition.

The traditional list of anniversaries follows

FIRST	*paper*
SECOND	*cotton*
THIRD	*leather*
FOURTH	*fruit and flowers, silk*
FIFTH	*wooden*
SIXTH	*sugar and candy, iron*
SEVENTH	*woolen or copper*
EIGHTH	*bronze or pottery*
NINTH	*willow or pottery*
TENTH	*tin or aluminum*
ELEVENTH	*steel*
TWELFTH	*silk or linen*
THIRTEENTH	*lace*
FOURTEENTH	*ivory*
FIFTEENTH	*crystal*
TWENTIETH	*china*
TWENTY-FIFTH	*silver*
THIRTIETH	*pearl*
THIRTY-FIFTH	*coral*
FORTIETH	*ruby*
FORTY-FIFTH	*sapphire*
FIFTIETH	*golden*
FIFTY-FIFTH	*emerald*
SIXTIETH	*diamond*
SEVENTY-FIFTH	*diamond*

Whether this schedule is used as a guide in selecting a wedding anniversary gift, however, matters far less than the spirit behind the gift I remember seeing an aged couple surrounded with expensive gifts that marked their fiftieth wedding anniversary But the gift which pleased them most was a potted cyclamen plant bought out of his savings by a small boy in the neighborhood whom they loved and who loved them.

21

Weddings

A WEDDING IS THE CEREMONY THAT MARKS THE JOINING of a man and woman as husband and wife.

The two terms "Marriage" and "Wedding" ought not to be confused. Many happy marriages have been solemnized by the simplest of ceremonies in which a minister, priest, justice of the peace, or even the captain of a ship at sea has read the marriage service and pronounced the happy couple man and wife before two witnesses, without fuss or fanfare. And often the most elaborate wedding has been followed by months of unhappiness and a divorce almost before the shine has worn off the wedding gifts.

I say these things at the beginning of this chapter and before making any attempt to explain the intricacies of elaborate weddings because I often think that young people—especially perhaps young women—whose parents cannot afford an expensive wedding and reception feel somehow cheated of a part of their marriage, and I want to make it clear that while a beautiful and dignified wedding is a fine thing, and something which many a woman remembers happily all her life, it is not, in itself, a "marriage" in the true sense of the word, but rather an added something that is good if the union between the bride and groom is a true union, and is worthless if it is not.

RELIGIOUS ATTITUDES TOWARD MARRIAGE

Roman Catholic

Roman Catholics, basing their conception on the teachings of St. Paul, consider marriage a sacrament that symbolizes the supernatural bond between Christ and the Church, the "mystical body of Christ," and believe that it is peculiarly blessed by God. Thus it assumes a special importance as a religious rite, can be legitimatized only by the Church, must be accompanied by an avowed intention to raise the children which are its issue as "members of Christ and of the Church of Christ," (that is, the Catholic Church) and, after consummation, can never be dissolved

The Catholic Church places great emphasis upon the home and the raising of children. It considers people as divided broadly into two groups, those who are unwilling to regulate their acts by "the revelation of God," but rather consider their own happiness as the sole criterion of behavior, and those who accept such revelations as the law of their life.

In the view of the Church the attitude of the first group inevitably results in unstable marriages and easy divorces For the second group the primary object of marriage is the raising of children, and the lifelong devotion of the parents to the children's welfare. Therefore marriage must be for life, and divorce is forbidden In extreme cases an unconsummated marriage may be dissolved by an annulment, or one that has been consummated, by a separation, but an actual civil divorce is not recognized by the Church.

Marriage between Catholics and non-Catholics is forbidden by the Church without a dispensation. A civil ceremony is not recognized.

Jewish

Based upon the divine admonition in Genesis, "Be fruitful and multiply," the Jew considers marriage and the home and family which result from it, basic elements of the good life, and therefore a religious duty. According to the Talmud one of the first three questions asked of a man in the world to come is "Did you raise a family?" A positive answer is counted to his credit, a negative to his discredit.

Judaism is singularly devoid of reticence or any sense of shame connected with sexual union, yet the sacred character of Jewish marriage (indicated by the term *kiddushin,* "sanctification") and the consequent religious importance of the marriage tie as the sound base on which the home is built have produced a high rate of fidelity and a low divorce rate among Jewish families.

Marriages between Jews and non-Jews are forbidden unless the non-Jew becomes converted to Judaism, and though they sometimes occur, they are viewed as a tragedy and it is a rare rabbi indeed who will officiate at such a marriage.

Divorce, while not forbidden in the Jewish faith, is considered a catastrophe and it is discouraged.

Protestant

To Protestants, as to Roman Catholics, marriage is also a sacrament not to be entered into lightly or with any intention save that it be so long as both parties to it live. But the Protestant concept is far less demanding than the Catholic, and that of Orthodox Judaism. Both mixed marriages (that is, marriages between Protestant and Catholic or Protestant and Jew) and civil marriages with no religious ceremony are considered valid.

In general also the attitude toward divorce is much more liberal. While it is against the canon of the Church of England, and Protestant denominations as a whole discourage it, save as a last resort when all attempts at adjustment have failed, it is accepted as a sometimes unavoidable misfortune. In most churches, civil divorce is recognized as valid, and remarriage for divorced persons considered valid.

MARRIAGE AND DIVORCE LAWS

Laws governing certain details of marriage vary from state to state. Every state has set minimum ages at which marriages may take place with and without consent The youngest age at which any state allows a man to marry with parental consent is 14. Both South

Carolina and Massachusetts permit this and both permit a girl to marry with consent at the tender age of 12. Ages at which marriages are permitted with parental consent in other states range from 14 for women and 15 for men to 16 for women and 18 for men. All states permit women and men to marry without consent at 21. In Minnesota, women do not require consent at 16 or men at 18. In other states both men and women may marry without consent at ages varying from 18 to 21.

Most states require that the absence of venereal disease be demonstrated by a blood test before a license will be issued.

The cost of a marriage license varies from nothing in Puerto Rico and forty cents in the Virgin Islands to six dollars in Kentucky. The fee is usually two or three dollars. In some states there is a short period between the application for the license and its issuance, and in some between its issuance and a permissible marriage. In planning their marriage the prospective bride and groom should inform themselves of the regulations of the state in which they are to be married.

Divorce laws vary even more widely than do the marriage laws. In New York only one cause, adultery, is recognized. Among the causes recognized by other states (some by some, others by others) are cruelty, desertion, nonsupport, alcoholism, felony, impotence, and drug addiction.

PREPARATIONS FOR THE WEDDING

No matter how simple the wedding ceremony is to be, some preparations and planning are necessary. Below are discussed plans and preparations which should be sufficient for any kind of wedding But let me emphasize that, save for complying with the laws of your state, obtaining a license, buying a ring, arranging with a justice of the peace, a minister, a priest, or a rabbi, and finding two friends who will act as witnesses, *none of them is necessary to a legal and meaningful marriage.* That is something that takes place within and between a man and a woman. Whether the ceremony is the simplest that will conform to legal requirements, or the most elaborate that tradition and desire may dictate has no bearing on the validity of your marriage. If you wish, because of the expense, or for any other reason, to avoid a conventional wedding and simply to be married quietly with no attendants save your witnesses, there is no sensible reason why you should not do so.

But if you are to have a wedding, and a reception to follow it, planning must begin as soon as the wedding date has been set. First of all you must answer such questions as these:

Where will you be married and when?

Will your marriage be simple and informal, semiformal, or formal?

How much may it cost?

How many guests will be invited? (Obviously the bride, the bride's family, the groom, and his family must decide this together.)

How many attendants and ushers will you have?

Will you have a reception? If so, where and how elaborate?

With these questions decided you are ready to make your plans.

A Word About Expense

To ask how much it costs to get married is a little like asking what an automobile costs. Many an adolescent has bought his first car with $50 saved from his earnings at odd jobs or an after-school paper route, and remembers it in later years as the car in which he took more pride and out of which he got more fun than any he has bought since. Yet it is possible to spend $10,000 or more for an automobile. So it is with the cost of getting married.

The comparison is not completely apt, for while the $10,000 car will undoubtedly go farther, last longer, be more comfortable, be better looking, and require less in the way of repairs (at least for a number of years) the $10,000 wedding joins a bride and groom no more soundly, nor carries with it any greater assurance of long happily married years than does the $50 one. Indeed if an expensive wedding is arranged at the cost of skimping on necessary furnishings for the new home, or going deeply into debt, it may actually sow seeds of discord and unhappiness which will produce bitter fruit.

Though the largest expense of the wedding is usually borne by the bride's family (see below), there are cases in which this is impractical and the prospective bride and groom must work out the problem of cost between them. In such cases they will be wise if they carefully consider relative values, with due thought for the amount of money they have saved and the amount of income to which they can look forward. The cost of furnishing and equipping a home is large; even a modest honeymoon trip is costly. Many a young married couple (wisely I think) feel that they would rather have at least a few days by themselves in some attractive spot away from home after their marriage, and a pleasant and comfortably furnished home to enter when they return, than an elaborate wedding

Even though the conventional custom is followed and the bride's family assumes the major wedding expenses there may be a choice well worth considering. Given the choice of an elaborate wedding and a comparatively small wedding present, or a simple wedding and a substantial contribution to the cost of furnishing the home, the wise bride may choose the latter. In no situation do convention and "what people will say" matter less.

With these considerations in mind it is a good plan for both the prospective bride and groom to sit down with their families and make an estimate of the cost of the kind of wedding which they have in mind before deciding definitely on how elaborate it will be.

Expenses Customarily Borne by the Bride and Her Family

Needless to say all the clothing worn by the bride at her wedding and on her honeymoon are purchased by herself or her parents before the wedding. In the past the trousseau also included all linens for the home, but the latter are now frequently bought by the bride and groom together as a part of the household furnishings.

All costs of the wedding ceremony, church fees and the sexton's fee, if it is to be a church wedding (but not the clergyman's fee), music, flowers (though usually not the bride's bouquet), church or home decorations are furnished by the bride's family. So also are all costs of the reception, if there is to be one, including decorations, music, whatever food and drinks are served, and of course the wedding cake. Also included are

Invitations and announcements.

Photographs.

Flowers carried by the bride's attendants, corsage bouquets for both mothers, and flowers for the buttonholes of both fathers, though these latter may be furnished by the groom.

Gifts for the bride's attendants.

The bride's gift to the bridegroom, if there is to be one, and the bridegroom's ring if it is to be a double-ring ceremony.

Transportation for the wedding party, including the bridegroom's parents, close relatives, and bride's and groom's attendants, to and from the wedding and the reception, and sometimes for the bride and groom to the train or plane as they start on their honeymoon

Hotel rooms, unless arrangements have been made for rooms in the homes of friends, for out-of-town members of the wedding party. The bride's parents also usually make reservations for members of the groom's family if they are from out of town, though whether they pay for them is optional.

The bridesmaids' luncheon.

Sometimes the rehearsal party, if this is not, as usual, assumed by the groom or his family.

The bride's health certificate, in states where one is required.

A wedding gift for the couple.

If the wedding is to be so elaborate that it is felt a secretary is needed to arrange the details, she or he is engaged by the bride's parents.

The Groom's Expenses

The groom obviously pays for his own wedding clothes, his honeymoon wardrobe, and his luggage If he can afford it he will probably want a completely new outfit for his wedding and for traveling, but if he cannot he will be married in the best that he already has.

He usually pays for accessories worn by the best man and the ushers, though not for the purchase or rental of their suits.

Gifts for the best man and ushers. These are generally balanced off by their gift, generally a silver cigarette box, to the groom.

The bride's bouquet and going-away corsage (The florist, if asked to, will arrange the corsage as a detachable part of the bridal bouquet, so that it may be taken off before the bouquet is thrown to the bridesmaids.)

Boutonnieres for himself, the best man, and the ushers.

Corsages for both mothers and boutonnieres for both fathers, unless this has been attended to by the bride's parents The groom and the bride's parents should decide this between them.

A gift to the bride

The bride's wedding ring

The marriage license.

His own health certificate, if required

The bachelor dinner if there is one.

The clergyman's fee. (This will vary with the groom's circumstances and the elaborateness of the wedding No clergyman, of
course, has any set fee for performing a service. If the wedding is a
small and simple ceremony the average fee is $15 to $25. If, however, it is obvious that several hundred or even several thousand
dollars have been spent on the wedding so small a fee as this would
constitute a marked discourtesy In such cases the fee would properly
be $100 or more.)

Usually the rehearsal party, though this is sometimes paid for
by the bride's parents.

All expenses of the wedding trip.

Variations from Custom

There is nothing sacrosanct about any of these customs. They
are usual when the bride and the groom are of conventional families
both of whom are financially able to bear without hardship the expenses traditionally allotted to them for whatever kind of wedding is
decided upon.

But as in all things special circumstances dictate special arrangements

It is quite conceivable that the prospective bride may be an
orphan, completely self-supporting and with an income limited to
her weekly earnings, or the daughter of parents of very limited economic means, and that the parents of the man she is going to marry
or the young man himself are well off, or at least in an income
bracket that permits a little extra spending for so special an occasion.
If they both want a more memorable and impressive wedding than
the girl's parents could be expected to pay for without sacrifice, there
is no common-sense reason why the prospective groom, in a frank
and friendly talk with his fiancée's parents, should not arrange to take
over some of the expenses which they would ordinarily assume. If it
is done graciously and with affection and understanding, and the
expenses taken care of unostentatiously so that no one except those
primarily concerned need know about it, there is no reason why
anyone should feel offended.

However, if it is apparent that such an offer might give offense,
then the two young people, if they are wise and considerate, will decide together that they want a simple, inexpensive wedding. It will
constitute a far better beginning for their marriage and a far better
memory than would allowing pride and the desire to do the expected

thing to persuade the girl's parents to spend more than they could afford.

Or it may be that two young people are both "on their own," both in moderate financial circumstances, and can expect no help in their wedding expenses from either family. In such a situation the natural and sensible thing is to begin at once, as I am sure many young people do, to pool their resources, and spend together on their wedding whatever they can afford with due regard to their plans for a wedding trip and the expenses of furnishing their home.

The conventions which dictate that wedding expenses be divided between the two families in a way prescribed by custom have a purpose and usefulness under ordinary circumstances. But actually they have very little importance in comparison with a sound sense of relative values and a plan that takes into account the financial ability of both families.

Inviting the Guests

How many guests you invite, whether you will invite all of them to both the wedding and the reception (if there is to be one), and how you will invite them will depend upon how elaborate a wedding you plan to have

If you are to have a small informal wedding at the home of the bride (which you may have if you are either Protestants or Jews—if you are Catholics the service must be performed in the church), with the reception also in the bride's home the question of invitations is easily solved If it is a first marriage, the bride's mother, if she is living, or if not her father, writes informal notes to the close friends and relatives who are to be invited (using, of course, the list that has been decided upon by the prospective bride and groom together) The note may be completely simple

> Dear Helen·
>
> Margaret and Gregg are to be married here at our home Saturday, June 14, at 4 in the afternoon. We hope that you and Bill will come.
>
> Ever,
> Jane

If the bride has no close relatives she will write the note herself.

The same sort of invitation is quite proper for a very small church wedding If there is to be a reception at the house following the wedding, that fact will, of course, also be mentioned in the note which you write to anyone whom you wish to invite to both the wedding and the reception. You may wish to invite some guests to the reception, but not to the wedding, in which case your note will mention the reception only.

If there is to be a large wedding with fifty or a hundred guests invited, with an elaborate reception following, the matter becomes more complex. In that case the number of possible guests should be decided upon, and lists made by both the bride and her family, and the groom and his family, each furnishing approximately half the names. If some of those to be invited live in distant cities and are almost sure not to come, a few more may be invited than the total number of guests planned for.

If all of those who are invited to the wedding are also to be invited to the reception a single invitation may be used for both events, and may read:

Mr. and Mrs. William Rainey Parker
request the honour* of your presence
at the marriage of their daughter
Margaret Sarah
to
(or "and" if you prefer)
Mr. Gregory Robert Marsh
on Saturday, the fourteenth of June
at four o'clock
The First Congregational Church†
Mapleville, New Hampshire
Reception at 123 Elm Street, Mapleville,
immediately after ceremony

"R.S.V.P." is not included on an invitation to a church wedding

If not all of those who are to be invited to the wedding ceremony are to be invited to the reception, mention of the reception is omitted from the invitation and separate cards are engraved and inserted for those whom you wish to ask to the reception. These may read simply·

Reception (If the wedding ceremony is held
in the morning, the reception is
called a wedding breakfast.)
immediately following the ceremony
at 123 Elm Street

* The English spelling "honour" is preferred here, but this is an unimportant detail.
† In a large city the address of the Church should be given If the Church has a name, such as "St. Paul's" or "St. Mark's," it should be used In that case the denomination need not be given unless it is a part of the name of the church

You may put "R.S.V.P.," "R.s v.p." (either form may be used), or "Please respond" at the lower left-hand corner of the card if you wish, but whether you do or not most people today will let you know whether they are able to come or not, and if the reception is a simple one and you have not invited a great many guests, it will not matter greatly whether you know the exact number or not. It is perhaps a subtle compliment to your invited guests to assume that they will let you know their intentions without being asked to do so

The invitations are engraved on the first page of a folded sheet of fine quality vellum, usually in script or shaded antique Roman type. They may be either of a size which slips without further folding into the envelope or twice this size, which must be folded once before insertion. The smaller size is customarily used for less formal weddings, the larger for formal.

The invitations may be personalized, if you wish, by having the engraver leave a blank space in which to write in the name of the invited guests, using black ink, or two names if a man and his wife are invited, thus:

Mr. and Mrs. William Rainey Parker
request the honour of

presence at the marriage of their daughter
Margaret Sarah
to
(or "and")
Mr. Gregory Robert Marsh
on Saturday, the fourteenth of June,
at four o'clock
The First Congregational Church
Mapleville, New Hampshire
Reception at 123 Elm Street, Mapleville,
immediately after ceremony

The bride and groom's "at home" card is often, though not always, enclosed with the invitation. It is engraved in the same type as that used for the invitation, and is usually about 4" x 2¾"

At home*
after the fifteenth of July
216 Cross Street
Wheaton, Illinois

* With very formal invitations the word "home" is sometimes capitalized.

For very formal church weddings to which a large number of guests have been invited church and pew cards are sometimes enclosed with the invitation to make sure that all the invited guests will have seats and that no one who has not been invited will be seated until all with cards have found their places. The church card is engraved:

> Please present this card
> at the First Congregational Church
> on Saturday the fourteenth of June

If the pew number is to be designated (though this is seldom done) the words "Pew number" are engraved on the lower left-hand corner of the card, and the number later written in with black ink. Or the bride's mother may enclose her calling card with one of the following written in, "Pew number four," "The Bride's reserved section," or "The Bridegroom's reserved section."

The invitation, with enclosures if any, is inserted into the smaller of two envelopes, after the tissue which has been supplied by the engraver has been removed (unless, in a damp climate or because of the lateness of delivery of the invitations, there is danger of smudging), and the name of the guest, without address, written on it. If it is to be sent to an intimate friend or friends or a close relative, the names may be written informally, as "Tom and Helen," or "Aunt Mary and Uncle Bill." If there are children in the family who are also invited, their names may be added here, "Roberta, Jane, and Peter." This envelope (which has no gum on the flap) is then inserted in the larger one, and the outside envelope formally addressed.

The usage "Mr. and Mrs. John Smith and Family" in an address is not approved, because it is too indefinite. Custom dictates that the names of daughters above the age of childhood may be included with those of their parents, as follows:

> Mr. and Mrs. John Smith
> The Misses Mary and Patricia Smith

But if there are young men above the age of twelve or thirteen a separate invitation should be sent to them, addressed.

> The Messrs. James and Peter Smith

Invitations to a double wedding of brides who are not sisters are issued jointly by the parents of the two brides, thus:

Mr. and Mrs. William Rainey Parker
and
Mr. and Mrs James Ellery White
request the honour of your presence
at the marriage of their daughters
Margaret Sarah Parker
to
Mr. Gregory Robert Marsh
and
Vera Ashton White
to
Mr. James Houston Loring
Saturday, the fourteenth of June
at four o'clock
The First Congregational Church
Mapleville, New Hampshire
Reception at Mapleville Country Club
Immediately after ceremony

If the bride is a divorcee she and her family will be guided by restraint, good taste, and the custom of the group and locality in planning the wedding and issuing invitations. Customs vary. Generally speaking, an elaborate wedding is considered in poor taste for a divorcee If she is very young her parents may issue the invitations and announcements as they would in the case of a daughter who had not been married before, but they would use the name of her former husband along with her own, thus

Mr. and Mrs. William Rainey Parker
request the honour of your presence
at the marriage of their daughter
Margaret Parker Harrison,
etc.

Or the bride-to-be may herself send the invitations, which in many groups is considered in better taste. If she and her fiancé are following the conservative custom of having a small informal wedding, the most effective invitations will be simple informal notes written by the prospective bride.

If the bride is middle-aged and a divorcee she will invariably send the invitations herself.

The usage dictating the sending of invitations for the wedding of a widow is similar to that followed in the case of a divorcee They may be issued either by herself or by her parents if she is young. and her name may be written in either of two ways, as "Margaret

Sarah Henderson," or as "Margaret Parker Harrison." An older widow usually issues her own invitations and uses her late husband's full name, "Mrs. Frederick Francis Harrison." (See also Chapter 22, "Separation, Divorce, and Second Marriage.")

Indeed any woman who has reached the years that are generally considered those of middle age usually sends her own invitations, even if to her first marriage. In such a case the invitation is usually as follows:

> The honour of your presence
> is requested at the marriage of
> Miss Margaret Sarah Parker
> to (or "and")
> Mr. Gregory Robert Marsh
> etc.

If the groom is a member of the United States Army, Navy, Air Force, Marine Corps, or a reserve service connected with one of these, it is customary to designate this on the invitation. If he has the rank of Captain or higher, the rank precedes the name instead of "Mr." If he is a commissioned officer of lower rank, the "Mr." is omitted and the rank noted below the name. If he is a non-commissioned officer, a petty officer, or an enlisted man, the "Mr." is also omitted, and his service is mentioned below his name, thus:

> Captain Gregory Robert Marsh
> United States Army
> or
> Gregory Robert Marsh
> Ensign, United States Navy
> or
> Gregory Robert Marsh
> United States Air Force

If a wedding must be postponed and a new date has been set, a formal combination postponement and invitation takes the following form:

> Mr and Mrs. William Rainey Parker
> announce that the marriage of their daughter
> Margaret Sarah
> has been postponed from
> Saturday, the fourteenth of June,
> until
> Saturday, the twelfth of July,
> at four o'clock
> etc.

If death or a serious illness in the family between the time the invitations are issued and the wedding dictates that a very small and quiet ceremony must replace an elaborately planned wedding, it is proper to recall the invitations by the use of a card engraved as follows:

> Mr. and Mrs. William Rainey Parker
> regret that because of a death* in the family
> the invitations to
> their daughter's wedding
> must be recalled

In this case the wedding may take place, but it will be an extremely quiet affair with only close relatives in attendance.

It is considered in poor taste for an elaborate wedding to take place less than six months after the death of a parent of either bride or groom.

The Wedding Ring

The traditional wedding ring for a woman is a narrow band of gold or platinum. The wise prospective groom will take his fiancée with him when he selects it, though if they follow custom she will not see it again until it is placed on her finger at the wedding Frequently it is engraved on the inside with the initials of both the bride and the groom, and the date of their marriage, thus "G.M. and M.P. (or G. M. to M. P.) June 14, 1962." The groom of course pays for it, and keeps it until the wedding day.

If the groom is to have a ring it will be a plain gold band, which he wears on the ring finger of his left hand as the bride does It is a gift from the bride, and she pays for it. If it is engraved the initials are reversed, that is, "M.P. and (or 'to') G.M." and the date.

The groom's ring is purely optional as is the time when the groom puts it on if he has one. In the Protestant double-ring ceremony the rings are exchanged at the proper moment in the ceremony itself. If this plan is not followed, and the bride has purchased a ring for him, she usually gives it to him at the reception.

Bride's Attendants

Whether the bride has any attendants, and if so, how many, depends upon the kind of wedding she is to have, and how elaborate it is to be For a small ceremony, whether at home or at a church,

* Or "illness"

the bride may have only one, generally known as the maid of honor or matron of honor. For a very elaborate church wedding she may have a maid of honor or a matron of honor, or both, and as many as ten bridesmaids, with a group of younger girls from seven to fourteen as junior bridesmaids, flower girls, pages, trainbearers, and even a ring bearer. But the wedding in which the bride seemed to be lost in the throng of her attendants is largely a thing of the past in this country. At a simple home wedding, the bride usually has only one attendant, generally a sister or intimate friend, and for an elaborate church wedding from two to six bridesmaids in addition to the maid of honor or matron of honor.

If you are to have a formal wedding you must bear in mind the expense to which a bridesmaid is typically put for her outfit before asking anyone to serve, and make sure that she can afford it, or if not that your parents can and are able tactfully to suggest that they pay for it. (This is occasionally done, though it is more usual for the bridesmaids to buy their own outfits, while the bride's parents may provide accessories, and are expected to buy the bridesmaids' bouquets.) Further, if any of those whom you ask to be bridesmaids live at some distance from the city in which you are to be married they will have the expense of traveling, though the bride's parents are expected to arrange living quarters for them, either at the homes of friends or at hotels, and if at the latter to pay for them. Since it is very difficult to refuse an invitation to be a bridesmaid, the prospective bride should be sure that she is not asking a friend to assume expenses which she cannot afford before asking her.

The bridesmaids are invited to the bridal dinner or luncheon, if one is given, before the wedding, attend the wedding rehearsal, where they learn that they will precede the bride up the aisle in the processional, and follow the bride and groom to the back of the church in the recessional, accompany the bride to the church, after having dressed at her house and received their bouquets, stand in the receiving line, and sit at the bride's table (if there is one) at the reception.

The maid or matron of honor helps the bride to dress, holds her bouquet during the ceremony, adjusts her train (if she wears one) as she turns to walk down the aisle after the ceremony, and if there is a double ring ceremony, keeps the bridegroom's ring until it is called for. Like the bridesmaids she stands in the receiving line and sits at the bride's table at the reception. She also signs her name to the marriage license as a witness, and usually gives the bride a substantial wedding present.

Junior bridesmaids, flower girls, pages, trainbearers, and ring bearers are seldom members of contemporary American weddings. A favorite small sister, seven to fourteen, however, may be given the honor of being a junior bridesmaid if you wish, in which case she is simply a small replica of the bridesmaids, and does as they do. Flower girls, in the rare cases in which they are included, carry baskets of flowers in the procession, pages simply march with it, with no other duties, trainbearers (two) carry the train of the wedding dress, and the ring bearer, traditionally a small boy, carries the ring on a pillow (usually pinned on so that he doesn't drop it off). But these members of the cast nowadays exist more in the memories of elderly society matrons than as actual participants in even the most elaborate weddings.

The Groom's Attendants

Just as the bride, even at the smallest and least pretentious wedding, has at least one attendant, so the groom has a best man. In point of fact even a civil marriage with no guests requires two witnesses. These of course may be picked up at random, but surely every couple wants at least one or two close friends to be present at the most important event of their lives.

The best man is usually brother or father of the groom, or a brother of the bride, or a close friend, and should accept the responsibility uncomplainingly for his duties, even at a small wedding, are numerous. For a large wedding he is extremely busy.

If there is to be a bachelor's dinner before the wedding the best man usually arranges it and, of course, attends it, though the groom pays for it. He attends the rehearsal. If it is to be a church wedding, and there are to be ushers (who are selected by the groom), the best man sees that they have proper clothes, which are almost an exact replica of the groom's in a formal wedding, sees that they come to the rehearsal, get to the church well ahead of the time set for the ceremony, and know what their duties are. He helps the groom dress and gets him to the church, or wherever the ceremony is to take place. He takes charge of the ring (the best place for him to keep it is on his little finger) and produces it at the proper moment Sometimes he has a spare, borrowed from the jeweler, to provide against the unlikely misfortune of not being able to locate the ring intended for the ceremony. The groom gives him the clergyman's fee in a sealed envelope, and he finds a propitious moment to hand it unobtrusively to the latter. He usually accompanies the maid or matron of honor in the recessional, or, in some cases hastens after the ceremony into the vestry, where he has the groom's hat and coat ready for him, meets the bridal couple, and sees them into their car. He signs the wedding license as a witness along with the maid or matron of honor. He attends the reception and remains the groom's companion there. If there is a bride's table he sits at it, traditionally proposes the first toast to the bride and groom, and opens and reads congratulatory telegrams. After the reception he helps the groom prepare for his getaway with the bride, sees that he has his car keys (if he and the bride are driving) or tickets (if they are leaving by rail or plane), sees that the luggage is all together, and gets it and the bridal couple into their car or cab.

Like the bridesmaids the best man should be chosen with consideration for the expense you have asked him to assume, for he must equip himself with whatever kind of clothes the groom is going to wear (save that the groom customarily furnishes his tie and gloves), he must pay his own transportation to and from the wedding, and, if he follows custom, give the bridal couple a substantial wedding gift.

Ushers

These are not necessary for a house wedding or for a very small informal church wedding. For a larger church wedding it is best to plan for at least one usher for about every fifty expected guests.

They are usually close friends or relatives of the groom, and may include a brother of the bride. If one is designated a head usher he should be preferably a brother or a cousin who knows the family well.

The ushers are dressed as the groom and best man are dressed. They outfit themselves, save for the tie, gloves, and boutonnieres, which the groom supplies. Today they may rent their outfits if they wish without any impropriety. Indeed this is also true today for the best man and even the groom. They pay for their transportation to and from the wedding, but they are the groom's guests while there, and are put up by him at the homes of friends or in a hotel. They customarily give the bride a wedding present, and often it is a fairly expensive one which the ushers as a group give her jointly.

Their duties are fairly standard. They go to the bachelor dinner if there is one. Arriving early at the church (wearing their boutonnieres to indicate their function) they wait in the vestibule for the guests (If they are given lists of the guests who are to sit in the bride's reserved section, and those who are to sit in the groom's section, it facilitates their seating If not they may quite properly ask whether the guests are friends of the bride or of the groom, so that they may seat the bride's friends and relatives on the left side and the groom's on the right.) Friends and family who are to be seated in the reserved seats may be identified by pew cards or by a seating plan that has been given the ushers. At a small wedding with a member of the family or a close friend acting as usher, such devices are usually unnecessary, for the usher will probably know by sight those who are to sit in the reserved section.

The usher offers his right arm to each lady whom he sees to her seat. If two ladies arrive together the usher escorts the elder, and the younger follows them down the aisle.

If ribbons and canvas are used (as explained later—see p. 315) the ushers manipulate them.

Junior ushers are almost never a part of contemporary American weddings, but if either the bride or the groom has a small brother whom they particularly want to include in the wedding he may be so designated and may be given the job of handling the ribbons, if they are used, or of just standing about looking pleasant, dressed in a dark blue suit, or in summer white flannels with either white or dark blue jacket, and wearing the same boutonniere as the senior ushers. If any of his young friends come to the wedding he might well escort them to their seats, but should leave the older guests to his senior colleagues.

The Bachelor Dinner

Whether a bachelor's dinner is given or not is entirely the choice of the prospective groom. Actually the reasons for it and the customs which have obtained at it in the past are all a little silly. It is supposedly a last fling, a frequently rowdy and drunken farewell to freedom and bachelorhood. Yet it may be a friendly and dignified gathering in which a man's male friends can give him especially warm wishes for happiness in his marriage, and I know of no rule which says that anyone *has* to get drunk anywhere, or under any circumstances.

It is at the bachelor dinner that the groom customarily gives the ushers and best man the presents that will express his gratitude and commemorate the occasion. These may be what he wishes. Small articles for personal use, such as cigarette cases, cuff links, belt buckles, or billfolds. These are put at the places of the recipients before they arrive at the table.

If the affair is given, the best man traditionally arranges it (and of course attends it, as do the ushers), though the groom pays for it, in a private room at a restaurant or a club. At the end of the dinner the champagne glasses are filled, the groom rises, as do the other guests, and proposes the toast "To the bride." The toast is then drunk by all, and if the groom wants to be very extravagant he may snap the stem of the glass from which he has drunk, in which case (but not otherwise) the guests will do the same.

The Bride's Party

It is even less common for the bride to signalize her changed status by a party than it is for the groom to do so She may, however, invite her attendants (if she is to have more than a single maid of honor) to tea, lunch, or dinner, at her home a few days before the wedding, give them the presents which she has bought for them, and, if she likes, propose a toast to the groom. Or she may invite both male and female attendants to a similar informal function.

The Rehearsal

Whether the wedding is to be the smallest possible affair with only the bride and two witnesses, or a few close relatives and friends present, it is essential that everyone connected with the wedding party know exactly what he is to do during the ceremony. In the case of a small informal wedding a visit of the bride and groom, and such attendants as there are to be, to the minister who will perform the ceremony, and careful attention to his instructions will doubtless serve the purpose. For an elaborate church wedding there should be a rehearsal at the church.

Since the procedure at the rehearsal is the same as at the wedding (except of course, that it is preceded by instructions, and halted for corrections and that the words of the service are not spoken, nor the ring used), I shall not repeat it here. (See p 318)

In general, however, it is well to remember that these are among the important things that must be decided and learned at the rehearsal: How the attendants should pair off, how the ribbons and canvas, if used, are handled, the distances that should be maintained between members of the wedding party, how fast the music should be played so that it will synchronize with the beginning and end of the processional and recessional, whether the bride should take the right or left arm of her father (if he is giving her away) in the processional (it is usually considered better for her to take his right arm, so that after he has played his part in the ceremony he may take his place in the front seat of the bride's section at the left without crossing the aisle), where each member of the party is to stand during the service, the parts of the bride and groom in the ceremony and when each does what, whether the groom is to kiss the bride at the altar or not, etc. Since the practices of different religions and denominations, and sometimes of different churches within the same denomination differ in some of these details, the clergyman will issue specific instruction concerning all of these matters.

THE WEDDING CEREMONY

A Simple Protestant Home Wedding

One of the loveliest, most intimate, and most dignified of all weddings is the informal, small, ceremony held in the home of the bride. For a Protestant home wedding no special equipment is necessary. The ceremony may be held in whatever is the most suitable room in the house—usually the living room. It, and probably the rest of the house, will be decorated with flowers. Traditionally these are white or pastel shades, but the beauty of an informal wedding lies in its informality, and any flowers which are in season may be used. The member of the bride's family who is most adept at flower arrangements should be given the responsibility of choosing and placing the flowers. If the bride's home is in the country, her own garden may furnish the loveliest flowers of all. Some people, feeling that floral decorations detract from the effect of the bride's bouquet, use simply smilax and other greenery.

A bay window, or a corner of the room, or an alcove, may be selected as a suitable spot for the ceremony itself, and this may, if you like (but need not), be made into a bower of flowers, or set off by potted ferns or palms. Here the clergyman will stand, facing the guests, as he speaks the words of the marriage service.

For an informal home wedding the bride wears a street-length dress or suit of any color she chooses (but not black). She customarily does not carry a bridal bouquet (though if the groom has furnished one, she will of course carry it), but does wear the boutonniere which the groom has given her. The groom wears a dark business suit, preferably Oxford gray or black, a white shirt with turndown collar and a conservative tie (in summer he may wear a Palm Beach suit if he prefers, or a light-weight dark suit), and black shoes (or if he wears a Palm Beach suit he may, if he likes, wear white shoes). His boutonniere is usually white

Whether or not there is music is purely a matter of choice. If there is, it may be furnished by a small orchestra brought in for the occasion, by a friend or relative of the bride at the piano, or even by phonograph records that are especially made to be used at weddings. In the most informal home weddings there is usually no processional or recessional, but incidental music before and after the ceremony may be played.

At the most informal house weddings the bride usually does not keep out of sight before the ceremony, but joins her mother in greeting the guests as they come. When the clergyman takes his place the guests rise, the bride approaches on the arm of her father or not as she chooses, and with her maid of honor beside her the groom joins her with his best man before the clergyman, her family take their places at the left and his at the right, and the ceremony proceeds When it is finished the groom kisses the bride and both turn to receive the congratulations of the guests.

There is no receiving line, but usually a table is prepared with refreshments (including, of course, the wedding cake) to which all turn after the congratulations have been given.

In the country, when the season and weather are favorable, the wedding ceremony may take place out of doors, with an especially effective background of flowers and greenery in their natural state. After the ceremony the entire party then usually enters the house for refreshments, or they may be brought to the guests out of doors.

The Formal Home Wedding

If the house is large enough a home wedding may be as formal as any held in a church, with as many guests as may be accommodated, with a number of attendants, and even with ribbons and canvas. In general the procedure follows exactly that of the formal church wedding (see p. 318), though obviously certain adjustments have to be made. Since there is no "aisle" as in a church, along which the processional and recessional will proceed, a passage must be arranged leading to the altar. And as there are no pews, enough chairs must be provided (these may be rented) to seat the guests, etc.

The Protestant Rectory or Parsonage Wedding

Informal weddings may be held at the rectory or parsonage of the bride's or groom's church. In such cases usually only the bride and groom, the best man and maid of honor (who will act as witnesses) and members of the immediate families of the two principals attend. The bride may, or may not, be "given away" by her father. Informal clothing is worn as at an informal home wedding. The ceremony proceeds as in the informal home wedding, save that if there is to be a reception, it takes place at the home of the bride or in a hotel after the ceremony.

The Protestant Church Ceremony

A church ceremony may be as informal as that earlier described for the home, or it may be as elaborate and formal as you desire.

In the informal ceremony with few guests the procedure is quite simple. The bride and groom dress as they would for an informal home wedding. There may be no attendants save the best man and the maid of honor, and the guests may consist only of the immediate families and most intimate friends of the bride and groom. The bride's guests customarily (as at a formal wedding) sit on the left of the center aisle and the groom's on the right.

A wide latitude of procedure is permissible in the actual ceremony. When there are only a few guests the processional and recessional are often omitted, though they may be used, in which case the procession (though much smaller) follows the routine described for a formal church wedding (see p. 318). Or after the groom and best man have taken their places before the altar and the waiting clergyman, the bride may enter with her maid of honor and with or without her father and proceed down the aisle to the altar. Or the bride and groom may enter together through a side door, followed by the maid of honor and best man. The bride may or may not be "given away" as she and her father decide. If this detail is to be observed, and the father has not entered with the bride, he may step to the altar from his pew at the proper time. After the ceremony, if there is to be no reception, the bride and groom usually pause in the vestibule of the church to receive the congratulations of their friends, or if there are so many of them that this would be awkward, may go to a small room in the church, to which the usher or ushers will direct the guests. Sometimes this practice is followed even when there is to be a reception.

The Formal Protestant Wedding

A formal wedding may be held in a church or at the home of the bride if it is large enough and if special arrangements have been made to allow for the processional and recessional (see p. 318). Save for modifications made necessary by the physical differences between a home and a church the procedure is the same. The following description concerns a formal church wedding, but may easily be adapted for use in a home.

The bride wears a full-length gown of any one of several materials. For a winter wedding, velvet, taffeta, chiffon, lace, or tulle are usual. If the wedding is in summer any of these may be used except velvet, and also organdy, dotted Swiss, dimity, or linen. The length of the train will depend upon the bride's taste, upon her height (a very long train on a very short woman is incongruous) and on the size of the church. A moderately short train is about a yard long. The gown should be conservative, according to old tradition with long sleeves and a high neck. Rigidity in this, however, has relaxed a great deal in recent years, and (save in some churches) a mild décolleté is permissible. If short sleeves are worn, it is customary to wear long gloves (though some brides today omit them), in which case the seam of the ring finger must be ripped before the bride enters the church so that it may be slipped back when the ring is to be put on.

If it is a first marriage the gown is traditionally white, but may be ivory or a pastel shade of blue, pink, green, or yellow. (If the bride is being married for the second time it is considered improper for her to wear white.)

You may, or may not, wear a veil (for a first marriage) as you like. If you do wear one, it should match your gown, and may be as long as you choose (Bridal veils are not worn at a second marriage, either by a widow or by a divorcee.) If you wear a face veil it is removed by the maid of honor before the recessional

Shoes, of silk or satin, should match the gown

"Something old, something new, something borrowed, and something blue, and a lucky sixpence in your shoe" are by old tradition supposed to bring good luck to a marriage. If you wish to follow the tradition it is very simple If your mother or grandmother has saved her wedding veil and passed it on to you, either it or a piece of it fulfills the first requirement. An old piece of jewelry or lace handkerchief will do equally well, provided the jewelry is inconspicuous "Something new" is provided by any article of clothing bought specifically for the wedding costume. A prayer book will fulfill the specifications for "something borrowed." If there is no blue in your costume a blue garter, or a piece of blue silk pinned to your slip will do the trick And a dime (fastened with scotch tape in your shoe, where it will not slip down under a toe and make you uncomfortable) will surely bring you as much luck as a sixpence would.

A flower circlet fulfills the need for a head covering required in many churches. In those which do not require any it may be omitted if you like But if you wish to wear nothing on your head ask the clergyman about the requirements in the church where you are to be married before planning your costume.

The bridesmaids wear clothing selected by the bride to harmonize with her own, of the same material or one which goes well with it. They may wear the same dress, but in a different material or color, or all white. In any case they are usually the same length as the bride's gown Or they may be in pastel shades, all the same, and differing slightly, or exactly alike in style, or they may wear slightly different pastel colors. Their slippers and the ribbons on their bouquets match their dresses They may wear hats or floral headpieces. They do not wear gloves except at a very formal wedding, in which case they do whether the bride does or not. They sometimes wear no veils, though they may wear short veils if the bride's is long.

The maid or matron of honor dresses with just enough difference from the bridesmaids to be noticeable. If she wears the same color dress it will be slightly different in style. Or if it is similar in style it should be of a different color. Or she may be set off by a distinctive headdress and bouquet.

The Formally Dressed Groom

What the groom wears for a formal wedding depends upon the hour of the day when the ceremony takes place. If the wedding occurs before seven in the evening he will wear a cutaway or the less formal sack coat with gray-striped trousers, a gray vest (for which natural or white linen may be substituted for summer). If he wears a cutaway he will wear a wing collar with black and white ascot or cravat, if he wears a sack coat he may wear a turndown stiff collar. He wears black socks and black shoes (the soles of which may be blackened so that they will not be noticeably off color if and when he kneels during the ceremony). His boutonniere, often lilies of the valley or a gardenia, may be a spray from the bride's bouquet.

For a formal summer wedding in the country he may substitute white or gray flannels and a navy jacket for the cutaway and striped trousers, with blue tie, white shoes, and a turndown stiff collar. For an outdoor wedding he may wear a Palm Beach suit, if he likes, with a white tie or one in a light color. Ushers may, for a summer wedding, wear dark trousers and white, or Palm Beach jackets.

If the wedding takes place after seven in the evening he wears a tail coat with an opera or high silk hat, if the wedding is very formal, or a dinner jacket if it is less so.

The groom's attendants wear what the groom wears with minor variations. In any case all the ushers dress exactly alike, and the best man is distinguished by some detail or details. For instance at a formal morning or afternoon wedding, when the groom wears a cutaway and wing collar, the best man will also But though the ushers will wear cutaways they will wear turndown collars. The best man's boutonniere will differ from that of the ushers.

The family of the bride and groom are also guided by the time of day the wedding is held in choosing what they will wear, the fathers of the bride and groom and other mature male relatives dressing as the groom does, wearing cutaways or sack coats and striped trousers for a morning or afternoon wedding, and tails and white tie if the wedding is in the evening, as will many of the male guests, though the latter need not dress formally unless they choose. Younger male relatives who are not actually members of the wedding party may properly wear dinner jackets if they wish.

The mothers of the bride and groom wear, for a daytime wedding, floor-length or shorter length dresses of pastel faille, taffeta, satin, or silk, with long gloves, if short sleeves are worn, or short gloves with long-sleeved dresses. Hats and shoes are chosen to match or contrast with dresses It is pleasant to have the dresses of the two mothers similar and harmonious, though not of course identical.

For a formal evening wedding the mothers will wear formal evening dresses or dinner gowns, with jacket or stole, and accessories the same as for a daytime wedding.

Church Decorations, Canopy, Ribbons, and Canvas

The decorations and appurtenances for a church wedding may be few or many depending upon taste, whether the wedding is small and informal or large and extremely formal. It should be remembered, however, that beauty, dignity, and restraint, not ostentation, are to be desired.

If the church permits decoration of the altar suitable flowers may be placed there, but the minister should be consulted as to what flowers may be used. The aisle posts of the pews are often decorated, sometimes with flowers, sometimes only with greenery, sometimes with both Frequently such decoration is confined to the posts of the reserved pews, or may be placed on every other post for the whole length of the aisle. Palms and ferns are often used effectively by a skillful florist, and if the decorations are to be at all elaborate a professional florist should attend to them.

A canopy is sometimes (though less frequently than formerly) erected from the curb to the church entrance, and the church aisle is sometimes especially carpeted for the wedding.

A canvas, the width and length of the aisle, and rolled, is sometimes provided to be put down (as explained later) by the ushers after all the guests and the bride's mother have been seated, in order to keep the bride's train clean, but this is not considered essential.

White satin ribbons, three or four inches wide, are sometimes used to separate the reserved sections (which are, of course, at the front of the church) in which the families and special guests of the bride and groom sit, from the rest of the pews. They may be managed in either of two ways. A ribbon may be stretched across the aisle, hanging by loops from the post of the last pew in the reserved section of the bride's side to the post of the last pew on the groom's side. In this case it is taken down by the usher each time he seats someone in the reserved section and replaced as he returns, and of course must be taken down after the bride's mother is seated and before the processional begins, for it makes a barrier across the aisle. Or two longer ribbons may be used, each stretching from the rear of the last pew in the reserved section on one side to the back of the last pew in the church. If this method is used the ribbons are left folded and lying at the side of the aisle at the last pew of the reserved section until the bride's mother is seated, and then put in place by the ushers before the processional begins. In either method, instead of loops the ends of the ribbons may be weighted so that they will hang in place over the backs of the pews

The canopy, the canvas, and the ribbons are usually furnished by the florist who decorates the church, though sometimes the canvas and canopy may be provided by the church.

Music is usually supplied by the church organist, or an organist engaged by the bride's family. It may consist simply of the processional (traditionally the *Lohengrin* Wedding March) and the Recessional (usually the march from Mendelssohn's *Midsummer Night's Dream*), but often incidental music is played while the guests are assembling. This should be dignified but not somber, and the selections must be discussed with the clergyman or the church's musical director if it has one, for there may be restrictions on the kind of music that may be played. If the church permits it you may, if you like, have a soloist, and perhaps the church choir.

Arrangements for these must be made some time in advance There will be fees for the organist, the soloist, and the choir, if used, and these will be paid by the bride's family before or after the ceremony.

The ushers should arrive at the church about an hour before the ceremony is to begin, wearing their boutonnieres, and take their places at the head of the aisles, ready to seat the families of the couple and guests, the family and close friends of the bride usually on the left, and those of the groom on the right.

One usher is designated "head usher" and it is he who seats the families of the bride and groom.

In most churches the pews are divided into only two sections, with a center aisle running between them, and an aisle down each side of the church. In some, however, there are three sections, and consequently in effect two center aisles. In such cases it may be decided to use only two adjoining sections, treating the aisle between them as the center aisle. Or all three may be used with the front pews of the left section and those of the left side of the middle section up to approximately its middle line used as the bride's section, and those of the right section and in the right half of the middle section, used for the groom's family and closest friends.

The mother and father of the bride are always seated in the front pew of the bride's section, and those of the groom in the front pew of the groom's section.

The groom and best man are the next to arrive at the church, coming about half an hour before the ceremony is to begin. They go to the vestry room, or to the clergyman's study, as arranged with him beforehand. Here the best man gives the clergyman a fee in an envelope, which has previously been given to him by the groom. (See p. 306.)

The guests should arrive at the latest fifteen minutes before the ceremony is to begin and are shown to their pews by the ushers (See p. 307.)

The bride, her parents, and her attendants, having previously assembled at the bride's home, now arrive in a prescribed order in cars furnished by her parents. The first car in the group carries the mother of the bride and one or two bridesmaids. The other bridesmaids follow in as many cars as are needed. The last car of all carries the bride and her father. If the bride's family wish to add a nice touch to the entourage they may outfit the chauffeur of this car with a white boutonniere and white gloves. If the timing is perfect the bride's car will arrive about a minute after the hour set for the ceremony.

All of the cars except that in which the bride and her father ride discharge their passengers at the door of the church and move off to the parking space The bride's car, however, stays at the door of the church waiting for the bride and her husband to enter it after the ceremony.

When the bride's mother has been seated the doors are closed and no other guests are shown to their seats. If there are late arrivals they must wait in the vestibule, or (if the doors have not yet been closed) quietly find places in the rear of the church, or if there is a balcony, sit there.

The canvas, if one is used (see p. 315), is then unrolled down the aisle by two ushers, and the ribbons (if used) adjusted. If the arrangement by which a ribbon has been stretched across the aisle has been adopted, it is taken down to permit passage of the processional.

If the other arrangement has been decided upon the ushers advance in step to the last pew of the reserved section where each picks up the ribbon waiting on his side of the aisle, slips the ribbon loop over the pew post on his side (or if the ribbon has been weighted, drops the end over the back of the pew), and carries his ribbon behind the posts of the other pews to the last pew at the back of the church where he loops it over the post of the last pew, or drapes it over the back of the pew. The ushers then return to the vestibule to take their places for the processional

The clergyman, followed by the groom, who in turn is followed by the best man enters the chancel from the vestry or study as the organist strikes the first chord of the wedding march. The clergyman takes his place directly in front of the altar, the groom, with his best man behind him, a little to the right, and with his eyes on the aisle watching for his bride. The guests rise.

The procession then enters the aisle, in step, each member of it starting on his left foot, and in the following order:

The ushers walking in pairs, arranged by height, the shortest first.

The bridesmaids in pairs also arranged according to height with the shorter preceding the taller.

The maid of honor, walking alone. If there are both a maid of honor and a matron of honor, they may walk together or the younger may precede and the older follow.

The flower girl (if any).

The bride on her father's arm (usually the right, though this will be decided by the clergyman).

If there are trainbearers they will, of course, come directly behind the bride, holding the train just high enough so that the lowest part will barely clear the floor.

If there is a ring bearer he will bring up the rear.

If the timing has been properly arranged the music of the processional will end precisely as the bride reaches the altar.

As the head of the procession reaches the altar it will divide in either of two ways, as has been decided at the rehearsal.

The ushers and bridesmaids at the right may turn to the right, pair off, and stand behind the groom and best man, while those on the left may do the same thing on the left, accompanied by the flower girl if there is one Or all the ushers may turn to the right, and all the bridesmaids to the left. The maid of honor proceeds to the altar with the bride and stands at her left.

As the bride and her father reach a spot (previously exactly determined at the rehearsal) a few paces from the group, she drops her father's arm, he stops and stands where he is, and the groom steps forward to meet her, taking his place on her right side, and they advance together to stand directly before the clergyman. The father stays where his daughter has left him until the clergyman says, "Who giveth this woman away?" Whereupon he steps forward saying, "I do," takes his daughter's hand and places it in that of the clergyman. He then takes his seat in the bride's section.

The bride has been carrying her bouquet or prayer book in her right hand and now shifts it to the left. She may, or may not, take the groom's arm, or even his hand, but customs as to this vary with different denominations, bride and groom will be instructed by the clergyman at the rehearsal.

The marriage service differs slightly in different denominations. The clergyman will carefully instruct all members of the party at the rehearsal so that each will be well versed in his part. During it the maid of honor holds the bride's bouquet so that it will not be in the way.

The recessional proceeds in reverse order to that of the processional, save that now the groom takes the place of the bride's father, who remains in his pew. As the organist begins the music (usually the march from Mendelssohn's *Midsummer Night's Dream* played in a somewhat faster tempo than was the processional) the train-bearers (if any) take up the bride's train, or if there are none the maid of honor arranges it, having handed the bride's bouquet back to her, the bride takes the groom's right arm, and followed (in this order) by the flower girl (if one has been used), the bridesmaids, in pairs, and the ushers, in pairs, they walk to the rear of the church.

Sometimes the arrangement is varied; if there are the same number of bridesmaids as there are ushers, the bridesmaids and ushers pair off, each bridesmaid on the right arm of an usher. If there have been other children in addition to the flower girl in the processional they join their parents in the pews and do not take part in the recessional.

If the church has three sections and thus two center aisles, and you have decided to use all three sections, the processional takes place along the right-hand aisle, and the recessional along the left-hand.

At a double wedding the arrangement is as follows.

The two bridegrooms, with their best men, follow the clergyman into the chancel from the vestry or his study together, and stand side by side at the right.

In the processional all the ushers lead as in a single wedding They are followed by the bridesmaids of the older bride, who in turn are followed by her maid of honor and flower girl (if any), and by the older bride on the arm of her father. Next are the bridesmaids of the younger bride, her maid of honor, and the younger bride on the arm of her father, or if the two are sisters, on that of a near male relative.

The couple which includes the older bride take their place at the right side of the altar, the younger bride and her groom at the left, with each father standing behind her. If they are sisters the male relative who escorted the young bride goes to his pew, and the father gives both brides away in turn.

The ceremony is read once for both couples, with the responses being repeated by the younger couple after the older has responded.

In the recessional the older bride and her husband lead off, followed by the younger bridal couple. The flower girl if any, comes next. (If there are two, they walk together.) The two maids or matrons of honor follow, walking together, and then either the bridesmaids of the older bride followed by those of the younger, with all the ushers bringing up the rear, or the bridesmaids of the older paired with ushers, those of the younger similarly paired, if there are an equal number of bridesmaids and ushers.

In a church with three sections, and thus two center aisles there may be two processionals and two recessionals, if you like, one for each couple, proceeding simultaneously, that of the older bride using the right aisle and the younger the left. This maneuver takes careful rehearsing as the two groups should keep exactly even with each other and in step.

The Roman Catholic Wedding

The order and physical arrangements are similar to a Protestant church wedding, though the ceremony is somewhat different, and is usually followed by a Nuptial Mass.

All Catholic marriages must take place in the church, save in certain special cases.

At large and important weddings the processional may be led by

singing choristers, but this is rare The rest of the processional is arranged as in the Protestant ceremony.

Although the bride walks down the aisle on the arm of her
father, he does not give her away, but genuflects at the altar, then
leaves her and takes his seat in the front pew on the bride's side

The grouping at the altar is the same as in a Protestant ceremony
save that the bride's father is not present and an acolyte, who assists
the priest, is.

The recessional proceeds as in a Protestant ceremony.

The Club or Hotel Wedding

Whether formal or informal, the club or hotel wedding follows in general the procedure prescribed for the home wedding, with
an improvised altar set up in the flower-decked room chosen for the
ceremony, and another room usually engaged for the reception and
refreshments

A Civil Marriage

Performed by a judge or justice of the peace this is always
informal, with the bride and groom in street clothes, though she will
probably wear a corsage and he a boutonniere. Usually only two
witnesses, and perhaps a few very close friends attend

An Elopement

This, by its very nature, is somewhat outside the subject of
etiquette and conventional behavior. I would be the last to condemn the practice under certain circumstances, and am sure that
many a happy marriage has begun thus.

Yet even though the eloping couple may (perhaps because of un-
changeable opposition on the part of the parents of one or both of
them) have decided to flout convention in this way, there are some
things that should be remembered.

If you are planning to elope because of parental opposition to
your marriage, try by every reasonable means to remove the opposition before you take the final step.

If your parents ask you merely to wait a reasonable time so that
you may be sure before you are married, give their wisdom the
benefit of the doubt. You have a lifetime ahead of you. Surely you
can afford to spend a little of it both in making sure that you are
right and in seeking the blessings of your parents.

If you are a mixed couple, Catholic and Protestant, or Jewish and Christian, and the Catholic or Jewish parents feel strongly opposed to your marriage because of that, one possible solution of the problem is the conversion of the non-Catholic or the non-Jewish member to the other's faith. I say that this is a *possible* solution. It could be for some, for others it could not. For anyone with deep religious convictions an acceptance of another faith purely for expediency must be repugnant and ineffective except to gain the end in view. It may well result in bitter regrets later on. Today to many young people, religion seems to be merely a matter of form and it makes little difference to them whether they are members of one church or another. But in this case parental opposition is unlikely to be based on religious grounds.

I do not recommend this sort of "conversion" (which, save in exceptional cases, is no conversion at all). But I do suggest that you will have a happier marriage if you can find some reasonable way to remove the opposition of your parents before you undertake it.

If you do decide eventually that you are going to elope, be sure that, in the state in which you plan to be married, the law permits people of your age to be married without consent. If you are under the required ages (they usually differ for men and women) and lie about them, your marriage will be technically invalid.

And regardless of the differences that may exist between your parents and yourselves, do not just disappear, giving them no word as to what has happened to you. Let them know as soon as possible by telegram, or telephone, or by deputizing a reliable friend to telephone them. Do it before the night of the day you elope. Night is the time of worrying, and the deeper the differences between you and your parents the more they will worry if you disappear without a trace.

Life is too short to waste any of it in hurting anyone unnecessarily, and later regretting it, or to close any gates against reconciliation with anyone from whom you may have become estranged.

THE RECEPTION

The reception, which may be held at the bride's home, or at the home of a friend, or at a hotel or club, may be small and informal, or large and as formal as the most formal wedding

At the Small, Informal, Home Wedding

Here the most effective procedure is the simplest. After the ceremony is over and the groom has kissed the bride, the couple simply turn to their guests as a group, and receive their congratulations and good wishes, as the guests surround them and talk to them in no prescribed order whatever. In the room in which the ceremony has taken place or in an adjoining room there is usually a buffet table on which refreshments (including the wedding cake) are set The traditional drink in which the best man at some time during the gathering proposes a toast to the bride is champagne, but champagne punch, which is much less expensive, or even good domestic white wine will serve as well, and in families that as a matter of conviction never serve alcoholic beverages, no such drinks will be served, and in my opinion the wedding will lose neither effectiveness nor beauty as a result of the omission.

At such an informal post-ceremony gathering as this the guests will eat standing up, or sitting wherever they may find seats, perhaps at small tables which have been placed here and there. But if there are toasts, and any are seated, all will rise to drink them.

After the toast to the bride the groom often proposes a toast to his bride's mother, and other toasts sometimes follow.

The wedding cake (which may be anything from a simple white homemade angel food or fruit cake to a towering creation furnished by a caterer who specializes in such things) is cut by the bride and groom after the other refreshments have been eaten. Traditionally the bride always cuts the first piece, with the groom's hand over hers, and then divides it for the groom and herself to share. She may then continue to cut pieces for the guests, or turn the task over to her maid of honor, one of the bridesmaids, her mother, a sister, a friend, or a servant.

The same informality usually is observed at a reception following an informal church wedding, the bride and groom together simply chatting with the guests, while the bride's mother welcomes others as they arrive.

The Formal Reception

After a formal church wedding, and often after a formal house ceremony, the reception begins with a receiving line. The pleasantest place to hold such a reception is at the home of the bride's parents, if it is large enough to accommodate the invited guests, and the arrangement of the rooms lends itself to the planning Otherwise it may be held in a private room at a hotel or club, or even at the home of one of the bride's friends.

The receiving line is best established in a room with at least two doors, so that the guests may come in at one and go out through the other. The room may be decorated with flowers—a few simple and well arranged bouquets are sufficient, too many often create a smothering effect.

The arriving guests are met by the bride's mother standing just inside the door. The positions of the groom's mother, the groom's father, and the bride's father are matters of individual choice. Frequently the groom's mother stands just behind, or beside, the bride's mother, where she may be introduced to guests she does not know as they arrive. Her husband may stand beside or behind her, and the father of the bride will usually be close at hand where he can chat with the guests and even wander about a bit with them if he likes.

At a little distance beyond the parental group stand the bride and groom, the bride on the groom's right, with the maid of honor and the bridesmaids standing at her right.

Having been greeted by the parents, the guests then pass on to the bride and groom, greeting first the one whom each knows (or perhaps both simultaneously, or the bride first and then the groom, if both are friends), congratulating the groom, wishing the bride the greatest happiness (it is not considered complimentary to congratulate the bride) and chatting with the maid of honor and the bridesmaids. The bride, of course, usually receives a kiss from each one who is a close friend, and often from one who is not. The guests then pass into the room where refreshments are waiting, at either a buffet table or tables at which some, or perhaps all, sit.

Light Refreshments

Refreshments served buffet style at an informal reception are customarily simple. The wedding cake dominates the center of the table, which is often decorated by vases of flowers. In addition to the cake there may be sandwiches, perhaps small cakes or cookies, tea or coffee or both, and champagne, punch, or wine, if one of these is served.

The Formal Wedding Breakfast or Supper

After a formal morning wedding, and often after one held in the afternoon, it is customary to serve a meal with at least a table for the bride and groom, their attendants, perhaps another for the parents, the clergyman and his wife, and a few especially honored guests, and sometimes small tables for the rest of the guests, though they may also be served standing.

Sometimes the bride's and the parents' table are combined.

Seating arrangements may vary somewhat, but here are two suggested arrangements, the first for an occasion on which there are separate bride's and parents' tables, the second for a combined table.

The bride's table. At each end a bridesmaid and an usher, with the bridesmaid on the usher's right. At the center of one side the bride at the groom's right. At the bride's right the best man; at the groom's left the maid of honor. Bridesmaids and ushers are paired at the remaining spaces.

The parents' table. A guest or guests at each end of the table. At the center of one side of the table the bride's mother, with the groom's father on her right and the clergyman on her left. At the center of the other side the bride's father sitting opposite his wife, with the groom's mother on his right and the clergyman's wife on his left. Guests at the other places, if any.

The combined table. The bride's father at the head, with the groom's mother at his right and the clergyman's wife at his left. The bride's mother at the foot, with the groom's father at the right and the clergyman at her left. At the center of one side the bride sits with the groom on her left and the best man on her right. The maid of honor sits at the groom's left. The bridesmaids and ushers do not ordinarily sit at this table, but pair off at smaller tables or eat standing.

The menu may consist of whatever you like, but is usually light and consists of two courses or possibly three. There may be a thin soup or melon, or this course may be omitted. There is usually a light meat dish with a salad, and a dessert consisting of ice or ice cream with, of course, the wedding cake.

If champagne or punch is served, it is usually poured as soon as the first course is served, and the best man rises as soon as all have had their glasses filled and proposes a toast to the bride, for which all the guests rise.

The best man then reads any telegrams of congratulation that have arrived for the bride and groom (These, incidentally, should of course be addressed to "Mr. and Mrs.")

The Wedding Presents

You may, or need not, display your wedding presents to your guests as you wish. If you do, arrange them as prettily as you can on a separate table, preferably in a room upstairs, or at least in another room from the refreshments Checks sent as gifts are not displayed, but for each one a card is customarily put with the other gifts, each card having written on it simply "Check from ————" using the name of the sender, but not the amount.

Dancing

If there is dancing, with music by a hired orchestra, a piano played by a friend, or even a record player, it begins after the company has eaten. No one dances with the bride until the groom has done so, and it is courteous to allow the bridal couple to take one or two turns around the floor without competition, after which the father of the bride with the groom's mother, and the father of the groom with the bride's mother, join them, and are followed by the guests. The groom should dance with his mother, the bride's mother, and the maid of honor, the bride with her father, father-in-law, best man, and if possible each of the ushers, and the ushers should keep the bridesmaids on the floor throughout the dancing.

The Getaway

As the bride leaves the reception to dress for her honeymoon trip, after having let the bridesmaids know that she is about to leave, she pauses at the door of the reception room, or on the stairs, if there are any, to throw her bouquet to the bridesmaids, so that the one who catches it may look forward to being the next to be married.

After the bride and groom have left to prepare for their journey they need not show themselves again to the guests as a group, but say good-by to their families and perhaps their closest friends privately. Then they are off in car or taxi, with the guests, having got wind of their departure, even if it has been through a back door, dashing out to throw rice, rose petals, or confetti after them, and sometimes, especially in rural communities, to follow in other cars.

This horn-blowing parade has always seemed to me a rude and inconsiderate accompaniment to a wedding. Perhaps I would feel differently about it if we used sweetly chiming bells on our cars instead of horns. But the sound of an automobile horn, under these circumstances, is raucous and seems derisive. By all means let this moment be a gay one, but dignity and kindliness need never be sacrificed for gaiety.

The considerate bride and groom will not neglect to send telegrams to their parents as soon as they reach their destination thanking them for the parts they played in the wedding, assuring them that all is well, and sending their love.

Thanks for the Presents

The considerate bride will write cordial notes to all who have sent her presents thanking them, and if she can remember what each present is, in her excitement, making some appropriate comment about it. She will do this within a week or two of the wedding, regardless of her reluctance to take on such a chore during her honeymoon The plan sometimes followed of having a card of general thanks engraved to send to each of the donors is highly improper unless sent by the bride's mother saying the gift was much appreciated and her daughter will thank the sender on her return.

The Jewish Wedding

Jews are divided into three religious groups with variations in their practices and beliefs, Orthodox, Conservative, and Reform, and even within these divisions there are some disagreements as to ritual.

The extent to which the Reform group (most liberal of the three) has departed from the old traditions of orthodoxy is illustrated by a story, typically subtle and exaggerated as Jewish humor is so likely to be. To understand its meaning you must know that a *bracha*, commonly called a *broche* (pronounced "bro-huh"), is an ancient word meaning prayer or benediction A *broche* is said over the candles when they are lighted on Sabbath eve, and in many other circumstances. It is the equivalent of a Christian "blessing"

A young man had just achieved his heart's desire buying a new Jaguar sports car. Devoutly religious, he wanted to start the car on its career by having it blessed, so he drove to his synagogue, which was highly orthodox, and said to the rabbi,

"Rabbi, I have a most unusual request to make. Will you say a *broche* over my Jaguar?"

The rabbi looked puzzled and asked, "What's a Jaguar?"

Embarrassed by the unworldliness of the holy man, the boy stammered and finally said, "Never mind. I guess it wasn't a very good idea," thanked the rabbi, and left.

Going to a somewhat less orthodox synagogue, he made the same request of the rabbi there, was asked the same question, and again left, without having accomplished his purpose.

Surely, he thought, a Reform rabbi will be modern enough to know what a Jaguar is, so he went to the most liberal Reform synagogue he knew, found the rabbi, and said, "Rabbi, I have a most unusual request to make of you."

"Anything I can do for you, my boy, I'll be glad to," the rabbi said.

"You see, I've just bought a new Jaguar—" the young man began.

"Splendid!" the rabbi said. "I've been thinking of getting one myself. How do you like it?"

"It's wonderful," the boy said. "I like it so much—I hope you won't think my request is silly, because it would mean a lot to me. It would make me so happy if you would say a *broche* over it."

For a moment the rabbi looked puzzled, then he asked, "What's a *broche?*"

I doubt that there is a Reform rabbi anywhere who would not know what a *broche* is, but the significance of the story is apt. Many of the strict regulations and colorful ceremonies of ancient Jewish orthodoxy have been abandoned by Reform Jews, and even by some who are Orthodox. But it seems to me worth while to describe a strictly orthodox Jewish wedding ceremony as it used to be, and as it sometimes still is in rigidly Orthodox congregations, both because it is so colorful, and because today many Jews might encounter unfamiliar practices if they attended such a ceremony. Also in case they are invited, Christian guests will be better prepared and will know what to expect and how to behave.

Jewish weddings, whether Orthodox, Conservative, or Reform, may be held anywhere, in a synagogue or temple, at the home of the bride, or in a rented hall. At Orthodox and Conservative ceremonies all men (including non-Jews if any are present) and all married women wear hats. As a matter of fact, though this is not required, mature, unmarried women also usually have their heads covered The women dress very modestly, with high-necked, long-sleeved dresses. In extremely Orthodox groups the men and women sit in separate parts of the hall The custom of dividing them by a curtain has been largely abandoned, yet in extremely rare cases of the most rigidly Orthodox congregations it is still sometimes followed. Contact between men and women is strictly avoided, and if you, a woman, attend an Orthodox Jewish wedding, do not offer to shake hands with a man—especially not with the rabbi, for if he is extremely religious it would embarrass him deeply.

The bride, dressed in white, will sit with her close female relatives in a room near the main room where she will receive wishes for her happiness, and compliments on how lovely she looks, before the ceremony. If the wedding follows strictly Orthodox custom only women, and no men—not even the groom—will enter the room during this period, save for the brief ritual held just before the ceremony called "examining the bride." This ritual commemorates the Biblical story of Jacob's betrayal by Laban, who substituted Leah for Rachel, and guarantees the groom that there has been no trickery, and that he is indeed getting the girl of his choice.

When all is in readiness the procession forms and proceeds down the aisle in the following order Ushers, bridesmaids, best man, groom walking between his father (on the left) and his mother (on the right), the maid of honor, flower girl (if there is one), and the bride (dressed modestly in white, and wearing a veil), walking between her father and mother (father on her left and mother on her right).

At the front of the hall there has been erected a *chuppa,* a canopy often covered with vines or flowers. All Orthodox and Conservative wedding ceremonies take place under a *chuppa,* as do most of those of a Reform congregation, though it is sometimes omitted by the latter. In talmudic teaching the bride's arrival at the *chuppa* symbolizes her voluntary assumption of the state of matrimony, in popular interpretation the structure is symbolic of the new home which the bride and groom are about to enter. Under the canopy the rabbi, the bride, the groom, the best man and maid of honor, . and if there is room, both pairs of parents stand, in Orthodox and Conservative ceremonies In Reform congregations the parents are not present at the altar In no case may one who is not Jewish stand under the *chuppa*

Now may come (though it is often omitted) one of the most colorful moments of a Jewish wedding ceremony when the bride, accompanied by her closest female relatives, circles the groom seven times in commemoration, it is said, of the storming of the walls of Jericho. (Another explanation is that the seven times symbolize the seven days of the week during all of which she will be a faithful wife.)

The actual ceremony then begins with the rabbi saying the "benediction of betrothal" over a cup of wine, in which he praises God for the institution of marriage. This is followed by the act of *kiddushin* in which the bridegroom, in the presence of two witnesses, places the ring (always a plain gold band) on the index finger of the bride's right hand, saying, "Behold thou art sanctified unto me by this ring according to the Law of Moses and Israel" (The bride, incidentally, usually moves it some time later to the ring finger of the left hand.)

The *ketubah,* or marriage settlement, is then read, which includes the promise from the bridegroom to the bride, "I will work for thee, I will honor thee, I will support and maintain thee, as it beseemeth a Jewish husband to do."

Seven benedictions of nuptials are then said over a cup of wine. These include praises of God as the creator of the fruit of the vine, the shaper of man in his image, the gladdener of friends, the giver of love, brotherhood, peace, and friendship, and include such lovely words as "Soon in the cities of Judah and the streets of Jerusalem will be heard the voices of the bridegroom and the bride, and the sounds of joy and gladness. Blessed be thou who gladdenest the bridegroom with the bride."

At Orthodox weddings the entire ceremony is in Hebrew, at Conservative, in English and Hebrew. Reform ceremonies are usually conducted in English, save that the prayers are sometimes said in Hebrew.

The wine over which the benedictions have been said is drunk by the couple as an indication of their readiness to share whatever destiny Providence sends them. A glass wrapped in a linen napkin is then given to the bridegroom (at all Jewish weddings, Orthodox, Conservative, and Reform) and he breaks this by stamping upon it. The rabbinical explanation of this is that it is in memory of the destruction of the temple, and a declaration that the bride and groom will obey the national pledge expressed in Psalm 137 not to forget Jerusalem, even in the most joyous moments of life.

This act ends the ceremony and traditionally all the guests then shout *"Mazel tov!"* (Congratulations and good luck.)

In the recessional the bride and groom go first, followed by the bride's parents, the groom's parents, the flower girl (if there is one), the maid of honor and best man walking together, and the paired bridesmaids and ushers bringing up the rear.

Usually a feast follows such a wedding, with dancing, eating, and drinking. In highly orthodox circles here, as at the ceremony itself, men and women keep themselves fairly well separated. The traditional toast, which is commonly drunk over and over, is *"L'Chayim!"* ("To Life!")

In Praise of Simplicity

During a long and eventful life I have attended many weddings, and have helped to arrange several. They have ranged in size and atmosphere from the smallest and most informal, to the largest and most rigidly formal and expensive. Among those which I remember with the keenest pleasure and that seemed to me to have the greatest dignity and the most beauty have been small informal affairs at which the light in the bride's eyes seemed to illuminate the proceedings, and the groom's quiet dignity strengthened my faith in the future of mankind. It has been at these that I have felt most strongly that I was witnessing not only a wedding, but a marriage in the deepest and truest sense.

Two small informal weddings which I have had a hand in arranging, I remember with particular pleasure.

In one, my daughter-in-law Mrs. John Roosevelt arranged to have the young couple stand in front of some climbing roses on the lawn near her gray stone cottage in Hyde Park. The couple came out from the cottage accompanied only by two little flower girls My two teenage grandchildren were the witnesses. The ceremony was of the simplest, and afterwards the couple merely turned around and were greeted by their relatives and friends. A friend of theirs played the piano by an open window; and this was the one contribution which I made, as my piano had to be brought over from my nearby cottage.

After the ceremony an unpretentious lunch was arranged on tables on the lawn.

In this case the bride had made her own dress, and the young couple's chief concern was putting what money they had into doing over an old village house nearby that had great charm but needed badly certain modern improvements.

The other wedding, which I arranged, was also very simple. It was held in my New York apartment. There were some flowers in front of the fireplace where the rabbi stood, but the ceremony was a quiet one and only the close family and friends were present Afterwards some light refreshments were served. Then the couple left for their own home.

In both cases, though the ceremonies were simple there was no question but that the couples involved were solemnly and happily entering into the responsibilities of a real marriage.

Just recently a young man, marrying a lovely girl from a family of moderate income, said to me, "That wedding is going to cost Helen's parents over six thousand dollars, and that would make a very nice down payment on a home."

Six thousand dollars was a very great deal of money to him Actually a wedding sometimes costs several times that amount, and I often think of how much human suffering might be alleviated by the money so spent.

I have felt it necessary to tell how elaborate formal weddings are managed, for there are, and undoubtedly will continue to be, many who insist on them. But I want to end this chapter with praise for the beauty of simplicity! And I caution you to keep your sense of relative values sound, and never let the meaning of marriage and a realization of the things which contribute soundly to it be obscured by the elaboration of wedding plans.

22

Separation, Divorce, and Second Marriage

THERE IS AN OLD AND WISE SAYING THAT EVERY HOME, TO assure success in marriage, must have two bears in it— bear and forbear. Without any question these two benevolent creatures have brought about adjustments in many essentially good marriages which would have been dissolved to the detriment of themselves and of society as a whole if the two parties to them had simply given way to impulse born of angry emotional upheavals, or the temporary attraction of one to an outsider of the opposite sex. I have known marriages that, periodically stormy for years, have finally settled down to constructive cooperation and a quiet contented joy, and others that have been terminated by divorce soon after the first quarrel. Such a divorce, incidentally, is as often as not one of a series in the life of one to whom marriage, divorce, and remarriage become simply a cycle of events in a firmly entrenched bad habit, demonstrating what Samuel Johnson called "the triumph of hope over experience."

For such a person the attempt to find happiness by changing the marriage partner is seldom successful, for the root of the trouble, as like as not, is within himself and taken with him from one marriage into another. It is, as the late Clarence Darrow once said, "like trading a carbuncle on the neck for a lame left leg."

Far wiser is the couple who, on finding disappointments and frustrations in their marriage, seek every possible way of adjustment, each examining himself for inadequacies, faults, and too little effort to understand the other, and making allowances for differences in temperament and preferences between them. Such a married couple will discuss their problems of adjustment frankly with each other, each willing to sacrifice some nonessential desires to the common happiness. If each is determined to go a little more than half way a successful adjustment frequently can be found. Sometimes seeking the advice of an understanding doctor, a clergyman, psychiatrist, or all three may help to solve the problem.

There are undoubtedly marriages, however, in which none of these efforts are successful and the home becomes a barren waste in which only unhappiness and despair grow.

Even then only the precipitate and the worst of pessimists will rush into divorce proceedings. Far better is a trial separation, agreed upon by the marriage partners in as friendly a manner as possible. Often in the objectivity which is the fruit of solitude the love that originally brought them together reasserts itself, purified and made humble by trial, and each realizes as never before the beauty and eternal goodness of that love which, as St. Paul described it,

> Suffereth long, and is kind . . . envieth not, . . . vaunteth not itself, is not puffed up, Doth not behave itself unseemly, seeketh not her own, is not easily provoked, thinketh no evil, Rejoiceth not in iniquity, but rejoiceth in the truth, Beareth all things, believeth all things, hopeth all things, endureth all things.

Often the reunion of a thoughtful married couple after such a trial separation becomes a second honeymoon, more joyous than the first, because both at last have learned the value of what they almost lost, and know that if each is intent on giving rather than receiving, both will receive more than either ever expected of marriage.

For devout Catholics, of course, to whom divorce is forbidden, the only choice is to find a way to live together as amicably as possible or to separate without divorce.

SEPARATION

Who Leaves the Home?

Two considerations, those of ordinary gallantry, and the wisdom of keeping the matter as quiet as possible, dictate that in case of a separation the husband will move out and the wife will continue to manage her home as she has done in the past.

Keep Your Own Counsel

When a trial separation has been arranged it is not only in poor taste, but unwise from the point of view of a possible reconciliation, to spread the news. Keep your own counsel even among friends, for as long as possible. Embarrassing questions from friends may often be evaded by some vague statement about a "vacation" or "taking a little time off." If the separation is prolonged the truth will undoubtedly leak out, but even then it is in poor taste for either the wife or the husband to talk about the difficulties that led up to the situation. In general, the least said about it the greater the dignity maintained, and the better are the chances for an eventual reconciliation. Gossip is like a fire that, intensified and spread by every breath of wind, may burn your bridges behind you.

Definitely no public announcement should be made by either the wife or the husband. In especially bad taste is the old-fashioned announcement which the husband placed in the newspapers announcing that he will not be responsible for debts contracted by the wife who has "left his bed and board."

Behavior during Separation

During the period when the two are living apart the wife continues to use her married name exactly as she did before, and to wear her engagement and wedding rings. She will send regrets in response to all invitations which she receives for her husband and herself, giving no explanation or simply saying that her husband will be away on the appointed day. She may of course carry on a certain amount of social life by herself, but she will be discreet in her conversation, avoiding every intimation that she and her husband have quarreled. And if she is truly desirous of an eventual reconciliation she will be even more meticulous in her conduct as a married woman with other men than before. She will forward her husband's mail to him, but not give the post office a forwarding address If he is within convenient phoning distance she will take phone messages and relay them to him, or give all who ask for him on the phone the number where they may reach him.

If they are socially prominent enough to inspire columnists to mention "rumors" that they are separated or seeking divorce, they will ignore such notices, and if newspapers ask for interviews will refuse to give them.

When no reconciliation seems possible, a permanent separation without divorce may be arranged by private agreement without court action if both husband and wife are amenable, or by a separate maintenance court action brought by the wife if she can show cause.

Obviously if the matter can be arranged without court action it is desirable to do so. An agreement is drawn up by an attorney, or by two attorneys, one representing the husband and one the wife. It should answer such practical questions as the amount of money which the husband will pay regularly to his wife for her support and for the support of the children (if any), the disposition of such property as the house in which they lived (if they own it), its contents, and the automobile or automobiles. If there are children, the agreement should state in whose custody they will remain (unless there is some reason why this is unwise they will no doubt stay with the mother), and usually grants the other parent certain privileges of seeing them either at their home or at his

Such an agreement does not dissolve a marriage, the two parties to it remain legally husband and wife, and if a reconciliation is achieved after it has been entered into they need simply to take up common residence again (in which case they will probably tear up the agreement which both have signed) and make a new and, it is to be hoped, more successful effort to find happiness together.

While they are living apart their behavior will be much as it should be during a temporary separation, save that more people will know about it and any pretense that it is a temporary state will probably be futile. The wife will continue to use her married name and wear her rings, and conduct herself as a married woman.

DIVORCE

❧ Though neither a temporary separation nor one that is intended to be permanent changes the legal status of either the wife or the husband, what should be the last resort of the unhappily married—divorce—does.

While divorce proceedings are under way, however, both parties to the marriage remain married persons and should act as such. The wife continues to use her married name and to wear her rings No announcement is made of the proceedings and no comment is made publicly by either husband or wife if the news leaks out and appears in the public prints Both members to the action should remember that many a divorce proceeding has been canceled while still pending because of a reconciliation.

If either member is contemplating a second marriage that fact too remains the business only of those primarily concerned. For a woman publicly to announce her engagement to one man while she is still married to another is the height of bad taste. Only when the final decree has been granted does either husband or wife regain the freedom of single persons. Even then if another marriage is pending, it is in better taste to wait a bit before hurrying into it like children running with a whoop and a holler from school on the last day before summer vacation.

After the divorce has been granted the woman may continue to wear her rings or not as she likes (so long as she does not remarry), or she may lay aside her engagement ring and wear only her wedding ring, or she may have the engagement ring reset and wear it on her right hand instead of on her left.

She no longer uses her husband's first name as a part of her own If her maiden name was Helen Randall and she has been married to Edwin Howe, she is no longer Mrs. Edwin Howe, but Mrs Randall Howe, and her signature becomes Helen Randall Howe. The usage "Mrs. Helen Howe" which was current in former generations is now considered in bad taste.

Life is a better thing for those divorced couples who can remain friends or, if that is impossible, at least can keep open the channels of communication between them, than for those in whom it breeds a bitter silence and enmity. Divorce is at best an unhappy affair, the admission of failure and the termination of a program which began with high hopes and expectations for a lifetime. It is especially important that the two remain able to communicate freely and at least without unfriendliness when children are involved. It is they, rather than their parents, who are often most deeply and tragically affected by the breaking up of a home that has hitherto been their chief security. If now the two to whom they looked for safety and comfort seem to hate each other, those who are too young to understand may be shattered indeed. One of the most serious obligations of each of the divorced parents is never by word or act to express scorn, contempt, or disrespect for the other to one of the children of the marriage.

And there is another—and a very good—reason for adopting a way of life that makes communication between the divorced couple possible. Having thought at the time the divorce proceedings were instituted that their marriage had been a mistake, they may find that their divorce is an even greater one and remarry with a stronger determination to adjust to each other and with an increased maturity that will make this possible. It has happened quietly more often than most of us realize.

Divorcees and Their Children's Weddings

If the daughter of a divorced woman who has not remarried is to be married, the mother (if the daughter is living with her) will issue the invitations to the wedding, using the name which she has assumed as a divorcee·

Mrs. Randall Howe
Requests the honour of your presence
at the marriage of her daughter
Helen
etc. (See p. 298)

If the girl is living with her father he will issue the invitations, thus:

Mr. Edwin Howe
Requests the honour of your presence
at the marriage of his daughter
Helen
etc.

In either case both of the girl's parents should make every effort to forget their differences for this one day so that both may attend their daughter's wedding without any sense of friction, and so that the father may give the bride away if that is planned as a part of the ceremony.

If Mrs. Randall Howe has married Mr. Harold Purdy the invitations are sent out in both their names:

> Mr. and Mrs. Harold Purdy
> request the honour of your presence
> at the marriage of her daughter
> Helen Howe
> etc.

In such a case Mr. and Mrs. Purdy sit in the first pew on the bride's side of the church and Mr. Howe, the girl's father, sits immediately behind them. At the reception, if there is one, the bride's mother and her second husband stand in the receiving line, and the bride's father is simply an important guest.

REMARRIAGE

The Wedding

A second marriage for a divorcee or a widow should be simple and quiet. It is usually a home wedding with only a few close friends attending, and without bridesmaids. If the bride prefers a church ceremony it should be a simple one also with only a few friends as guests.

Invitations

Invitations for a second marriage are not engraved but are issued by informal notes or phone calls by the prospective bride

Announcements

No engraved announcements are sent out after the second marriage of a divorcee, though an announcement may be sent to the newspapers after the event. In this case the bride will use the name she has used as a divorcee. The newspaper announcement may read. "The marriage of Mrs. Randall Howe to Mr. Harold Purdy is announced." (A widow may, if she likes, send engraved announcements after her second marriage)

Rings

The first wedding ring and engagement ring marking the divorcee's or widow's first marriage should of course be removed before the second marriage, and will not be worn again.

Dress

The bride-for-a-second-time, whether widow or divorcee, does not wear a long white gown, the bridal veil, orange blossoms, or myrtle wreath, which are reserved for a first wedding, and though she wears a corsage she usually does not carry a bridal bouquet. Since a very informal second marriage is appropriate, her best course is to wear the simple street clothes which any bride would wear for such an informal wedding

The groom dresses also as he would for any informal wedding.

The Young Widow or Divorcee

All the above rules (save that of discarding the rings and that which prohibits wearing a veil) are frequently relaxed for the second marriage of a very young widow or divorcee In such cases all the procedure (with the two exceptions noted above) common to first weddings is frequently followed. Yet if there is any meaning in the rules at all it seems to me that it is not changed by the age of the bride.

If only to avoid the risk of offending the family of the first husband, or the first husband himself if he is alive, it seems to me that the second marriage of a young bride as for an older one is in better taste if it is simple, small, and quietly arranged.

When the Groom Has Been Divorced or Is a Widower

None of the above rules apply to a marriage in which the groom has been divorced or is a widower and the bride is being married for the first time. In such a case the procedure is exactly the same as for a first marriage.

Stepchildren

In many circles it is considered bad taste for the children of a first marriage to attend the second marriage ceremony of their parent But as I have said earlier in this book this seems to me a case where the rules of etiquette conflict with those of kindness and wisdom. Adjustment to a stepparent is frequently most difficult for any child. If he is barred from the ceremony which confers a stepparent upon him his resentment of the second marriage may be increased to alarming proportions. A much wiser plan, it seems to me, is for the prospective stepfather or stepmother to make friends with the children of the one who is to become wife or husband before the marriage, and win approval beforehand, and then to have the children take part in a small and simple ceremony.

23

Funerals

WHEN THE DEATH OF A LOVED ONE OCCURS THE MOST effective consolation which the bereaved will have is a realization of the goodness of the life that has been lived, and the privilege of having shared it. Robert Louis Stevenson, in his story *The Pavilion on the Links*, expresses this beautifully in the words of the narrator who says of his dead wife, "Now that she is taken from me . . . I recall our old loving kindness and the deep honesty and affection which united us, and my present loss seems but a trifle by comparison."

And there is something more difficult to explain than this; a discovery of strength at the depth of one's being which, laid bare by grief, supplies support for the stricken. I think that this is perhaps what Jesus meant when he said, "Blessed are they that mourn. for they shall be comforted"—not by any outside agency, but rather by the something indescribable born of the grief itself.

The most sadly bereft are not those who have lost greatly loved ones with whom they have formed ever deepening unions which have glorified their lives, and so have loving happy memories to support them, but those whose memories are of frustrations and perhaps even bitterness in their relationship. It is a strange but true paradox that the greater the loss the greater the comfort that is born of memory.

It is well for friends who seek to soften the blow by words to remember this, and to emphasize the goodness of the past rather than the grief of the present. It is a more helpful thing to say to a widow who has just lost a devoted husband with whom she has spent years in a happy and constructive marriage, "What a wonderful person he was, and how fortunate you are to have such beautiful memories of the years you spent together," than to multiply grief by expressing it.

In any case, death places upon the family and friends an obligation to carry out certain necessary details with gentleness, consideration for those most deeply affected, respect for the deceased, and dignity, and to ease as much as is possible the difficult adjustment of the chiefly affected. A funeral may be harrowing or have within it elements of comfort for the mourners, depending upon how it is managed.

ARRANGEMENTS FOR THE FUNERAL

It is desirable that some member of the family other than the one most deeply affected by the death, a relative or friend, assume responsibility for all funeral arrangements. Even for the simplest funeral there are many details to attend to, some of which might be extremely painful to the one most sorely afflicted.

Arrangements will vary according to the religious faith of the deceased and his family, and possibly according to their financial state. The one who takes charge of the funeral arrangements should obtain as tactfully as possible the answers to such questions as these:

Will interment be in the earth or in a vault? Or is cremation desired? (The last question is necessary only in case the deceased is a Protestant Christian or a free-thinker.)

Is a family plot or mausoleum available, or must arrangements be made for this?

How much money can the family afford, and does it desire, to spend?

Do they wish a religious funeral with the service conducted by a priest, clergyman, or rabbi, and if so, would they prefer to have it held from the church (always if it is a Catholic family), the home, or a funeral parlor? If the deceased was a member of a church, the clergyman of his church will be the natural choice to conduct the services. If not, the surviving family will indicate a choice Or if they do not wish a religious service but would like to ask a friend or friends to speak at the services, they will give the name or names of those they have in mind to the one who has taken responsibility for arranging the details and he will ask them to do so.

In most modern funerals the casket is usually carried by bearers furnished by the funeral director, and four or more—sometimes as many as ten—male friends of the deceased are asked to serve as honorary pallbearers, but do not actually touch the casket. This, however, is not always the case Especially in small communities friends are still sometimes asked to carry the coffin to the hearse, and from the hearse to the graveside. The friend or relative who arranges the funeral should ask which plan the family wishes to follow, take from them the names of those who are to be asked to serve either as honorary or actual bearers, and arrange with them to do so.

If they are to serve as actual bearers there should be six, and a practical consideration enters here in the combined weight of the coffin (which, if it is lead-lined, as it sometimes is, may be extremely heavy) and the body. I remember one awkward moment when six frail friends had been asked to be actual pallbearers for a very heavy man whose family had selected an extremely heavy coffin. When they came to lift it into the hearse they found that it was beyond their combined strength, and the clergyman and several male attendants at the funeral had to step forward and help them.

A funeral, like a marriage, is a highly personal thing, and the ceremony that will seem the most dignified, the most honestly representative of the convictions and nature of the dead, and the most comforting to the bereaved, is the one that will be the most fitting in each case. The simplest of ceremonies may be the most impressive.

Indeed, one of the most moving ceremonies which I have ever seen was the funeral of a young married woman who had lived with her husband in a town to which they had recently moved, and in which they had few friends Both deeply religious by nature and with a strong faith in the goodness of life, their lack of any church affiliation was the outcome of their convictions rather than of indifference. Knowing his wife's convictions, the young widower felt that any sort of formal religious service would be hypocrisy. As a consequence, he asked to the funeral only the immediate members of his family and hers, three or four intimate friends, and six men who had known and been fond of her to act as pall-bearers When all had assembled, at a wordless signal from the widower the funeral director closed the casket and the six friends carried it from the house with no words having been spoken. Only as the casket went through the door into a beautiful sunlit day did the father of the dead young woman, with tears streaming down his face, say spontaneously, "You see, she goes into the sunshine!" I have never forgotten the dignity and beauty of that impressive moment.

The one who is to arrange the funeral will also learn from the family whether they desire music, and will note their suggestions for specific hymns or psalms, or even a favorite poem. Often they will suggest a piece of classical music which was a favorite of the one who is gone.

Thus at the funeral of King George VI at Sandringham there were played "Abide with Me," "The King of Love My Shepherd Is," the great Scottish lament, "The Flowers o' the Forest," and "The Land of the Leal," all of which had been favorites of the King.

Notifying Family and Friends

It may be that members of the immediate family living in distant cities will have been notified by telephone calls or telegrams before the person who is to arrange the funeral has been called in. If not, he will offer to take over this sad task. Even if it has already been done, he will make a list of their names and addresses so that he may notify them of the time and place of the funeral after arrangements have been made.

He will also make a list of other friends who are to be notified, and will send word to them, and a notice to the newspapers after arrangements have been made for the funeral. The short notice that appears in the "Death" column of the newspapers is paid for at classified advertising rates, and customarily is very brief, simply giving the name of the deceased, whether husband, wife, son or daughter of whom, the date of the death, and if the funeral is to be public, its time and place If it is to be private, the notice customarily ends with the words "Funeral private."

If it is a Jewish funeral the request that no flowers be sent is usually included, for to Jews flowers are associated with joyousness and are quite incongruous as concomitants of mourning. Even if the request does not appear in the death notice and you know that the family is Jewish, it is quite improper to send flowers to either the funeral or the home, or to send them on any anniversary of the death.

This notice is also sometimes included in notices of deaths of non-Jews with the added request that flowers may be sent to a named hospital, or that money be donated to a certain charity in lieu of flowers. In such cases if either money or flowers are sent, a card should be enclosed saying that the gift is in memory of the one who has died, and a note of condolence to the family may mention that this contribution has been made.

If the deceased has been prominent, and therefore newsworthy, the newspapers will probably already have on file enough of the salient facts concerning his life to make it possible for them to write a news story to accompany the death notice. But even if they have, they will probably want to check it by a phone call and acquire any late facts which they may not have. In order to be prepared for this, the one who is in charge of the arrangements should have an autobiographical sketch written and at hand to which he may refer.

The Death Certificate

No arrangements can be made with a funeral director without a duly signed death certificate If a doctor was in attendance at the time of death, or in the last illness (as is usually the case), he will have executed and signed one. In the rare cases where death occurs without a doctor in attendance, the coroner or public medical examiner or health officer must be called in to issue one.

After the one who is to arrange the funeral has learned as much as possible about the family's desires, he should be prepared to take complete charge, make minor decisions himself, and trouble those most closely affected by the death with as few questions as possible.

Seeing the Clergyman

His first call will be to the clergyman (if one has been selected) who will be asked to conduct the service. With him he will arrange the time and place, the use of the church (if it is to be a church funeral), and discuss such details as the music, whether there is to be a soloist, etc. He should not discuss the matter of the clergyman's fee Theoretically, no clergyman sets a fee for conducting funeral services After the funeral, however, it is customary to send him a check made out to him as a contribution to the church fund. This may be anything from ten or twenty-five to a hundred dollars, depending upon the family's financial ability.

The Visit to the Funeral Director

The next call which the one who is in charge of the funeral will make is to the funeral director. Here he will tell the director what plans have already been made by the family, where interment is desired, or if cremation has been decided on, and select the coffin. If the family has expressed a preference as to the kind of coffin to be used, he will of course be guided by it. If not, he will remember that, regardless of the financial ability of the family, a simple coffin is in the best taste.

Arrangements for the burial plot (unless there is already a family plot), the grave digging, or vault interment, or cremation, and cars for those attending the funeral are made by the funeral director, though this is not invariably so. And it is still not uncommon, especially in smaller communities, for friends who have closed cars (preferably black, certainly of a dark color) to be asked to use their cars for the funeral cortege. Arrangements for the plot may also be made by the family if they wish The funeral director of course always furnishes transportation for the body and the pallbearers, unless the friends who have been asked to serve are actually to carry the casket instead of acting merely as honorary bearers.

The cost of the funeral should be discussed with the funeral director and a definite agreement reached.

THE FUNERAL

The Protestant Home Funeral

The home funeral is private; in that only the family, relatives, and invited friends attend. It is usually held in a room selected with a view to accommodating the number of persons who will attend it, often the living room. The coffin, resting on a stand supplied by the funeral director, may or may not be open, as the family decides. The funeral director also supplies chairs.

The principally bereaved (widow, widower, or mother and father) usually stay out of sight until the service is about to begin, though guests are greeted at the door by another member of the family, a relative, or perhaps the friend who has been in charge of funeral arrangements. If they wish, they may pay their last respects to the deceased by going to the casket (if it is open) and standing before it a moment before they take their seats. It is not improper (though unusual) for a highly religious friend to kneel before the casket and say a prayer. Then they take their seats, but not in the front row which is reserved for the family and the pallbearers.

When all have arrived the principally bereaved take seats in the front row and the service begins There may or may not be music furnished by a friend at a piano, perhaps in another room, or by some of the excellent recordings of organ and choir music which are now available.

After the service the funeral director, clergyman, pallbearers, and family and relatives proceed to the cemetery. The other guests ordinarily do not, unless they have been specifically asked to do so; they keep their seats until the funeral party has left, and then leave the house quietly.

A Protestant Church Funeral

A church funeral differs only in details from one in the home. The family customarily occupies the front right pew, and the pallbearers the left. Others take seats as they choose, close relatives usually going toward the front and others sitting farther back. Sometimes there are no ushers, sometimes male members of the family act in this capacity. In this case, though an usher escorts guests to the pews he does not offer his arm to a lady, as he does at a wedding.

The casket is usually placed at the front of the church, or may be placed in the vestibule, where arriving guests may pause a moment if they wish before entering the chancel. The latter arrangement has the advantage of speeding the departure to the cemetery and avoiding the harrowing waiting while the coffin is carried down the aisle after the service.

The pallbearers customarily walk down the aisle together and take their seats just before the service is to begin. Family members, who have been waiting in the vestry or clergyman's study, now enter and are seated, and the clergyman begins the service.

When the service is over the family may retire again to the vestry or, if they choose, follow the casket. If there are honorary pallbearers as well as those who actually carry the coffin, they precede the coffin. No guest leaves until after the casket and the family have left.

The organist, incidentally, should be paid, usually about $25, for his services. The sexton may present a bill for the use of the church. If he does not, he should be sent a check, usually also about $25.

A Catholic Funeral

A Catholic funeral is always held in a church. It begins with a processional led by altar boys and sometimes a choir. Following them are the priest, the honorary pallbearers, the casket, and the family, usually with those nearest to the deceased in front—the widow, for instance, on the arm of a son, and other members of the family following.

After the funeral mass (which is somewhat more elaborate than a Protestant service) there is a recessional which follows the same order as the processional, save that the choir does not take part in it.

One way which friends may express sympathy for the bereaved is to make a contribution to the church, ask that a mass be said for the dead, and receive a card saying that this will be done, which is sent to the family. Checks are drawn to the church, not to the priest.

A Mortuary Chapel Funeral

Many Protestant funeral services today are conducted in mortuary chapels or funeral homes which provide small non-sectarian chapels in which simplicity and good taste prevail. At such services there are no ushers, no honorary pallbearers, and no processional or recessional. In many such chapels there is a small room, set off from the main room by a gauze curtain. Here the family may sit in seclusion, hearing what is said, but unseen by the other guests. If no such room is available, they will take their seats at the front of the chapel, as in a church, and the other guests will seat themselves toward the front or rear, depending upon the closeness of their relationship to the deceased.

As at a church or home funeral, guests remain in their seats until after the family has left and the coffin has been removed—unless it is to stay in its place for later disposition.

Cremation

If the family has decided upon cremation (perhaps in carrying out the previously expressed wish of the deceased) they may or may not attend the actual process as they choose. In either case other guests ordinarily do not. There may, however, be held on the same, or another day, a memorial service to which relatives and friends are invited. This will resemble the ordinary Protestant funeral service save that the body of the deceased is not present.

Cremation is not permitted by Jews (who believe that the body should return to God and to the earth in its original form) nor by Catholics (as a matter of ecclesiastical policy rather than of Divine law), chiefly because of its association with the idea of eternal fire, but also perhaps because of a belief in the eventual physical resurrection of the dead.

MOURNING

The wearing of black exclusively for a period after a death in the family, the widow's bonnet, the black arm band for men, and the black-bordered notepaper are fortunately only memories for most Americans. We have come to feel (rightly, I think) that it shows no disrespect for the dead, no lesser grief, to appear in public within a week or so after the funeral, or even sooner, dressed as usual and engaging, for the most part, in the everyday activities of life.

Social activities may be curtailed to some extent for a time. If elaborate entertaining has been planned to take place within a few weeks of the time when death has intervened (a formal wedding, a dance, or a party of any kind) it will be canceled, though a wedding may proceed if it is simple (see p. 303). A young widow or widower will see friends quietly and attend small gatherings, go to the theater or to concerts, but will probably not be seen publicly with the same person of the opposite sex frequently for several months after the funeral. Even in this the old convention that no second marriage could take place until more than a year after the death of the first spouse is less strictly observed than in the past.

We are realizing more and more, I think, that true mourning is a very personal, private, and inward matter that cannot be shared with others and that is not measured by outward show, that we are less than considerate if we dampen the happiness of others by continuous evidence of our own sorrow; and that we pay a tribute to those who have made life rich by sharing theirs with us in returning as quickly as possible to the stream of life after they are gone.

Jewish Funerals and Mourning

The funerals of Jews vary as do their other religious ceremonies depending upon the degree of orthodoxy practiced.

According to strictly orthodox practice the body is not embalmed and cremation is not permitted, for Jews believe that the body should return to God in its original form and by way of the earth of which it was made. The body is washed and wrapped in a linen shroud after the nails have been pared, and after prayers it is taken directly from the home to the cemetery and buried before sunset on the day of death (if the strict orthodox custom is observed), unless it is the Sabbath or a holiday. Even in such a case, in highly religious families preparation of the body may begin immediately after sunset, and the burial take place late that night.

At a Jewish funeral held at a chapel, the casket is placed in the chapel proper, the mourners enter first, pay their last respects to the dead, and then go to a small reception room while the guests assemble. Relatives and close friends usually visit the chapel and offer their sympathy before the service begins. All the men and all the older women at any save a Reform service will wear their hats, and even at Reform services many male heads may be covered.

After the mourners have entered the chapel and seated themselves at the front, the casket is sealed and the rabbi recites the mourner's prayer, the *kaddish,* and usually one or two of the Psalms of David. One frequently used is a favorite of both Jews and Christians, the beautiful Twenty-third Psalm, "The Lord is my shepherd; I shall not want." The prayers and Psalms are in Hebrew.

Sometimes friends and relatives will rise and speak in praise of the dead.

I include the *kaddish* here because of its beauty and the courage which it displays, having in it no word of sorrow but only praise for the Lord "who giveth and who taketh away."

Magnified and sanctified be his great Name in the world which he hath created according to his will. May he establish his kingdom during your life and during your days, and during the life of all the house of Israel, even speedily and at a near time, and say ye, Amen.

Let his Great Name be blessed forever and to all eternity.

Blessed, praised, and glorified, exalted, extolled and honored, magnified and lauded be the Name of the Holy One, blessed be he, though he be high above all the blessings and hymns, praises and consolations, which are uttered in the world, and say ye, Amen.

May there be abundant peace from heaven, and life for us and for all Israel, and say ye, Amen.

He who maketh peace in his high places, may he make peace for us and for all Israel; and say ye, Amen.

The religious spirit of Judaism which pervades the *kaddish* is expressed in a very old talmudic story:

A devout rabbi and his wife had two young sons who were the joy of their life. On a Sabbath when the rabbi was at the synagogue the two boys died suddenly. His wife, not wanting to dampen his Sabbath happiness, did not tell him of their great loss until after sundown. Then she said to him quietly:

"Some time ago I was entrusted with two precious treasures. Now the one who asked me to keep them for him has asked for their return. What am I to do?"

Her husband looked at her in astonishment.

"I am amazed that you should ask," he said. "You will return them immediately, of course, and thank the Holy One, blessed be he, that you are one worthy of a trust."

Then she led him to the room where the bodies of their sons lay. The rabbi gazed at them for a moment with tear-dimmed eyes, then said softly, "The Lord giveth and the Lord taketh away. Blessed be his Holy Name."

There are brief services at the cemetery where, after a prayer by the mourners, the oldest and nearest relatives dip earth from the ground with their fingers (each three times) and drop it onto the coffin. The rabbi then sometimes asks who will throw the first earth onto the coffin, and a few relatives and close friends will each put a spadeful into the grave. But no matter how close a friend to the deceased a non-Jew is, though he may attend the funeral and even, if he is very close, go to the cemetery, he will not take part in this ritual, for the prohibition against this, as is the tradition that no one who is not a Jew will touch the body of one of their dead, is strongly held even by Jews who are not strictly orthodox.

After the services close friends and relatives go to the home of the mourners. Before entering the house after a funeral, Orthodox, Conservative, and many Reform Jews will wash their hands, but not dry them. This custom of "washing the dead off their hands" persists even among Jews who consider their thought highly modern

Mourning Jewish families traditionally "sit *shivah*" for seven days after the funeral, though when this imposes severe inconvenience the period is sometimes reduced to three days. During this "sitting" period the door is left unlatched. All who wish to call and offer condolences walk in without ringing the bell or knocking. The caller and the sitters do not greet each other. The caller (who has usually brought a gift of food—which may be only cookies or candy—for if custom is strictly followed the mourners do not prepare any food for themselves during the period of sitting *shivah*) simply expresses his sympathy to each mourner, spends a little time sitting with them, and leaves. In lieu of a gift of food the caller may donate money to a Jewish charity, and a card will be sent to the family indicating that a contribution has been made in memory of the deceased.

During the entire period of sitting *shivah* a mourning candle (today often replaced by a simulated candle which is really an electric light) is lit and the *kaddish* is said every morning and evening. If a non-Jewish friend is present at the time when the *kaddish* is recited he need feel no embarrassment, for the family will not feel that he constitutes an intrusion. He will simply bow his head in silent respect. (The *kaddish* is also repeated on each anniversary of the death throughout the lifetime of the next generation.)

VI

OFFICE ETIQUETTE

24

Company Manners

ALMOST A QUARTER OF A CENTURY AGO, MARY ALDEN Hopkins wrote an excellent small book called *Profits from Courtesy: A Handbook of Business Etiquette*. The implication of the title and the message of the book was, of course, that the business that observed the rules of courteous behavior within its offices and in its dealing with the public would make more money than the one that did not.

No one, I think, would dispute this. Nor, needless to say, do I quarrel with the profit-making objective of business. Yet I think that there is more to be considered in thinking of courtesy in business than its relation to monetary profit. In the first place I very much doubt that what one might call an overlay of courtesy, consciously assumed for the sole purpose of increasing profits, can ever be fully effective. The overcordial salesman whose voice seems to be slapping your back even if the palm of his hand is not, the obsequious executive who asks about the health and well-being of your wife and children when you know that he really has no interest in them whatever, and the officer of a company who speaks rudely to his secretary as you enter his office and then turns to you with smiles and an outstretched hand very often defeat their purpose. In business as everywhere else true courtesy and proper social behavior arise from a sincerity of feeling for others, a genuine desire to be helpful and kind, and a realization that your own happiness and satisfactions in life are closely dependent upon the happiness and satisfactions of those with whom you come into contact.

Every justifiable business is a part of the world's work, supplying the public with a product (or products) or services that contribute to the welfare of the human race. If the owners, the executives, and all the employees of such a business are genuinely desirous of doing this well, if in short there is deeply embedded in the purposes of the company the ideal of public service, and if this ideal is implemented with sound organization and training, the influence of which will be felt from the highest officer in the company to the least of the office boys or mail clerks, the details of business courtesy will come about almost as a matter of course, and every member of the organization will feel a satisfaction in his association with the company which will go far beyond the matter of his salary or profits. Further, he will be a pleasanter person to know, and one who will be more courteous and considerate in his contacts with others outside of business.

Throughout the United States the employees of the Bell Telephone System are noted for their courtesy, and the system itself is justifiably famous throughout the world for the efficiency of its service. A telephone public relations man and one of the customer's service consultants were asked this question "Why, when you are to all intents and purposes a monopoly furnishing an essential service, do you still spend so much money training your personnel in courtesy, and put so much emphasis on it generally? Surely your courtesy program does not materially increase the number of phones in operation nowadays when practically everyone feels that he must have a phone."

Both looked a little startled, for so thoroughly was courtesy a part of the telephone company tradition that neither had ever thought that it needed any justification save itself alone. Finally the public relations man said, "I think that it all goes back to Theodore N. Vail who insisted on it," and the customers' service consultant added, "I think that it is *because* we are a monopoly and so have a greater obligation."

Both of these seem to me to be valid answers, yet I believe there is more to it than that. I think that over the years of the Bell Telephone System's existence, during all of which the tradition of courtesy has held sway and has grown, the huge family of Bell employees, literally thousands of men and women, have learned that the instilled habits of courtesy have not only made it easier to collect bills and to adjust subscribers' complaints, but made their working relationships within the company pleasanter and more rewarding things and have carried over these habits into their personal life. Even if the indoctrination which the Bell System still promulgates were discontinued, I cannot believe that those who have learned the lessons of courteous living would give them up any more than they would abandon running water for the old oaken bucket that hung by the well.

Theodore Vail (from 1878 to 1887 general manager of the National Bell Telephone Company and its successor companies, and from 1907 until his retirement in 1919 president of the American Telephone and Telegraph Company) realized that (the quotations are his words), "It is the duty and obligation, as well as self-interest, of a public service corporation to give efficient service up to the limits of reasonable practicability and to furnish such service at a reasonable price," that "our interests are best served when the public interests are best served," and that "in all times, in all lands, public opinion has had control at the last word . . . it is based on information and belief. If it is wrong, it is wrong because of wrong information and erroneous belief." He knew that any business could function only as well as the organization as a whole, and that its efficiency depended largely upon fair treatment and the resulting happiness of the employees as a whole.

The Chicago and North Western Railroad, one of the principal commuter lines of the Middle West, recently converted its commuter service from a losing enterprise to a profitable one by a combination of new, money-saving equipment, and a carefully indoctrinated program of employee courtesy which has induced many commuters who had in desperation been traveling to and from work in their cars to go back to the railroad.

The great hotels have long known how essential courtesy is to their very survival. Every member of the staff of such a hostelry, from the manager down to the cleaning women, is carefully trained

in general courtesy and in meeting graciously the special situations
that are a part of hotel life.

One of the most trying situations for both the hotel management
and the disappointed guest arises when a guest who has made a
reservation arrives and finds that there is no room vacant for him.
It is inevitable that this should sometimes happen. No successful
hotel is able on one day to say exactly how many vacant rooms it
will have the next. The probable number is carefully calculated on
the basis of known averages. Some guests do not announce when
they are going to leave, others stay longer than they had intended
when they checked in. These and other factors are taken into
account and when the number of expected vacancies has been
exhausted for a day the hotel ceases to make reservations for that
day. But guests do not always behave in an average manner, and
sometimes a guest who has made a reservation which the hotel has
confirmed arrives to find that no room is available to him. He is
invariably disappointed and not infrequently quite justifiably furious.

The manager of New York's Waldorf Astoria has told how he
manages the situation.

"Whenever a guest who has reserved a room we are unable to
supply arrives," he says, "we do not leave the explanation to the
room clerk. The guest is brought directly to my office and directly
to me. A phone call while he is on the way makes it possible for
me to call him by name. I see him at once regardless of what I may
be doing at the time, and keep two things firmly in mind as I begin
to talk to him. The first is that he has a very real grievance and is
quite justified in being angry. The second is that I must make him
feel that I, rather than the impersonal Waldorf Astoria Hotel, am
his host, that (however unintentionally) I am guilty of a breach
of hospitality, and that, in addition to the sincere apology which
I give him at once, I am eager to compensate for it to the best of
my ability. The truth is that I am probably more unhappy about the
situation than he is, for I know that we are in the wrong and that
any explanation I can give him will be inadequate.

"Frequently the disappointed guest upbraids me in a loud tone
of voice. I consciously keep my voice at a very low pitch so that
he must come a little closer to me to understand what I am saying,
as I explain to him exactly how the unfortunate circumstance came
about, and tell him that we have transferred his reservation to a

nearby hotel that has comparable accommodations. Soon he has lowered his own voice and nine times out of ten is agreeing with me that the problems involved in running a large hotel are complex.

"When he is quite smoothed down and ready to go to the other hotel I do not call a bellboy, but carry his bags myself and go with him onto the street and to the hotel, where I introduce him and see that he is comfortably settled.

"Many guests who have thus been disappointed have become staunch supporters of the Waldorf, and not a few have become personal friends—through courtesy that not only is a matter of words and intonations, but is composed of sincere feeling and action too."

A manual of rules issued for the employees of Marshall Field and Co. of Chicago some years ago contained this wise paragraph·

Back of these rules we wish all employees to see our earnest desire to conduct this great institution in the most harmonious manner, to give them the benefit of long experience, to save them the retracing of unguided steps, and to help them grow in the knowledge and application of sound business principles.

Saks and Company, of New York have gone even farther than this in explaining to its employees the values of courtesy:

It pays in the friends it makes you personally and as a representative of the company. It pays in minimizing the friction of your life, as well as that between the company and its patrons. It pays in raising your standard with the company. It pays in the personal satisfaction resulting from having done the right and kindly thing by your neighbor.

THE FUTILITY OF LIP SERVICE

Though I know that I am repeating here what I have said before it seems important to me to emphasize the fact that, in business as elsewhere, courtesy to be effective must be given much more than lip service. The old saying, "Your actions speak so loudly that I cannot hear what you say," is soundly based in life. What might be called proper social behavior in business must arise from a genuine desire that pervades the organization. It must reflect a sound business policy which includes honesty, a firmly rooted purpose to be of useful service, a willingness to admit mistakes frankly and take responsibility for them, and a genuine interest in the business and in the people whom it serves.

The factory salesman who is the epitome of courtesy to his customer will have wasted his breath if the company behind him does not carry out efficiently and well the order which he takes. The personnel director who treats the new employee with the height of consideration will have but added a discontented and ineffective member to the staff if the working conditions, duties, and salary are not as he has represented them. The employee who is obsequiously polite to his superiors and his colleagues will have accomplished nothing by what is after all only a pseudo-courtesy if he does not conscientiously carry his share of the work load.

ORGANIZATION

Nor is courtesy both within an organization itself and between the staff and the public effective if it is not backed by a sound organization of business routine and an orderly designation of areas of authority. True courtesy is action as well as words

The gas and electric light company that spends large sums of money indoctrinating its employees in courtesy to the public has accomplished little if its inter-office routine is so inefficient that it takes two or three months for a change of address to become effective. The president of a company may send a Christmas card to every employee and all the executives may in personal contacts treat every employee with consummate consideration, but if no employee knows exactly from whom he is expected to take orders, exactly what his responsibilities are, or of events and changes of policy that affect his work, the "courtesy to employees" program will be only fractionally effective.

H. P. Miller, public relations director of Pan American World Airways, has said that employee courtesy is basically a matter of employee morale, to which a good internal communications system is essential. Informing employees of company objectives and problems helps them identify their future with that of the firm. A satisfied employee with a sense of loyalty to, and pride in, his company will naturally do a good job and be well mannered in doing it.

25

The Employer, the Executive, and the Staff

THE PRINCIPLES OF BUSINESS ETIQUETTE ARE BASICALLY no different from those that should guide the individual in his personal relationships, but their implementation is in some respects more complicated. For in any business it is desirable for the personnel—whether it consists of a few or several thousands of people —to act as nearly as possible as a unit, each reflecting the character, attitudes, and policies of the firm of which he is a part. It is the responsibility primarily of the owners, officers, and executives to see that conditions within the firm are such that a united front will be presented to the world, that the organization and routine within the firm is such that every member of the staff will know exactly what his duties are, to whom he is accountable, and how much initiative he may safely take in exceptional circumstances when following the ordinary routine is impractical. He must also have full assurance that if he acts responsibly his action will be supported by the firm. If he makes what should be justified promises to customers or other members of the organization and the firm fails to carry them out his courtesy is meaningless

In business courtesy and efficiency have a symbiotic relationship. There is no question that courtesy increases efficiency, it is equally true that without efficiency of organization and procedure true courtesy is impossible.

The customer who phones asking for information or to discuss a detail of his relationship with the firm and is shifted from one department to another, perhaps two or three times, because no one really knows who is competent to discuss the matter, will quite justifiably charge the firm with discourtesy and inefficiency. If a letter passes from one department to another perhaps three or four times, because no one knows who really ought to take care of it, and so is not answered for two or three weeks, no amount of courteous language in the eventual reply will compensate for the discourtesy of the delay.

HIRING

The relationship of every employee with his firm obviously begins with his initial employment. Nowhere is the old saying, "well begun is half done," more applicable than here The worker who understands as clearly as is possible before he begins what his duties will be, what working conditions he may expect, the kind of people with whom he will work, and the general policies and objectives of the firm, so that he may look forward to being a part of it and feel confidence in his ability to fit into it constructively, has been given a proper start.

I understand that there are several methods of hiring. In some businesses the head of each department hires those who are to work under him; in some the head of the business does all the hiring In some a personnel director hires and sends the employees to the department to which they are assigned without their having had any previous contact with the one under whom they are to work.

I am not a businesswoman but the latter procedure seems to me discourteous both to the new employee and to the one under whom he is to work, and one that invites disaster. In all human relationships there are intangible, unexplainable elements from which arise

liking, respect, and sympathetic understanding, or antagonism. The
old quatrain:

> I do not love thee, Dr. Fell,
> The reason why I cannot tell,
> But this I know, and know full well,
> I do not love thee, Dr. Fell,

is descriptive of a phenomenon with which we are all familiar.

A working relationship is first of all a human relationship, and
if it cannot be entered into with pleasure and hopeful expectancy by
all involved it is better not undertaken.

The personnel director, properly trained and experienced, may
be much more competent than the department head to weed out
those applicants who are obviously not suited to the position to be
filled, and to evaluate the ability of those who are, and should use
this ability so that only the most promising applicants are interviewed
by the department head. But before the actual hiring is done the
applicant and the one under whom he is to work should have a quiet
interview and each be given the opportunity to "feel out" the personality of the other. If there is any doubt in the mind of either that
they will be able to work harmoniously together it will be more courteous to both and more conducive to the welfare of the firm, if
someone else is found to fill the position.

The Hiring Interview

Whether the head of the firm, the department head, or the
personnel director conducts the hiring interview, it should be frank,
courteous, and with a marked respect for the applicant's point of view.

Pertinent questions should be asked by the representative of the
firm, of course, but the applicant's questions should be encouraged
also. As nearly as is practical there should be left no questions in the
applicant's mind as to the duties that will be expected of him, the
working conditions, the kind of colleagues with whom he will work,
the prospects for advancement, and such matters as vacations, pensions, medical insurance, etc.

An applicant who has no questions is not necessarily incompetent. He may be shy and may not immediately make his personality
felt, but an employer who is asked searching questions about his
firm's policy and its relationship with the public by a prospective em-

ployee will probably have found someone who will take a genuine interest in the business.

Getting Started

When a new worker arrives at work for the first day he should be shown about the office by his department head, the personnel officer, or some suitable designate of one of these, and introduced to all the other members of the staff with whom he will come into contact in his work. Where the office force is a small one he should be introduced to every member of it. This should include the working officers of the firm who—if courtesy is more than a word to them, and if they expect their employees to be courteous to one another and to the public—will make him feel as welcome as they would a guest in their homes.

If the new employee is made to feel that he is really wanted, if special attention is given to seeing that he is given courteous, friendly instruction in the routine of the firm and in his particular duties, if the foundation stone of his training in courtesy is the example set by the treatment which he receives from the outset, then his own development in courtesy and efficiency will be a natural and pleasant one.

BUSINESS COURTESY IS A CHAIN

The general tone of every organization is set by its head. If the president of a company is surly, ill-tempered, unfriendly, unfair, and inconsistent in his dealings with his department heads, the atmosphere he creates in his office is almost sure to be reflected in the heads of departments, among the employees themselves, and between the company and the public. This is not simply because we all tend to follow a leader, but perhaps even more because under such a president no executive can ever be sure of his own position or know what effect on his relations with his superiors any act of his may produce. Thus his uncertainty, his frustration, his sense of insecurity will almost inevitably be passed on to his subordinates, who will in turn pass them on to their colleagues and to the public with whom they come into contact.

Business courtesy is a chain that is only as strong as its weakest link.

EMPLOYEES' PROBLEMS

Employees should be trained to take their problems, questions, and complaints to their immediate superiors, who should listen to them courteously and understandingly, and respond to them frankly and helpfully. Even when reprimands are necessary, when the employee is obviously in the wrong and must be told so, the obligation to be courteous is not abrogated Many an employee who has somehow got off on the wrong foot in working for a firm, and has shown signs of becoming a chronic complainer and an inefficient worker, has been set right and made into a valuable and pleasant member of the staff by a wise department head who has shown him frankly and with understanding (but without rudeness) how wrong he has been and helped him to understand the ways of working harmoniously with others. No one, I firmly believe, was ever helped to anything by discourtesy.

Availability of Officers

Although the proper person for the employee to see when he is discontented is his immediate superior, every officer in the firm should on occasion be available to every employee, especially, it seems to me, the personnel officer and the head of the company. Though the latter may quite properly refuse to discuss the specific matter that is worrying the employee, telling him to talk with his immediate superior about it, he will do so courteously and in such a way that the employee will see that his welfare and contentment are of interest to the head of the firm. And the president, by skillfully turning the conversation into general channels which do not conflict with the department head's jurisdiction, may so convince the employee that the firm is genuinely interested in the welfare of every member of the staff that the matter will end right there.

Jurisdiction

High-level officers should in all things respect the jurisdiction of their department heads if they expect good relations between them and their subordinates. If an individual employee is selected for advancement, a raise in salary, or transfer to another department, it should be his department head, not a higher officer, who tells him so.

Whether a department head has the power to discharge an employee on his own judgment may well be a matter for careful decision in forming the overall general policy of the firm, but in either case if an unhappy decision has been made that an employee must go, the department head should assume the unpleasant task of telling him. Taking such matters as these out of his hands not only constitutes a discourtesy to him, but also exhibits to those working under him the weakness of his authority and his unimportance as their leader.

TRAINING IN COURTESY

I do not intend here to outline a specific course of training in courtesy for employees. Indeed I believe that far more important than any specific word-of-mouth instructions as to the forms of courtesy are the two things which I have already mentioned—an organization and routine that make courtesy not only possible but almost inevitable, and the example set by the officers and department heads.

But I would like to emphasize two essential elements in any such training. One is sound information about the function and purposes of the business which will give every employee a proper pride in it. The other is the firm impression made on the employee that the habit of courtesy, once acquired, will be an asset not only in his business career but in every aspect of his daily life.

Correctional Interviews

All correctional interviews should be conducted in private with only the employee and the department head present. The department head should be completely frank, but courteously so, and should give the employee every opportunity to state his point of view. If as a result of this the superior is convinced that he has misunderstood the situation and been unjust, he should say so and express regret for the misunderstanding. If he is convinced that the reprimand is justified, he should go a step further and make sure that the employee understands why he is being reprimanded, and in every way possible, through explanation and instruction, help him correct his mistake. No employee should ever be discharged without first having had his errors or inefficiency called to his attention and without being given a chance to improve.

THE EXECUTIVE AND HIS SECRETARY

The degree to which that extremely important asset to any firm, the executive's secretary, functions efficiently and courteously depends not a little upon the habits of her superior and the example which he sets for her.*

Every intelligent officer and executive knows the value of a good secretary. She is the intermediary between him and the other members of the firm and the office staff. She is in many ways the creator of the image which others form of him and of the firm. It is of the utmost importance that she be proud of the firm for which she works and of her immediate superior, that she be happy and contented in her job. If she knows, from bitter experience, that the man for whom she works is a boor, without consideration or courtesy for herself or others, unreliable, unstable, and lacking in human understanding, she should try to compensate for his bad manners by being more courteous herself, even though she may find this rather difficult.

The intelligent, conscientious executive will be courteous to his secretary not only in his manner and speech but also in the way in which he arranges the work which they do together and which she is expected to do alone.

He will treat her not as an underling at whom he growls orders and gives commands, but as a lady who is his colleague, one whom he directs but does not dominate. He will use "please" and "thank you" in speaking to her as automatically as he would to his most distinguished friend.

He will dictate in a clear voice, enunciating carefully, and having learned her speed in taking shorthand notes, will try not to exceed it. Further he will arrange his work so that he may dictate all letters which he wishes typed on that day early enough in the day so that she may complete them within office hours. Only under the most special circumstances will he dictate five minutes before closing time and expect her to transcribe his dictation that day.

He will not ask her to do personal shopping for him during her lunch hours, nor to entertain male customers from out of town.

He will quite properly delegate certain tasks to her in which she will act as his proxy, but he will do so only when it is clear that she

---

* The secretary may of course be male or female, but since a woman usually fills this post, I use the feminine pronoun.

may act for him without misunderstanding and with good judgment, and then he will support her in her action.

Men differ in their ideas of how impersonal a relationship with their secretaries should be, and I suppose this difference in ideas arises somewhat from differences in temperament. There was a time when the courteous executive supposedly never called his secretary by her given name; she was always "Miss Smith," never "Mary." I am sure that this is still true of many, and that often the practice is a wise one. Yet it seems to me not a matter about which one can safely make a hard and fast rule.

I once heard an executive say, "To me the perfect secretary is a woman whom I would not recognize if I met her on the street." That seemed to me a rather chilling statement. There are degrees of familiarity which do not breed contempt, but on the contrary, understanding and friendly cooperation.

I for one would find it impossible to work long with a secretary or anyone else if I did not find that we could be friends, and that our working relationship included a dignified but cordial personal relationship.

This, it seems to me, is the measure of any successful relationship between employers and executives and the staffs that work under them—that they should be friendly, dignified, respectful, and courteous The degree in which personal friendships may be added to business relationships will in all times and places depend upon the personalities of the people involved, their compatibility, and the individual circumstances of their lives.

Making Appointments

It is the secretary who usually makes appointments for her employer. When someone phones asking to see the man for whom she works she often needs considerable tact. She should as graciously as possible learn what the purpose of the proposed visit is. She will do this not by saying, "What do you want to see him about?" or "Can't you tell him what you want to say in a letter?" thereby intimating that the call will be unwelcome, but rather by something that indicates a concern for the other's welfare, such as, "If you could tell me a little of what you wish to talk about, I shall see that Mr. Smith has the information which he needs before you come." This should precede any definite discussion of setting a time for the appointment, so that if it becomes apparent that the one who wants it is likely merely to be a nuisance, the secretary may find some plausible reason why her employer will not be able to see anyone on that day, and may suggest that the caller write a letter. This will save time and make a later appointment more fruitful.

The secretary to the editor of a publishing house whom I know has an unvarying technique for dealing with the ambitious author who phones saying that he wants to come in to talk to the editor about a manuscript he wishes to submit. She asks him whether the manuscript is ready for submission, and if it is, she says, "Mr. Smith will be very glad to read it, I'm sure, but you can see that he would be unable to talk about it intelligently, or even to discuss your point of view about it with understanding, until he has done so. Why don't you send it in and he will get in touch with you after he has read it?" Many a fruitless appointment and much wasted time have been avoided in such a circumstance by a courteous rejection letter following reading of the manuscript. In case the manuscript is not ready to submit, she suggests that the editor will be able to discuss the idea much more intelligently if he has a written outline to study before the interview.

When the secretary does make an appointment for her employer she will ask the caller if he knows the location of the office, and if he does not, will tell him how to reach it.

She will make a note of the appointment on her employer's calendar pad, and each morning she will examine the sheet for that day to see that any appointment which she makes will not conflict with any which he has made without telling her about it.

So far as is possible she will collect any information which her employer may need in his discussion with the one who is coming and see that it is on her employer's desk in time so that he may study it before the appointment.

She will treat persons from outside the organization and those within it with equal courtesy, but she will remember that as a general rule it is easier for those within the organization to adjust their time to that of her employer than it is for those from the outside, especially if they are from out of town.

The tone of voice used by a secretary is most important. She can make her voice sound warm and pleasant so that even a refusal will be softened.

Handling Mail

Men differ in the way they want their incoming mail handled The careful and courteous employer will instruct his secretary

in this matter, as in others, when she begins her term of employment
with him. If he does not do so she may at least well ask him whether
he wants her to open his obviously business letters. If he says that he
does, and goes no further in his instructions, she might well adopt
the following program

She will open all envelopes that plainly contain business letters,
clip the envelopes to the backs of the letters, place them in a neat
pile with what she considers the most important letters on top, clip
a blank sheet of paper on top of the pile, or put it in a filing folder
(so that the top letter will not be visible to anyone entering the
office), and lay it on his desk. Letters that are marked "Personal" or
that are contained in nonbusiness envelopes, addressed in longhand,
and look as though they were personal, she will place unopened on
the top of his business letters.

In some offices the secretary to the president, the office manager,
or the business manager opens the mail for the entire office, and
after reading and making notes of its contents for her employer, sends
it on to the persons concerned or sometimes puts it onto her employer's desk for him to read first, so that he may be informed of matters in the various departments. In this case she will also be careful
not to open letters that seem to be personal letters, but will send
them on at once to those to whom they are addressed.

Keeping in the Background

The courteous and efficient secretary does not allow her personality to intrude upon her employer's consciousness any more than
is necessary. Though I cannot imagine any successful and happy
working relationship that does not include some of those elements
of mutual respect, pleasure in association, and even a dignified affection, which are elements of a good personal relationship, an employer
and his secretary should be first of all a working team in which the
employer must take the lead and the secretary complement him as
efficiently and unobtrusively as possible.

She should comply with his requirements in such a way that she
will call no more attention to herself than is necessary. She will not
start conversations with him beyond taking to him messages which it
is her responsibility to pass on to him.

If he says "good morning" to her when he arrives, and "good
night" to her when he leaves (as he will ordinarily do if he is cour-

teous) she will of course respond courteously If he does not, she will remain silent.

When he summons her for dictation she will enter his office with her notebook and pencil ready, take her seat (not expecting him to rise and seat her, as he would if they met at a social gathering), and wait for him to speak.

If she must take him a message when he is talking with someone she will not interrupt him, but will wait until he acknowledges her presence. The message, incidentally, will be written on a slip of paper which she will hand to him (unless it is the most routine sort of thing), so that he need not share it with his visitor unless he wishes to.

She will not expect him to solve her personal problems for her, nor to be allowed to weep on his shoulder—either literally or figuratively.

She will call him "Mr. Smith," not "Ted," even though he drops into the habit of calling her by her first name.

Lunching with Her Employer

There are times when, in the midst of a busy day, an employer may be justified in asking his secretary to lunch with him so that they may discuss necessary working arrangements, and in such a circumstance the secretary may quite properly accept his invitation. If, however, it becomes a habit and she finds that his talk of "business" is merely a mask for paying her personal attention, especially if he is a married man, she will do well to have other engagements or other plans and to decline his invitations as courteously as possible, even at the risk of being asked to find another job.

I do not mean to say that a sound and lasting affection may not properly grow between an unmarried employer and his secretary. It it quite natural that this should be so. In few relationships may two human beings come to know each other better than in that in which they work together. Many happy marriages have come about thus. If an unmarried employer and his secretary fall in love with each other they will of course see each other outside the office and frequently at lunch, at dinner, and at other times.

In such a situation, however, whatever their relationship outside the office, it should remain so far as all outward evidence goes an impersonal business relationship during working hours.

Trips with Her Employer

It is sometimes necessary for the secretary of an executive to accompany him on business trips that take them out of town and may keep them in another city for several days and nights. If her presence is obviously necessary and she knows that her employer's request that she accompany him is not merely a ruse, if their relationship is one of mutual dignity and respect, and if proper arrangements are made for their hotel accommodations, she may take the trip with him with complete propriety. She must herself judge whether these conditions are met.

In arranging for hotel accommodations for her employer and herself on such a trip she will see that he has a room or a suite on one floor, and she on another. If she wires ahead for accommodations for her employer "and secretary" most hotels will automatically see that the rooms are on separate floors, but she will do well to specify this If she finds when they arrive that they have been given adjoining rooms she will ask that she be given a room on another floor.

Her attitude toward lunching and dining with her employer (if he asks her to) while they are on such a trip will depend largely on the reasons for his asking her to do so, the frequency of his invitations, and his conduct. It might well be that the business necessities of the trip might suggest that they dine together in his suite and continue their work into the evening In such a case there would be no impropriety in her doing so, as long as he plainly had nothing in mind except their working relationship.

The care which she takes to see that her dress is neat, smart, and attractive but inconspicuous and businesslike, that she retains her dignity and impersonal workmanlike behavior, and that in all actions she will never give him any cause to believe that she would welcome personal attention, will be her best assurance that nothing will happen on the trip which is contrary to the rules of propriety.

THE WELL BEHAVED EMPLOYEE

The employee who rates an A for behavior carries his full share of the work load—or a little more—cheerfully and efficiently, is at pains to learn everything he can about all phases of the operation of which he is a part, is willing to help others and to do extra work in emergencies, gets along well with his colleagues, is respectful but not servile to those in authority over him, and is equally courteous to the mail clerk, to the president of the firm, and to the public. In this list of qualities I have put the element of courtesy in its usually understood meaning last, because it is meaningless without the other qualities which I have mentioned.

Attitude Toward Work and Employer

The basis for your behavior as an employee is your attitude toward the firm for which you work and toward those in authority over you. Roughly, I should say that your attitude and resultant behavior fall into three possible patterns.

(1) You love your job and feel that there could not possibly be a position anywhere in the world in which you would rather be. You have the greatest respect, admiration, and even affection for those under whom you work and those with whom you work, you are completely satisfied with your salary and working conditions, find the business of which you are a part of engrossing interest to you, and hope for nothing better than to spend the rest of your life in it. You are one of a very fortunate minority, and efficiency, courtesy, and happy cooperation with the staff and the public are almost automatic for you.

(2) You find that your salary, your working conditions, the details of your work, and the personalities of the people with whom you work are less pleasing than you would like them, but realizing that perfection is seldom found, you accept the things that displease you, adapt yourself to them, better what you can, and devote yourself to doing the best job you can. With this attitude and under these conditions you are also among the fortunate ones, and probably typical of the large majority of successful office employees. The essential combination of efficiency and courtesy (which, let me repeat, go hand and hand in any office operation and are the mainstay of the good business life) are well within your reach You will need more adjustment than you would in the circumstances described in (1), more self-control, a greater self-discipline in overlooking things which you cannot change, and a continuing determination to return courtesy for discourtesy, whether in word or act. But your attitude, which is adult and constructive, will dictate courtesy and make your success in the firm possible.

(3) You may hate every minute of your work day, instinctively resent every order and detail of instruction, believe that your superiors go out of their way to make things difficult for you, that your colleagues refuse to cooperate with you, and that you are unappreciated and not being given a chance to do a decent job. If this is your attitude you undoubtedly go home every night exhausted, have indigestion and perhaps headaches, and rise in the morning with a groan, wishing that you were going anywhere in the world except to your office.

You are one of the unfortunates who feel this way. I should say that without change, either in yourself or of your job, it is impossible for you to be efficient in your work or courteous to your superiors or to your colleagues. Not only your success in your work, but your physical well-being and happiness depend upon your either adopting a new attitude to your job or leaving it and finding another.

Your first task should be to weigh carefully the advantages and the disadvantages of your position, the nature of the firm for which you work, your superiors, colleagues, working conditions, salary, and prospects for advancement. You must do this with as great objectivity as you are capable of bringing to the problem, without paying too great attention to the personal factors that irritate you the most.

If an objective analysis convinces you that the disadvantages far outweigh the advantages, that the job and the firm are of such a nature that you can never possibly fit in harmoniously, that you are in short in an unpleasant blind alley from which there is no exit short of resignation, then the sooner you begin to look for another job the better. But meanwhile for the sake of your own self-respect and your business reputation, perform the duties of your present position as efficiently and with as great courtesy to others as you can, consoling yourself with the ancient truth (I believe that, like so much wisdom, it is Chinese) that "this is only temporary."

On the other hand, if you decide, in spite of flaws in the work pattern of your life, that the advantages of your job outweigh the disadvantages and that if you can adjust to the conditions as a whole, you can do as well and be as happy there as you could in any position you are likely to obtain, then you must find a way to adapt yourself and accept the things which you don't like and stop letting them poison your life. Until you can accept inevitable imperfections and live with them you are not emotionally an adult. If you are honest with yourself, your analysis may show you that some of the trouble may be of your own making.

Many adults qualify for the designation only by reason of their chronological age; in many ways they still act like unruly, badly brought up adolescents. They find a twisted satisfaction in breaking rules, in acting contrary to instructions, and in defying their superiors, as if it were necessary for them to prove that they are laws unto themselves and as good as or better than those who give them their orders.

These are the employees who are always trouble spots in any organization, who cannot work harmoniously with their colleagues or their department heads, who constantly criticize the firm for which they work, both inside and outside the organization. If they are able to retain their positions they seldom are advanced If they are by some mistake given authority they issue instructions and orders in an authoritative manner that irritates and offends, and they become less satisfactory executives than they were clerks.

If you feel that any of this description fits you, your first step should be to examine yourself with as much honesty and objectivity as you can muster. Perhaps you were dominated in childhood by an unsympathetic father or mother who established in you a resentment against all authority which you have never overcome. Perhaps through comparing yourself with a brilliant older brother or sister, or because of childhood illnesses or other disadvantages, you early in life convinced yourself that you had less ability than the normal average individual, that people did not like you, and that you would have to fight for everything you got. Your lack of cooperation with others, your truculence, your unpleasantness, your resentments of those in authority over you may all be unconscious efforts on your part to prove to yourself that you are as good as anyone else, and perhaps a bit better.

You may even be carrying over from childhood a habit of spoiled children—that of seeking to win attention by misbehavior. The child who habitually seeks attention by interrupting others, by talking in a loud voice, by ostentatiously disobeying, by fretfulness and complaining, by dramatizing himself, by self-pity and acting the part of a martyr is a classic behavior problem. Some children never abandon these techniques even when their age signifies that they should have reached maturity. In office staffs the adolescent-adult may manifest his immaturity by all of these actions. In addition he may try to turn over to others responsibilities that are rightfully his, have an inexhaustible reservoir of excuses for his own derelictions, take offense easily and go about exhibiting his hurt feelings as though he were proud of them. He may indulge in spells of working overtime which he carefully publicizes in order to prove how the management takes advantage of him and how unfairly he is treated.

Another troublesome employee is the one who makes his job, superiors, and colleagues the butts for his resentment at some frustration in his personal life. I remember one young man, happily married, with a pleasant home and two children whom he adored, and a compatible job in which he was doing very well until he became infatuated with a woman who worked in the same office. For several months they saw each other secretly at frequent lunches together, and sometimes in the evening when he resorted to the age-old device of telling his wife that he had to work overtime.

The quality of his work constantly deteriorated; he became curt to the point of rudeness in his contacts with the office staff, and neither he nor those with whom he worked found any joy in his connection with the firm. Deeply committed to his wife and family by both desire and principle, he finally faced the situation honestly and objectively, saw exactly what was happening to him, resigned, and stopped seeing the woman who had made such a devastating impact on his life. He is now a responsible executive in another firm doing the fine job which it is his nature to do, and making others feel that it is a privilege to work with him

It is not easy for an individual to discover damaging personality factors within himself without help or, having discovered them, to undo their harmful power over him Yet an honest search for them is in itself a wholesome thing, and the first step toward controlling them is to recognize them.

Of this I am sure: However you do it you must either accept your job and work with it rather than against it or find another where you can be happy, if you are to be an efficient, courteous employee.

Keeping Office Hours

A basic factor in office courtesy is the habit of being punctual. The man or woman who habitually disregards this rule (and there are several ways of doing so) violates the tacit agreement into which he entered when he accepted employment, and is being unfair and discourteous to his employers and his colleagues.

Under no circumstances is John Donne's statement that "no man is an island" more applicable than in the operation of a business office. It is not sufficient for you to do your job if you do it only at your own convenience and as though you were a solitary worker An efficient and harmonious office force works as a team. Nothing is more irritating or hampering to an executive or a colleague when he needs information or cooperation from you half an hour after the office has opened in the morning, to find that you have not yet arrived—or that you have left half an hour before closing time. It is a bit as though a quarterback in a football game, trying to execute a play by passing the ball to an end, finds that the end is not there. Failing to keep your appointment with your job is as personally discourteous as to keep a lady with whom you have an engagement for lunch waiting at a restaurant for half an hour.

Arriving and Leaving

The basic element of punctuality is arriving at the office at the time it regularly opens (not a half hour or even ten minutes late) and staying at your desk until closing time. Exceptions are possible, of course, when emergencies arise. Late trains, subways, or buses are acceptable excuses if they do not occur regularly. If they do, you had better revise your estimate of the time which it takes you to get from your home to the office and start a little earlier, even if now and then this will result in your being ten minutes early.

If you are going to be more than a few minutes late, and you have the opportunity, call the office and announce the fact

The employee who habitually leaves the office before closing time is as guilty of a breach of courtesy as the one who arrives late. In the same class is the one who cleans up his desk half an hour before closing time, washes up, and spends the last half hour of the work day gossiping with his colleagues or smoking and looking out the window.

Arrive Ready for Work

You may arrive at the office on the stroke of nine, yet if you are not ready to begin work until half an hour later you are as guilty of discourtesy as you would be if you arrived thirty minutes late.

If you get up so late that you cannot have breakfast at home or on the way and still arrive at the office on time, and so have fallen into the habit of having coffee and rolls sent up to you as soon as you arrive, change your rising habits. Set your alarm clock fifteen minutes earlier and have breakfast before you go to work.

Your toilet should be carefully made before you leave your house or your apartment. If you are a woman and spend half an hour in the washroom finishing what should have been done at home you have accomplished nothing by arriving at the office on time. One business friend of mine tells me that he not infrequently encounters girls in the elevator in the morning with their hair still in curlers, hurrying to check in on time only to go immediately to the washroom and spend the next half hour making themselves presentable. Obviously someone ought to give them a little basic training in ordinary manners.

The man who arrives unshaven at his desk is a similar case. He may shave in his office with an electric razor or slip out to a barber shop for a shave, after he has demonstrated that he can arrive at the office on time. Whether he or the one who remains unshaven all day has committed the more serious breach of office etiquette, it is hard to say.

Coffee Break

The midmorning "coffee break" has become almost as much an expected part of office routine in metropolitan America as is afternoon tea in English offices. In many offices the management furnishes the coffee, which is brought around each morning by an employee to whom this chore is regularly assigned. In others the employees have an arrangement with a caterer who brings it around, and the expense is shared by those who participate. Or the coffee can be sent up from a neighborhood drugstore or restaurant, of course with the employer's permission.

It is a legitimate and wholesome custom so long as it is not abused. It should not be made an excuse for a complete stoppage of work that may last for most of the rest of the morning, or for the gathering of employees in social groups in order to gossip. Properly it is a brief moment of rest and refreshment to be enjoyed quietly at your desk, and should be followed by a renewal of energy and a greater efficiency. If two employees happen to be sitting together discussing a matter connected with their duties at the time the coffee arrives they will properly enjoy it together and go on with their discussion. If an employee has at his desk someone from outside the office with whom he is discussing business, he will of course invite his visitor to join him.

Properly managed, the coffee break lightens and makes more pleasant the business routine, but remains a part of it. It is not a social event in favor of which business is set aside.

The Lunch Hour

Unlike the coffee break the lunch hour is, or should be, at the employee's option, as much a release from business duties as the evening, the weekend, or his vacation. In actual practice this principle is frequently disregarded, and a very great deal of business is conducted across the luncheon table Yet I think no employer is justified in expecting an employee to make a habit of spending his lunch hour in this way. When the weekly working hours in any office are calculated, they do not include the time allowed the employees for lunch.

But by the same reasoning the employee is obligated to take his lunch hour at a time designated by his department head or personnel officer and not materially or habitually to overstay the hour allotted to him. Life members of the "three hours for lunch club" are being not only unfair but also discourteous to their employers and their working colleagues.

Some employees bring their lunches to work with them, and unless there is an office rule prohibiting it, there is no reason why they should not do so. Indeed some offices provide conveniences such as a refrigerator, running water, and equipment for making tea and coffee for the use of those who want to eat in. If you do eat in, either in the room set aside for the purpose or at your desk, and there is a considerable portion of your lunch hour left after you have eaten, there is no reason why you should not leave the building to do personal errands or to take a walk and get a breath of air. But you should bear in mind that your lunch hour starts when you stop work and begin to eat, and that you should be back at your desk and at work when the hour ends. Eating your lunch first in time that properly belongs to the company for whom you work, and then leaving to spend the whole of your allotted lunch time away from the building is not, as the English would say, "quite the thing" It is not playing fair It is not being courteous.

When employees lunch at a restaurant together, the simplest and most approved method of handling the check is for each to pay his part of it, not forgetting to include his share of the tip. Otherwise you will find yourself in a tangle of luncheon obligations that may be very confusing. This is one situation in which a lady, lunching with a mixed group from the same office, is quite justified in insisting upon paying her own check even if she has been specifically asked to lunch with a male colleague alone. She may well suggest that she pay her check, though perhaps not insist against his firm opposition.

Office Dress and General Appearance

There are no specific and exact rules for office dress as there are for formal social occasions, but there are some general ones that are important For both men and women the basic essentials are simplicity, neatness, and cleanliness. But in addition to this there are some details to be observed.

For Women. I am constantly moved by admiration of the simple beauty of dress achieved by the average office girl in metropolitan America. The taste which such women bring to selecting their clothing, and the care which they give to keeping it clean, well pressed, and attractive, is usually beyond reproach. This does not mean that they spend large amounts of money on it, for today the wise shopper can buy most attractive dresses, blouses, skirts, and jackets at prices that are quite within the range of an office worker's salary. I do know, though, that such girls maintain their inviting appearance at the cost of vigilance and a great deal of work, washing, pressing, and altering clothing during the evenings and weekends, and taking care to hang it carefully that it may be worn another day without added effort. I am sure that the impression of dignified attractiveness which they achieve is worth all the effort

But here and there an exception proves the rule—the careless girl who dresses sloppily in ill-chosen garments or garments which she does not take the trouble to keep in shape Or she may go to the other extreme, overdressing in costumes that might be suitable for a lawn party or even an evening theater party, but are quite out of place in an office.

I am reminded of a story told me by a friend, which, though it has nothing to do with an office, is in its significance pertinent to what I want to say here. It is, in its way, one of the saddest little stories I have ever heard.

The young son of my friend had become infatuated with a sweet but almost illiterate girl who waited table in a cheap restaurant where he occasionally ate, and had gone out with her several times, then brought her home to spend a weekend at his parents' and his home. The girl had no luggage and brought her nightclothes, toothbrush, and cosmetics in a paper grocery bag. But having become quickly devoted to the boy and wanting to make as good an impression on his parents as possible, she wore for that weekend in the country what was obviously her best dress—a cheap party dress covered with gold thread, a tragic contrast with the pitiful little paper bag which she carried in her hand, and as unsuitable to the occasion as a garment could possibly have been.

If only someone could have told her that the clothing which she wore to work daily, clean and pressed, would have been far more suitable, I am sure that both she and the family which she visited would have had a pleasanter weekend.

It would be unrealistic to condemn women who under some circumstances make a conscious attempt to dress seductively. But a business office is under no circumstances the proper place for such an attempt. Every woman working in an office should take pride in her personal appearance as in the efficiency and neatness of her work and the graciousness of her behavior in relation to her co-workers. But in choosing her clothing she should remember that she is choosing a working, not a party, costume. Her clothing should be conservative, neat, and well designed, and she should wear only simple and inconspicuous jewelry.

Men. While I think it likely that more business women offend by dressing too elaborately for the office than by dressing too carelessly, I think the opposite is likely to be true for men. For every foppishly dressed dandy in an American office there are probably several who look as though they had slept in their clothes or had worn them without changing during a long weekend in the country, and had come straight to work upon rising without even combing their hair. I remember a friend's graphic, if inelegant description of one of her male office colleagues. "He always looks," she said, "like a used pipe cleaner."

The rules for male business dress are actually simple and general. Suits should be conservative, preferably of a dark color and without noticeable pattern in the fabric. In summer light-colored Palm Beach or similar suits may be worn, though today tropical worsteds and suits made of synthetic material enable a man who prefers dark suits to be as cool and unhampered in them as in the lighter colored material, and are more easily kept presentable.

It used to be considered ill bred for a man to discard his jacket in the office. Today it is a commonplace for male employees to work in their shirt sleeves—especially in the summer if they work in offices not equipped with air conditioning Some men prefer the freedom of movement which discarding the jacket gives them all the year round, and in most offices will draw no criticism if they work thus, so long as they do not have habitual contact with the public.

It is still considered courteous for an employee to put on his jacket before talking with a customer or other visitor, or when going to the office of an executive for a conference. But even this custom varies in different offices. If the executive himself habitually works without his jacket, the employee cannot be criticized for appearing with similar informality.

The basic requisite for men, as it is for women, is neatness, cleanliness, and a general appearance of alertness that can be expressed by his clothes almost as much as by his manner. The suit should be kept well pressed and in repair, the shoes (which may be brown or black, but should not be sports shoes, although loafers are now permitted) should be well shined. The shirt and handkerchief must be clean. The hair should be cut frequently enough to be always neat, fingernails should be kept trimmed and clean, and the morning shave should never be neglected.

Excessive Body Odor. One of the most annoying causes of offense to working colleagues is the unpleasant body odor with which a few people are afflicted. I am sure that many an office career has been retarded and many a budding romance shattered by a condition that arises from a slight physical difference for which the offending individual is in no way responsible Yet it is one that demands special attention, and though the condition apparently cannot be changed, its effects may be controlled.

Here and there throughout the body are the apocrine glands, the secretions of which become active during adolescence and continue throughout life. It is their secretions that emit offensive odors from anyone who does not keep his body scrupulously clean. In a few unfortunate individuals there may be many more of these glands than in the average person, and for these ordinary cleanliness is not enough Such a person may leave home in the morning after a thoroughly cleansing bath and, especially in hot weather, be offensive by noon. Both men and women may be thus afflicted

But there are some things which the sufferer can do to eliminate or at least minimize the unpleasant effects of the condition.

It goes without saying that if you are one of the unfortunate ones you will be especially careful about personal cleanliness. A daily bath is essential. Since bacterial action alters the glandular secretions and increases their odor, medicated soaps are often helpful Deodorants, too, that reduce or prevent the secretions are helpful, but some skins are sensitive to them and for these certain preparations may produce a rash. If you find this to be the case change your deodorant, or talk it over with your doctor. Ordinary rubbing alcohol is as effective as anything you can use and as safe

I know one woman who has been afflicted with this condition since she was in her teens, though none of her friends know it, for she has controlled it. She has found two clothing rules helpful to her She wears light cotton clothing whenever possible, and she avoids closely woven nylon.

Do not hesitate to consult your doctor because of a sense of shame, for no blame can possibly attach to you It means simply that you were born with more apocrine glands than most people have. It is not even an abnormality. It is simply that you are a little different from most people. But do find a way to cope with it, and you and all with whom you work will be happier.

Probably the worst possible approach to the problem is one which some women make—that of using an excess of perfume. This is a case in which the remedy may well be worse than the disease, for the combination of body odor and perfume can be overpowering

Indeed the woman who uses too much perfume at any time in business or in the evening should be politely told that she does not require this added allurement. A good perfume, used with extreme restraint, can be charming. But the office is not the place for it. If you are a businesswoman restrict yourself on working days to cologne, which is refreshing and pleasant, but vanishes quickly and leaves no perceptible scent.

THE RECEPTIONIST

❧ One of the most important persons in any office is the receptionist. She is frequently the human façade of the business and often creates the image of the organization as a whole which the visitor will retain. She is the greeter, the hostess, the welcomer to visitors She is also the buffer between unexpected and undesired callers and the executives and officers of the company. She is the one who may sometimes be faced with the necessity of keeping a crank or even a deranged invader of the office from disrupting the morning's or afternoon's work.

Qualifications

The ideal receptionist is naturally friendly and likes people. She has more than the average human being's share of an ability to judge people quickly. She need not of course be a flaming beauty, but she should have the attractiveness that illuminates a face from the inner light of character, intelligence, forthrightness, friendliness, and good nature. She should have a good memory for faces and names, be quick-witted, and have infinite patience and tact. She should be a good conversationalist, but know where the line is between expressing friendly interest and indulging in long gossipy chats with callers, and should allow no conversation with a caller to pass it. She should dress conservatively, but give rather especial attention to the neatness and cleanliness of her appearance.

Greeting a Caller. When a man or woman approaches her desk, she will smile and say, "Good morning," or "Good afternoon," if she has time to do so before the caller speaks. If he says, "I have an appointment with Mr. Smith," her procedure is simple. If there is a chair by her desk, as there should be, she will say, "Won't you sit down while I tell him you are here? May I tell him who is calling?" She should avoid such abrupt questions as, "Who are you?" and "Who is calling?" She will then phone Mr. Smith's office and say, "Mr. Brown is here to see Mr. Smith by appointment." She will then, having had the appointment confirmed, address Mr. Brown, giving him whatever information is pertinent. "Mr. Smith will be out at once." Or "Will you go right in, please. Do you know the way to his office?" (If he does not she will either take him to Mr. Smith's office, or give him explicit directions as to how to reach it.) Or "Mr.

Smith asks me to apologize to you, but he has someone with him. Do you mind waiting a few moments?" (Actually Mr. Smith's most courteous behavior will be to come to the reception room himself to greet Mr. Brown and take him to his office, or if this is impossible or seriously inconvenient, to send his secretary to the reception room to do so.)

When a caller arrives without an appointment and asks to see an executive or officer of the firm, or arrives in a dudgeon asking to see "someone in a responsible position to whom I can give a piece of my mind," the receptionist's task will call for a high degree of tact and ingenuity.

If the caller gives the name of a specific person, the receptionist will ask as tactfully as possible what the caller's name is. She will not say, "What's your name?" or even, "Your name, please," but "May I give your name to Mr. Meyers?" Even if he refuses to give it she will call Mr. Meyers' office and say that a visitor is there to see him. She may then report to the caller, "I'm sorry, but Mr. Meyers is in an important meeting just now (or not in the office today) Perhaps you could phone him and make an appointment for some time tomorrow."

If the caller simply demands to see "someone in authority" she may quite correctly say, "Could you tell me a little of what you want to see him about, so that I may find the proper person for you?" If she has enough tact and intelligence and knowledge of the business she may herself so soothe the complainant that he will leave satisfied. If she is unable to do this she will choose some one in the organization who she knows will be able to handle the matter, and turn it over to him.

Sometimes the receptionist is called upon to handle tactfully a dereliction on the part of one of the executives. I remember the story of an incident in which an executive had completely forgotten an appointment which was handled with consummate tact by a receptionist.

It was during the noon hour when Miss Brown, a woman executive of a company with whom the receptionist's firm did a great deal of business, entered the office saying that she had a luncheon appointment with Mr Smith. The receptionist knew that Mr. Smith had left the office a few minutes earlier to lunch with someone else. Nevertheless she phoned Mr. Smith's office while the visitor waited. Since Mr. Smith's secretary had also gone to lunch she received no answer, as she had expected. She then asked the visitor to excuse her, disappeared, and returned a moment later with Mr Jones, Mr. Smith's assistant who apologized for Mr. Smith, saying that he had been called out in an emergency, had phoned Miss Brown's office only to find that she had already left. He ended his explanation with a gracious invitation (as the receptionist had suggested). "Will you permit me to take you to lunch? I have wanted for a long time to meet you."

The luncheon was a great success, and the rudeness of an executive which might have seriously damaged the cordial relations between two firms was turned into a negligible incident by the quick-witted stratagem of a good receptionist.

SOME GENERAL RULES FOR OFFICE BEHAVIOR

Conversation

It would be unrealistic and ridiculous to say that nothing but business should be discussed in a business office. The organization in which the individuals of the staff are not friends is an unfortunate, an unhappy, and almost certainly an inefficient one. Your friends are interested in what interests you—in the health and welfare of your family, in the way your garden grows (if you have one), in where and how you spent your vacation when you return from it, in the especially good movie which you saw last night, and in other things. A reasonable sharing of such interests (when discussion of them does not interfere with the smooth operation of the work) is natural and right, and undoubtedly contributes to the *esprit de corps* of an organization.

But the employee should never forget that he is in the office to work, and any indulgence in personal conversation should be brief and unobtrusive. The practice of groups gathering at the drinking fountain, in the rest rooms, around a desk or elsewhere for long gossip sessions is in the worst of taste and should be avoided.

Even if a justifiable conversation about personal affairs is being carried on between two colleagues and a third enters with a business matter to be discussed, the personal discussion should stop at once, to be continued at some later time.

Courtesy in speech among office colleagues at whatever level of responsibility and authority—"Please," "Thank you," "I'm sorry," not interrupting, etc.—should be as strictly the rule in business offices as at the most formal social affairs.

One of the obligations of courtesy in conversation is to use your language correctly and as exactly and economically as possible. (See Chapter 30, "Conversation.")

Suggestions for the proper use of the telephone will be found in Chapter 31, "The Telephone."

Remembering Names

Drill yourself to remember the names of your superiors, your colleagues, and any customers of the firm with whom you have constant contact, and use their names when speaking to them. Following certain practices will help you to do this. When you meet someone and learn his name make sure that you have it correctly even if you have to ask him to repeat it If it is a difficult name you will not offend him by asking him to spell it. This will enable you to impress a visual image of it on your memory. Use it several times in your first conversation with him. If it is a name which itself suggests a visual image such as a color (Brown, Green or Black), think of the color in association with the person. If it suggests an occupation such as Smith, Carpenter, Farmer, form an image in your mind of a man shoeing a horse, sawing a board, tilling a field. If it suggests an object (Castle, Street, Ball), think of the object. Try to pick out some special feature of the other's appearance, a prominent chin, an exceptional width between the eyes, exceptionally heavy eyebrows, or protruding ears, and think of them and the name at the same time. One of the most useful tricks in memory training is learning to associate what you wish to remember with a visual image. It may also help you to write down the name after your first meeting, and even note one or two of the physical characteristics to which you have paid attention. The very act of writing these things on paper will help your memory.

One of the most remarkable people I have ever known was a telephone operator my husband took with him to the White House. She headed the White House telephone staff for many years and there was no one who called whose voice she did not recognize on a second call, so that she could respond immediately with the individual's name.

She was also remarkable in the way she found people. Of course it may be easier to do this from the White House than from even a very important business office, but one could say to her, "Miss Hackmeister, I want the man who called from Denver, Colorado, a week ago. I do not remember his name and I do not remember his address." In half an hour she would have the man on the phone. How she ever trained her memory to sound no one could understand, but she was an invaluable individual in the working machinery of the White House so long as my husband was there.

Social Life. Your social life should not be allowed to intrude upon your office hours. Both incoming and outgoing personal phone calls are sometimes unavoidable (though there are some firms who forbid the latter and ask their employees to discourage the former), but they should always be kept short and in the nature of giving and receiving essential messages. There is no excuse for the employee who calls his friends simply to gossip with them, or encourages long gossipy conversations with friends who phone him.

Similarly the well mannered employee will not encourage his friends to pay social visits to him at the office. There is no reason why a man's wife (or any one else for that matter) who is having dinner downtown and going to the theater with him should not meet him at the office at the end of a work day, but she should time her call so that she will not arrive noticeably before the work day is over, or if she does, will wait quietly in the reception room until he is ready to leave.

Personal Correspondence

Generally speaking an employee should ask his personal correspondents to address their letters to him at his home. I suppose that receiving an occasional personal letter at the office is inevitable, but the man or woman who regularly receives personal mail at the office not only uses office time for reading his private mail, but quite naturally creates the suspicion (rightly or wrongly) that he writes his personal letters during his working hours, which of course is quite improper.

Maintaining the Toilet

All employees, both male and female, should maintain their appearance of cleanliness and neatness throughout the work day.

Hands that become soiled should be washed, fingernails kept clean, hair combed, and feminine makeup kept in repair. But these things should be done in the retiring rooms Hair should not be combed, fingernails cleaned, or makeup repaired at the desk.

Suggestion Box

If your office has in it a "Suggestion Box" for the use of employees, as some have, use it only for suggestions which you think will improve the methods or the product of the organization for which you work, and never as a way to complain of other employees or your immediate superiors.

SOME DON'T'S

Don't push into or out of elevator doors in front of older persons, whether they work in your office or other offices in the building, or if you are a man, in front of ladies. Indeed don't push. If through being courteous you find it impossible to get onto the elevator which you intended to take without overcrowding, wait for the next one.

Don't remain seated when an officer of the firm, a materially older person than yourself, or a lady (if you are a man) enters your office to talk with you. The same rule applies when you greet any visitor from the outside.

Don't be irritable with your colleagues. They may also have slept badly the night before, or perhaps are suffering from indigestion.

Don't act (because you are older, have a bit more authority, earn a little more, or have been longer with the firm) as though you felt that you were superior to the other members of your department. Remember they may get promoted over your head, and they will not forget how you behaved to them.

Don't be obsequious or behave as though you felt inferior to your superiors in authority and responsibility. Your behavior toward them should exhibit respect and the desire to cooperate, but should also reflect your sense of self-respect and personal dignity.

Don't refuse help to a beginner who knows the office routine and personnel less well than you do. To do so is not only discourteous but also to fail in your obligation to the firm for which you both work.

Don't gossip.

Don't let your ambition for advancement lead you into currying favor with your superiors at the expense of your colleagues. Let your ambition be to do your own work as well as you possibly can and, when possible, to help others.

Don't go over your immediate superior's head to make complaints, or to show those at the top what a clever person you are. If you find that sometimes your department head has taken credit for an idea of yours, or something you have done, remember it only long enough to resolve never to adopt his method yourself. Don't make an issue of it.

Don't be a habitual cadger of cigarettes or borrower of money. If in an emergency you borrow a small amount of money, remember that you have done so and pay it back at the earliest possible moment Write the sum and the name down on your pad so that you don't forget it.

Don't be a destructive critic of the work of your associates. In business as well as in personal relations take every opportunity to build up their self-respect rather than tear it down. Remember the wise advice which Lord Chesterfield gave his son "Make other people like themselves a little better, and I promise you they will like you very well."

VII

SOME
SPECIAL PEOPLE

26

V. J. P.'s

EVERYWHERE SINCE THE DAWN OF CIVILIZATION SOCIETY has paid special marks of respect to certain people, through forms of address, and through established orders of precedence which have dictated, according to their rank, their places at public functions or even private gatherings.

Jesus acknowledged this special type of respect when he said

When thou art bidden of any *man* to a wedding, sit not down in the highest room, lest a more honourable man than thou be bidden of him, And he that bade thee and him come and say to thee, Give this man place, and thou begin with shame to take the lowest room

In government and diplomatic circles, especially in these days when the representatives of sovereign governments from all over the world meet with our own government in Washington, at the U.N., or in private homes, the problems of protocol have become more and more complex. To many people in democratic America, "conceived," as Lincoln put it, "in liberty, and dedicated to the proposition that all men are created equal," where we shun titles and consider every man as good as his neighbor, this intricate business of determining who ranks whom and what is the proper form of address for each may seem to be pretentious nonsense.

But when we make any such judgment, we fail to understand that what appears to many of us a ridiculous bowing to rank and privilege is in fact homage paid not to the individual involved but to the position for which he stands. In any administration, Republican or Democratic, a citizen may not respect the character and qualifications of the person who holds the office of President of the United States. Yet any breach of etiquette in our forms of address or conduct toward him is an act of disrespect not to him but to the nation of which he is the Chief Executive.

In Theodore H. White's magnificent book, *The Making of the President,* the author recalls John F. (later President) Kennedy at dinner in his home at Hyannis Port waiting for the results of the election on November 7, 1960. Reminiscing about the campaign the candidate (as he then was) remembers a vignette "out of the tumult and storm and noise." When he had traveled in the big cities and the cheering crowds had filled the sidewalks he could look up to the office buildings above them and see the white-collared executives staring down at him. In city after city, as if by common instinct, they all were giving him the "bent-arm, clenched-fist gesture of contempt." Now this they did and felt free to do because then John F. Kennedy was the Democratic candidate and they were entitled to express their feelings in any way they pleased. They were exercising their rights as citizens. But today these same men, were they privileged to meet him, would greet him respectfully as "Mr. President."

Or to take an example from a sister nation; when immediately after the death of King George VI (which made his daughter Elizabeth, Queen of England) the young Queen came face to face for the first time with the Dowager Queen Mary, her grandmother, the latter made a low curtsy and said, "Your Majesty." Queen Mary was not curtsying to her youthful granddaughter; she was paying homage to the British Crown, symbol of a mighty sovereign state.

In some respects the English are especially careful to make this distinction. For centuries the Lord Mayor of London, head of that segment of the great metropolis known as the City of London, which is so jealous of its traditional distinction as an entity that the Queen of England when she wishes to enter it in state must ask permission to do so, has been given the title "The Right Honorable." The form of address places the emphasis upon the honor due his position rather than the man himself. The present incumbent is not "The Right Honorable Sir Bernard Waley-Cohen," but "Sir Bernard Waley-Cohen, the Right Honorable, the Lord Mayor of London."

In other usages this distinction is less apparent. Hereditary titles of nobility descend to eldest sons regardless of their character, usefulness to the world, or economic status. (It is probably this element in British aristocracy that led the newly founded United States of America to forbid all such titles in American society.) Yet even in this custom there is inherent a certain element of respect for something behind the person who bears the title—a select body of men and women committed, by the fact of their positions, to wise leadership and the principle of *noblesse oblige*. That not all the members of the class fulfill their obligations does not in itself negate the principle.

Perhaps the British custom that is most difficult to explain in terms of honoring the position rather than the individual is the one that dictates to whom the term "Esquire" and to whom the term "Mr." should be used. Most Americans know that in writing a letter to an Englishman the envelope usually should be addressed not to "Mr. J. P. Robinson" but to "J. P. Robinson, Esq." "Esquire" is an old rendering of the word "Gentleman." Many Americans do not know, however, to whom it is not properly applied. The carpenter, the plumber, the tailor or the mechanic is never addressed as "Esquire." The reason is that no one who works with his hands is properly entitled to be called "Esquire." Probably for this reason a British surgeon, no matter how distinguished, is never "Dr. John Brown," but "Mr. John Brown." Unlike his other medical colleagues, he works with his hands. In this instance, the principle is carried beyond the point at which an American, born to a classless society where the skilled workman is respected, can sympathize with it. Yet it is an essential part of the British respect for rank.

The British system of inherited titles and the importance given it by some persons has caused amusement and sometimes scorn not only in our own country but in England itself. In *Persuasion*, that masterpiece by Jane Austen, the great early nineteenth century English novelist, there is an excellent example of this, beginning with the first paragraph ·

Sir Walter Elliot, of Kellynch Hall, in Somersetshire, was a man who, for his own amusement, never took up any book but the Baronetage;

there he found occupation for an idle hour, and consolation in a distressed one, there his faculties were roused into admiration and respect, by contemplating the limited remnant of the earliest patents, there any unwelcome sensations, arising from domestic affairs, changed naturally into pity and contempt as he turned over the almost endless creations of the last century, and there, if every other leaf were powerless, he could read his own history with an interest which never failed.

Reading this, we must not forget how flattered Miss Austen was when she learned that King George IV "read her works with pleasure!"

Later in the same novel she demonstrates how seriously the matter of precedence was taken by members of her own class.

Again, it was Mary's complaint that Mrs. Musgrove was very apt not to give her the precedence that was her due when they dined at the Great House with other families, and she did not see any reason why she was to be considered so much at home as to lose her place And one day when Anne was walking with only the Miss Musgroves, one of them, after talking of rank, people of rank, and jealousy of rank, said, "I have no scruple of observing to *you* how nonsensical some persons are about their place, because all the world knows how easy and indifferent you are about it; but I wish anybody would give Mary a hint that it would be a great deal better if she were not so very tenacious, especially if she would not be always putting herself forward to take place of mamma. Nobody doubts her right to have precedence of mamma, but it would be more becoming in her not to be always insisting on it. It is not that mamma cares about it the least in the world, but I know it is taken notice of by many persons."

Fortunately for all concerned we do not have in this country the problems created by a hereditary baronetcy or peerage, and the complicated matters of precedence which they create. Yet anyone who has moved in Washington society, or even the society of Albany or other state capitals, or to a lesser extent in that of the great cities knows how complex and frequently embarrassing even in our America the matter may become, especially when it concerns a Cabinet member and his wife or a distinguished guest from another nation. Every experienced hostess in Washington has learned that sometimes there is only one foolproof solution to the problem involving two almost equal foreign dignitaries, and that is never to invite them to the same function. But even this may cause offense, unless the uninvited guest is asked to a similar function, quickly arranged for a later date. This can be more than a nuisance, it can be expensive.

At the Vienna Congress on June 9, 1815 (at which the United States was not represented), an attempt was made to establish by codification the order of precedence for diplomatic agents in international relations. The representatives of foreign governments were divided into three classes, (1) ambassadors, legates, or nuncios, (2) envoys, ministers, or others accredited to sovereigns, and (3) chargés d'affaires accredited to ministers of foreign affairs. In 1818 another class—resident ministers accredited to sovereigns—was added and inserted between envoys and chargés d'affaires. The regulations, which were agreed to by the plenipotentiaries of the eight powers who signed the Treaty of Paris in 1886, provided further that diplomatic agents of the same classes from different countries would take precedence according to seniority—the one with the longest service, no matter how insignificant his country, being given first place. Substantially these orders of precedence have been followed ever since.

Amusingly enough, though the code provided that in signing treaties between several powers lots should be drawn to determine the order in which the signatures should be affixed, no lots were drawn to determine the order of the signatures to the agreement itself. The plenipotentiaries simply signed in the order in which they sat about the table—which proves, I suppose, that common sense sometimes overrides protocol. (The lot-drawing plan was abandoned, incidentally, in 1818, in favor of the simpler method of signing in alphabetical order.)

PROTOCOL IN GOVERNMENT CIRCLES

Rank

The question of rank and precedence has always been a touchy one in government circles, yet these apparently ridiculous or archaic rules agreed upon among the nations have a strong practical reason for their existence In 1661 a sword battle in London between the attendants of the French and Spanish ambassadors, over whose carriage should precede the other's, brought France and Spain dangerously close to war. In 1756 a violent quarrel between the French and Russian ambassadors at a ball in London over precedence led to a duel and a serious threat of war between Russia and France.

A slight to an ambassador is not a personal affront, it is an insult to his nation.

Even in the democratic United States of America, where rank is of less importance than it is in Europe, many famous quarrels over precedence have occurred in Washington. During the administration of President Theodore Roosevelt, when Miss Helen Cannon, daughter of "Uncle Joe" Cannon, a widower and Speaker of the House, demanded precedence over the wives of senators and representatives and was overruled, she announced that she would send regrets to further invitations to the White House if she were not given at least equal status with the wives of members of the Congress. During the Hoover administration Dolly Gann, sister and hostess of Vice-President Curtis, created a long-drawn-out controversy by her demand that she be given precedence over Alice Roosevelt Longworth, wife of Speaker Nicholas Longworth. Admiral of the Navy George Dewey precipitated a similar commotion when he demanded (in vain) that he be given precedence over foreign ministers because he rated a salute of seventeen guns as compared to only fifteen for the foreign ministers.

Some of these controversies have brought about modifications in the orders of precedence; others have left them unchanged. Sometimes other factors have brought about modifications. The intent has always been to arrange the order of precedence in such a way as to indicate properly the degree of vested authority represented.

The official order according to the list I have before me, and which I believe is correct as I write, is

> The President of the United States
> The Vice-President
> The Speaker of the House
> The Chief Justice and retired Chief Justices
> Former Presidents
> The Secretary of State
> Ambassadors of Foreign Powers (in order of the length of time they have been officially in the United States)
> Widows of former Presidents
> U.S. Representatives to the United Nations
> Ministers of Foreign Powers
> Active and retired Associate Justices of the Supreme Court
> The Secretary of the Treasury
> The Secretary of Defense

The Attorney General
The Postmaster General
The Secretary of the Interior
The Secretary of Agriculture
The Secretary of Commerce
The Secretary of Labor
The Secretary of Health, Education and Welfare
The Director of Defense Mobilization (Cabinet rank)
The Director of Foreign Operations Administration (Cabinet rank)
The Director of the Bureau of the Budget
The Governors of the States, in order of seniority
The Senators, in order of seniority
The Assistants to the President
Acting Heads of Executive Departments
Former Vice-Presidents
Members of the House of Representatives
Under Secretaries of State
The Deputy Secretary of Defense
The Secretary of the Army
The Secretary of the Navy
The Secretary of the Air Force
The Under Secretaries of the Executive Department and Deputy
    Secretaries
Chairman, Joint Chiefs of Staff
The Chief of Staff of the Army
The Chief of Naval Operations
The Chief of Staff of the Air Force
Generals of the Army and Fleet Admirals (5 star)
Chargés d'affaires *en pied* of Foreign Powers
Chargés d'affaires *ad interim* of Foreign Powers
Chairman, Atomic Energy Commission
Director, Central Intelligence Agency
Federal Civil Defense Administrator
Deputy Assistant to the President
Secretaries to the President

THE WASHINGTON HOSTESS AND HER GUESTS

Now it is not likely that as a private hostess you will invite *all* of these distinguished men and their wives to dinner on the same evening. It is not likely that the President himself will, except perhaps to a Presidential reception where the order of precedence will be almost entirely relaxed and the guests will mingle freely among themselves. To me today the extraordinary interest of this list, now only occasionally personally useful, is the order of importance of the offices and titles themselves. Why for instance in this our modern world should the Chairman of the Atomic Energy Commission be outranked by the Governor of Alaska? He is. Why should the Postmaster General outrank the Secretary of Labor? He does Cabinet officers rank according to the dates when their departments were created. In the United States, as opposed to Great Britain, the Army always outranks the Navy because it is the older service; but again in this our modern world, why should the Air Force always follow the Army, the Navy and the Marine Corps because it is the youngest? Thus, to be socially correct, when you give a dinner party and both Navy and Army of *equal rank* are present, the Army Colonel always precedes the Naval Captain.

The obvious importance of new departments and differences of interpretation can and does bring about revisions in the order of precedence. The wise diplomatic or social hostess will make sure to check the latest rules of precedence before issuing invitations to an affair to which she intends to ask several government officials or foreign diplomats This can be done by telephoning the State Department Protocol Officer.

Planning the Guest List

In planning the personnel of any dinner party, whether formal or informal, in honor of an individual, the hostess must remember that the code of precedence *always* determines the seating at table Therefore she will not invite anyone of higher rank than the guest whom she wishes to honor, for if she does he will find himself seated not in his proper place as guest of honor, but below another guest or guests of higher rank.

The hostess will be equally careful not to invite two guests of equal rank, unless she knows one of them well enough to be sure that he will not be offended if she gives him place slightly below the other. In some cases there are determining factors that may solve the difficulty. Governors of states and senators, for instance, rank according to their time in office. If, however, two governors have been in office exactly the same length of time, the one whose state was first admitted to the Union takes precedence

No invitations to a luncheon or dinner in honor of any person should be sent out without first consulting the one who is to be honored

If a hostess plans to ask the Vice-President, or the Chief Justice, or the Speaker of the House to dinner she will ask him first, giving him the option of two dates, and not issue other invitations until he has accepted one of them. It is considered improper for any host and hostess to ask any one of these to more than two affairs in a single season.

A diplomat and his wife may not be asked to dinner until the hostess has called on them or left cards. Ambassadors expect to be seated next to the hostess. Because of this only one may be invited to a dinner to which anyone who ranks him is asked, two if no other ranking guest is asked, but never if two or more ranking guests are asked.

Seating of Guests

Seating arrangements at formal or informal dinner parties are based as nearly as possible upon the order of precedence of the guests. However, the Protocol Staff of the State Department has pointed out that the rules which it has established are for official affairs only, and that they vary for different affairs. The private hostess must, of course, arrange her seating in such a way that no honored guest will be slighted, but if for a formal dinner party she violates some of the rules of strict protocol, the success of her evening will be judged by the quality of her hospitality and not by how closely she follows the book. In general, however, she will do well to follow one of several accepted plans of seating at her table.

If she is entertaining with her husband she will sit at one end of the table or at the middle of one side of the table, and he will sit directly opposite her In either case, the most honored male guest will sit at her right, and the next most honored at her left, while the most honored lady will sit at her husband's right, and the next honored at his left. Other guests, with men and women alternating, will sit in the order of their precedence. Sometimes, at a small dinner party given for a guest of honor the host will give his place opposite the hostess at the center of the table to the guest of honor and sit at one end of the table on the same side as the honored guest

At a large dinner party when the table is arranged in the form of a square or rectangle with one side open, two arrangements are possible The hostess may sit at the center of the outside of the closed end of the square with the principal male guest at her right, and the next most important man at her left. Her husband may sit opposite her with the principal lady guest at his right and the next most important at his left. The others will alternate (men and women) in the order of their precedence around the outside and down the inside, with the lowest in precedence at the ends of the two legs of the open square.

Or the host may sit at the left of the hostess on the outside of the closed end of the open square or rectangle. In this case the principal male guest will sit at the right of the hostess, and the principal lady guest at the left of the host, the others alternating in the order of their precedence as in the other arrangement.

Place Cards

The custom which is prescribed for place cards used at formal dinners to which government officials have been invited dictates the following forms:

For the President of the United States
The President

For the Vice-President of the United States
The Vice-President

For a Cabinet Officer
The Secretary of ———

For the Under Secretary of a Department
The Under Secretary of ———

For the Assistant Secretary of a Department
Mr. Smith

For the Secretary to the President (if with military rank)
Major General James Smith

For the Comptroller General
The Honorable James Smith

For the Director of the Bureau of the Budget
The Honorable James Smith

For the Speaker of the House of Representatives
The Speaker

For a Senator, or Senator Elect
Senator Smith

For a Member of the House of Representatives
Representative Smith

For a Resident Commissioner
The Resident Commissioner of Puerto Rico, James Smith

For a Territorial Delegate
Delegate Smith

For the Chief Justice of the Supreme Court
The Chief Justice

For an Associate Justice or Retired Justice of the Supreme Court
Mr Justice Smith

For the Governor of a State
The Governor of Illinois

For the Secretary of State of a State
The Secretary of State of Arizona

For the Commissioner of the District of Columbia
The District Commissioner (or) Mr. Smith

For a State Legislator
The Honorable James Smith

For the Mayor of a City
The Mayor of ——

The list of government boards and commissions, and of organizations, the personnel of which may be guests of the Washington hostess, is far too long to include here. A complete listing, however, may be found in the *Congressional Directory* or *The United States Government Manual*.

The Armed Services

The Army, the oldest of the armed services, has always precedence over the Navy, the Marine Corps, and the Air Force. Individual officers in the same service take precedence according to their rank, or if their ranks are equal, according to the length of service in the rank In the Army retired officers rank next to the same grades of active officers, in the Navy retired and active officers rank equally for the same grade, precedence being determined by the dates of their commissions In all of the services women rank equally with men according to grades

The order of precedence for officers in the five services follows

Army	Navy	Marine Corps	Air Force	Coast Guard
1. General of the Army	Fleet Admiral	No Comparable Rank	No Comparable Rank	No Comparable Rank
2. Chief of Staff	Chief of Naval Operations	Commandant of the Marine Corps	Chief of Staff U.S. Air Force	No Comparable Rank
3. General	Admiral	General	General	Admiral
4. Lieut. General	Vice Admiral	Lieut. General	Lieut. General	Vice Admiral
5. Major General	Rear Admiral	Major General	Major General	Rear Admiral
6. Brig. General	Rear Admiral (Lower Half)	Brig. General	Brig. General	Commodore
7. Colonel	Captain	Colonel	Colonel	Captain
8. Lieut. Colonel	Commander	Lieut. Colonel	Lieut. Colonel	Commander
9. Major	Lieutenant Commander	Major	Major	Lieutenant Commander
10. Captain	Lieutenant	Captain	Captain	Lieutenant
11. First Lieutenant	Lieutenant (j.g.)	First Lieutenant	First Lieutenant	Lieutenant (j g.)
12. Second Lieutenant	Ensign	Second Lieutenant	Second Lieutenant	Ensign

FORMS OF ADDRESS

There is no fixed rule that determines arbitrarily how you should speak or write to all persons who have earned the distinction of an office or title. In some cases the designation of the office itself is used, preceded by "Mr." or "Madam" ("Mr. President", "Madam Secretary"). In some cases the title of the office is used with the proper name following ("Senator Smith," "Doctor Makewell"). In some cases a specific title of honor is preceded by "Your" ("Your Majesty," "Your Grace," "Your Honor"). In some cases, in correspondence, the proper name is preceded by "The Honorable." There is no general rule that will cover all cases, and so I have listed below a variety of important personages with the proper forms of address you should use in speaking or writing to them.

The President

"Mr. President" in spoken address; formal letter begins "Sir"; informal, "My dear Mr. President." Envelope, if mailed in the United States, is addressed "The President, Washington, D C.", if mailed abroad, "The President of the United States of America, Washington, D.C."

The Vice-President

As above, save, of course, that "Vice-" precedes "President."

Chief Justice of the Supreme Court

"Mr. Chief Justice" in spoken address; formal letter begins "Sir"; informal, "Dear Mr. Chief Justice"; envelope address, "The Honorable, the Chief Justice, Washington, D.C."; if mailed abroad, no change.

Associate Justice of the Supreme Court

"Mr. Justice" in spoken address, formal letter begins "Sir"; informal, "Dear Mr. Justice Harrington." Envelope address, "The Honorable A. B. Harrington, Justice of the Supreme Court, Washington, D.C."

Member of President's Cabinet

"Mr. (or "Madam"—whether Miss or Mrs.) Secretary" in spoken address; formal letter begins "Sir" or "Dear Sir" (or

"Madam"), informal, "My dear Mr. (or "Madam") Secretary"; envelope address, "The Secretary of ————, Washington, D C." or "The Honorable James C. Smith, Secretary of ————, Washington, D.C."

Mayor of a City

Spoken address, "Mr. (or "Madam") Mayor"; formal letter begins "Dear Sir" (or "Madam"), informal, "Dear Mayor Harrington", envelope address, "His (or "Her") Honor the Mayor, City Hall, Walla Walla, Washington."

Ambassador

"Mr. (or "Madam") Ambassador" or "Your Excellency" in spoken address; formal letter begins "Your Excellency", informal, "Dear Mr. (or "Madam") Ambassador", envelope address, "His Excellency, the American Ambassador, London, England."

Minister Plenipotentiary

Spoken address, "Mr. Minister" (though in the United States he is more often called by his surname, thus "Mr Saint John"), formal letter begins "Sir" or "Your Excellency", informal, "Dear Mr. (or "Madam") Minister" or "Mr. (or "Miss" or "Mrs ") Saint John", envelope address, "His Excellency, the American Minister, London, England" or "The Honorable John S Saint John, Embassy of the United States of America, London, England."

United States Senator or State Senator

Spoken address, "Senator Spokesman"; formal letter begins "Sir" or "Dear Sir" (or "Madam"); informal, "Dear Senator Spokesman", envelope address, social, "Senator John C. Spokesman," home address; official, "The Honorable John C. Spokesman, Senator from Utah, Washington, D.C."

Governor of a State

Spoken address, "Governor Stately", formal letter begins "Your Excellency" or "Sir" (or "Madam"); informal, "Dear Governor Stately", envelope address, "His Excellency the Governor, Springfield, Illinois" or "The Honorable James C. Stately, Governor of Illinois."

High Ranking Officers in the Armed Services

(Commander, or higher, in the Navy, and Coast Guard; Major or higher in the Army, Marine Corps, or Air Force.) Spoken address, "Admiral Jones"; formal letter begins "Dear Sir"; informal, "Dear Admiral Jones"; envelope address, "Admiral David Jones."

Protestant Bishop

Spoken address, "Bishop Goodword"; formal letter begins "Right Reverend and Dear Sir"; informal, "My dear Bishop Goodword"; envelope address, "The Right Reverend John B. Goodword" or "The Bishop of Illinois."

Protestant Minister

Spoken address, "Dr. Smith" if he has a D.D. degree, "Mr." if he has not (when in doubt use "Dr."), if he is a Lutheran, "Pastor Smith", if he is a high church Episcopalian he may expect to be addressed both personally and in correspondence as "Father Smith"; formal letter begins "My dear Sir"; informal, "Dear Dr. Smith"; envelope address, "The Rev. James Smith."

Rabbi

Spoken address, "Rabbi Torah" or, if he holds a doctor's degree, "Dr. Torah"; formal letter begins "Dear Sir"; informal, "Dear Rabbi (or Dr.) Torah"; envelope address, "Dr. (or Rabbi) Moses Torah."

The Pope

Spoken address, "Your Holiness"; letter (always formal) begins "Your Holiness"; envelope address, "His Holiness, the Pope" or "His Holiness, Pius VII, Vatican City."

Catholic Cardinal

Spoken address, "Your Eminence"; formal letter (always formal) begins "Your Eminence"; envelope address, "His Eminence, Arthur Goulding, Archbishop of ———" if he remains an archbishop or "His Eminence Arthur Cardinal Goulding" if he does not.

Catholic Archbishop

Spoken address in the United States, "Your Excellency" (in England, "Your Grace"), formal letter begins "Your Excellency" or

"Most Reverend Sir", informal, "Most Reverend and Dear Sir", envelope address, "The Most Reverend James Worthy, Archbishop of ———."

Roman Catholic Bishop

Spoken address, "Your Excellency", formal letter begins "Most Reverend Sir"; informal, "My dear Bishop Pius"; envelope address, "The Most Reverend John Pius."

Catholic Monsignor

Spoken address, "Monsignor Kelley"; formal letter begins "Right Reverend and Dear Monsignor Kelley", informal, "Reverend and Dear Monsignor Kelley"; envelope address, "The Right Reverend Monsignor Kelley."

Catholic Priest

Spoken address, "Father" or "Father Jensen"; formal letter begins, "Reverend and Dear Sir"; informal, "Dear Father Jensen"; envelope address, "The Reverend James Jensen "

Mother Superior of a Catholic Order

Spoken address, "Reverend Mother", formal letter begins "Reverend Mother", informal, "Dear Reverend Mother Elizabeth"; envelope address, "Reverend Mother Elizabeth" with the initials of her order, if you know them.

Member of a Religious Order

Spoken address, "Sister Mary" or "Brother William"; formal letter begins "My dear Sister" (or "Brother"), informal, "Dear Sister Mary" or "Dear Brother William"; envelope address, "Sister Mary" or "Brother William" (with initials of order).

University Professor

Spoken address, usually "Professor Sessions" if on the campus, and "Mr." elsewhere, though both are correct in any situation. If the professor has earned, as today he must, a Ph.D , you may call him "Dr. Sessions" if you like, though in many circles it is considered better taste not to use the title for the holder of an academic doctorate; formal letter begins "Dear Sir"; informal, "Dear Professor

Sessions" ("Dear Dr. Sessions" should never be used), envelope address, "Professor Sessions"

The following are addressed as "Mr." when spoken to, and in formal letters. ("Dear Sir" or "My dear Sir" in formal salutations.) Envelope addresses:

Officers of the Navy and Coast Guard with ranks lower than that of Commander

Envelope address, "Ensign John Jones."

Instructors in Colleges or Universities

Envelope address, "Mr. John C. Teacher."

Consuls

Envelope address, "Mr. James Envoy, American Consul" (or "James Envoy, Esq." if he is British).

Members of the U.S. House of Representatives or State Assemblies

Envelope address, "The Honorable William F. Smithers, House of Representatives, Washington, D.C."

Reigning Sovereign

Spoken address, "Sir" or "Madam"; salutation—always formal —"May it please your Majesty"; envelope address, "His Most Gracious Majesty, the King" or "Her Most Gracious Majesty, the Queen." (Queen Victoria in her old age in conversation with one of her Prime Ministers, Lord Rosebery, corrected him. Rosebery had remarked that English princes or kings were always addressed as "Sir." "Not the King, Lord Rosebery," replied the Queen. "The King of England is always addressed as 'Sire.'" But not today.)

Other Members of a Royal Family

Spoken address, "Sir" or "Madam"; formal letter begins "Your Royal Highness"; informal, "Sir" or "Madam"; envelope address, "To His Royal Highness, Prince (or Crown Prince, or Princess, with 'Her' instead of 'His') ———" (or "Duke of ———" or "Grand Duke Peter").

Duke or Duchess

Spoken address, "Duke" or "Duchess" if informal and speaking as equals; if formal, "Sir" or "Madam"; an official formal letter begins "My Lord Duke"; social letter, "Dear Duke of ———"; informal, "Dear Duke" or "Dear Duchess"; envelope address, "To His Grace the Duke of ———" (or "Her Grace the Duchess of ———").

Marquis (or Marquess) or Marchioness

Spoken address, "Lord (or Lady) Castle", formal letter begins "My Lord" or "Madam"; informal, "Dear Lord (or Lady) Castle"; envelope address, official, "To the Most Honourable, the Marquis (or Marquess) of Castle"; social, "The Marquis (or Marquess, or Marchioness) of Castle".

Let me here interpolate a piece of advice. Under no circumstances, meeting on an equal basis as human beings, should a titled foreigner in conversation ever be addressed by you as "My Lord" or "My Lady." This is a tacit admission by you of his or her social superiority. Unless you really mean to work as his valet or secretary or chauffeur or underling call him anything you please, but never "My Lord."

There are some general rules that may help you to remember proper forms of address if you meet, or have occasion to write to, persons who have either honorary or hereditary titles.

In the United States the right to the title "Honorable" is conferred on the following upon their assumption of office, and remains theirs through life, though they do not use it when referring to themselves in speaking, or on their letterheads, visiting cards, or with their signatures: The President and Vice-President of the United States, members of the cabinet, senators and representatives, federal judges, ministers plenipotentiary, ambassadors, and the governors of states. The wife or husband of a person with an honorary or official title does not have the title of the spouse, but remains plain "Mrs." or "Mr." Similarly, in England the wife of a Duke or Lord who is entitled to be called "His Excellency" is "The Duchess of ———" or "Lady ———," not "Her Excellency."

The eldest son of a Duke receives his father's second title, Earl, or Marquis.

Thus for instance, the younger son of the Duke of Marlborough was the famous Lord Randolph Churchill, whose son in turn was the even more famous the Honourable Winston Churchill.

The younger sons of a Duke or Marquis are called by their given (not family) names, to which "Lord" is prefixed, that is, "Lord James Hightower," not "Lord Hightower." This is purely a courtesy title Lord James's wife is called "Lady James," never "Lady Helen," unless she herself is the daughter of a Duke or a Marquis, in which case she is "Lady Helen," whether married or not.

The younger son of an Earl is called by his given name to which "The Honourable" is prefixed, a daughter also by her given name and "The Honourable." So also is the eldest son of a Baronet, and sons of younger sons of a Duke or Marquis.

If the daughter of a Duke, Marquis, or Earl marries a commoner, she is "Lady Helen ———" (her husband's surname) but he remains "Mr. ———."

AN AUDIENCE WITH THE POPE

Four kinds of audiences are granted by the Pope:

At a *Private Audience* the Pontiff receives an individual visitor in his study. Such an audience is granted only to cardinals, heads of state, ambassadors, or others of special importance.

A small group may be received in a *Special Audience,* usually in one of the parlors adjoining the Pope's study.

At a *Semipublic Audience* the Pontiff, seated on his throne in one of the large reception halls in the Vatican, receives a much larger group of persons than at a *Special Audience.*

A *Public Audience,* at which several hundred people of mixed nationalities may appear, is held in the piazza of St. Peter's, or in the basilica itself, or in the courtyard of Castel Gandolfo, the Pope's summer residence.

Arranging the Audience

Arrangements of an audience may be made through the American Embassy in Rome, the Ufficio del Maestro di Camera di Sua Santitá, in Vatican City, or The North American College, Via dell' Umiltà 30, Rome. No request for an audience is ever refused, though unless your position is such that one of the first three classes of audience will be automatically granted, or you have an especially important mission, you may be granted only a public audience.

Actually in many ways the large public audience is the most interesting—especially if it is held in the sunshine and joyous atmosphere that prevail at the Castel Gandolfo audiences, where the mixed throng of visitors and their happiness at seeing the Holy Father smiling down at them from his balcony make an unforgettable experience.

Dress

For a Private Audience or Special Audience men wear evening dress with white tie and tails or a uniform, and women wear long-sleeved, black dresses and veils over their heads. For a Semi-Public Audience or a Public Audience formal dress is not expected. Both men and women, however, should dress soberly and with the same dignity as they would for church. Women must cover their heads, and must not have bare arms or legs.

Behavior at an Audience

When the Pope enters the audience chamber it is customary for Catholics to kneel, others may do so or not, as they choose, but if they stand, they will do so with dignity and in a respectful attitude.

At the type of audience in which the Pontiff meets his visitors individually and speaks to them, it is customary for him to extend his hand and for each visitor to kiss his ring. No visitor shakes hands with him.

Rosaries, holy medals, or other religious objects which a visitor has on his person when the Pope blesses him are considered also to be blessed.

I remember a lovely episode in connection with this. A friend who was an eminent Jewish surgeon came back from Rome having attended a Public Audience with the Pope. He told me that before going to the audience he had bought twenty-five small religious medals and put them into his pocket so that they could be blessed.

Somewhat puzzled, I asked him, "What are you going to do with them all?"

"I've given them all to my nurse, who is a Catholic," he told me. "I often have Catholic patients and I thought that if she could have these and give one to each Catholic before I operate, it might be of some comfort and reassurance."

INTRODUCTIONS

✍ The rules of introduction are simple and fairly easy to remember. Either a lady or a gentleman is always introduced to a king, a member of a reigning dynasty, a chief of state, or a high church dignitary ("Mr. President, may I present Mrs. Harris?"). All other persons of title or rank are always introduced to a lady ("Mrs Harris, may I present the Ambassador of Italy?" or ". . . Senator Smith?"). But Senator Smith, having a lower rank than the Ambassador of Italy, is always introduced to him ("Mr. Ambassador, may I present Senator Smith?").

LEAVING A LUNCHEON OR DINNER

✍ After a luncheon or dinner the lady at the right of the host is the first to leave, and it is discourteous, even if there is a gentleman present whose rank is higher than hers, to precede her. If she follows the accepted rules of etiquette she will leave a formal dinner at approximately ten o'clock, an informal one at about ten-thirty, and a formal luncheon by three o'clock The rules concerning the order of departure after the highest-ranking woman has left are less rigid than they once were, yet it is still considered courteous for no one to leave until after the highest-ranking male guest, and those who rank close to him, have gone.

ABROAD

✍ The rules of protocol and the orders of precedence in countries other than ours vary widely If you are planning to meet and perhaps entertain or be entertained by royalty, the aristocracy, or other important personages abroad you will do well to consult the American Embassy or an American Consulate in the country you are going to visit. If you have friends already living abroad who are likely to know the rules, do not fail to consult them. They can give you invaluable advice.

THE UNITED NATIONS

Protocol at the United Nations headquarters is a complex problem because of the large number of delegates and visiting dignitaries from many countries whose rules of precedence often differ from one another. In general, diplomatic protocol is followed. But visiting diplomats are seated for general U N. business in the alphabetical order of the countries represented.

The U.N. Secretariat has established a Protocol and Liaison Section as a part of the Office of the Secretary General, and there is an Information Office that will help you with difficult problems of protocol.

INVITATIONS

Invitations from the head of any state, whether the President of the United States or another country, a reigning sovereign, or for that matter from a member of a royal family are always accepted unless ill health or some other unavoidable circumstance makes acceptance impossible.

27

Thirteen to Nineteen

I HAVE HESITATED ABOUT WRITING THIS CHAPTER AT ALL, for in doing so I may seem to intimate that I think a special code of behavior is necessary to young people in their teens. Of course I think nothing of the kind. The rules of proper social usage, good manners, courtesy, kindness, and consideration are fundamentally the same for people of all ages and in all places. Adolescents are simply human beings who are not children any longer, nor yet quite grown up. Even the term "young adults" which is so often used today seems to me a misnomer, and one which, if taken seriously, may lead the adolescent into misunderstanding as to his nature and his role in life. "Young" he is, "adult" he is not. He is in a confusing period of overlapping impulses and desires, in which the tendencies of childhood often find enlarged expression through physical development and widened freedoms, yet are hampered by the strictures imposed by authority that, with increasing maturity, tend to be more and more irksome.

To most teenagers, life is a strange uncharted land filled with a mixture of new joys, intensely felt, and painful confusions for which they know no anodyne. They have neither the experience of past events to guide them, nor the knowledge that other people older than themselves have been through the same agonizing frustrations and have not only survived but can look back on them with gentle content.

The young resent authority, even though they know within themselves that they need its steadying influence and the guidance which it provides. This knowledge, too, they resent. They are passionately eager to be wholly on their own, to form their own judgments and even to make their own rules.

Both health and danger are in this. The good part of learning to stand on one's own feet is that it helps to build character later on. But when this desire for independence is allowed a completely free rein, when young people renounce all authority and make their own conditions, when good conduct and good manners are flouted, then if they are not very careful indeed or wise beyond their years they become what their contemporaries call "a mess." The harm that they do to themselves is bad enough, this can be repaired and, if they are lucky, will mean only a certain loss of time in their gaining of maturity. What is more important is the harm and pain which they inflict on others—their parents, their teachers, harmless strangers, the girl or boy selected for special devotion.

It is this overconfidence, this desperate need of independence that puts these young people—teenagers, adolescents, young adults, or, in some cases, juvenile delinquents—whose ages range from thirteen to nineteen, in a class by themselves.

The general recognition of this fact in our day has given them a disquieting importance The rules that govern their behavior should be no different from those that govern the behavior of anyone else. Yet they are in the grip of physical and spiritual drives which they have not known as young children, and which will not affect them in quite the same way when they grow up. Their situation is special, and for that reason they deserve a chapter.

IDEALISM AND THE URGE TO LEADERSHIP

To the teenager (and this is exactly as it should be) the world and its prizes are simply an opportunity waiting to be seized in his hot young hands. The difference over the last fifty years consists in this—that where earlier the teenager was brought up to believe that these prizes could be won only by hard work and a high moral character, today he knows that these are not the only methods frequently employed in getting ahead. Of course he is right. Sometimes a teenager today is convinced that he can take the things he wants from life by methods certainly not in the books of Horatio Alger.

This is not the proper stuff of idealism, but nevertheless it carries enough validity to be attractive. What it neglects or denies is that it is not possible for any human being to live happily to himself alone, and that obedience to sound rules of conduct is essential to the happiness of everyone, whatever his age.

In a sense the young learn this early, but often without recognizing what they have learned, for there is no more gregarious group of human beings in the world than a group of teenagers. Who else finds it so difficult to spend an evening at home alone? Who else is so eager for the approval of his contemporaries? Who else longs so ardently to be voted the leader in the group?

This very need to be popular, to be a leader, often makes the young man a follower instead, committed to the customs and attitudes of the group of which he is a part, insisting on "going steady," smoking too much because others do, begging for the family car because others have cars, flouting the authority of his parents, his school, and sometimes the law, in his need to win acceptance. The same of course is true of the girl.

I have perhaps stated this too positively, as though I were writing of *all* young people, when assuredly I am not. Great numbers of young people in America and elsewhere throughout the world, among whom will be found the future leaders in the eventual victory of civilization, have no part in this rebellion of the teenagers. I am speaking here of the confused ones who have lost faith in the wisdom of their elders and seem unconsciously determined to remake the world after their own pattern, or destroy it in the attempt

I believe that essentially this effort, twisted as it often is, arises from a genuine idealism, an impulse which, properly directed, has accounted for much of humanity's progress There are times when considered disobedience to authority and violation of established rules are essential to self-respect and loyalty to one's principles of social conduct. Confucius said,

The linen cap is that prescribed by the rules of ceremony, but now a silk one is worn. This is economical, and so I follow the common practice. The rules of ceremony prescribe bowing below the hall, but now the practice is to bow only after ascending it. That is arrogant. I continue to bow below the hall, though I oppose the common practice.

Here is another wise saying from the East "If your enemy has a wise custom, adopt it, if your friend has an unwise custom, shun it."

William James, one of the wisest, kindest, and best of men, said, in speaking to young people:

There is only one way to improve ourselves, and that is by setting an example which the others may pick up and imitate till the new fashion spreads from east to west. Some of us are in more favorable positions than others to set new fashions Some are much more striking personally and imitable, so to speak. But no living person is sunk so low as not to be imitated by somebody . . . there is no human being whose example doesn't work contagiously in *some* particular. . . . If you should individually achieve calmness and harmony in your own person, you may depend upon it that a wave of imitation will spread from you, as surely as the circles spread outward when a stone is dropped into a lake.*

This is the true way to leadership, and the only kind of popularity worth having. Among you, the young, are the future leaders of the world.

A recent message from the Jewish Theological Seminary of America on the occasion of the Jewish New Year says this well

Do you say—"There's nothing I can do about the problems of the world?" This is a common mistake, for there isn't a world problem which doesn't begin where you are. And always you can diminish or add to it. . . .

We often think the problem is ignorance. Yet the real problem is our unwillingness to learn. . . . Only when we are willing to listen to others can we hope they will learn with us and from us. When we do this, when we concern ourselves with listening and learning, we diminish ignorance in the world right where we are. . . .†

Here is the basis and reason for all rules of social conduct whatever your age, for etiquette at its soundest and best.

---

* William James, *Talks to Teachers on Psychology: and to Students on Some of Life's Ideals* New York, Henry Holt and Co , 1916.
† *The New York Times,* September 13, 1961

RESPONSIBILITY

These are the years when your ability to accept responsibility will be tested and developed. How you meet the test will be the measure of your ability to conduct yourself properly in your social relations. The basis of every proper code of social behavior, let me repeat, is a recognition of the individual's responsibility to other human beings.

Responsibility to Your Parents

You are no longer a child for whom your parents assume full responsibility. Instead, you are approaching the time when you must stand on your own feet, make your own decisions, and discharge your own obligations. Your home is a proving ground for your ability to assume them wisely and responsibly and graciously. Never forget that you have definite social obligations toward your parents How well you fulfill them now will be the measure of your success in other relationships in later life.

Your responsibility to your mother and father is a mixed thing. You may chafe over the authority which they have always exercised over you, and feel that it should now be relaxed. Yet, in fairness to them and to yourself, you must remember that until you have reached the age of legal maturity they *are* responsible for your acts, and may be held to that responsibility by the law This, in itself, justifies their placing certain restrictions on you.

Further, it may be assumed that their increased age and experience make them wiser than you are This may not always be the case, they also are human beings and make mistakes, but in general you owe them the respect and consideration that is due age from youth. If their rules for you seem too strict or unreasonable, do not simply disregard these rules and disobey them secretly, but do your parents the courtesy of being open with them. Argue out with them the reasons for your objections, and pay them the compliment of listening to their point of view. If nothing else, it will be good practice for similar situations later in life.

There is another way you may properly (as one who is nearing maturity) regard at least some of the rules which your parents make for your guidance, if you are living at home with them. It is your home, to be sure, and no proper parents would want their children of any age to feel otherwise about it Yet in a special sense it is primarily *their* home. Their money has bought it and maintains it. Your mother and father are responsible for its upkeep, and for all of the day-to-day details that make it possible for you to be comfortable in it.

If as a properly behaved adult you were a house guest in the home of a friend, you would have due regard for the routine of that household. You would be as neat as possible in your own room and elsewhere. You would pay strict attention to mealtimes and be punctual and comport yourself with courtesy at table. You would not invite your own guests into the house without first making sure that it was convenient for your host and hostess. You would not, if you had guests, allow them to conduct themselves boisterously or destructively. You would not take your host's car without permission, nor ask for such permission at a time when you knew that it would be inconvenient for your host to grant it. And if you did take it, you would be careful not to damage it, not to violate any traffic law, not to damage another car or other property—knowing that for all of these things the owner of the car would be legally responsible, even though you were driving it. You would be helpful, in any ways that you could, while staying in your friend's house.

Your adjustment to the responsibilities and the social situations you will have to meet in later life will be much easier for you if you have learned early how to consider the feelings of others. You cannot be a barbarian until you are nineteen and then suddenly become a well behaved adult without the most painful transition.

And there is immediate gain to be sought. You will find that as you assume and discharge your responsibilities, your parents will grant you increasing freedom and will allow you more and more to regulate your own actions.

Responsibility to School

Your school affiliation represents several overlapping relationships. Most important is your relation to the future, to the adult world of which you will soon be a part. Learning to discharge your responsibilities to your instructors, to your schoolmates, and to your parents will help to shape your ability to accept and discharge the responsibilities of adult life

You owe your instructors the respect and consideration due their position, regardless of your feelings about them as persons. Some of them may be inadequate, but don't make the mistake of judging their ability to instruct you solely by their personalities, the way they dress, or the way they speak. They will respect you by giving you a chance to prove yourself in their classes. Give them the same opportunity. You may find that the instructor whom you most feared or cared least for at the beginning of school is the one whom you most respect and trust at the end of the term.

This does not mean that you must always agree with everything an instructor says. Every observer of the educational process has known students who were more intelligent and in some cases better informed than some of their instructors. Some particularly able and articulate students are able to outreach their mentors quite rapidly. But if they were mindful of their social responsibilities, they were able to do this with grace and modesty and without discourtesy. Many a scholarly mind has been developed in a "poor" school and many an intellectual drone holds a diploma from a school of high standing. To a large degree you will get out of your school and your instructors just exactly what you put in, in terms of your own ability and your willingness to achieve an education.

You may say that this has little or nothing to do with a book about the common sense of etiquette, but improving your mind, developing the ability to analyze a set of facts, improving your understanding of people and the forces that come into play between them are all basic qualities in helping you to develop yardsticks with which to measure your own conduct.

Responsibility to Your Schoolmates

Your relationship with your schoolmates is an important rehearsal for the real drama of your adult life to come. Your performance here is generally an accurate barometer of how you will accept the responsibility of adult relationships a little later. Once again the key is the ability to respect others. One of the greatest of teachers, William James, had much to say on this subject. Here are some of his thoughts which I think you will find particularly helpful:

We are practical beings, each of us with limited functions and duties to perform. Each is bound to feel intensely the importance of his own duties and the significance of the situations that call these forth. But this feeling is in each of us a vital secret, for sympathy with which we vainly look to others. The others are too much absorbed in their own vital

secrets to take an interest in ours. . .   Hence the falsity of our judgments, so far as they presume to decide in an absolute way on the value
of other persons' conditions or ideals .   .

The first thing to learn in intercourse with others is non-interference
with their own peculiar ways of being happy, provided those ways do not
assume to interfere by violence with ours. No one has insight into all
the ideals No one should presume to judge them off-hand The pretension to dogmatize about them in each other is the root of most human
injustices and cruelties, and the trait in human character most likely to
make the angels weep.

Every Jack sees in his own particular Jill charms and perfections to
the enchantment of which we stolid onlookers are stone-cold. And which
has the superior view of the absolute truth, he or we? Which has the more
vital insight into the nature of Jill's existence as a fact? . . . surely, to
Jack are the profounder truths revealed, surely poor Jill's palpitating little
life-throbs *are* among the wonders of creation, *are* worthy of this sympathetic interest, and it is to our shame that we cannot feel like Jack. . . .
We ought, all of us, to realize each other in this intense, pathetic, and
important way.

If you say this is absurd, and that we cannot be in love with everyone
at once, I merely point out to you that, as a matter of fact, certain
persons do exist with an enormous capacity for friendship and for taking
delight in other people's lives, and that such persons know more of truth
than if their hearts were not so big. The vice of ordinary Jack and Jill
affection is not its intensity, but its exclusions and its jealousies *

Your Part-Time or Vacation Job

Recently a daily newspaper in a Connecticut city of some
30,000 population did what seems to me a wise and fine thing. For
a week, immediately following the close of school in June, it offered
free advertising space to boys and girls who wished to find work
for the summer. The response was so great, the newspaper devoted
almost a full page each day to the project. I was surprised and delighted to see so fine a response and to know that so much of this
city's teenage population was eager to do something constructive
during the summer vacation. I suppose the motives were mixed.
Some were probably saving for their educations, or were motivated
by a desire to help out their parents. Others wished merely to increase their own spending money. But in any case I am sure all of
them learned that going out and finding a job and then accepting the
responsibility of it and being paid for it is a satisfaction in itself, an
accomplishment that will help pave the way for more important

* William James. *op. cit*

experiences. And this is so, regardless of the purpose for which the money is being earned.

The young people who obtained jobs this way found a purpose for which to get up in the morning No matter how much a teenager may praise the state of idleness, no one of us likes to be idle for long.

It is also a nice feeling to be wanted, and you get that feeling when you are hired. To taste this experience and gain the satisfaction of earning money by performing a day's work when you are still quite young helps to give you an appreciation of what a job really means.

It is not surprising to find that a young boy or girl, after a week or so on a part-time or vacation job, will suddenly find a new appreciation and respect for the efforts of his parents. He or she may find a new level of mutual understanding about the problems of the day "on the job," and why it is that Dad occasionally is preoccupied and silent during dinner.

Most of the young people who found jobs through these newspaper ads did very nicely. In some cases there was a hard lesson to be learned. A friend of mine hired one of the eager young job-seekers, a lad of thirteen, whose nickname was Skippy or Skip His job was the weekly mowing of a large lawn. For the first two mowings his employer kept track of the time and paid him at the rate of $1.50 an hour. After this had established an average time for the job, they settled on a regular fee for the assignment. It was then that the boy began to live up to his nickname by failing to do as thorough a job as he had when paid by the hour. Each week my friend patiently pointed out the ridges of still unmowed grass and the areas near the lawn furniture and at the borders that had not been touched. But, though Skip was capable of doing a good job, as he had already proved, he continued to be careless and so my friend had no choice but to discharge him.

This boy, about to be a young man, had not learned that how a job is done is important not only to the employer but also to the worker. My friend pointed out to Skippy that someone else could be hired who would do a good job, or my friend could do the job himself. But only Skippy could establish his own reputation for reliability and learn the satisfaction of having done a job as well as he knew how. In being irresponsible, in failing to fulfill an agreement implicit in his original acceptance of the work, he was courting habits that could hamper him in his work relations for the rest of his life. His failure in this case was a very basic one.

Do not even attempt a job if you do not plan to do the best you know how. The money you may make is never worth the loss of self-respect and honor that comes when you do not fulfill the obligation you have made to someone else.

I believe thoroughly in part-time jobs for young people who are still in school. The dollar you make by your own labor can mean more to you than five given to you by your parents. More than what it may buy for you is the pride you will have earned along with it, the pride in your own ability, in helping others, and in having made some small contribution to helping the world conduct its business. You will also have advanced the process of building sound human relations, of meeting new people and having new experiences in a world you may have only heard or read about before.

Unless you learn something of these things, all of your superficial expressions of courtesy, all of your observations of the formal rules of etiquette will be meaningless. And in your new experiences you will have wonderful opportunities for putting into practice some of the manners, formal and informal, that you have been developing.

Note to Parents

All of the situations in which the adolescent's ability to accept and discharge responsibility are tested are valuable experiences for him in his progress toward maturity. The part you play in helping your son or daughter to benefit from them is highly important. You should always respect his problems; never make fun of them. Help him to achieve a perspective in looking at his problems and, above all, help him to develop a sense of humor and balance about his life.

As in all else, the example which you set for him in fulfilling your own responsibilities—to him and to others—is more important than all of the instruction you may give him.

It is also important that you try to understand the forces that are operating within him and often provoke inconsistent results. For example, you may find that he resents and shirks the chores which you set for him at home. At the same time he will discharge very well the duties of his part-time job outside. This is not an unusual situation. It has its roots in the young person's need to organize his life in a pattern which he himself forms, rather than one imposed by his parents. This need is part of his learning to stand on his own feet and proceed on his own momentum.

The chances are that he may consider the jobs assigned to him at home to be dull routine tasks, while those he finds outside (even though they may be similar to home chores) have about them a certain atmosphere of adventure. He will find greater personal challenge in them because he has found them himself

Certainly it is desirable for every young person to take on a share of the household duties, but parents should try to be patient with a lack of thoroughness. It is far sounder to praise your son on the day when he has mowed the lawn efficiently, or your daughter when she has washed the dishes and left the sink spotless, than to nag at them daily for not doing their tasks in a thorough fashion.

If you find habitual resistance to the idea of doing any work at home, try to talk to them in an adult way, get their views of the matter, the reasons for their distaste, and explain to them that the smooth operation of your household must be a joint effort to be successful. You can tell them that when each member does his part, each benefits from the efforts of all the others.

You should also make an effort not to patronize, but ask them to suggest a more equitable distribution of the work. You may find that they will actually want to take on more difficult tasks, feeling that those they had been asked to do are "kid stuff." If this is so, try to expand their responsibility. When practical, allow them to share with you some of the planning for your household. Give consideration to their ideas. Don't dismiss their suggestions too lightly. Just because they are younger and less experienced doesn't mean that they won't frequently find a good solution to some household problem. And when you show them that you are indeed willing to try their plans, you will be rewarded in seeing them glow with the excitement and discovery that they are making a very real contribution to the household. Young people need to feel this sense of their own worth and importance, especially during the years between their childhood and maturity.

If they are not doing as well as you feel they should in school it is a cause for concern. But it is not their academic record alone that marks their accomplishments in school. The prime aim of education is adjustment to life and society. Many a brilliant and accomplished adult has come from a youth marked by scholastic mediocrity. Many a winner of high marks throughout his school career has done little to fulfill that promise later on.

Try not to place too great an emphasis on this phase of your child's development. Try to measure your satisfaction with your children in terms of their overall development. The manner in which they accept responsibility, the way they rise to meet a crisis, the kindness and consideration they show are all equally important marks of their development.

You should also be quite sure that you let your children know how satisfied you are with them. Frequently, though they seem to be rebelling against your authority in almost every way, though they may drive you to distraction with their negativeness, they still are hungry for your approval, for a sign from you that you are their closest ally and will always be there if they need you. If you have ever closely observed a group of very young children playing in the park you will know what I mean. You will see little Susie, at the age of two or so, run off from her mother to play. Moments later she will come running back and for no apparent reason wish to be taken in her mother's lap and hugged for a moment. Then she will run back to her play again. At the same time she is tasting the independence that has come with learning to walk and run and play with other children, she still wants the comfort and security that only her mother's arms can provide. So it is on a different level now with your teenagers. The lure of complete freedom is still competing with a strong desire to be protected and praised and loved by you. Do not deny these things before your children are ready.

DATING

During the dating years your associations with your contemporaries of the opposite sex will be a preparation for the most important of all adult relationships, marriage. In addition, you will be gaining experience in general social relationships. In establishing a pattern of consideration for others and a sense of responsibility for your behavior, you will, in a large measure, be establishing your ability to move smoothly into the adult social world. These years will help to determine just how successful you may be in achieving the respect and admiration of your adult contemporaries later on.

When to Start Dating

I think it is really quite impossible to say that a certain age is exactly the right age for every youngster to start dating. Just as one cannot say in what month a child will cut his first tooth, or exactly when it is normal for him to speak his first words, it is unwise to pronounce the precise age at which every young person will be ready to begin his or her dating career

Each of us is an individual, conditioned by heredity, environment, and purpose. Each of us responds in his own way and in his own time to the attractions of the opposite sex and the desire for an enlarged social life. Each of us matures at his own rate. The boy or girl whose physical growth outstrips that of others may or may not have also developed a sense of responsibility essential to proper conduct while dating. The various facets of a young person's personality and his or her own skills and desires rarely grow at an even or equal rate.

A recent survey conducted at Purdue University found that many youngsters begin to date before they are fourteen years old—thirty-one per cent of the boys and forty per cent of the girls. The same survey found that about twelve per cent of those questioned never dated until they had finished high school. This tends to prove that there is a wide variety of habits and customs in this respect. Environmental factors are, in some ways, even more important influences than physical maturity. The boy or girl living in a city or a village near a number of contemporaries will probably begin dating earlier than one who lives in a more isolated rural or farm area. Some adolescents carry such a heavy burden of school and outside work that they have little time for dating. And some, of course, are deterred by rigidly enforced parental authority.

It seems to me that a boy is ready to date when he has the desire to do so and has learned to accept several kinds of responsibility. First, there is an obligation to see that work to which he is committed, whether schoolwork, work around the house, or an outside job, is satisfactorily accomplished before he indulges in social pleasures. Second, he has an important obligation to take care of the girl with whom he goes out, by treating her with respect and consideration, by accepting the fact that he is responsible for her welfare. Third, he has a responsibility to her parents and to his own to return at the time agreed upon and to behave at all times in a manner that will lead to a mutual respect between the two young people.

The boy also has an obligation to arrange the financing of the date sensibly and honestly, not attempting to do more than he can comfortably afford and frankly letting the girl know his situation if there is any question about it.

A girl is ready for dating, it seems to me, when her sense of responsibility complements that of the boy. She will not accept a date unless she knows she can fulfill her other responsibilities without difficulty. She should know how to do her part in establishing a good relationship by treating her date as a lady treats a gentleman. She should bear in mind any financial limitations that her date may have and should not hesitate to propose a less expensive evening when her date suggests one that may be too costly. If the boy is forthright enough to tell her that he can take her either to dinner or to an evening's entertainment, but that he cannot afford both, she should welcome his confidence and either make a choice or show him that she will not be disappointed whichever he chooses.

Above all, a girl will be ready for dating when she has a feeling of confidence in her own ability to handle virtually any situation on the date and when she knows that she will only accept a date with a boy in whom she has confidence. The temptation may be very strong at the beginning to accept a date simply for the sake of having one and not because she wishes to spend time with the boy who has asked her. She should avoid this temptation. Other dates will come. It is always wisest for a girl to avoid making a date with someone in whom she doesn't have confidence and trust. (See sections on Blind Dates, Pickups.)

When youngsters have sufficiently developed a confident and common-sense attitude about their responsibilities in dating and when they feel strongly that they are ready to cope with the unexpected and sometimes the undesirable or embarrassing, then they have begun to show their readiness. An awareness of how and *why* they are expected to adhere to the rules agreed upon between them and their parents and the general customs of their social group is highly desirable. A willingness to do so at all times will mark the boy or girl who is ready to begin dating. The ability to mix fun with responsibility, balance consideration of others with natural desires, and to cope with one's own sometimes almost overpowering impulses—these are the basic things upon which all ground rules of etiquette and social behavior rest. And this is really true for all ages.

Some General Suggestions

No one of school age should allow dating to interfere with schoolwork. During the school term you should be sure *before making a date* that you can properly finish your homework before going on it and that you will be home from it in time to get the necessary rest. In fact, midweek dating should be kept to an absolute minimum and reserved for special occasions.

Try to have some understanding of the natural and actually quite desirable anxiety of your parents when you first begin to go out on dates. They are experiencing several different emotions, and if you are the first child in your family to reach dating age, they are perhaps learning something brand new themselves. They are proud of you—proud that you have arrived at another milestone on your way to adulthood. They are also concerned over your well-being, both physical and emotional. They do not want you to be placed in embarrassing or compromising situations that may hurt you.

Work out a sensible plan with your parents ahead of time. Make certain that they know exactly whom you are going out with, where you will be spending the evening, and when you are returning. Try to avoid conflict over the time of your return home by placing confidence in their judgment about the hour, and by respecting it. If the time they set seems unreasonable to you, then talk it out with them. When a time has been agreed upon, be sure to observe it. Their trust in you will be all the greater if you always live up to the promises you make. In time they will relax enough to permit you wider and wider latitude in your social life. One of the secrets is to make haste slowly. If you go by gradual stages you will be sure to get there. If you rush into situations before you are ready or constantly try to gain privileges you are not ready for, then you will surely run into conflicts. The smartest boy or girl avoids these conflicts by developing the gentle art of compromise to a fine degree. But once you establish principles, live by them.

There is something else which, I think, should be emphasized. I have been discussing the dating of a single couple, in the main. This is never the way for young people to begin dating experience. During the early years of dating, both boys and girls should be restricted to group dates, gatherings at the home of one of the young people or at the school dance or at an athletic event or similar group activity. Gradually, from this stage, the young man will call the girl for a movie date. One set of parents may wish actually to bring them to the movie of their choice and the other to bring them home again. This may be some extra bother to the parents, but it will help to establish the importance of adhering carefully to the rules agreed upon.

Two other things are important here (1) A general acceptance of fairly well fixed customs by all the members of your group will make proper conduct for all of you easier and make your social lives as a whole proceed more smoothly and graciously. (2) You owe your parents consideration and respect, as you acknowledge their authority now, you condition yourself both for the necessary authority to which you must submit yourself in adult life and for assuming authority yourself.

Making a Date

For young people, most dates are usually informal. Most often the boy asks the girl when he meets her at school, while walking her home, or by phoning her. If the girl has arranged a party at her house or planned an evening at home with one or two friends, it is quite proper for her to invite the boy. Or if she has been given two tickets to a football or basketball game, or a similar affair, she may ask a boy if he would like to go with her. As I have said earlier (see Chapter 19, "Engagements"), a girl should be fairly sure that the boy would like to go with her before asking him, since it is much more difficult for a boy to say no to an invitation than for a girl to refuse a boy.

Because the status and behavior pattern of women in our society is still changing rapidly, there has been a perceptible change in the view that a girl must never ask a boy for a date. I see nothing basically wrong with a girl calling to ask a boy to take her out, provided that they know each other quite well and that their relationship is such that it permits her to do this without any special embarrassment. If in doing so the girl will feel she is "chasing" the boy, or making any improper gesture in his direction, then it is wise for her to refrain from such a direct approach. If, on the other hand, she feels that he will understand that she would just like to have a date with him and that he will not interpret her having asked him as a sign that she will bestow any special favors upon him, then I do not feel this is undesirable. But the reputation of the young lady in her own social circle is also important and she should not make a practice of this; particularly since it may lead other potential dates to arrive at an entirely mistaken notion of what she may be like.

When a boy telephones a girl to ask for a date (or for any other reason), he should identify himself immediately to whoever answers the phone. He should say, "This is Jim Brown. May I please speak to Nancy?" He should do the same if Nancy answers the phone, unless he is sure that she will recognize his voice. "Guess who this is?" is not amusing. It is simply rude and boring.

If one of Nancy's parents answers the telephone and the boy recognizes the voice, he might very well say, "Hello, Mrs. Smith. This is Jim Brown. How are you?" Then after Mrs. Smith answers he may ask to speak with Nancy. There is nothing quite so disconcerting to a parent and rude as a young voice on the phone saying what frequently sounds like, "HellomayIspeaktoNancy?"

Once Nancy is speaking do not preface your invitation with such a phrase as, "What are you doing next Friday night?" Come right to the point and ask Nancy at once whether or not you may see her on Friday night. Do not wait until Thursday night to ask Nancy to go out with you on Friday night. The date should be made a week in advance, unless you have unexpectedly acquired tickets for an event that is to take place within a day or so. In this case, explain the lateness of your call.

Once having been asked, Nancy should answer at once without coyness or hesitation by saying either, "Yes, I'd love to," or "I'm sorry, but I can't." If she would like to go but must get her parents' permission first, she should say so frankly and say when she will be able to let him know. She should never make some imaginary excuse for her delay. If the invitation is for an evening in the middle of the week and she has agreed to a no midweek dates rule during the school year, she should say so. Jim Brown will probably respect her adherence to a set of rules. If he does not, then Nancy will be wise if she recognizes a flaw in his character. But not to give Jim some reason for her refusal is humiliating to him.

If this is the first time Jim Brown has called and Nancy really does not wish to go out with him, but has no parental rule to fall back on, then she should say she is sorry as gracefully and gently as possible, and offer the excuse that she already has a date for that particular time, if this is true. In the event that she does not, but still does not wish to accept, then she might say that she must remain at home that evening—and indeed, she is then obligated to do so! No well bred girl will say no or postpone giving her answer simply because she wants to wait for another offer that may be more attractive. She must never cancel an invitation because a later and more desirable one comes along

If you should ever consider this type of behavior or try to justify it on the grounds that a little white lie never hurt anyone, be assured that sooner or later your maneuvering will be found out and you will suffer for it when you least wish to. Beyond the practical considerations of the matter is the very simple rule that in all personal relationships complete honesty is always the simplest and best way.

Meeting Your Date

If you are a young man you should always call for your date at her home, unless there are special circumstances involved Never make arrangements to meet her on some street corner or at a favorite hangout to begin a date. The young lady's parents probably have never met you and they want very much to see who their daughter's escort is and what he plans for their date. They want to be sure that you understand the rules they have agreed upon with their daughter and that you will graciously abide by them. You may not choose to believe it, but they genuinely want to help you to have a good time with their daughter and they are sometimes able to make suggestions about your plans that will help you do just that. By being properly introduced to them and by listening to them and respecting them as you would your own parents, you are performing an important part of your responsibility as a young man.

Remember always to be prompt. Nothing is quite as irritating to the parents of the girl you are calling on as sitting in their living room watching their daughter in her best party dress listening and looking for you while the clock ticks slowly on. It is equally infuriating to the young man to be asked to wait in what may be very unfamiliar and uneasy surroundings for any length of time while you finish doing your hair or are adjusting that party dress

If you drive a car, you will not, of course, park in front of your date's door, sound your horn, and wait for her to come out. Go to the door and ring or knock. Then be prepared to be greeted by your date and her parents and to exchange a few minutes of conversation before getting started.

Find out before you ask the young lady for the date what kind of dress is expected at the party you may be attending. If she will require any special clothes, tell her when you ask for the date and be sure to conform yourself. Nothing can be quite so humiliating as finding yourselves the only couple wearing an afternoon dress and a sports coat to a formal affair.

Introductions

Young people's introductions to one another or to adults should almost always be informal. "May I present," or "May I introduce" are stiff and make you seem affected. "Mary, this is Jim Brown" is just fine and you may introduce him to your parents the same way. The young man's most courteous answer would be "Hello, Mary," or "How do you do, Mrs. Smith." Avoid the four words "Pleased to meet you," and the phrase "Glad to make your acquaintance," which has the additional drawback of being ungrammatical.

Double Dating

Especially during the early years, dating in groups of two boys and two girls or larger groups is an excellent plan and often is more fun. The four provide a sort of built-in chaperonage of one another and this arrangement can be a particular blessing to the shy boy or girl who will be more at ease with three others than with one. It is also an excellent way to share the companionship of another couple with whom you feel close.

Blind Dates

As with so many other human situations, one cannot generalize easily about blind dates. Accepting an invitation to one may be wise or foolish, depending on the circumstances. There is almost never any way of eliminating in advance a certain possibility of error. But let us say that Mary and Jane are good friends who have known each other for some time and have a mutual respect and affection for each other. One of Mary's friends, Bob, is known by both young

ladies as a nice, responsible young man with good taste and judgment. If he has an out-of-town friend, Bill, visiting him and suggests
a date with Mary and asks if Jane would like to have Bill escort
her, there is no reason why she shouldn't accept if she wishes.

If, on the other hand, she scarcely knows Mary or Bob, or has
some hesitancy about them and their kind of behavior or reputation,
then she will probably be wise in refusing the invitation politely,
or perhaps in suggesting that she will ask some other friends to her
home for that evening and that they all come there if this is
practical.

In any case, if you are a girl and have committed yourself to a
blind date, it is extremely wise if you insist that he call for you at
your home and that your parents meet him at that time. Then,
without embarrassment to you, he will be made aware of the rules
of conduct you have agreed with your parents to abide by, and there
can be no question that you can feel more confident about the
evening ahead.

Pickups

It has always seemed absurd to me that two human beings,
especially if they are young, should be forbidden to speak to each
other without the benefit of a formal introduction. In today's world,
on the college campus, in high school corridors, on a bus or plane
trip, even in a restaurant, chance may throw two people together
who find each other "sympathetic looking" and enter into a conversation in a quite spontaneous way. There is nothing wrong in
this and, in my opinion, it is one of the good things about our
modern freedom of manners. A young girl today can bring home
and introduce to her parents a young man whom she has met in just
such circumstances, without feeling that the lack of a formal introduction means she has gone beyond the bounds of good taste.
And the same is true of the boy. There is no reason to suppose that a
relationship begun this casually may not develop into a fine and
lasting one.

Of course both sexes should avoid entering into any relationship
that has been plainly invited at the outset with the purpose of se-
curing immediate attentions or favors. The boy who stands on
street corners whistling or mumbling small phrases of admiration
at passing girls—or the girl who by word or act plainly invites strange

young men to pay attention to her are as unpleasant and undesirable today as when our parents and grandparents were young.

Many of those lonely and unhappy boys and girls who do engage in this sort of thing seem to do so in couples or even in groups, and invite others to join them. Few parents realize the pressures put on their sons and daughters, especially if they are popular or attractive, to "go along" on those long spring or summer evenings when there seems nowhere to go and nothing to do. If this happens to you, your best course would be to talk immediately with your parents, telling them plainly what the invitation may mean and the consequences if you refuse. Above all, they will want to help you work your way out of an awkward situation. With their experience, they may be able to offer excellent suggestions.

Dances. When a young man takes a girl to a dance he should dance the first and last dance with her and at least one or two of the others. But he should not insist upon dancing all of them with her. He should introduce his date to his friends if there are any present whom she does not know, and dance with other girls if other boys ask her to dance. After each dance he should stay with his partner until the boy with whom she has the next dance claims her. But a young man should never abandon his date and wander off to dance with another young lady, unless his partner has been engaged to dance by another boy.

If "cutting in" is practiced in your group you should cooperate gracefully when your dancing partner is taken from you The act of cutting in should be accomplished courteously Approach a dancing couple without interfering with others on the dance floor, touch the boy on the arm and say, "May I cut in, please?" or "Do you mind?" And it is never wrong to thank him for being cooperative. When another boy has cut in on you and your partner do not attempt to cut back in on them. Wait until the end of the dance or until she has another partner. In any case, allow others a reasonable length of time to enjoy their dancing.

According to current social custom, I understand that when a boy and girl are "going steady," it is not proper for either to dance with anyone else. They seem to carry this artificial display of loyalty farther than most sensible married couples do. It seems extremely shortsighted to me. Still if this is the accepted custom in your group, then you should try to respect that custom by not attempting to cut in on a "steady" couple if it will cause any of you embarrassment.

If there are chaperones at a dance or any other party, it is expected that each couple speaks to them as they arrive. On leaving it is proper to say good night to the chaperones and to thank them for their part in the affair.

Going Steady The custom of going steady as practiced by many of our young people today is of comparatively recent origin. It is not the exact counterpart of what our grandparents called "keeping steady company," which meant that the couple was obviously on the road toward marriage, whether or not there was a formal engagement. The term would never have been used to refer to a couple who merely seemed to prefer each other's company on a virtually exclusive basis, without any prospect of marriage. In such a case, if one partner were to be seen with another member of the opposite sex, the fact would cause no social or emotional crisis and elicit no criticism from contemporaries.

The present attitude of some groups of young people today is nicely illustrated, I think, by a story told to me by a friend whose twelve-year-old daughter was going steady Concerned about the possible implications, the mother asked her daughter why she didn't see some of the other boys now and then. The child looked at her with a combination of astonishment, anger, and pity and then replied, "Do you think I'm a rat?"

I recently asked one thirteen-year-old just what going steady meant. "Does it mean that you are engaged to be married?" I asked. "No," she said thoughtfully. "It means you're engaged to be engaged Or sometimes only that you're engaged to be engaged to be engaged." If one can become disengaged from the syntactical difficulties present in that answer, I think it is easy to see that such youngsters have very little idea of the real meaning of being engaged, or what responsibilities are involved in making a permanent human relationship

Going steady is apparently not a universal phenomenon, and there appears to be growing a considerable controversy about it not only among parents but among young people themselves. Recent surveys seem to show that youngsters are not really happy when forced to restrict themselves to such limiting arrangements. Yet many feel compelled to in order to preserve their popularity or social standing in their group. Few teenagers are emotionally capable of withstanding the severe pressures of their group and of resisting the temptation to take what seems to be the easy way out. It is not easy to go against the group, and most teenagers are too concerned with consolidating their place in a group to risk the chance of criticism by voicing dissatisfaction with the way it is.

So it seems to me that in practice one must be guided by common sense and consideration for the feelings of all concerned. Your thinking might be something like this

No human being of whatever age, or in whatever relationship, can ever "own" another, monopolize another, or completely govern another's thoughts or actions. Even engaged or married people who attempt to do so will seriously endanger their relationship.

At any age or station of life it is always necessary for us to consider, in determining our own course of action, the social customs of the group in which we move. We cannot live successfully outside these conventions. Yet we must not follow them blindly and without conviction wherever they may lead us. Whenever the conventional rules of behavior conflict with our own understanding of kindness, consideration, fairness, and honesty, we should bypass these rules and follow the more important ones which we believe point the way to a good life.

There is no more precious experience in life than friendship. And I am not forgetting love and marriage as I write this, the lovers, or the man and wife, who are not friends are but weakly joined together. One enlarges his circle of friends through contacts with many people. One who limits those contacts narrows the circle and frequently his own point of view as well.

If two young people genuinely prefer each other's company to that of anyone else and they have already had some experience in seeing and dating others, then it would be quite sound if they date each other frequently and see a good deal of each other. There is nothing unwholesome in this. But it should not be expected that neither will ever be seen with anyone else. Even in engagements and marriages, prohibiting any contact with others outside the partnership is shortsighted practice and most probably a danger signal that one should learn to recognize.

During the exciting and sometimes tempestuous years between thirteen and nineteen, you are an explorer of life. What you find in this time, how you develop your own sense of values will materially affect your happiness as an adult. Do not limit your friendships during those precious years.

Behavior on Dates. No one can possibly judge what constitutes proper or improper behavior for two young people on a date. But there are a few generalities which I am sure are sound and will help you to establish your own code.

I cannot say too often or too emphatically that the basis of all proper social behavior is kindness, courtesy, consideration, and a respect for the needs and desires of others. This truth applies equally to two young high school students going to the movies or an informal dance, or to a group of adults at the most formal gathering The basic attitude is far more important than the detailed rules of conventional etiquette. The young people who keep these things firmly in mind and govern their actions by them will not go far wrong.

I do not propose to discuss here detailed rules concerning the physical expressions of affection—whether they are wise and proper, when they are dangerous and how far young people should go in petting. It is utterly hopeless to set down rules that will apply to all young people caught in the magnetism that flows between them, experiencing for the first time the desire to yield to the forces that sway them.

I cannot imagine a genuine youthful affection that does not find some physical expression, and no one of us is in a position to state how all of the situations that may arise should be handled. But I can state with conviction three principles:

(1) Long-term considerations are far more important than momentary gratifications. Do not, by abandoning all taboos and yielding completely to the desires of the moment, commit yourself to a relationship which you may spend the remaining years of your life regretting.

(2) The basic test of friendship or love lies in the extent to which the well-being of the friend or loved one is of greater importance than one's own desires.

(3) No gentleman or lady presses unwanted attentions upon another. As a girl your "no" should mean just that and be supported by your attitude and actions. If you must be firm, try to be kind as well. As a boy, you must respect the "no" of a girl whom you are with. If, as sometimes happens, she is the aggressive one, do not let a mistaken sense of chivalry influence you to what you know would be an unwise acceptance of her spoken or unspoken invitations.

LOVE

Note for Parents

I do not feel adequate to give young people in their teens any general advice about the subject of love But there are a few things that should be said to parents, I think. Many older people do not take love among the young seriously. I have no patience with older people who attempt to laugh off their youngsters' love affairs with such terms as "puppy love," "infatuation" and the like. Love is love, and it is a matter of simple fact that boys and girls in their teens may fall in love as deeply, as seriously, and as devastatingly—perhaps even as lastingly—as when they are older.

I beg of you to take the matter seriously if your daughter or son falls in love at an early age. Treat this relationship with the respect which you would if it were shared by two of your contemporaries You must stand by with a sympathetic ear and a strong shoulder to support them in case it should end unhappily.

A young man of seventeen who has honored me with his friendship and confidence has recently gone through such an experience and he has written me about it. He has given me permission to quote just a portion from his letter.

"It is the thought of the happiness that could be that tears me apart—the pain of knowing that now is the time she needs me the most, and yet, if she were to see me, it would simply make things more painful. I can never say 'I love you' to another girl as long as this one is alive and haunting me. I will hear the bitter-sweet voice she used to sing in. I can't look at her picture or listen to many of my records. I can't even cry any more. Having to say good-by to the first downright good experience I have ever had was very hard. There are moments every day when I turn round a corner and run into something that has an association; there was so incredibly much that we discovered together and about each other that I see things in every phase of life in every dimension of it. Sometimes I cannot face them; there is such a thing as too much beauty."

Could anyone possibly read that paragraph without feeling the depth of the boy's love, the dignity, the beauty, and the maturing quality of it? My young friend is obviously more articulate than most of his contemporaries—or, for that matter, than most of us.

Fortunately he can find some outlet for his emotions by expressing them eloquently and convincingly in words. He will, I am sure, be able to say "I love you" to another young lady or perhaps, under more favorable circumstances, to the same one. But his pain at the moment is very real and very deep and very important.

A young man—or woman—such as this, even more one incapable of giving such fluent expression to his emotions, needs the support, the sympathy, and the gentle guidance which you can give at the time of what may be the first really serious crisis of his or her life. The parent who can help at a time like this will have performed a human service greater than he or she may ever realize.

THE FAMILY CAR

Almost every boy looks forward to the time when he may drive the family car and even more to the day when he will have his own. Often his eagerness leads him to begin a period of almost unrelieved cajolery before it would be either wise or legal to permit him to drive.

The wise young man will bide his time, learning all that he can about the safe, efficient, and courteous operation of motor vehicles. If a course in driving is offered at his school, he should take it and work hard to develop his skill. He should be completely familiar with the rules of safety before he attempts to take the car out alone. He should impress upon himself that *the only smart driver is the safe driver.* The young man who believes that he can distinguish himself, show his skill, and prove his courage by driving a car far above the safe or legal speed limits, or by performing various feats of driving that have a place only on a race course has not yet attained the degree of maturity which makes him fit to sit behind the wheel of an automobile. He is a danger to himself and to anyone he encounters on the road.

Physically, a girl or boy in the late teens is capable of being an excellent driver. The reflexes of youth are quick, the eye is alert, and the body vigorous. But in the matter of judgment, the sometimes uncurbed desire for thrills, the carelessness and lack of appreciation of how tragic and final a split-second mistake can be, teenagers are frequently not ready for control over so potentially lethal a piece of machinery.

It is natural and right that your parents should be unwilling to let you take out the car on your own until they are convinced that you have a combination of the skill, the judgment, and the sense of responsibility that will make you a safe driver Remember that they are not only responsible for your safety, but as owners of the car they are also legally responsible for any damage which you may inflict on property or on others, including those who ride with you.

When the time finally comes when you are allowed to use the family car, you will be wise not to abuse this privilege and thus lose it. And remember that it is a privilege and not a right. You are fortunate that your parents have a car which they permit you to drive. Do not forget that on occasion they will want to use it themselves So do not press your requests to use the car at times when other than you require it.

Never take the car without permission. When you have permission, be sure you always inform someone where you are going and exactly when you intend to return. If a time limit is agreed on, be very careful about observing it. I am fully in accord with parents who retract their permission for a young daughter or son to use the family car if the obligation to return at a certain time is not regularly met.

You will also be wise to make a special effort to show by your careful driving, your observance of the rules of the road, and the effort you make to help with the upkeep and appearance of the car that your parents have not made a mistake in trusting you with it. Driving carefully while still in sight of your home and then allowing your urge to break the law to take over on other streets is a poor indication of your level of maturity.

Remember that the alarmingly high percentage of accidents involving drivers under twenty-five has made insurance companies charge higher rates for cars driven by young people. Try to prove that, in your case, the assumption of the insurance companies is wrong.

When you take the car out, remember that the cost of the gasoline used while you drive is part of the expense of your afternoon or evening You should plan your money matters so that you will be in a position to replace it Your parents may be lenient about that when you are hard up, but you should make some effort to pay your own way with your allowance or the money you earn on a job

In no case should you leave the car with an empty or nearly empty gas tank In an emergency, the delay caused by this might have very unfortunate results.

Remember that consideration for your parents in the use of the car, obedience in getting it home when they tell you to, and establishing a record for safe, legal, and considerate driving are the surest ways to gain greater freedom in your own driving.

(You will find a detailed discussion of safe and courteous driving practices in Chapter 13 of this book)

Note to Parents. The family car presents a very real problem whenever there are young people in the family It would be unrealistic to think that the problem could be evaded by never permitting your young people to drive your car. But if you allow them to use the car before they have proved their readiness to do so well, and if you place no restrictions on their use of it, you are failing in your responsibility to them and to the community Their eagerness to use the car and prove to you that they are ready may be greater than their own inner confidence about the matter. Deep down they may not be too sure that they will know what to do if there's a flat, or if something else should go wrong. In fact, they may not even be absolutely confident about their own ability to drive well under all road and weather and traffic conditions. You must try to judge carefully when you think they are ready. You will always be much more at ease if your teenager has had the benefit of a high school driving course or, if you can provide it, proper instruction by a reliable professional instructor. In places where an instructor is available he may be able to do a far better job than you could, for young people will frequently pay closer attention to instructions from another adult than to those given by a parent.

The personal example of legal and careful driving that you set yourself will have more good effect than almost anything you may say. If your teenagers see you exceed speed limits, ignore rules of the road, and drive discourteously you can hardly expect anything better of them.

Be realistic in reserving the car for yourself when it is necessary. If your son asks for it on an evening when you had planned to use it yourself, tell him so and say that you are sorry but he will have to make other arrangements. One of the most important social lessons he has to learn is adjusting his plans to the convenience and needs of others. It is no kindness to him if you deprive yourself in order to keep him from disappointment On the other hand, if you have clearly given him to understand that the car is his on a given evening you should not arbitrarily and capriciously decide to use it yourself.

Try also to give him a sense of importance and helpfulness by occasionally asking him to do useful errands for you in the car. It will help him to understand that the car is to be used for purposes other than just having fun—that it is not merely a toy—and this should help to make him a better driver. And if a problem or dispute should arise, try not to be arbitrary. Talk it over and try to understand his point of view before you make a final decision. With the family car as with many other things, the importance of a disagreement can be blown up out of all proportion to the real issue. Remember too that the car is not the only means of locomotion available for short trips. Walking as a way of getting from place to place seems to be in almost total disfavor, particularly among many groups of teenagers Once your youngster's "honeymoon" with the car is over, you might suggest that he reacquaint himself with walking just as a change of pace.

Actually, the main point is not to be so thoroughly dependent on the car that its use is always a bone of contention. Be flexible, but stick to your principles.

FOR YOUNG LADIES ONLY

Two subjects of particular concern to girls entering their teen years are clothes and makeup. These matters may be the cause of more battles between daughters and their parents than anything else at this age. Once more, I do not wish to set down a list of rules that should govern everyone's thinking in regard to these things. For me to do so would be impractical, and arrogant as well. But there are certain guideposts that may be helpful.

First let us take up the matter of wearing lipstick or other makeup. When a young girl is finally able to use a lipstick with the permission of her parents and approval of her school, she has arrived at a certain milestone that is very important to her. Her status is changing She is no longer just a girl, she is now a young woman.

Unfortunately, I believe that today because of the tremendous pressures imposed by television, the movies, and the advertising of so many different products, a girl is frequently overprepared for the assumption of the role of young woman She is constantly being led to believe that this is a time of life which she must hurry to attain, that she must not lag behind, that she must take immediate steps to catapult herself into this state. And many young girls feel that the simple application of lipstick and some eyebrow pencil will transform them almost miraculously overnight into women. This seems to me too ridiculous. But there is no doubt that young people are being urged to become older faster and faster in our present world. Their natural urge to grow and mature is being artificially stimulated.

I should like to ask young girls not to be in such a hurry about their lives. There is time enough for everything, and your willingness to assume gradually the outward social manifestations will make your transition much more graceful.

If your school has a rule about the wearing of lipstick, then you should abide by this rule. Once you and your parents have agreed that you may begin wearing lipstick, by all means do so judiciously. Ask your mother to help you learn to apply it properly. Save your experimenting for an afternoon or evening date with your mother in which you can try your hand and let her help. Always use any cosmetic or beauty aids with discretion. If you feel you have on the right amount, take off a little and then you'll probably be just about right.

Remember that it is unattractive to apply your lipstick in a public place. Always do it where you have the required privacy. Keep your portable beauty paraphernalia to a minimum and make a place for it in your handbag so that you don't have to empty the entire contents each time you wish to use it. Never use your lipstick for anything except the purpose for which it was intended. Don't write notes with it or use it in art class.

Aside from a light dusting of face powder now and then to help combat the oily skin that many teenagers quite naturally have, I cannot think that there are any other beauty aids which a young girl would find absolutely necessary. Anything else that concerns your grooming routine you should talk about quite frankly with your mother. And try always to use common sense about these things.

I have heard stories about young girls who would wear lipstick despite a parental injunction, making certain that they removed all traces of it before walking into their homes. In one particular instance, the girl quite unexpectedly ran into her mother who immediately noticed that her daughter's mouth was painted a bright red. The confrontation was so sudden that the girl hung her head sheepishly and said, "I'm sorry, Mother." And her mother replied, "I am only sorry that you didn't ask me to help you. The shade you've chosen is wrong and you don't know how to use it. I am sorry that you disobeyed me; but even more importantly I am disappointed at your lack of good taste."

Such an embarrassing moment can easily be avoided by honestly approaching the situation.

When it comes to stockings and high heels, all of us are familiar with the picture of the little girl who loves to dress in her mother's shoes and stockings and parade around very proudly pretending that she is grown up. This behavior is a natural conditioning process in which a girl begins to identify herself with the role that she will play later on. But there is nothing quite so awkward as the girl just entering her teen years trying to cope bravely with high heels and pretending that she can handle them properly.

Once again, a good rule to follow is practice. When you and your mother decide that you are ready, make a slow and sure approach. Practice with fairly low heels at first until you are completely comfortable and at ease with them. Gradually work your way toward the high heels you will want to wear at a formal dance or other affairs. Above all, remember that if you are not comfortable, the chances are that you won't look comfortable or walk gracefully, and you will then not be making the simple and attractive impression you are striving for.

You should never have to be embarrassed about looking your age. An artificial attempt to look older than your years will usually result in giving a tasteless impression. You are you and if anyone, including a special young man, doesn't wish to accept that, then you needn't concern yourself with trying to impress him. The rest of your wardrobe should be built with these principles firmly in mind. Foolish fads, extremes of dress are indications of a poorly developed sense of taste. Dress neatly, simply, and in a manner that will match your age, and you will usually be dressed right.

DRINKING

Vast numbers of words have been written and spoken about this subject by expert and layman alike. Every state in our country has its own law setting the age at which one may legally buy an alcoholic beverage in a public place. Teenagers, except in very unusual cases, are interested in drinking more as a matter of curiosity than out of a genuine need or desire to take a drink. They often feel the need to display their maturity by drinking when they are physically repelled by the results. Without debating the merits of accepted customs of social drinking, let me say that I feel that no teenager should ever consider drinking alcohol in any place outside his or her home, and then only on special occasions. Even in the late teens, it should only be with complete parental approval that any young person should accept a drink. The dangers of teenage drinking are apparent for all of us to read about in the newspapers. These accounts do not exaggerate the perils of an inexperienced young person becoming involved in a situation which he or she is simply not equipped physically or emotionally to handle. If any of your friends find it amusing or daring to drink while out on dates, do not be afraid to be quite definite in your refusal to join them. There is nothing clever about their drinking and you will not lose one iota of self-respect by your simple refusal. In the event that anything about drinking is not clear to you, a frank discussion of this subject with your parents should help you to understand just how important it is for you to avoid making a mistake here.

SMOKING

This is another accepted social habit that is full of conflict for many teenagers. Fifty years ago, a lady of virtually any age was considered improper if she smoked a cigarette. Very gradually, people accustomed themselves to seeing the most proper and best brought-up ladies smoking in public places. I cannot but think that in almost every case a young person begins to smoke merely to help establish himself as a grownup. The desire to be accepted as a full-grown member of society has prompted more than one young boy or girl to become a habitual smoker. Why taking a cigarette, lighting it, and puffing on it should be considered a special sign of maturity I do not know.

No one will look at you with any special favor or attention if you smoke, or consider you a weakling or odd if you do not. No one will claim that smoking, at any age, is clean or neat. What you do about smoking at a later stage of your life is far less important than your willingness to skip it for a while right now. You cannot possibly gain anything in terms of poise, physical gratification, or approval by early smoking. It would seem to me that the case is pretty overwhelming for your simply not bothering. And in view of the mounting evidence of a relationship between cigarettes and lung cancer, if you do not smoke the time will undoubtedly come when considering the matter with the objectivity possible to your more adult years, you will be very glad that you have not acquired an unhealthful habit that is most difficult to break.

CONVERSATION

The Use of Your Language

No language has yet been invented that is a perfect medium of communication. Many expressions in one language virtually defy accurate translation into another. Often a word may have quite different meaning in two usages, depending on the context in which it is spoken and the tone of voice or expression of the speaker. And there are times when the meeting of eyes or the pressure of hands can say far more than any words. Indeed, there are times when silence can convey a meaning most eloquently.

The English language, properly used, is a delicate and, at times, beautiful instrument that should be kept sharp and clean by its users. Through proper use you are able to communicate your ideas and feelings to others, to learn to know and understand them, and thus to find ways of living with them more happily and constructively.

Learn to use your language as carefully and precisely as you can. Try to keep it free from meaningless expletives and vulgarities that are merely evidences of an unimaginative mind. Try to avoid the constant use of such meaningless phrases as "You know," preceding everything you say, and "See what I mean?" following your statements

A friend of mine who is well known for the precision with which he uses the English language told me that he has never forgotten how the president of his college, Henry Churchill King of Oberlin, used to say over and over in his chapel addresses, "Learn to report facts accurately." This so impressed the boy that now, years later, his friends call him "John, the literalist." But though they sometimes laugh at his meticulousness, they know what he means when he speaks. Sometimes you will find that despite every intention to be completely honest, you have distorted a set of facts in speaking to someone and thus caused yourself or someone else trouble or pain.

Subjects of Conversation

There is no fact of life that may not be a proper subject of conversation between persons of any age so long as it is discussed with respect and dignity. Young people today are much more frank and outspoken than they were when I was young and I feel that they are the gainers. Subjects that would have been highly improper fifty years ago, now enter conversations quite casually without causing anyone to raise an eyebrow or blush. This seems to me to be an excellent sign of progress. I think that young people are learning that the complex and exciting phenomenon of life in all its phases is ever-absorbing and that interest and knowledge are increased by frank discussion. They have learned the wisdom of Alexander Pope's remark that "The proper study of mankind is man," and, as A. G Street put it, that "It is not the rabbit out of the hat, but the rabbit out of the rabbit that is amazing."

It is not the choice of subject itself, but the manner in which it is introduced and the context of time and place that make a conversation proper or improper. The off-color remark, that is made with no pertinence to the subject under discussion. but simply for the sake of sensationalism or in an attempt to prove that the speaker has some sophistication, should be avoided. So should the vulgar, gutter-born word or phrase, dragged in pointlessly or used instead of a more dignified and meaningful term. The mere fact that you are aware of certain words and phrases or have heard others use them is no reason to make a practice of using them yourself. You do not prove anything about the level of your maturity when you do, and you may run the risk of offending or embarrassing someone as well.

Between the ages of thirteen and nineteen boys and girls are becoming increasingly aware of sex. Their minds are full of questions concerning it. It is perfectly natural that boys will talk with boys about it, and girls with girls. Sometimes there will be mixed discussions It forms the basis for many stories that are in highly questionable taste. Yet, must they always be so considered? I think it depends a great deal on the content and the attitude of the teller and the listeners.

If a story is told with the genuine desire to appeal to one's sense of humor and the listener receives it in the same spirit, that is one thing. If, on the other hand, it is the kind of story that is being told merely to excite or stimulate other more prurient interests, then it is an entirely different and unwholesome matter.

(For a more detailed discussion of the use of your language, see Chapters 30, "Conversation"; 31, "The Telephone"; and 32, "Correspondence.")

AT BOARDING SCHOOL

If you go to boarding school, you will have a major adjustment to make. You will be living and working with a new group of boys or girls, or both, some of them from social climates very different from your own. You will be subjected to the authority of the masters and mistresses and the fixed rules of the school, not only during your hours for class and for study, but for twenty-four hours a day while you are in residence. You will probably have a roommate—perhaps for the first time in your life—with whom you will have to share and for whose convenience and comfort you will have to be concerned.

Far more than is true if you attend a public school, you will be a part of a closely knit school body, the total welfare of which is affected by the behavior of each of its members. I believe it was Benjamin Franklin who said, "We must all hang together, or assuredly we shall all hang separately."

This also may be your very first experience in being away from home, away from the authority and influence of your family. It will demand a greater confidence in your own ability and a sense of responsibility about everything you do for you to make a success of it.

Getting Off on the Right Foot

At most boarding schools, the students are expected to arrive a few days before classes actually begin. Make full use of this breathing space by getting acquainted with your new roommate and arranging with him how you will share your quarters. Space should be divided roughly in half, but if your roommate is an "old boy," do not argue with him in case he seems to be taking a little more than his share. Be willing to go not only half way, but a little more than that, if necessary. If after a few weeks you find that he is really impossible for you to get along with (which is unlikely), you may quite properly ask for a change. But this should be a last resort. If you are driven to it, do not be too specific in your denunciation of him when you approach the appropriate master to make your application for change. Your attitude may be much more a reflection on your own inability to adjust—and talebearers are never popular. But at the outset, give your roommate every benefit of the doubt, every chance to prove that you and he can live harmoniously together. And be sure that you give him no just cause for complaint

Learn to know the rules of the school. Most schools have handbooks or manuals containing a history of the school, often with a list of the faculty members, addresses and phone numbers of the various rooming houses or dorms, a calendar of events for the coming year, and a listing of the school rules. A copy of this book or its equivalent is usually given to each new student as he enters. Read this carefully. Be sure that you understand the rules and make up your mind, as a young lady or gentleman, that you will abide by them. If you are ever in doubt about the meaning of any of them, clear the matter by asking the proper authority or one of your classmates to explain them to you.

Learn to know your way around the campus as soon as it is practical for you. If you are supplied with a manual or handbook, it will probably contain a map or directions for getting to the halls where you will attend classes and the other important buildings of the school. If you learn the key locations quickly, it will help you to be prompt for your classes and you can organize your schedule more efficiently.

Write to your parents as soon as you are located and know the name of the hall in which your room is situated and the number of the telephone nearest your room. If there are hours when a phone call from them would inconvenience others, explain this in the letter and ask them to confine their calls to other hours, except in times of emergency.

All of the hints given here are designed to make your beginning of school period as free from needless frustration and tension as possible. Try to be quick and efficient in everything you do and make a special effort during the first hurried and confusing days to be particularly well organized

Personal Finances

Your parents probably will have arranged to give you a stated amount of spending money each week. Perhaps they will do this by depositing a sum at the school treasurer's office from which you may draw weekly the sum specified. Unless they are extremely well endowed and overly generous, you will probably wish it were more. You may find that some of your schoolmates do have larger allowances. Try to adjust your personal expenditures to the amount of your allowance without complaining about it or feeling unhappy when you are in the company of friends who have more to spend than you.

If you feel unable to return in kind the entertainment which schoolmates offer you, try to avoid accepting it as gracefully as possible, or make it quite clear that you yourself cannot afford such an expenditure. Those who will later be real friends will respect you for it. Trying to "keep up with the Joneses" either now or later is a sorry business in which to be trapped and it will put you in danger of losing a sound sense of values.

Try also to think of your parents' point of view. Boarding school is usually quite expensive and your parents may very well be sacrificing some comforts or pleasures of their own in order to send you there. Try to cooperate with them.

Your Manners

At boarding school your manners are always on display and you should make a special effort to pay attention to them. Your personal habits of cleanliness, how you take care of your own clothes, how you are dressed and groomed—these things will bear particular watching. Be sure that you do your share in your room by keeping your things in proper order.

You will probably eat your meals in a community dining room and your table manners will be a subject of scrutiny by your classmates and members of the school's faculty I have discussed table manners in general in Chapter 10 ("The Family Is Entertained") and you may find this helpful. You will no longer have the leniency of your family to fall back on and many of your time-honored excuses will no longer serve you. See to it that you don't have to find excuses at any time. Abide by the rules of the dining hall and try to remember that eating is not a contest of some sort. Make it a pleasant and relaxed time for you and your tablemates.

Working Out School Problems

Do not carry every complaint or dissatisfaction to your parents, expecting them to find the solutions for you. Try to work them out yourself by reasonable and fair consultations with anyone else who is involved. If your problem concerns relations with your roommate, then talk it out with him. If you are in difficulty with one of your courses, then the instructor should be consulted. If you have personal problems that you have been unable to work out, then take the matter to your advisor, or the master, or the dean who is experienced in these matters. Do not go to the headmaster (except in cases that specifically require you to report to him, of course) unless all your other attempts to settle the difficulty have failed and the matter is extremely important.

Carry your troubles to your parents only as a last resort. Your experience at boarding school is an excellent preparation for the assumption of full responsibility, for being entirely on your own. Make the most of it by approaching that state as closely as you can.

Some General Suggestions

Don't be a habitual borrower of books, clothing, or money. When you do borrow, be sure to pay back promptly. Do not assume that it is perfectly all right for you to wear your roommate's ties, shoes, and sweaters without his permission—and do not ask for this permission often.

Remember that you owe the same courtesy to the janitor, the

cleaning lady, and the man who takes care of the grounds as you do to the headmaster or your roommate's parents.

The truculent contradictor is a boor and a bore. Don't get into the habit of contradicting things which your schoolmates say simply to exhibit your own knowledge or to show off your independence of mind.

If you should miss one of your possessions, be very careful before you insinuate that your roommate is, let us say, a thief. The probability is strong that you have lost or mislaid the object yourself. Be very certain before you make another person's character the object of your suspicions.

When conversing with members of the faculty, whether male or female, be respectful. Avoid a flat "yes" or "no" in speaking to them. Use "Yes, sir," and "Yes, ma'am." Or use the appropriate surname. For example, "Good morning, Mr. Masters" or "How do-you do, Mrs. Masters?"

Try in all of your life at boarding school to be respectful and considerate of everyone. The waiter at your table should be thanked for his service. Your roommate is much more likely to respond favorably to your "please" than he would to a "hey." Try always to observe the rules. The reason they have been established is to make life easier and more pleasant for everyone at the school.

A Note to Parents

At no time is the admonition to "let go" more applicable than when you send your son or daughter to boarding school. You cannot impose your authority or give your child your protection all of his life. His period at boarding school and college should be most valuable in teaching him to accept authority outside the home and in assuming responsibility himself. When you enrolled him in boarding school, you transferred much of your own authority to the faculty of the school and made him subject to school rules. Support the faculty and the rules and help your child to observe them. Do not openly disagree with the rules or encourage him to flout them.

Try to develop a sixth sense about good-bys. Don't make them tearful when you part. Tell your son good-by cheerfully, with a firm handshake and a kiss if he still permits you this; if it embarrasses him, omit it. Even if you feel a special tenderness and sense of loss at leaving him, don't show it. This may give him a feeling of fear.

If you feel so badly about leaving him there, you must be abandoning him to a terrible experience Once you have made the choice, be confident that you have chosen well. He will be in good hands. There is nothing to worry about

You should get a copy of the school rules and learn to support them. Try to confine your telephone calls to convenient hours and a frequency that will not serve to embarrass your child.

The headmaster is a very busy man Don't drop in for a chat without making an appointment first. If you wish to pick up your son or daughter for the weekend, be sure to make arrangements ahead of time. Leaves of absence must be arranged and are usually strictly regulated. The school, which has accepted responsibility for your child, must know where he is at all times. So don't just drop in and pick him up. He must obtain permission to leave—even with you—and check out when he goes.

School schedules are important. Do not ask for extra days off for your boy or girl, or for extra travel time because he or she has a long way to go.

Do not complain because the room assigned to your boy or girl is not as luxurious as you think it should be. He is there to receive an education, not for a luxury vacation.

Visit the school sometime during the sessions, but try to do so when it is convenient for you to visit classes. Some schools have special days on which mothers, for example, are encouraged to visit. If you attend on such a day, remember that your presence in the classroom creates an artificial atmosphere. Try to be as unobtrusive as possible and remember that the boys or girls may be tense and not quite up to standard.

A headmaster's wife has told me a charming story about one master's technique for combatting this On the day before "Mother's Day" he said to his boys·

"Tomorrow several of your mothers will probably be here to visit and of course we all want to make a good impression. So, whenever I ask you a question I want all of you to hold up your hands. Those who are sure that they know the answer, hold up the right hand. Those who are not sure, hold up the left hand. I shall call only on those of you who raise your right hands "

I am sure this man was a good master and got excellent co-operation from his students.

In short, cooperate with the school in every way you can. If you feel that you cannot, you have made a wrong choice for your son or daughter and you had better make a change.

Your adolescents are no longer children and should not be treated as though they are; and as they are not adults you should not expect them to behave like adults. They are in their threshold years now and you must encourage and support them in every way. Though they may seem to resent your authority, they still cling to it, lean upon it, and expect it to save them from making too many mistakes. It is your difficult task to exercise it with discretion, relaxing it gradually as your sons and daughters prove that they are more and more able to accept and discharge responsibility. You must learn to let go of the one who was such a very short time ago your child. Yet you must not let go too soon so that you shirk the responsibility you have to one who will always be your son or daughter.

It is often difficult to find a middle ground between too great domination and too much freedom. The path to it, it seems to me, lies in full and frank discussion with your youngsters on all matters about which you disagree. Such discussions should be kept on a courteous and adult level Let your children see that you respect their points of view and their personalities; that you are ready to take guidance and learn from them, just as you expect them to learn from and be guided by you. Be willing to be convinced that, on occasion, you have indeed been wrong. Tell them so and change your attitude.

Develop a sensitivity to impending conflict, or to their sometimes mercurial changes of temperament. Turn aside, whenever possible, their wrath. Avoid head-on clashes and show-downs by catching the trouble before it becomes a full-blown scene. When a little thing goes wrong try not, as your adolescent himself might so expressively put it, to "make a production of it."

Welcome your children's friends to your home, even those (if any) of whom you don't approve. The more wholesome character of your family circle will probably bring about a gradual sloughing off of undesirable relationships Your refusal of admittance may only provoke clandestine meetings. Encourage parties in your home, especially for your younger adolescents. Plan the arrangements with them and stay home on the evenings when they occur. Generally speaking, it is not a good idea to try to participate in the party itself, beyond welcoming the guests and perhaps helping with the refreshments.

All rules you adopt should be the products of your mutual thinking. Be sure that you are fair at all times, that you never play favorites when there is more than one teenager in your house Try not to impose your will on them arbitrarily. If you have to say to them, "Because I say so," the chances are that you haven't really thought through your reasons for imposing a rule.

Always try to look back and remember how it was with you Your teenager is between two worlds, but the world has itself changed a good deal since you were a teenager. Keep that in mind too. You will want your children to look back on the years between thirteen and nineteen with warmth and happiness. Whether they will or not depends largely on how you help them cross the threshold.

28

The Handicapped

IN MEETING THE HANDICAPPED THERE ARE SPECIAL ELE-
ments to be taken into consideration if one is to treat
them with the understanding and the courtesy that are the basis for
all proper social behavior.

One who is sincerely interested in human communication and
cooperation, in being genuinely helpful, will pay only so much attention to the disability as is necessary to give the other the help he
needs and wants, will not call undue attention to it by extravagant
gestures of sympathy and elaborate offers of undesired help, will
give such help as is asked for or indicated in a matter-of-course
way, neither evading nor emphasizing the fact of the disability, and
will in general keep his companionship with the other on a basis
that will keep communication and companionship between the
handicapped and the unhandicapped as nearly normal as possible.

BLINDNESS

The history of society's attitude toward the blind is a
strange commentary on man's inhumanity and his lack of human

understanding. For centuries the blind were ostracized, considered a group apart and unclean. Blindness was regarded as a punishment from God for sins and therefore to be avoided. In several instances recorded in the Old Testament, God is called on to punish evildoers by making them blind. King David (II Samuel 5 8) offered special rewards to those of his men who killed the blind and the lame. And in at least one instance (Malachi 1·8) it is intimated that the blind were actually killed on altars as sacrifices to God.

As late as the seventeenth century in Europe blind men and women were thought incapable of serving any useful purpose, and it was considered impious to attempt to help them to do so. Consequently they were shut up and concealed from public view in asylums. Even as late as the beginning of the nineteenth century to most people "to instruct the blind was considered impossible, and some fanatics even held it to be a great sin to attempt it, for they saw in every blind person the trace of God's hand."*

During the nineteenth century, however, a beginning was made in a halfway scientific attempt to give the blind their rightful place in society and in training them to assume that place. Since then, material progress has been made both in Europe and in the United States, in teaching the blind to do useful work and to meet the ordinary situations of life with a minimum of help. But little improvement in the attitude of sighted persons toward blindness has been shown. Mr. Chevigny and Miss Braverman say.

The machine should have made the position of the blind person today a fundamentally different one from any that he occupied in the past. He has, in theory at least, permission to take his place in society. But there is that in his situation which still defeats him as a person, and it is not the physical drawback of sightlessness. It is the effect of his sightlessness upon the sighted world There is still an emotional barrier against him, a survival of the times when a silent prayer against catching his affliction was said by sighted men on touching his hand It is still vaguely more fitting to give a check to a social agency for the blind than to give jobs to its clients, a memento of the times when it was impious to make a blind man work but pious to give him alms.†

---

* Dr. Jacob Koloubovski, reporting on the status and history of the blind in Russia, before the 1914 International Conference Cited in *The Adjustment of the Blind,* by Hector Chevigny and Sydell Braverman (New Haven, Yale University Press, 1950), p 93. I am indebted to this book and to Mr Chevigny who has been most helpful in personal interviews, for other information in this chapter.
† *Op. cit.,* p. vii

Obviously the first obligation of any sighted person who has close or casual contact with blind people is to see that no trace of this attitude motivates his relationship with them, and that he does everything possible to correct the attitude when he encounters it in others.

The Group Concept and Discrimination

One of the fallacies that underlies the negative attitude toward blindness held by many sighted persons is that the sightless form a group which are, per se, physically, mentally, emotionally, and morally inferior. Those who are capable of discrimination against other minority groups discriminate against the blind, both socially and in the matter of job placement. Both the group and the inferiority conceptions completely neglect demonstrable facts, which seem so obvious that they ought not to need stating.

The personalities and characters of the blind vary as widely as do those of sighted persons and have been in no way basically changed by the loss of sight. The advent of a great misfortune affects different persons in all walks of life in different ways. To some it becomes a crushing blow under which they cower, give up, and spend the rest of their lives in ineffective misery. To others it becomes a challenge that calls forth and strengthens the bedrock courage and determination that is within them, and results in successful accomplishments which they would not have attempted before. So it is with those who become sightless after years of seeing.

Most of those who have become blinded in youth or early adult life can be, and have been retrained to most skills for which they have been accustomed before they became blinded, and to others for which they are fitted by nature and inclination. These vary from manual craftsmanship to the following of professions and achievements in scholarship. Tape recorders, the telephone, the typewriter (most blind persons learn to use the touch system), and Braille keep the avenues to information and communication at a distance open.

The old conception that such things as basket making, weaving, chair caning, and certain kinds of needlework were the only physical occupations open to those who have lost their sight has long since been displaced. These skills are still taught and are extremely useful, especially in the initial phases of training and for those blinded at advanced ages. But today trained, able-bodied blind persons operate circular saws, wood-turning lathes, drill presses, shapers, and other power tools (sometimes modified) efficiently and safely. They work in the fabrication and casting of plastic materials, in metal crafts and jewelry, in ceramics, as inventors, as musicians (both instrumental and vocal), as piano tuners and typists, and in other occupations, including photography. Sometimes these occupations are taken up merely as hobbies, sometimes as means of earning a livelihood.[*]

Recently thirteen blind persons who had made outstanding successes in their careers were introduced at a fund-raising luncheon at the Light House. Among them were a producer of Shakespearean plays, a newspaper editor, a concert pianist, a college professor, a practicing chiropractor, and a man who owns and operates his own business.

Pity. One of the greatest obstacles which the sighted place in the way of blind persons is "pity." I have put the word in quotation marks for I have always used it as meaning very much the same thing as compassion, from which springs genuine kindness and helpfulness. But the blind make a clear distinction between "kindness" and "pity," considering the first among life's greatest graces and the latter an inverted expression of cruelty, sadism, and a sense of guilt, "a magical gesture to satisfy the conscience when confronted by objects arousing instinctual aggressive wishes, no doubt to banish the object from sight or destroy it."[†] It is, as Chevigny and Braverman put it,

born . . . of the need to master fear . . . the unmasked impulse would be to banish from sight, or kill, the individual who, by exhibition of misfortune, mobilizes fear and hostility, all of which, in turn, arouse the sense of guilt. . . . Pity for another implies inferiority. . . . Pity avoids contact. It explains the man who will not employ the blind man, even if he is proven as fit as the next man for the job, but instead makes out a check to the nearest blind service institution—his form of magical gesture to exorcise guilt.[‡]

Plainly our basic attitude is far more important in the matter of our proper behavior with the blind than any detailed rules of physical or verbal approach.

You should have a clear understanding, however, of the special

[*] Charles G Ritter, *Hobbies of Blind Adults*. New York, The American Foundation for the Blind, 1953
[†] Ludwig Jekels, "The Psychology of Sympathy." Cited by Hector Chevigny and Sydell Braverman, *op. cit.*, p 148.
[‡] Hector Chevigny and Sydell Braverman, *op. cit*, pp. 149–150.

needs of the newly blinded in their progress toward readjustment, and of the ways in which you may show courtesy to all blinded persons. If someone close to you has been blinded or if you come frequently in contact with others who have lost their sight, your understanding and thus your behavior will be helped materially by reading some of the extensive literature on the subject. One of the best of the basic books is *The Adjustment of the Blind,* by Hector Chevigny and Sydell Braverman, from which I have quoted. In addition to its penetrating text it contains an excellent bibliography that will suggest further reading to you. Most helpful also is the educational series of publications issued by the American Foundation for the Blind, 15 West 16th Street, New York 11, New York.

Here I shall make only a few suggestions:

Do Not Be an Obstacle-Placer

Sighted persons sometimes place two kinds of obstacles in the way of the blind, small and large. The small ones are physical, the large psychological.

If there is a blind person in your home or in a home which you are visiting, be careful not to move the furniture from its accustomed places. The blind person has learned at the cost of more than one collision where various articles are placed and finds his way about the house by means of them, touching them with his hands, but avoiding bumping into them. Even the placement of rugs is important to him, for he feels them through his shoes.

If you pick up an ashtray to empty it or use the phone, put it back exactly where it was.

If you are cleaning out the closet and move a blind person's hat or topcoat, return them to the places where you found them. Do not leave doors partially open. If a door to one room is customarily closed, keep it closed at all times. If it is usual to keep it open, see that it is always wide open.

These are the little things which ordinary consideration should dictate to anyone. The psychological obstacles are somewhat more complex. Chief among them is the tendency to overprotect and give too much assistance to the newly blinded. Both the sightless and those who are close to him and wish to give him all the help possible must learn at the outset that the difficult task of reorientation must be accomplished largely by the blind man himself.

The mother, wife, or sister of the newly blinded man is hindering the handicapped rather than aiding him, and perhaps yielding to that dangerous impulse which the blind call "pity," by crying out or rushing to his aid every time he seems about to bump into a chair or a wall, thus implying that he is truly helpless, which he is not Help when he asks for help or when it is quite obvious that he must have it, but do not try to save him from the minor bumps and frustrations that are his best tutors. When in doubt ask him quietly and casually if he wants help, as you would anyone else, but do not make an emotional issue of it.

The newly blinded is faced with the extremely difficult task of learning anew the everyday skills of living which as a sighted person he took for granted as all of us do. He must find a way to re-enter the stream of community life from which he has been temporarily washed ashore by the loss of his sight. He must reachieve the ability to move independently, avoid danger, eat, dress and undress himself, use the telephone, write, and do many other things that are simple for sighted persons, and now extremely difficult for him until he learns his new techniques. All these things he can learn to do with proper training, if he has the will, the courage, and the ingenuity. But he must acquire adeptness in these relearned skills by himself. He should be encouraged to go to a school for training the blind operated by one of the agencies established for this purpose. His training should then be left to the school and to himself Helping him too much, sympathizing with him too much, maintaining an atmosphere of emotional tension in your relationship with him will tend to undermine his morale and slow the process of his reorientation.

Do not, if he is able-bodied and adaptable, attempt completely to rearrange your home in order to give the newly blinded special aids, such as placing guide wires under rugs and along garden paths, gates at the tops of stairs, etc. Of course he may get hurt. He might also if he were sighted and playing football. He cannot, if he is to live a satisfying life, confine himself to the home, and he will not find such aids elsewhere. Let him learn to use the aids that are in the average home—the placement of rugs and furniture, the sounds that come from a ticking clock or through the windows, the wall or banister rail that runs to the head of the stairs. (An exception to this rule should be made for those who become blind in advanced age, and for whom retraining is impractical.)

Current among the myths held by sighted people are that the blind have a sixth sense, that they have abnormally acute hearing, and that they can tell color by touch. None of these is true. What is true is the old adage that necessity is the mother of invention, a truth which the blind demonstrate every day. Those who have been deprived of their sight learn to listen for sounds to which they would have paid no attention when they were sighted, and use them as guides. The blind woman who says, "I think I shall wear my blue scarf today," goes to her dresser drawer and unerringly selects it from several of different colors has probably learned to recognize it by its texture, or by a small Braille label or other identifying device which she has fastened to it. The one who knows whether she has handed a grocery clerk a one-, five-, or ten-dollar bill has simply folded them differently before placing them in her wallet

If there is any question of hearing loss in the newly blinded one, be sure that he has a hearing test and, if necessary, procures a hearing aid. Do not, because you do not want to force upon him the realization that he has two handicaps instead of one, ignore the matter. Many persons with a slight hearing loss unconsciously do a certain amount of lip reading. Not only can the blinded person no longer do this, but also he must now depend upon his hearing as well as his sense of touch for orientation.

Do not shout at the blind For some not understandable reason many sighted persons do this, as though blindness automatically connoted hearing loss It is not only annoying, but it is also one more indication of how painfully aware you are of your friend's affliction, and so constitutes one of the physchological obstacles you are placing in his way.

When talking to a blind person remember that he is interested in the same things that you find interesting. You need not avoid the subject of blindness, but you need not, either, substitute it for other topics. Use the words "see" and "look" as you would if talking to a sighted person.

When escorting a blind person into a strange place tell him where things are in the room and who is there so that he may feel at home. If you are at a party try to see that he finds friends to talk to, but don't force people on him any more than you would do if he were sighted.

In a restaurant, read the menu to him, with the prices if there is a reason for doing so. It is quite proper to ask him whether he would like to have you cut his meat and put sugar and cream into his coffee, but accept his answer literally without argument. Also you might tell him what is on his plate and approximately where each article is But offer no more help than is necessary.

If you live with a blind person, read his mail to him promptly, but do not comment on its contents unless he wants to discuss them with you, and forget them as soon as you can Within the limits of possibility grant him as much privacy as you would a sighted person

The most serious of all the obstacles that sighted persons may put in the way of the newly blinded in the family is the assumption that now it is impossible for him to enter most of the ordinary activities of life, and so, tacitly or outspokenly, to lessen his desire to make the great effort necessary to adjustment If those among the sighted who are concerned with his welfare give up for him, his own tendency will be to give up and accept defeat. The line between making too little and too much of the blind man's handicap is a thin one and sometimes difficult to find Exactly where it is will depend somewhat on the nature of the blind man and the quality of your relationship and your ability to understand each other. Your greatest service will lie in your encouraging him in every way possible to depend on himself as much as he can and to learn as quickly as may be the new skills which he needs to become again a constructive member of society. The extent to which he will be able to do so will depend somewhat upon your ability to bolster and increase his hope, his aspiration, his courage, and his confidence in himself.

Courtesy to the Blind in Special Situations

If you see a blind person without a guide dog waiting at a street corner, it is courteous and kind to offer to help him. But do not rush up and take his arm without speaking to him. Approach him quietly and ask, "May I help you?" before touching him. If by chance he answers, "No thank you," do not insist. The fact that he is waiting at a crossing probably means that he wants someone to make the offer you have just made, but may not. If he accepts your help, do not take his arm, but offer him yours—holding it just so that it will touch his hand as he extends it Walking with you in this way his steps will be just far enough behind your own so that he can follow the motions of your body Hesitate momentarily (but do not stop) just before stepping down or up at a curb, saying "curb" or "step up," or when you come to a deep crack or hole in the pavement. If you have to go through a narrow passage, turn slightly sideways, letting the arm which your blind companion is holding move a little behind you.

If you go to a restaurant, or concert, or lecture with a blind friend, back your friend gently to his seat so that its edge just touches the back of his leg. If this is awkward, place his hand on the back of his chair.

If you are in a restaurant with a blind person and the waitress takes your order and then asks you what your friend would like, suggest courteously that she ask him. One of the minor annoyances with which the blind have to contend is the apparent assumption of others that they can neither hear nor talk. Incidentally this, of course, should be remembered if you have a blind guest who comes with a friend to your home for a meal Speak directly to the blind person, making it clear that you are doing so by calling him by name, rather than to him through his companion.

If you meet a blind person with a guide dog do not offer your help unless it is quite clear that he has become confused and, as it were, lost. In that case ask if you may help, but do not insist if the answer is no.

Never touch a guide dog when he is in harness. His mind at that time should be on one thing only—the difficult job which he is doing and, if he is a good dog and well trained, doing well A part of the dog's training is not to pay attention to strangers on the street, save as obstacles to be avoided, and to attempt to pat him while he is working is a little like urging a person to abandon carefully formed, good, and necessary habits. If his harness is off and he is on leash, it is quite all right to ask his master if you may pet him, but do not touch him without the master's permission

Hector Chevigny, whose career as a writer was interrupted in his early forties by sudden blindness, and who has retrained himself so that he has been writing successfully and well ever since, has called my attention to one small thing which I would never have thought of.

"Not one person in two hundred and fifty," he said, "will tell a blind man that he has egg on his shirt front, or that his tie is in the soup. They refrain out of self-consciousness, whereas if they would only speak up in a matter-of-fact way without making a production of it, they would help him to help himself and save him from embarrassment."

In talking with the blind remember that your sole method of communication is through your words, whereas with sighted persons you add meaning to what you are saying by facial expressions and gestures. Your audience cannot see the smile or shrug of the shoulders which tell the sighted person that you are using sarcasm or speaking in jest. Say literally what you mean, and if there is any indication that you have been misunderstood repeat it perhaps in slightly different words which you know will be comprehensible. Speak in a natural tone of voice. In a group, address the blind person by name so that he may know you are speaking to him.

When listening to him remember that he cannot see the nod that would tell a sighted person that you understand or agree with him, or the smile which shows that you appreciate the humor of the thing he has just said. An occasional "yes," or "no," or a gentle laugh or even a grunt, when appropriate, will let him know that he has your attention.

A Note to the Blind

I would not myself presume to give the blind any advice on proper behavior. But Mr. Chevigny has asked that I mention two things to them, and given me his permission to quote him.

"Tell them," he said, "to make sure of the state of their hearing If there is any hearing loss, urge them to get hearing aids. Not to do so is not only dangerous for them, but also inconsiderate of others.

"Tell them also, if they have guide dogs, to keep the dogs in proper training and under control. Quite properly a guide dog may go many places with his master where other dogs are not allowed— on streetcars, subways, buses, and in restaurants. But many blind persons take advantage of this privilege and let their dogs lie down anywhere and become obstacles to others. The place for a guide dog on a bus or subway is seated between the knees of his master. If one is sprawled in the aisle where others have to step over him it is quite proper for a sighted person to tap the blind man on the shoulder and say, 'Will you please get your dog out of the way?' The blind man who resents this and refuses to cooperate is among the rudest of the rude."

The Deaf-Blind

Fortunately the totally deaf-blind are rare. I discuss them here less in a desire to outline rules of behavior in meeting them than in order to demonstrate the almost incredible feats of adjustment that have been performed by the severely handicapped, and thus I hope to demonstrate further the absurd stupidity of an attitude of negativism toward the blind.

Among them, the blind who have learned to speak before losing their hearing are the fortunate ones, for they may express themselves orally. Yet even for them communication would be a one-way affair were it not for no less than sixteen ingenious and easily learned methods which sighted persons may use to speak to them. (I shall mention only one here. If you ever have occasion to communicate with a deaf-blind person and have not learned one of the other methods, try the simplest of all—printing in the palm. Hold the other's hand lightly in yours, palm up. With your free index finger outline capital letters as large as the other's palm permits. At the end of each word lay your palm flat on the receiver's palm. If you have made a mistake, rub the other's palm with your own as if erasing it. It is a slow method, and one that may be difficult at first, but it may be used with a fair degree of success by anyone without previous training. If you have frequent contact with a deaf-blind person learn one of the faster methods)*

Like the hearing blind, the deaf-blind have been trained to useful occupations that range from simple handicrafts to the operation of power machinery. I have just read a letter from a remarkable deaf-blind man who lost his sight at the age of three, began noticing a hearing loss at the age of twelve, and since the age of thirty has been able to hear no voice except his own. He began his readjustment to a productive life by learning to cane, rush, and repair chairs at a school for the blind For a number of years he conducted his own chair-repair business, and made a good living During the latter half of World War II, when materials were hard to get, his business fell off and he sought an outside job. Given a trial at a routine task of tying square knots in the ends of pieces of string, he was later moved on to other jobs that included cutting strings to two-foot lengths, inspecting various parts of flashlights, inserting springs in flashlight

---

* Annette B Dinsmore, *Methods of Communication with Deaf-Blind People*, Rev. Ed. American Foundation for the Blind, 15 West 16th St, New York 11 Price 50 cts

caps, assembling nuts and bolts, operating a wire cutter, a stripper (which removed the insulation from the ends of wires), a staking machine, a tapping machine, and a drill press—and he did all of them well. He habitually found his way to and from his home with no help save that which was offered to him on the streets.*

Such stories as this should shame anyone who believes that the blind are inferior.

THE HARD OF HEARING AND THE DEAF

The Historical Attitude

Like blindness, impairment of hearing has in the past carried with it the stigma of implied inferiority, brought about by the apparent lack of mental development in the afflicted persons who could not understand what others said and whose speech was often unintelligible. As far back as the second century B C. the deaf were classified with children and fools. The Justinian Code barred them from the rights of citizenship.

Not until the middle of the sixteenth century was any systematic effort made to understand and help those with partial or total hearing loss, when Girolamo Cardano of Padua, Italy, demonstrated, by teaching the hard of hearing to associate written symbols with related objects, that they could be educated if a proper psychological approach were used. Cardano's method is the basis of the teaching methods of today.

During the past three hundred years tremendous advances have been made in helping those whose hearing is below normal, and with increased understanding there has been an improvement in the public attitude. Yet a residue of the ancient stigma still exists. One evidence of it lies in the fact that in many languages a single word, such as our "dumb," means both stupid and mute; and muteness is of course associated with impairment of hearing.

Hearing impairment is a less dramatic handicap than blindness, but is far more widely spread. Surveys show that in the United States alone from ten to fifteen million (or one in every fifteen persons) suffer a major hearing loss. Yet of these only about a mil-

* *Training and Employment of Deaf-Blind Adults.* American Foundation for the Blind, 15 West 16th St , New York 11 Price 45 cts.

lion have sought treatment or correction. The hard of hearing, even
more than the blind (for whom concealment is impossible) seem
reluctant to acknowledge their handicap, probably because of the
ancient stigma.

Terminology

Those with serious hearing problems are extremely sensitive
to the designation used when referring to them. To them "deafness"
means a total inability to distinguish sounds In speaking of those
with a partial hearing loss use the term "hard of hearing," not "deaf."

Especial Difficulties of the Hard of Hearing, and What You Can Do about Them

Some people depend entirely on lip reading to learn what
another is saying to them. But even those with partial hearing loss
who have not been trained in lip reading consciously or unconsciously depend on it to some extent. When talking with one who
has any hearing impairment face him directly and see that the light
is on your face so that he can follow the movements of your lips.

One with normal hearing will pick up the subject of your conversation as you go along. The hard of hearing may have difficulty
doing this. Be sure that he knows what you are talking about before
proceeding with detailed remarks. "Clue him in" at the outset.

Some words are more difficult to understand than others, and
sometimes two words ("wash" and "watch," for example) require the
same lip formation and so may be indistinguishable to the lip reader.
If one who is hard of hearing does not understand you, change the
wording slightly in repeating what you have said. Instead of saying
again "I'll walk you to the corner," say, "I'll go to the corner with
you"; instead of repeating "I'll see you at three," say, "I'll meet you
at three o'clock."

The hard of hearing have difficulty with many names. Spell them
out when necessary, and whenever possible spare those with a hearing loss the task of introducing another person whose name may be
in doubt.

Many persons with normal hearing have difficulty understanding
over the phone, those with hearing impairment find it especially difficult. In a phone conversation with one who has any hearing problem
make sure that he understands what you have said. Repeat tactfully

or emphasize such matters as addresses, times and places for meetings, etc.

One of the worst barriers to understanding for anyone with a hearing impairment is background noise. Keep the radio and television turned off when talking with one who has difficulty. If street noises are coming in through an open window, close the window

Persons with normal hearing have a "global sense," that is, they can hear sounds that come around corners. For the hard of hearing this is more difficult. Corridors, walls, doorways, distance, all are barriers. When you speak to one with a hearing loss, come to him, do not shout from a distance.

Those with hearing losses sometimes find it impossible to localize a sound. If you are one of a group of three, one of whom is hard of hearing, and the other is speaking, look at the speaker, thus directing the attention of the one who is having difficulty toward the sound.

Some General Suggestions

When sitting or walking with someone wearing a hearing aid, place yourself on the side on which you can see the ear mold. In modern hearing aids the microphone itself is tucked behind the ear and almost invisible. If he wears the type of aid that is concealed in the bows of his glasses, and you know it, ask him which side is the best for him.

If you are with a hard-of-hearing friend in a group, and the others laugh at something he has not heard, explain the joke to him or tell him you will do so later. People with hearing loss are often hypersensitive and your friend may think that the others are laughing at him.

Speak clearly and distinctly, but do not shout.

Sit or stand not more than four feet away from the person with hearing difficulties when you are talking with him.

Write key words—especially proper names—when necessary.

Helping the Child with a Hearing Problem

If you have a child who shows signs of seeming inattention, or of misunderstanding what you say, or of being unaware of ordinary sounds, take him to your family doctor, and if he suggests it, to an otologist. If his hearing is impaired the sooner this fact is recognized and he is given help, the more nearly complete may his adjustment be.

Do not make so much allowance for his impairment that he feels that he is different from other boys and girls. Within reason expect the same things from him that you would from a child with normal hearing.

Be sure always to let him know that you love him, that you have confidence and pride in him. Any handicap has a tendency to give a child a sense of inferiority.

Remember the rules which you should use in talking to all who are hard of hearing—face him directly, let your face be in the light, speak distinctly, do not shout at him, do not expect him to hear when you are in another room or are speaking to him from a distance, but stand or sit near him when you speak to him.

If he was born with a hearing loss or if it occurred before he had learned to speak well, he will inevitably have a speech difficulty. Help him with patience and kindness to learn to speak, but let him see that you expect him to speak, and give him especial praise when he utters a new word properly.

Don't apologize for him or act as though you were ashamed of him, and don't keep him from other children because of his handicap. They may be among his best teachers.

When you talk with him, show him by your expression and your alertness that his conversation is of the greatest interest to you

Do not assume that his hearing loss accounts for every minor difficulty in his behavior. Approach his behavior problems as you would those of any child. Use your ingenuity to include him in all group family activities.

THE CRIPPLED

As work with the handicapped becomes more and more fruitful, it becomes increasingly clear that their psychological and emotional problems are greater than the physical ones. Says Dr. E. D. Witkower:

Irrespective of the nature of their disability, disabled persons have in common that they are—and feel—different from the fit population. Most persons are anxious to conform to the laws of uniformity. For good or evil many persons do not like to make themselves conspicuous. . . . If they lack something the possession of which is taken for granted by others, they feel underprivileged and are afraid of being despised and laughed at. Hence disabled persons not only feel different from, but also inferior to, the nondisabled population.*

Like blindness a crippling accident or disease is a visible disability and thus more shattering than one that can be concealed, for the handicapped know through memory of their own former attitudes that they form a minority group against whom there is an almost automatic prejudice.

It is not surprising that one who has suffered a severe handicap goes through an initial stage of deep depression. The first task of anyone who has the care of such a person is to help him to overcome this depression. The soundest approach to the problem contains a mixture of sympathy—but not too much—encouragement to achievement, and help in establishing a wholesome set of relative values. He must learn to consider what he has lost as of lesser value than formerly, what he has left as of greater importance. If he has lost the ability to walk without help, he must come to realize that walking is a convenience rather than an essential, the loss of it a hardship, not a catastrophe.

Disabled children are in many ways more fortunate than those who become disabled in adult life, for they are more adaptable and, not having yet taken their places in adult life, can be given the special training necessary for them to do so before maturity.

Yet with them as with the adult disabled, the formation of a wholesome and constructive attitude as early as possible is of the utmost importance.

What their attitude will be will depend largely on that of their parents. If the older people think of the handicap as an irremediable tragedy, and feel helpless and guilty about it, so will the child, and his life will probably be warped in consequence. If the parents on the other hand have a healthy and constructive attitude and see the handicap as a challenge, and find ways for working out compensations, the child will follow their lead and his disability will become merely an inconvenience.

I know one boy of nine or ten who seems quite unaware of the partial disability of a slightly atrophied left leg, considerably smaller and weaker than the right, the effect of early polio. Indeed I had

* "The Emotional, Social, and Occupational Aspects of Disablement," a paper delivered at the third annual meeting of the Canadian Association of Physical Medicine and Rehabilitation, June 25, 1955 Reprinted in *The Canadian Medical Association Bulletin,* Vol. 73, 371–376.

known him for over a year before I noticed one day, as he was running after his older brother, that he had a very noticeable limp, and dragged his left leg slightly. But as if there were no difference whatever between him and the older boy, he climbed a tree with him, going as high as his brother did, laughing and taking his part in the play with no recognition whatever of his handicap.

His parents had obtained for him every available advantage of physiotherapy, but beyond that had made as little as possible of his disability, letting him know that they expected as much from him as from his older brother—and getting it.

Sympathy

As the blind abhor the word "pity" so do the disabled cringe at certain kinds of "sympathy." There is, according to them, a "good and bad kind of sympathy." Here are some quotations from several crippled patients which may guide you in approaching similarly unfortunate ones with courtesy and helpfulness:

"You can always take encouragement. More than sympathy, it is the cheerful look, not a sorrowful look—a feeling of raring to go kind of infects you—not the idea that the world has gone wrong."

"I think it's all right for someone to say he's sorry on first meeting. I think I would say the same thing. If he would let it go with saying he was sorry and not rave on about it. . . . It's all right if they don't overdo it."

"A person can say he's sorry it happened, but I don't want him to say he's sorry for me. . . . It's in the time element Sorry it happened refers to the past and it doesn't mean he keeps right on feeling sorry. Pity and being sorry *for* a person suggests looking down."*

Suggestions

A disabled person in a wheelchair usually needs help getting up or down a curb, and up or down steps. Do not, however, rush up and seize the back of the chair without warning. Ask the occupant whether you may help, and if he says no, do not stand over him insisting that he needs it. If he accepts your offer, and you are in any doubt as to his need, ask him what he would like you to do, and if you have not formerly handled a wheelchair, how to do it. If he is waiting at a street corner he will probably want you to

* The above statements are cited in "Adjustment to Misfortune," by Tamara Dembo, Ph D , Gloria Ladieu Leviton, Ph D , and Beatrice A. Wright, Ph.D , in *Artificial Limbs, A Review of Current Developments,* Autumn, 1956.

negotiate the curbs for him. This is done by backing the chair off the curb, and facing it forward, tipping it up onto the opposite one. There is a rear brace put on the chair for the latter purpose, but if you are unfamiliar with it ask the person in the chair just how to do it.

Taking a person in a wheelchair up or down steps is a far more difficult task, and requires at least two people. Do not attempt it without proper help, and without receiving instructions from the wheelchair occupant. Obviously a slip in this circumstance can be disastrous.

Some paraplegics successfully drive specially fitted automobiles, but may have difficulty getting themselves and their folding wheelchairs in or out of their cars, or up steep inclines. If you see one in apparent need, offer your help, and if it is accepted ask exactly how you can help best, and follow instructions. If your help is rejected, accept the refusal without protest. The disabled want to do as much for themselves as they can, and it is more courteous and helpful to allow them to do so than to insist upon supplementing their own efforts.

Those who walk with crutches are in most things more independent than the wheel-chair bound. But they must use both hands and arms to manipulate the crutches and need assistance in some situations. Offer to help them through difficult doors, to carry packages for them, and to seat themselves by holding their chairs firmly until they are securely seated in them.

THE ALCOHOLIC

Alcoholism is today regarded by medical, psychiatric, and social work groups as an illness which, like diabetes, cannot be cured but may be arrested. The phenomenon differs from that of simple "heavy drinking" in several ways. The principal difference is in the matter of control. The normal heavy drinker is able to stop when he chooses. The confirmed alcoholic drinks compulsively. One drink sets up within him a craving against which he is powerless and may be (and often is) followed by days of incapacitating drunkenness.

Typically the alcoholic is one who is emotionally insecure, who because of this feels a sense of inadequacy, who feels himself rejected, and believes that because he is unworthy he should be rejected. He is egocentric and reacts poorly to states of strain He has discovered that alcohol relaxes his tension, creates a state of elation in him, and makes him feel omnipotent Gradually his drinking increases and his ability to control it vanishes. He is then a very sick man for whom there is no specific cure, but whose disease may be arrested and made ineffective if he recognizes it, has the will, learns the effective techniques by which he may escape his compulsion, and has the support of those who are close to him.

The National Council on Alcoholism has listed the "thirteen steps to alcoholism." The first three, the Council points out, are not necessarily the beginning of alcoholism, but they may be. The last ten definitely describe the behavior of an alcoholic. Familiarity with them should be useful to anyone who is beginning to be concerned with his own drinking or with that of one who is close to him.

1. The beginning You start drinking Once in awhile you drink too much, but in the morning you can't stand the sight of a drink, and after you have recovered from your hangover you have no abnormal craving for liquor. Statistically the odds are very good that you will not become an alcoholic. They are better if you stick to beer and other drinks of low alcoholic content.

2. Blackouts. You periodically get drunk and, the next morning, can remember nothing that happened the evening before. You have not "passed out" (that is, lost consciousness). You have simply suffered a form of amnesia. If you are wise and still in control of your drinking you will see that it does not happen again. If it does happen several times, you are in danger.

3. Liquor becomes important. You find that you are gulping drinks rather than sipping them, feeling the need to make them effective quickly. Liquor means more to you than it does to others. You become secretive about it, sneak extra drinks at a party when no one is looking, and sometimes have one or two before going to a party to be sure that you will have enough. At this point you should still be in control and able to stop drinking if you really want to, but if you don't stop, or manage to restrict your drinking to moderate amounts, you are in great danger of becoming an alcoholic.

4. Out of control. You find that almost every time you take a drink you go on from there and drink more than you intended to. You may be able to stop for a given period, say "I won't have another

drink for two weeks," and stick to it, but once you have taken a drink you go on drinking until you have completely numbed your feeling of anxiety. This is a crucial phase. If you recognize it you can stop But if you refuse to, and begin to find specious excuses for your drinking, it is probably too late for you to manage it without help

5 Excuses. You feel guilty about drinking and tell yourself that you really can handle it any time you want to, but keep making excuses to yourself and to your friends if the question comes up

6. Eye-openers. You feel that you can't get started in the morning without a drink as soon as you get up, and take it to steady your nerves and give you the courage to meet your family and your job.

7. Drinking alone. You begin to drink alone because you actually prefer to do so, indulging in the fantasies of well-being which liquor brings you without sharing them with anyone else.

8. Antisocial behavior. When you have drunk enough you become abstractly revengeful, picking fights with strangers, throwing rocks at windows, striking your own children. Your desire to cause damage is compulsive. Or you may turn your destructive impulses inward, castigating yourself, feeling afraid of people, believing that they are criticizing you and laughing at you. Your sense of right and wrong has been drowned by alcohol.

9. "Benders." You go on periodical drunks, usually lasting several days, during which you drink blindly, helplessly, completely disregarding your family, your friends, your job, and even food and shelter. You have no sense of pride and your moral sense is dulled. You will beg, pawn your most cherished possessions, even steal, in order to get money for drink

10 Remorse You have sober moments of deep remorse and self-castigation. You call yourself a no-good bum and a failure. But in other moments your resentment against yourself is turned against others. Your drinking is the fault of an unsympathetic wife, of an unreasonable boss, or of society as a whole. The world is against you!

11. Fear and trembling. You feel constant, deep nameless anxiety You walk in terror with shaky steps, trembling hands, and a glassy stare. You begin to hide your liquor supply for fear it will be stolen. Only in drinking can you escape your terror.

12. Realization. You admit that you can't handle liquor without help. All your excuses are a tissue of lies You are licked unless someone or something gives you a hand.

13. A way out. You get outside help—or you are lost. Some alcoholics are helped by religion, some by medicine or psychiatry. The program of Alcoholics Anonymous has been more successful in arresting alcoholism (they do not speak of "cures") than any other.

If Your Husband or Wife Is an Alcoholic

Learn the facts about alcoholism. There is much sound literature available today. In addition to books which you will find in the public library helpful pamphlets and papers are issued by the following:

The National Council on Alcoholism, Inc.
New York Academy of Medicine Building
2 East 103rd Street
New York 29, New York

General Service Headquarters
Alcoholics Anonymous
P. O. Box 459
Grand Central Annex
New York 17, New York

Publications Division
The Yale Center of Alcoholic Studies
New Haven, Connecticut

Having learned the facts accept them, emotionally as well as intellectually. Regard your alcoholic spouse as a sick person in need of help, rather than as an immoral weakling who should be scorned and censured. It would be as unrealistic to say of a child with pneumonia, "If he loved me he would not have pneumonia," as to believe that an alcoholic who loved you would not drink.

Do not increase the sense of guilt and inadequacy (which is one of the causes of his alcoholism) by preaching, nagging, lecturing, or even trying to reason with him when he is drunk, or adopt a "holier than thou" attitude.

Do not hide his liquor or pour it down the sink. It is not only a waste of time and money, but will also stir resentment in him that will probably increase his drinking (for he can always find liquor elsewhere).

Don't let him persuade you to drink with him on the grounds that he will drink less, he won't, and by thus condoning any drinking on his part you may merely help him delay doing anything about it.

Examine yourself and your attitudes carefully for inadequacies that may have damaged your marital relationship, and when you find them try to correct them. If you are a woman make sure especially that you do not unconsciously welcome the helplessness which alcoholism brings about in him so that you can "mother" him. One of the strangest of phenomena in alcoholism is the wife who becomes depressed and anxious when she sees her husband conquering alcoholism, and may even offer him a drink now and then, saying that he has proved that he can take one occasionally, but actually unconsciously wanting him again to become helpless and dependent upon her.

Learn to be as sensitive as you can to your alcoholic's mental attitudes. Make it your objective to have him go to a treatment center or join Alcoholics Anonymous, but do not press the issue. If you feel he will not resent it give him some of the literature on alcoholism which you have obtained. But remember that he must himself make the decision to seek help. The first of Alcoholics Anonymous' famous "Twelve Steps" is: "We admitted that we were powerless over alcohol—that our lives had become unmanageable." Unless your alcoholic spouse has deeply and meaningfully taken this step of his own accord treatment will probably be worthless.

If he is taking treatment, or trying to work out his salvation through Alcoholics Anonymous, do not expect immediate success. Try to accept his relapses, if they occur, with the same tolerance and understanding which you would give to one who had a relapse after any other illness. But as he progresses try to hand back to him some of the responsibilities which you have been obliged to take over during his incapacitation. Ask his advice, and get him to share in making family decisions with you, showing him in all possible ways that you have confidence and believe in him. The alcoholic is a person with a badly shattered ego, and one who has been afraid to take responsibility. His salvation lies not only in stopping drinking, but also in achieving self-respect and accepting responsibility.

Don't try, by warning his friends not to offer him drinks, to protect him from alcohol, thus stirring up his old feelings of resentment and probably pushing him into a relapse. He must learn to say "no" gracefully and positively, but of his own free will.

Encourage his interests and activities, and share them as much as you can.

But with all of your sympathy and understanding and desire to help, do not be bullied by the arrested alcoholic who exploits his achievement and holds it as a threat over his family. If he is one of the rare ones who feels that he deserves special consideration because he has won a hard fight, and in word or by implication threatens to start drinking again unless you do so and so, call his bluff.

If You Have an Alcoholic Friend or Guest

Your attitude and actions toward an alcoholic friend should be the same as those adopted by the wise wife or husband of an alcoholic.

Whether you will invite an arrested alcoholic to a party at which you intend to serve drinks or not should depend somewhat on your understanding of how effectively he has won his fight. If you know that it is a commonplace for him to be with others who are drinking and that for a number of years he has refused to take a drink, there is no reason why you should not do so. If, on the other hand, he is in the initial stages of conquering his compulsive thirst, better not.

But never, under any circumstances, say to one who you know is an arrested alcoholic, "Oh, come on. You're not really an alcoholic. One drink isn't going to hurt you." Every enlightened alcoholic knows that the first drink is disastrous, for it sets up in him a craving which he cannot control.

And if you have asked one to a gathering in which you serve drinks to others, ask him, as you do the rest, "What will you have?" Do not label him before the others by serving the rest of your guests with alcoholic drinks, while saying to him, "I'll get your tomato juice for you in a moment, Bill."

VIII

COMMUNICATION

The Importance of Communication

W HEN WE SPEAK OR WRITE, WHEN WE READ OR LISTEN, we are using a skill which is one of the important distinguishing characteristics of man—our ability to communicate with one another to an extent far beyond that known by any other living thing

A dog may express fear, anger, hunger, pleasure, pain, and affection. But only man can communicate abstract thought, memories of the past, hopes and plans for the future. Only man can make promises. Only man is able to record his experiences and leave a written record of his accomplishments and his failures. Only man can give future generations the chance to acquire a heritage and a tradition, to profit from what those who have gone before have learned and experienced.

Without verbal communication there could be no education more specialized than that which a mother bear gives her cubs. Without our ability to express abstract concepts there could be no scientific progress, no human culture as we know it. We live our lives through communicating with others, and so our own individual ability to do so with consideration and courtesy, with an awareness of the effect on others is vital The ways in which we make known our thoughts, our feelings and our goodwill toward others constitute more than just social grace or the lack of it, through communication we contribute to or detract from the very progress of human civilization.

WORDLESS COMMUNICATION

When Polonius asked Hamlet, "What do you read, my lord?" the Prince of Denmark answered, "Words, words, words." Yet, when *Hamlet* is produced, what Shakespeare had to say to us is conveyed not only by his words, but by the gestures, movements, and facial expressions of the actors. Even their silence may be eloquent.

Many communications are without sound, and in all of them we may be courteous or discourteous. Pliny, in his *Natural History,* wrote,

Other animals have eyebrows, but only man's express grief and joy, mercy and severity, by moving together or singly to signal from his soul. They show our agreement and disagreement, and supremely our contempt. Haughtiness enthrones herself in them, and though conceived in the heart, rises to the eyebrows and there hangs in the loftiest and steepest part of the body which it can occupy alone.

A sudden firming of the lips may express obstinate refusal without a sound, a shrug of the shoulders indifference, a grimace disgust, contempt or similar displeasure. Perhaps the most varied of all expressions in its potential meanings is a smile. The centuries have failed to agree on just what the Mona Lisa's smile really means. A smile may say, "I like you and I am glad to see you." It may say, "I am amused," or "I find what you just said somewhat ridiculous." It may mean, "You're doing fine, keep it up," or "I'm sorry." It may be a thinly disguised mask for cruelty and hatred, a warning of future retribution, a way of saying, "I've got the best of you." And it may say many other things.

When used with spoken words, a smile may modify, emphasize, or negate what is spoken. Some expressions are taken as affectionate compliments when accompanied by a friendly smile, as unforgivable insults without a smile.

In music, a rest or silence may be as significant as a sounded note. So, silence in communication may also convey an eloquent meaning. Every reader of detective stories knows how avidly a favorite sleuth will seize upon a momentary silence, a hesitation on the part of a suspect. To the trained investigator, this silence has meaning. Your words of welcome to a guest who has "just dropped in" will be meaningless if after a few moments of desultory talk, you are wordless, clearly telling your guest that you wish he would depart.

Even our general appearance may speak volumes to the trained observer. The right hand of one Jabez Wilson, slightly larger than the left, said to Sherlock Holmes (in *The Red-Headed League*) that Wilson had for some time done manual work, the shiny cuff of the right sleeve of his jacket and the patch near the elbow of the left that he had been doing a considerable amount of writing, and so on.

Similarly, by greeting invited guests in uncleaned shoes, a soiled shirt and unpressed clothes, you are saying, "I really didn't think you were worth the trouble of cleaning up."

Over and over again your actions may speak more clearly, may even contradict your words. If you are consistently late in keeping appointments with a certain acquaintance, it will probably be difficult for you to convince him in words that you enjoy his company. Many a wife, rightly or wrongly, has interpreted her husband's failure to remember their wedding anniversary as an announcement that his love for her has dimmed. Fidgeting, coughing noisily, or rising from your seat while someone else is speaking to you may say clearly, "You are boring me." Failing for weeks or perhaps months to answer a letter intimates, "I don't really care to keep up a correspondence with you."

Of course there are times when what may seem rude to another is the only way in which you can make your feelings and your intentions clear. But the wise person who wants to express courtesy, kindness, and goodwill must always consider the meaning of what he does as carefully as the meaning of what he says.

DIFFICULTIES IN COMMUNICATING

I believe it was Louis Armstrong who said, "You can say anything with a trumpet, but when you begin to use words, you've got to be careful." Music may be a universal language. But the barriers between men of different tongues are sometimes all but impenetrable. And this is true despite the common origins that many vastly different languages have. For example, philologists tell us that English, Russian, Irish, Spanish, Latin, Italian, Greek, Albanian, Armenian, Persian and Hindustani have common roots. Here are four words which bear evidence of this:

English	mother	father	sister	brother
German	Mutter	Vater	Schwester	Bruder
Russian	mat'		sestra	
Latin	mater	pater	soror	frater
Italian	madre	padre	sorella	
Greek	meter	pater		phrater
Irish	mathair			brathair
Sanskrit	mata	pita	svasr	bhrata

This little tabulation shows the great similarity that exists between languages. Yet what vast differences there are!

Every literate Briton and American knows what Bernard Shaw meant when he said, "England and America are two countries separated by a common language." Elsewhere I have written about some of the differences between the British and American versions of the English language (see Chapter 15, "When in Rome Do as Rome Does"). Today approximately one person in every ten throughout the whole world speaks some variety of English. It is the most widely studied language in countries to which it is not native. It has become the predominant language of trade and business. Three-fourths of the letters of the world are written in it and over half of the world's newspapers and scientific and technical journals are printed in it. It is spoken over three-fifths of the world's radio stations. More nearly than any other it is the *lingua franca* of the modern world.*

Despite the wide use of English by many people all over the world, the barriers between those who speak it not only in different countries but even in the same country are very real. If you would be courteous and effective in your speech and writing, you must learn to be sensitive to the different meanings that words have to different people.

The Variable Meanings of Words

"Before I discuss anything with you, you must define your terms," said the French philosopher Voltaire. Attempts at commu-

---

* *The Story of Language*, by Mario Pei. New York, J. B. Lippincott Co., 1949. Also Mentor Books, New American Library, 1960.

nication are often unsatisfactory because words are used vaguely or ambiguously. Often the user does not realize that a word means one thing to him and another to the listener. To the English "corn" is simply a cereal grain, which may be wheat, rye, or barley. To an American the word invariably means Indian corn or maize, a painful growth on the foot, or, in slang usage, something that is cliché-ridden or contains fulsome sentimentality. I have heard New Yorkers speak of Chicagoans as "living in the West." To Californians, Chicago is "in the East." In political terminology, "the West" consists of the democratic states of Europe and the Americas. Unless the context makes it perfectly clear, what does the term mean without definition?

Sometimes words have special meanings to special groups of people To most people (including the makers of both Webster's and the Oxford dictionaries) the words "pity" and "compassion" are synonymous. Yet the blind, who consider compassion a part of commendable kindness, abhor "pity," which they feel imputes inferiority to them and is tinged with a sadistic cruelty.

Those who suffer from a partial hearing loss are sensitive about being called "deaf." Though Webster defines the word as "wanting, or deprived of, the sense of hearing, either wholly or in part," to the hard of hearing it means only "totally deaf." So it is offensive when applied to those with a partial hearing loss.

When abstract concepts are involved the matter of language becomes most complex. One of the tragedies of misunderstanding between the communist and democratic nations is their lack of a vocabulary in which the same words have precisely the same meanings for both. The very survival of man may hinge on this.

In my own work at the United Nations, when we were first trying to set down on paper the Charter on Human Rights, I came to know firsthand the terribly complex problem of settling on words and phrases which each country's representative felt would reflect the true intent and purpose of our work. Often we would spend many hours exploring the meaning of a single word with each of us offering to "define" that word, or to find another word with which all of us would be satisfied. Each sentence was gone over in detail. Compromises had to be made. Yet I am not at all certain today that each of the representatives who met to frame these documents would interpret them with precisely the same meaning.

I frequently marvel at the ability of the United Nations trans-

lators to convey quickly the meaning of a speech from one language
to another. They deal not with words, grammar, and construction
alone; they must constantly struggle in an attempt to convey the
"spirit" of the speaker's words into another tongue.

Thucydides tells us [Plutarch wrote in "Flattery and Friendship"]
that during revolutions and wars "words had to change their ordinary
meaning and to take that which was now given them. Reckless audacity
came to be considered the courage of a loyal ally, prudent hesitation,
specious cowardice, moderation was held to be a cloak for unmanliness,
ability to see all sides of a question inaptness to act on any." . . . Plato
somewhere remarked that the lover calls a snub nose cute, a hawk nose
royal, brunettes virile, blondes children of the gods, "honey-pale" he
says is the coinage of a lover who cheerfully tolerates a greenish com-
plexion and gives it a pet name.*

Humpty Dumpty may say, as he does in *Through the Looking
Glass*, "When *I* use a word it means just what I choose it to mean—
neither more nor less," but this attitude is just why many heated
and futile arguments take place. The two who take part may use
the same words, yet they are actually talking about very different
things.

Ambiguity

All of us have an obligation to use our own language as correctly and accurately as we can. Some words have more than one
meaning to everyone, according to standard dictionary definitions.
When we use these words we must be careful that our meaning is
accurately conveyed. If we say, "John Smith is a poor athlete," do
we mean that he has little money or that he is not a competent
athlete? A friend has told me of a sign which she saw over the entrance to a New England Rest Home. It read "For the Sick and
Tired of the Episcopal Church." The home was quite obviously for
ill and exhausted persons who happened to be Episcopalians, not for
those who had wearied and "become sick" of the Church. This sign
would not have been the butt of ridicule if it had been worded
differently.

Some word combinations are ambiguous though the meanings of
the individual words are quite clear. If a friend asks you to do a
somewhat onerous errand for him and you write in reply, "I shall

* *On Love, the Family, and the Good Life Selected Essays of Plutarch*, translated
with an Introduction by Moses Hadas New York, New American Library, 1957

lose no time doing as you have asked me to do," do you mean that you will do the errand at once or that you will not do it at all?

We all remember the story of the man who insisted that he could answer every question with a yes or no. A friend demonstrated how wrong he was by simply asking, "Have you stopped beating your wife?"

In writing, when you do not have the advantage of accompanying your words with gestures and facial expression, it is particularly important that you strive for accuracy. There is a story told about the Czar of Russia who left a brief message on the table. It read· PARDON IMPOSSIBLE, TO BE SENT TO SIBERIA. The Czarina happened to see the message and, moved by one man's fate, she merely changed the position of the comma. The altered message then read. PARDON, IMPOSSIBLE TO BE SENT TO SIBERIA.

Know What You Think before You Speak or Write

Descartes suggests in his *Discourse on Method* four simple steps by which we may learn to think logically and thus communicate clearly:

1. Accept as true nothing which you do not clearly know to be so, avoid hasty judgment and prejudice.
2. Divide every problem into as many parts as possible, or into as many as are necessary for your specific consideration.
3. In examining any problem begin with the simplest and easiest parts of it and progress to the more complex.
4. Make your enumeration so complete, and your review so thorough, that you may be sure you have omitted nothing.

René Descartes lived over three hundred years ago, but his advice is still perfectly sound. If we all clarified our thoughts *before* attempting to put them into written or spoken words many misunderstandings and hurt feelings could be avoided.

When I first began to speak on the radio I submitted scripts that were returned to me time after time with the suggestion that my audience would understand me better if I used words of two syllables instead of four or five. While I found it difficult to express myself simply and clearly I did find that simple speech was far more effective in getting across what I wanted to say.

This first bout with radio scripts was perhaps one reason why some years later a student writing a term paper on columnists said that in order to read Arthur Krock or Walter Lippmann one needed

at least two years of college education, but anyone who had finished
fifth grade could read Eleanor Roosevelt.

My children teased me about this for a long time, but I didn't
mind, counting it an advantage which I had gained from my training
in radio.

Stick to the Point

Many years ago I first heard the story of the child who felt
she was losing an argument with her brother. Though their argument had nothing to do with cleanliness, she ended it by saying,
"Well, anyway your face is dirty." Many people resort to this kind
of trick when they feel they are on the losing end of an argument.

Perhaps even more discreditable is the practice of asserting as
"facts" matters which have not been proved, or using as "evidence"
something that is the product of illogical thinking and the drawing
of an invalid conclusion.

John says he *knows* James is a communist because he has heard
him praise the Russian writer Dostoevski and his novels. Besides,
James is an advocate of socialized medicine. The same man is sure
that a man on trial for murder is guilty because he is cross-eyed,
scowls, speaks broken English and *looks* like a murderer. Also, he
is known to have been arrested previously for theft.

Language Is a Changing Thing

All language is fluid, a living, changing thing. The patterns
of speech, the expressions, indeed, the words themselves change
from generation to generation. This is particularly true of colloquial
and informal speech. Because of the rapid march of science, the fact
that the world is constantly shrinking and we are feeling the influences of many peoples we have never had such close contact with
before, our language is in a particularly changing state today. When
these changes make communication simpler and serve to clarify and
deepen our understanding, then we are enriched by them. When
through ignorance or carelessness they obscure meanings, then they
are to be deplored.

Correct Usage

A good dictionary is an essential tool for every literate person. One of the standard unabridged works is of course the best, but
there are several small desk dictionaries that will serve ordinary pur-

poses. If you wish to speak or write meaningfully, clearly and, therefore, courteously, use your dictionary whenever there is the slightest doubt in your mind as to the spelling or meaning of any word. Of course, you will have to have a general idea of the spelling before you can find the word. I recall a story told to me by a publisher friend about one of his authors, an eminent physicist, who was such an incredibly bad speller that, in despair, the publisher sent him a dictionary and suggested that he use it. A few days later a letter arrived from the physicist saying, "Your dictionary is no good. Wanting to thank a friend for some fruit he sent me, I tried to find 'appel' in it and it isn't there!"

There is one other book, referred to by those who have come to use it and rely on it as "the little book," which I think is one of the most helpful in checking faults of grammar, usage, style, spelling and punctuation. It is called *The Elements of Style*, by William Strunk, Jr. and E. B. White (Macmillan, 1959). Armed with this book, guided by its principles, one can hardly go wrong.

Simplify Your Language

Many writers and speakers apparently believe that by using complicated words and phrases they demonstrate an especially advanced literacy and an ability to be impressive. They never use one word when ten will do. They use the six-syllable, little known word instead of a one- or two-syllable synonym which everyone knows. They draw liberally on their knowledge of foreign words and technical phrases, often plucking out words at random just to create an impression.

I recall a story which appeared some years ago in a now-defunct magazine. There was a photograph of a woman rural mail carrier astride her horse. The caption said: "Every day she delivers the mail to fifty farmers. *Ex officio* she is the mother of five fine children." The confused caption writer meant to say that in addition to her job as a mail carrier, the woman was a successful mother. But *ex officio* means "by virtue or because of an office." So, the caption actually meant that she was a mother as a result of her job!

There is one other important fault that seems to be on the increase today, perhaps because we are constantly being plied on all sides by superlatives. This is the school of the redundancy. There are many examples of this sort of thing Such phrases as "round circle," "funeral obsequies," "audible to the ear," "the whole point" or "one son, a boy," "one and the same," "estimated at about," "joined together," "sink down," "rise up," "the true facts" and so on.

Radio and television announcers seem to be particularly guilty of using unnecessary words. They are heard by millions who tend to follow their example, and thus our language is debased.

The man who gives us the weather report is likely to say, "There will be rain shower activity today." He means there will be rain. We are told, "Things are happening at this time" or "at this hour" (and I have even heard "at this time and hour") instead of "now." Awkward phrases take the place of simple expressions. The word "and" becomes "likewise" or "furthermore" or "in addition"; "so" becomes "for this reason," "accordingly," or "consequently"; "about" becomes "in reference to"; "like" becomes "along the lines of," and so on.

Style

Keep yours simple. Let it reflect you and your ideas. Keep it free from artificiality and superficiality. The loftiest sentiments and most noble purposes of man have usually been expressed by the great men of history in the simplest and most direct way.

Consider this imaginary version of how a memorable speech might have been worded:

"We firmly intend to oppose them in every way possible and in every place where it may be necessary to do so. It is our purpose to give them battle on the soil of our Allies, the French. Our gallant Navy will challenge them to battle on the oceans. Every hour and every day our air arm is growing which gives us increased and growing confidence that we shall meet them successfully in aerial combat in the skies. If they ever land in the British Isles, whether by sea or by air, we shall spare no expense or cost to defend our homeland, meeting them in determined combat whether they land in boats on the beaches, or in airplanes on airfields. We shall fight them in the wide open spaces of the countryside, in the farmlands and the fields. If they should enter our cities we will give them battle on the streets and the avenues, between the houses, on street corners and in the squares. If they appear in the hills we shall do them battle there At no time, at no hour or day in the future shall we raise the white flag, throw in the towel and surrender to them."

Now read what Winston Churchill said to the House of Commons on June 4, 1940:

We shall fight in France and on the seas and oceans, we shall fight with growing confidence and growing strength in the air. We shall defend our island whatever the cost may be, we shall fight on beaches, landing grounds, in fields, in streets, and on the hills. We shall never surrender. . . .

If the speech had been delivered as I have so clumsily rephrased it, I am sure it would have been buried in the records of the House of Commons.

No one who heard or read Churchill's words during the critical time when they were spoken could fail to understand their import or could forget their impact. This has become one of the classics of English oratory along with Lincoln's simple and equally forceful Gettysburg address.

The reverse of the above process is equally to be deplored. There are those who attempt to "popularize" a beautiful literary passage and proceed to ruin it completely. I remember a shocking example of this which I read some years ago in a modern translation of the *New Testament*. The passage which so offended me went something like this

"Think of the flowers that grow in the meadows. They don't do any work. Nevertheless, Solomon was never dressed as beautifully as they are " This is a colorless and pointless rendering of the magnificent passage in the Sermon on the Mount which in the King James version reads "Consider the lilies of the field, how they grow; they toil not, neither do they spin: And yet I say unto you, That even Solomon in all his glory was not arrayed like one of these."

Learn to know your language as well as you can. Use it naturally, clearly and economically Then you will achieve the basis of courteous, meaningful, and effective communication.

30

Conversation

How often have you heard that familiar childhood refrain, "Sticks and stones may break my bones, but words will never hurt me"?

Children may find this useful in turning taunts aside, but there is no question that words can be the cruelest of weapons. The bruises made by a stick or stone will disappear in time; those inflicted by a thoughtless or bitter word may never heal.

I remember to this day the words spoken to me by one of my aunts on the subject of not being a popular belle, which had been the achievement of all of the Hall sisters. I think that her remark that I was the ugly duckling of the family, while entirely true, certainly stayed in my mind longer, and made me shyer, than even a beating could have done.

Anyone genuinely concerned with enjoying good relationships will always avoid causing others pain through inconsiderate words. And he will go further than this by attempting to be courteous and understanding, and by trying to keep the flow of communication going *both ways*. He will not monopolize the center of the stage and will avoid discussing subjects obviously outside the interests of the listener. He will always try to speak clearly and simply, using his language correctly and with due regard for established social custom.

As in all other aspects of human relations, the formal rules of etiquette in conversation have an obvious usefulness in making meetings between two or more persons graceful rather than awkward, in helping others to overcome their shyness, in furthering our understanding and appreciation of others. The basic rule is the rule of kindness. Without it, all other rules are meaningless.

INTRODUCTIONS

Which Name First?

In introducing people, the name of the person to be accorded the greater courtesy should be given first. A man is introduced to a woman by saying the woman's name first, then the man's name. There are a few exceptions to this: When women are introduced to a head of state, an important male member of a royal family, a church dignitary, a governor or a mayor, the order is reversed. When a young girl is introduced to a mature man, his name is spoken first. When she has reached an age that entitles her to be called a young lady, even a much older man is introduced to her. There is another exception: parents always introduce their children to friends by giving the friends' names first. This is true even when the friend is a man and the child a grown woman. On the other hand, sons and daughters introduce friends to their parents, even when introducing a girl or young woman to a father.

In any organization in which there is a clearly established rank, as in the Armed Forces, a government staff, a college faculty or a business office, the person of lower rank is introduced to the one of higher position: A sergeant to a lieutenant, a captain to a colonel, etc.—or a newly hired department head to an officer of the firm, an instructor to a professor, a professor to a college president. There are certain exceptions to this where protocol is considered less important than in most government circles. The president of a college or business organization is introduced to a distinguished visitor, the name of the visitor being given first. Here, the rule of courtesy to a guest would take precedence over rank. But in government circles and the Armed Forces, the rule of rank would usually be observed even when it was in conflict with normal courtesy to a guest.

Forms of Introduction

What you say when you introduce people depends, of course, on the circumstances of the introduction and who the two people are. The most formal introduction is "Mrs. Mason, may I present Mr. Carpenter?" Such formality is seldom used today and is generally saved for introductions to dignitaries. Much more common in contemporary American usage is a simple, "Mrs. Mason, this is Mr. Carpenter." If a little more formality seems to be called for, it is quite acceptable for you to say, "Mrs. Mason, may I introduce Mr. Carpenter?" If you are introducing two good friends of yours who have not met before, you might add warmth to the introduction by saying something like. "You already know a lot about each other from what I've told you both." You also may add a bit of information which will tell Mrs. Mason something about Mr. Carpenter. For example. "Tom is a business associate of my husband."

In introducing your spouse, say "This is my husband, John," or "my wife, Mary." To use "Mr." or "Mrs." in such an introduction is not good form. Adding the last name to the first is not necessary and is stuffy.

In introducing one married couple to another, it is awkward to divide them and introduce each separately. Here, because it is simpler, you may ignore the rule of introducing the man to the woman and treat each couple as a unit If one couple is older, introduce the younger couple to the older. If there is anything which indicates that a greater courtesy should be shown one couple, let that couple be the one to whom the other couple is introduced. You may say simply "Mr. and Mrs. Mason (or Frank and Helen Mason), this is Mr. and Mrs. (or Tom and Edith) Carpenter."

Sometimes it is easier to introduce one person to a group than to go through a separate introduction with each individual It is quite proper to do so without regard to the rules of precedence. Simply look at the person who is being introduced and speak his name. Then, turning to the group, give the name of each person in it: "Tom (or Mr.) Carpenter—Miss Nannine James, Peter Scott, Bill Trotter, Larry Smith, Miss Rita Whiteson, Jack Mullen, and Miss Sue Weston."

Generally speaking, it is not necessary to say, "My friend, Mr.

Carpenter." It may be assumed that he is your friend, or at least an acquaintance, or you wouldn't be introducing him However, if you are introducing a relative, or someone with whom you have a special relationship, it helps to clarify matters if you explain the relationship.

If you are a man or an unmarried woman, "My brother, Tom," is sufficient, unless your last names are not the same If you are a married woman, use the last name as well as the first Your friends may not know your maiden name and will therefore not know your brother's last name automatically. (This is, of course, also true if you are a married woman introducing your parents)

If you are introducing a brother, sister, or parents of your mate, you may say, "This is my mother-in-law, Mrs. Price" (or father-, sister-, or brother-in-law). But it is more specific and perhaps more gracious to say, "This is my wife's mother, Mrs. Price," or "my brother's wife, Mrs. Holden."

If the person you are introducing is a friend with a special relationship, you may mention this in your introduction. For example. "This is Dr. Stone, our family pediatrician," or "Miss Rust is Sally's teacher."

Titles such as Judge, Doctor, Captain, etc , are always used in introducing those who hold them Titles of nobility are always given as well (see Chapter 26, "V.I.P.'s").

Forms to Avoid

Do not say, "Mrs. Mason, I want to make you acquainted with," or "I want you to make the acquaintance of," or "Mrs. Mason, shake hands with Mr. Carpenter," or "Mrs. Mason, meet Mr Carpenter." And avoid the awkward routine of a double introduction, "Mrs Mason, Mr. Carpenter—Mr. Carpenter, Mrs. Mason."

At a very large party do not attempt to introduce a newcomer to everyone there. See that he meets and knows the names of a small group of people so that he will feel comfortable. Then let the guests follow their natural instincts and introduce themselves to one another.

When you bring a friend to a party introduce him to the host and hostess and let them manage the proper introductions after that.

On the street it is not necessary to introduce someone you are walking with to every acquaintance you may meet and with whom you will exchange no more than a few words of greeting. By doing so you might only complicate matters and invite an awkward silence after the introduction. The same rule applies to a chance meeting with a friend when you are in a restaurant dining with someone. If your friend simply pauses to say hello when passing your table, let it go at that. If the friend sits with you to chat, an introduction is proper.

Acknowledging an Introduction

The proper acknowledgment of an introduction is "How do you do?" or, less formally, "Hello." Especially among younger people, "Hi," accompanied by a smile, is perfectly fine. Remember that a smile is a proper accompaniment even in formal introductions and should be eliminated under only the most solemn of circumstances.

"I'm pleased to meet you" is quite stiff and formal and should be avoided If the person to whom you have just been introduced is someone of whom you've heard or someone you admire or whose work you are interested in, you may quite properly say something like: "I've wanted to meet you for a long time," or "I'm very glad to meet you, I've heard (or read) so much about you."

Handshaking is a matter of confusion to many people. When a man is introduced to a woman, he should not offer his hand unless and until she does so. When a man is introduced to a man, each should offer his hand, unless he is willing consciously and openly to show contempt. Generally, if the person you are being introduced to is older, you should wait until he or she has offered to shake hands. Of course, if you are the host or hostess you will be expected to offer your hand in greeting the guests. On the matter of a woman offering her hand, there does not seem to be a set custom. I think it is a warm gesture for a woman to put out her hand when introduced to someone of either sex.

Shaking hands is a very natural physical expression of greeting people or congratulating them or offering condolences. Some people have told me that they can form an idea of a person's character by the way he shakes hands, and I have no reason to doubt it. Warm, outgoing, and hearty people shake hands in an enthusiastic fashion. Shy, introverted people who lack confidence tend to give quite the opposite impression. Try to avoid any special mannerisms when you are introduced to another. Don't be too athletic in your approach, don't seize the other person's hand in a viselike grip. Avoid prolonging the handshake and, by all means, do not offer your hand limply and allow the other person to shake it without any participation on your part. A smile, a firm handshake (but not a bone-crusher), and a friendly "hello" are always proper.

How to Save Your Own Bones

If you ever happen to be faced with a long line of people whose hands have to be shaken, perhaps the advice given by my uncle, Theodore Roosevelt, to my husband and to me will be useful to you. He told us never to let anyone else take the initiative. "Always put your hand out," he said, "and take that of the other person so firmly that he is unable either to squeeze your own or to insist on holding it and pumping it up and down for several minutes." If you forget this rule and wear a ring you may find your hand squeezed so firmly that the ring cuts into your finger, and even if you don't you may find yourself exhausted by overenthusiastic well-wishers who treat your hand and arm as though they constituted a pump handle.

Well intentioned signs of warmth can be most painful, but they can be made harmless by the one who takes the initiative and clasps the other hand first.

AFTER THE INTRODUCTION

After you have met someone do not stand in silence. If the other person begins to talk to you, try to listen with interest and respond with something equally interesting if you can. If he does not launch a conversation you should do so yourself. If you know anything at all about the other person's interests try to talk about them or to ask questions so that you may draw him into a conversation. If you don't feel comfortable with these subjects you can comment on an interesting news event or what a pleasant gathering the party is. If the weather has made you a gift of a dramatic subject such as a blizzard, a cloudburst, or an especially brilliant display of the aurora borealis, you are most fortunate. But try not to fall back on such clichés as "Lovely weather, isn't it?" Almost anything is better than such a forced "ice-breaker."

Overcoming Shyness

If your palate dries and your heart begins to palpitate at the thought of meeting people or talking to strangers, try to relax. Remember, talking too much is a far greater social fault than talking too little. Many persons remembered as "fascinating conversationalists" are not those who had the most interesting things to say, but those who listened with the greatest show of interest Being a good listener is an almost sure road to popularity, especially if you are a woman and those to whom you listen are men.

Talking, as every child of four knows, is easy once you get the hang of it. It's a little like swimming or driving a car or knitting. Learn the rules, try them out, practice until you have mastered them, and then you will find yourself automatically following them. Be pleasant, use correct grammar, do not misuse words, avoid clichés, control facial expressions and gestures so that they express your meaning—these things are all important. But do not stop and run over them in your mind every time you are about to say something Avoid being self-conscious about these "rules" Don't try too hard. Just relax and you will be all right Not all of us are naturally so glib and articulate that we can become polished conversationalists overnight. The mind of the good conversationalist is occupied nine-tenths with what he wishes to say and one-tenth with the way he says it. If you *think well and thus have something to say,* you will almost automatically talk well.

I personally know the terrors of shyness, for I was a painfully shy girl As I grew up and took on the responsibilities of a hostess and a guest I had to find ways to overcome this shyness. I adopted a simple plan which made it possible for me to enter into a conversation with almost anyone. I used the alphabet as a subject file. I would think first of a number of things beginning with the letter "A"—apples, accidents, art, ancestors and so on. Each of these words suggested related subjects and I would choose the one which I thought most likely to interest my companion of the moment. If there was nothing under "A" that seemed to provide a conversational spark, I investigated the "B's"—baseball, business problems, buttermilk, busses, etc. Usually, before I got through "C" I managed to strike a responsive chord.

One of the pleasant things about this system is that it takes your mind off yourself and your shyness. If, for example, you should be talking to a clergyman and you think of "Beelzebub" or "Bingo" you may find yourself wanting to giggle In such a mood you can hardly be afraid or sorry for yourself.

Try to be natural and unaffected. Do not talk too much in an effort to prove to yourself and others that you are really not shy. By skillful questions and expressions of interest keep the conversation as much as possible in the area of the other person's interests rather than your own. Then you will soon find that there is really nothing to fear and probably you are having a good time.

Selfish Interests and Interrupting

Two of the most unfortunate conversational habits are interrupting and talking excessively about yourself and your own interests. Often the same person is guilty of both. If a story your companion is telling reminds you of one you would like to tell about yourself, do not interrupt, but hear him out. While he is talking, you may want to reconsider your own story. Is it of real interest or does your desire to tell it stem from your pleasure in talking about yourself? Often you will find that it is better not to tell it at all, but rather to stimulate your companion to continue talking. Certainly a good listener cannot be accused of rudeness.

ARGUMENTS

There is a time and a place for almost everything. Intelligent, calm, and carefully thought-out discussions, in which you support a special conviction, have a proper place in the lives of all of us. But, generally speaking, a social gathering is a more rewarding and relaxed affair without arguments—at least heated and prolonged ones. It is best to avoid starting them yourself and to evade any which others have started. This is particularly true of personal arguments that should be strictly private affairs.

This does not mean that you should agree with everything someone else says to you merely to flatter him. Such remarks as "You took the words right out of my mouth" are not only boring, but may also constitute a negation of some of your most dearly held convictions, or may involve you in a disloyalty to persons in whom you believe.

There are some questions, I feel, which are of such deep importance to all of us that we each have a responsibility to make our influence felt at every opportunity. This can sometimes be a rather delicate matter and it is hard to be tactful. If someone tells you how inferior certain racial groups are, or how much better fascism or communism are than democracy, or that everyone in our government is corrupt, I think you owe it to your self-respect, as well as to society, to say quietly something like this "Perhaps my experience has been somewhat different from yours, but I cannot agree with you." It seems to me there are certain questions on which there exists an obligation which supersedes that of keeping social conversation always on a pleasant and noncontroversial level.

Even in such a difficult situation, you will accomplish nothing by angry rudeness If you make your point quietly and courteously, your words may have an effect, even though they do not seem to at the moment. If you are respected, your words may plant a seed that will bear fruit later. If you keep your voice well modulated and do not lose your temper, you will inevitably gain more respect than if you shout angrily and contemptuously.

If you are caught in a contradiction during an argument, or if your "opponent" makes a good point or manages to prove that you are wrong in any particular, don't be ashamed to admit that you are wrong. Conceding a point or two won't break down your whole argument. If it does, then you have lost fairly. In any case, your companions will have a greater respect for you if you don't act like a "know-it-all," or stubbornly hold out when you have been bested.

Do not be too positive about questions that are matters of opinion and personal preference. "It seems to me," or "Tastes and convictions differ. My own feeling is——" will keep the atmosphere much more pleasant than being authoritative or overbearing.

AVOID OFFENSIVE SUBJECTS

Avoid subjects that might be embarrassing or offensive to anyone in the group. If someone else launches into a subject which you know may offend someone present, try to guide the discussion along other channels or to divert the matter by simply switching to something else.

If you do unwittingly start talking about a subject which you find is painful to someone else, simply say, "I'm sorry," and change the subject. Do not go into a long explanation of how you came to be talking about it, or enter into an extended act of contrition which will only increase everyone's embarrassment.

HEARING LOSS

If you have difficulty with your hearing, do not be hesitant about telling people. It is more courteous to ask pleasantly that a companion raise his voice than to ask him continually to repeat what he has said. If your hearing loss is acute, by all means get a hearing aid. It should no longer be embarrassing to resort to one. Most people are not ashamed if they require eyeglasses. (For suggestions on helpful behavior when talking to one who is hard of hearing, see Chapter 28, "The Handicapped.")

FOREIGN WORDS AND PHRASES, QUOTATIONS

It is a fine thing to be familiar with other languages and to be on speaking terms with the world's great books. But it is boorish and immature to flaunt your learning. Do not sprinkle everything you say with foreign words or phrases and illustrative quotations from the classics. This is as lacking in taste as the constant use of clichés and proverbs in commenting about anything. If you learn how to use the English language as effectively as possible, you will be a far better conversationalist than if you superficially garnish your speech with phrases that merely indicate an affectation.

"TALKING DOWN"

Another offensive conversational habit is "talking down" to someone younger or who has (in your opinion) less intelligence or education than you have. This is a practice that often begins in families when the children are infants. If you believe that your children will learn to speak more quickly if you indulge in "baby talk," you are quite wrong. A child learns to speak by imitating the sounds he hears. If he hears his parents mispronounce the words he is struggling to learn because they think it is "cute," he will offer them back in the same fashion. Even when a child tries to imitate correctly spoken English, but still cannot quite do it, the surest way to help him is to speak clear, simple English. By all means, keep your vocabulary simple when talking to children whose own is still very limited. But the tone of your voice, your syntax, and your pronunciation should be the same as you would use if you were talking to a Ph.D.

Some writers and speakers, in addressing adolescents, adopt what is in effect a sort of glorified "baby talk" The person who opens a message to young people with: "Now, boys and girls, let's all sit down in a circle with our Cokes and have a heart-to-heart talk" will probably be greeted with a mixture of giggles and sneers, or at best a stony silence. He will be getting what he deserves

Be very careful about carrying with you an air of superiority as you engage in conversation. If you feel it, you probably will display it, even though you don't intend to. This haughtiness often crops up in conversations with those who have had less education or cultural advantages than the speaker. Such statements as, "You probably aren't aware of this, but . . . ," or "You obviously don't understand, so I'll explain this to you," will serve only to build a barrier of antagonism between you and your listener If there is a special technical vocabulary that applies to your work and is not a part of common speech, avoid it when talking with those who cannot be expected to be familiar with it If your listener asks you to explain something you have said, do so graciously and as a matter of course. But do not "talk down" to anyone of any age or position.

GIVE YOUNG AUDIENCES CUES

I find that in talking to young university and high school groups it is useful to bear in mind that with added years one remembers and uses quite naturally illustrations that may mean nothing to one's more youthful audience unless they are explained. For instance, the depression years and the years of World War II seem to me almost contemporary, but the young student was not born in the days of the depression and is too young to remember much about World War II, so I give some illustration of what the depression years really meant. Otherwise my audience would not understand the points I am trying to explain to them.

BE CONSIDERATE ABOUT LEAVING

It is well to remember that in almost any group the younger people will hesitate to leave before the guest of honor, particularly if the guest of honor is older. If you are a guest of honor you will do the rest of the company a favor by departing at a timely hour. They can then leave or stay longer if they wish without feeling that they are rude.

SOME IMPORTANT DON'T'S

Don't be noisy in your conversation, even when you are enthusiastic. Keep your voice down to a level at which your listeners can understand you, but which will not attract the undue attention of other persons in the room.

Don't give an opinion or repeat the witty saying of another person without giving the source. There is an anecdote about James McNeill Whistler and Oscar Wilde. While having lunch with a friend, they were amused by something the friend quoted. "I wish I'd said that," Wilde remarked. "You will, Oscar, you will," replied Whistler. By all means, if it is worth repeating, repeat it. But mention who said it first.

Don't, if you are a man, call a woman whom you have just met by her first name. Wait until she suggests it. If she does not, then she should remain "Miss" or "Mrs." to you.

Don't correct another person's grammar or pronunciation in public. Even in a completely private conversation this is just not considerate unless the person happens to be your young child or student. If you have occasion later to use the word you think has been mispronounced or the same phrase which your companion has butchered, use it correctly, of course. But don't go out of your way in order to give a special example or set yourself up as an authority. For one thing, you may be very surprised to find that you have not been correct after all

Don't be so eager to offer compliments that it will make them meaningless. If others compliment you, do not adopt a mock modesty and say that you don't deserve them (in a not-so-subtle effort to hear them again!). Simply say "thank you" graciously and let it pass.

Don't chatter about "nothing" just to keep talking

Don't pretend to know more than you do. If you are asked whether you have read a book on the Best Seller List which you have not, simply say "no" without an apology or explanation. If you are asked a question and you don't know the answer, say so.

Don't end a conversation on an unpleasant note, if you can avoid it. Keep discordancy out of conversation if you can. If, in spite of your efforts, a conversation should become difficult, try to resolve it with at least a few moments of pleasantness before you leave your companion. St. Paul wrote wisely to the Ephesians, "Let not the sun go down upon your wrath."

Don't whisper or indulge in private asides at a social gathering Also, don't engage in extended conversations about personal matters with one person when there are others in your conversational group If you are "caught" in a threesome in which the other two have some personal matter that is engaging them, excuse yourself graciously and simply turn away. Don't eavesdrop on others.

SAYING GOOD-BY

❧ When it is time to leave your friends, do so graciously, courteously and simply. The simplest way is to say, "Good-by." "Good afternoon" or "Good evening" are quite proper though a little more formal. "Good night" is simple and adequate if you are leaving an evening gathering. Once you have signified your intention to leave and are on your feet, shake hands with your host and your hostess (if she offers her hand) and thank them. If there is a large group of people still present you may offer a general good-by to the group and then go. Do not keep the men who have courteously risen when you rose standing while you make a long, drawn-out departure.

Unless you are a close personal friend of the host and hostess, it is never wise to be the last to leave a party. Try to be sensitive to the moment when the party is drawing to a close. Don't light up another cigarette or ask for another drink and settle yourself in comfortably when it is obvious that most of the guests are about ready to depart

31

The Telephone

AMERICANS ARE THE GREATEST TELEPHONE USERS ON earth. In Europe, there is only one telephone for every twenty-eight people. In the United States, there are approximately two phones for every five. Consider the fact that almost every phone serves more than one person and it becomes obvious that, with very few exceptions, any resident of the United States may speak to any other regardless of the distances between.

Because of the demands of business and the ever-quickening pace of modern life, more and more telephone calls are taking the place of personal meetings, letters, and telegrams. In a very real sense, a telephone call is a meeting between you and another person. So, all the basic rules of courtesy should apply to telephone calls. But since neither party to a telephone call is visible to the other, there are some special rules of etiquette which take this into account.

There should be no difference in the basics of courteous usage in either social or business calls. But there are special circumstances which attend each. First, some general rules which are applicable to both.

Answer Your Phone Promptly

When your phone rings, answer it as promptly as possible. No one likes to be kept waiting. If you are reading a book, it is not necessary to finish the paragraph before you pick up the phone. The book will wait. If you have just put food on the stove, halt your cooking when the phone rings rather than risk having to interrupt your conversation later on. If you are in your office, dictating to your secretary, or discussing a business matter with someone, ask to be excused and obey the summons of the phone. In short, try always to answer your phone as soon as it has begun to ring.

Telephone Speech

When you pick up the telephone, hold the transmitter about an inch from your mouth and speak directly into it. Over the telephone your voice is carried by rapidly changing electrical currents that are controlled and changed by the way you talk. The sound of your voice will be either distorted or made unintelligible if you hold the instrument at too great a distance or if you do not face it directly.

Be careful to enunciate clearly and do not speak too rapidly. Avoid evasions such as *er* and *uh* and say "yes" and "no" rather than *uh-huh* and *unh-unh,* which are difficult to distinguish by sound alone. Remember that the listener cannot see you nod or shake your head, cannot see your facial expressions or gestures which might clearly convey your meaning in a face-to-face encounter. Your voice alone must make your meaning clear.

If it is difficult for you to hear because of background noises at your end, cover the transmitter with your hand while listening. Be sure, of course, to remove it when speaking. The noises at your end as well as the voice at the other end reach your ear through the receiver. By shutting them out of the transmitter you will also shut them out of the ear at which your receiver is placed. If your difficulty in hearing is because you have a hearing loss, you may want to ask the telephone company to install an instrument to compensate for this.

If the person to whom you are talking has difficulty in hearing you because of noises at your end of the call, cup your hands around your mouthpiece while you are talking. This will help to concentrate the sound of your voice and shut out background interference.

If you have a radio or television set on, turn down the volume so it does not intrude on the conversation If there are others present and you do not have an extension phone in another room, then you may ask to have TV or radio sound lowered

While you are on the telephone, you owe your caller the courtesy of your full attention Even if you are not completely fascinated by what your caller has to tell you, don't read a magazine or book during a conversation or continue watching a TV program or engage in side conversations. Nothing is quite as confusing to the person on the other end of the line as being aware that you are giving him only part of your attention and that you are otherwise diverted by something of which he has no knowledge.

The more clearly you speak, the more chance that you will have a pleasant phone call that will be free of misinterpretations and misunderstandings. Speak clearly in a well modulated, natural voice. Whispering or shouting are annoying to the listener and make it more difficult for you to be understood. If it is your habit in conversation to speak rapidly, try to slow down. "What did you do?" and "going to" can easily become "wadjado" and "gonna" when the rapid speaker says them over the telephone.

In spelling out a name on the phone you may resort to the excellent device of saying "A as in Alice," and so on. Make sure that the words you use are clear and familiar to your listener. "A as in aardvark" and "L as in llama" may be funny to you and your closest friends, but are not recommended for general use. The New York Telephone Company recommends the following.

A as in Alice	N as in Nellie
B as in Bertha	O as in Oliver
C as in Charles	P as in Peter
D as in David	Q as in Quaker
E as in Edward	R as in Robert
F as in Frank	S as in Samuel
G as in George	T as in Thomas
H as in Henry	U as in Utah
I as in Ida	V as in Victor
J as in James	W as in William
K as in Kate	X as in X-Ray
L as in Lewis	Y as in Young
M as in Mary	Z as in Zebra

There is nothing sacrosanct about this list and any number of other words would do quite well. Just make sure that the ones you use are clear and easily recognized by everyone.

Wrong Number

If someone calls you and wants some other number, don't shout into the phone "Wrong number" and hang up. Also, asking "What number do you want?" in an angry voice is not pleasant or efficient. Usually a caller's first remarks will show that he has the wrong number, and you have only to say, "I'm sorry, but you have the wrong number." If you want to make it definite, then tell the caller what your number is, though this is not necessary. If you are the caller and get a wrong number, say that you are sorry to the person that answers without giving him the impression that you think he is to blame. Asking angrily, "What number is this?" is rude and futile. If you repeatedly receive or make a wrong number call, it is wise to get the operator on the telephone and ask her to help you straighten out the problem.

Consider the Person You Are Calling

If you are making a business or a personal phone call and are planning to speak at some length, it is courteous to ask at once whether you have called at a convenient time. If you ask, "Have you a few minutes to talk?" and the person you have called tells you that he is just rushing out to keep an appointment or that the family is about to sit down to dinner, don't say you'll only be a minute and then go on for ten. Rather tell him that you will call him later when he is free, then you say the first "good-by" and prepare to hang up. Since you are the caller, the other person will not, if he is courteous, end the conversation. He will wait for you to do so. If you do not do it quickly, you will have taken unfair advantage of him.

Saying "Good-by"

Say "Good-by" clearly and pleasantly when the conversation is over and make certain that the other person understands before you hang up. A casual "Okay" and the click that indicates your receiver has been put in its cradle may serve to cut someone off in mid-flight. Many annoyances have been created by someone hanging up without first making it clear to the other person on the telephone.

If You Are Cut Off

If you are the caller and you are cut off, hang up briefly, then try the call again. If you are talking long distance, signal the operator, explain what has happened and ask her to help you re-establish the call. If you have been called and a cut-off takes place, hang up at once and wait. If you keep your phone off its cradle and futilely say, "Hello, hello," your caller will only get a busy signal when trying to reestablish the call.

Identify Yourself

When you call someone, whether in business or socially, identify yourself as soon as you are answered, unless you are absolutely certain the person you are calling is quite familiar with your voice. Do not count on everyone to recognize you just from your "Hello." And do not be offended if a friend fails to recognize your voice immediately. "Guess who this is," or some similar phrase is not cute or funny. It is just plain rude.

Practical Jokes by Telephone

It is probably not necessary for me to mention this, but I have heard too many stories about practical jokes in which perfectly innocent people have been annoyed or harassed by others whose warped sense of humor compels them to waste people's time in this very unfunny pursuit. Most of us are, I am sure, familiar with the various "standard" telephone practical jokes and, indeed, there are some rather elaborate ones. People are rarely entertained by this sort of thing and most often the only results are frustration and a perfectly justifiable fury. Don't waste time and money by indulging in this sort of childish behavior.

The Telephone Operator

I doubt that there is a more consistently courteous group in America than telephone operators. The courteous phone user should be equally gracious to them. Use your directory if you are not sure of a number. Don't take a chance by dialing a number you are not certain is right. You may disturb someone by ringing a wrong number and waste your time and money. If you must call information or talk with an operator about a long-distance call or some difficulty you are having, remember that "please" and "thank you" are the three most important words you can use.

Operators are human and sometimes make mistakes The highly efficient and tremendously complex electronic system of the modern telephone sometimes makes a mistake too. Do not blame the operator personally for every difficulty you encounter. If you are cut off on a long-distance call, or you find it impossible to hear your party, signal the operator, explain courteously what is happening and thank her when she volunteers to help you. If you have ever had occasion to use the telephone a great deal, particularly in making long-distance calls, you will know how resourceful and persistent the telephone company personnel can be in serving you. If you should find an operator especially helpful and ingenious in connecting you with someone who is difficult to reach or in serving you in an emergency, you may demonstrate your gratitude and goodwill in a rather special way by writing the telephone company a note, telling them the story and mentioning the date and time you called and the number from which you called In this way the operator who helped you can be identified Such letters are prized by the ladies about whom they are written and have a very real influence on their standing with the company.

SOCIAL CALLS

Answering Your Phone

In spite of the Telephone Company's insistence that the proper way to answer a telephone is to speak your name, I feel that it is a little pompous when you are answering the telephone in your own home. "Hello," or even a questioning "Yes?" spoken in a pleasant and friendly way seems to me to be preferable.

If you have a maid who will be answering your phone, she should use your name. "Mrs. Smith's apartment" or "Mrs. Smith's house" will do very nicely. "Mrs. Smith's residence," which used to be considered proper usage, now seems a bit florid and fortunately has been abandoned along with a good deal of empty elegance in conversational speech and writing.

If a caller asks to speak with you, the maid should say, "May I give her your name, please?" (The form, "May I ask who's calling?" is actually unrealistic. Of course the maid may *ask*. The question really means, "Are you willing to have me give your name?")

If you are at home and in a position to take your own telephone calls, it will be especially gracious if you do so. This is impractical for some people who, because of their prominence or because of special demands, are harassed by more phone calls than they can possibly manage to take without serious encroachment on their time. But if you are not in this category, and most people are not, then it is gracious to talk with anyone who calls you.

In any case, the maid should be instructed to inform callers that you are out—when you are—*before* asking for the name of the caller. This will avoid the impression that you are "out" only to the person who has made the call. However, if you are the frequent victim of unwelcome calls, then you may instruct the maid to say, "I'll see if Mrs. Smith is in. May I tell her who is calling?"

Telephone Visiting

We all phone friends to visit with them, to learn their news and to tell them ours. It is inconsiderate, however, to allow such a conversation to consume too much time. You would not ordinarily drop in on a friend unannounced and stay for an hour or more. For the same reason you should not "drop in" by phone for a chat that may keep your friend from something which he or she has planned to do. Such lengthy chats will also prevent others from completing a phone call to either of you.

Children and the Telephone

Some people think that it is "cute" to allow their very young children to answer the telephone and engage in long, sometimes monotonous and frequently unintelligible speeches. It may amuse the proud parents, but it seldom does the person calling. If the caller is a relative or close friend who asks to speak to your offspring, call the child to the phone and let him say a few words. But until a child is old enough to use the instrument properly do not assign him the task of picking up the phone when it rings.

Teenagers and the Phone

There are many thoroughly frustrated and resigned parents who feel that their teenagers "live by phone." The teenage phone call is a living legend and the teenager who regularly monopolizes the family phone is the source of much humor. But, in actual fact, it is not at all funny. Allowing the teenagers in your house to engage in frequent and interminable phone conversations is to encourage them in a lack of consideration for others. Teach them to keep their phone calls short and insist that they do not use the phone just as a means of filling spare time or because they are looking for something to do. This is particularly important if you are on a party line.

Using Another Person's Phone

If you are obliged to use a neighbor's phone for a long-distance call, or place a toll call from a house in which you are a guest, always ask the operator to report the charges to you at the end of your call so that you may offer to pay for it. This is not necessary if you make a local call.

The Party Line

If you are on a party line, you are sharing it with probably no less than three other persons and possibly as many as ten. While you are using your phone, no one else on the line is able to make or receive calls. Unnecessarily frequent or long conversations are both discourteous and unfair.

If you have a number of calls to make, allow time between them so that someone else on the line may make or receive a call. If you find the phone in use when you wish to make a call, quietly replace the receiver at once and wait three minutes before you try again An emergency provides an exception to this rule. In case of one, you may quite properly interrupt by saying, "I am sorry, but this is an emergency. May I have the line, please?" Do not shout "Get off the line." Make your request courteously. If anyone ever makes the same request of you, comply with it instantly and graciously. Most states have a law requiring you to do so. But your common sense should compel you to yield without the need of this pressure.

Do not be a telephone eavesdropper. Listening in on a party line is like peeking through a keyhole In the case of a party line, the rudeness is compounded by the fact that when two or more phones on a line are off the hook, the audibility of the conversation is diminished.

If you should be plagued by others on the line listening in, you might be guided by a story told by a farmer who was on an old-fashioned, ten-party line on which each phone had its own ring. All the phones rang when any one of them was called. Those who shared the line with this man made a practice of listening in to his calls. One day he answered a long-distance call that concerned important business. As he talked he heard one click after the other, each one announcing that another neighbor had begun to listen. With each click, it became harder and harder for the farmer to hear

Finally he said, "Excuse me a minute, Bill, while I try to get rid of some obstructions." Then, speaking to the eavesdroppers, he said, "Neighbors, this is an important business call and I doubt that you can hear any better than I can with all your receivers off their hooks. If you will hang up now, I shall call you back when we have finished talking and tell you exactly what was said."

Immediately there was a series of clicks which told him that his neighbors had complied with his request. When his business con versation had ended, he kept his promise, calling each of the others on the line. All of them either apologized or tried to deny that they had been listening. But he never had any trouble with "listening in" after that.

One other thing to remember if you are on a party line. be sure to hang up correctly when you have finished a call. If you do not and your receiver is off its hook so that you have not really disconnected, no one on your line will be able to use the phone.

(For further tips on telephone procedure see Chapter 6, "The Family Entertains," Chapter 7, "Living Alone and Sharing," Chapter 9, "Getting Acquainted," Chapter 10, "The Family Is Entertained," and Chapter 27, "From Thirteen to Nineteen.")

BUSINESS

Answering

The main phone at a place of business is properly answered by giving the name by which the business is known to the public. "Good morning," or "good afternoon," spoken after the identifying name, adds a note of warmth.

A Prompt Answer Turneth Away Wrath

The phone should always be answered promptly, for a slow answer may turn away business. If your place of business has a switchboard, the operator should not merely plug in an incoming call without speaking when she is busy on another call. The ringing stops as soon as the new call is plugged in, and if the caller hears no voice answer him at this point, he may believe that he has been cut off and hang up If the operator is unable to handle the call at once, she should plug in and say, "Will you excuse me a moment, please?" and then take care of the call she was dealing with When she comes back to the person who was asked to wait in this fashion, she should then use the identifying greeting and apologize for keeping the caller waiting

The switchboard operator should always make it clear to the caller that she has understood his request by a reply that confirms it: "I'll connect you with the Production Department," or "I'll ring Mr. Smith's office."

If There Is a Delay

If the extension which the caller wishes is busy, the operator will say, "I am sorry. Mr. Smith's line is busy Would you care to wait or shall I ask Mr. Smith to call you back?" A good operator will always have a message pad and pencil handy so that she can take a message or jot down a number without causing any delay. If the caller elects to wait and the wait is a long one, the good operator will come back on the line every half minute or so to say, "I'm sorry, Mr. Smith's line is still busy." When the line is free she should say to the caller, "You may have Mr. Smith now," or "I'm ringing Mr. Smith. Thank you for waiting."

Answering an Extension

An extension in a business office should be answered by identifying the department or the executive whose office has been called, and then giving your name. For example "Production Department, Raymond Wheaton," or "Mr. Smith's office, Miss Dillon " To add "speaking" after this is not necessary.

Transferring a Call

Calls should be transferred only when it is necessary and desirable, not as a means of "getting rid" of a call. The caller should always understand why the call is being transferred. If the person in the Production Department says, "I'm afraid that we do not have that information in this department, but the Sales Department does.

May I transfer you?" then the caller will feel he has been treated fairly and courteously.

When you transfer a call, the projections on the phone's cradle should be moved up and down slowly. If it is done too rapidly, the switchboard operator may not see the signal. Once you get the operator on the line and you have the name of the caller, use it "Will you transfer Mr. Jones to the Sales Department, please?" And be sure to wait for the operator's acknowledgment before you hang up.

In any case, try to be helpful when speaking to someone on your business telephone and remember to be courteous no matter how busy you are. You would not want a prospective customer to be irritated or put off, and there is never an excuse for lack of courtesy.

Leaving the Line

If it is necessary to leave the line during a conversation, tell the caller courteously and ask him if he wishes to wait or to have you call back Don't just abruptly say, "Wait a minute" and leave the other person hanging on for five minutes. If he elects to wait and you find that it will take you longer than you anticipated to find what you are looking for, then be sure that the caller is informed. Never let anyone dangle so long that he begins to wonder whether you've forgotten about him.

When a Secretary Answers

When a secretary screens the calls of her employer she should exercise the greatest tact If the executive will accept calls, but wants to know the caller's name before being connected, the secretary should say "May I tell him who's calling, please?" She should avoid such abrupt forms as "What's your name?"

If the executive has told her that he will be available only to certain persons and others call, she should say. "I am sorry, but Mr. Brown is unavailable just now. May I tell him who called?"

If the secretary is in doubt, she might say, "Mr. Brown is not in his office right now, but I'll see whether I can locate him. May I tell him who called?" To say that he is unavailable after she has asked for the caller's name may give the impression that he is there but does not wish to speak to the caller

If a call comes in from another secretary who is placing it for her boss, the wise secretary will get the name of the caller and pass it on to her boss who, if he wishes to take the call, will pick up the phone at once. One of the most futile and time-wasting arguments is that between two secretaries jockeying to see which of their bosses will come on the phone first.

If the executive is actually out of the office or does not wish to speak with the caller, the secretary will (unless she has other instructions) ask the caller if she can be of help. Asking the caller to phone later without first offering to help is rude.

Placing Calls

The most courteous executive will place his own calls and be ready to speak to those he has called as soon as they come on the line. However, I am sure it would be unrealistic to expect all executives to do this under all circumstances. Indeed, there are many good reasons why this is sometimes impractical.

When a secretary is asked to place a call, she will tell the person being called (or his secretary) the name of the company and the name of her boss and *put him on at once*. The executive who asks his secretary to place a call for him and then keeps the person called waiting is being rude. Perhaps the worst offense an executive can be guilty of in phoning is to place a call and then leave his office so that when the person called is on the phone his secretary is forced to say, "I'm sorry, but Mr. Brown has left his office, he will call you later."

And Finally

Whether it is a business or a social call, always try to remember that courtesy is imperative. Some people vent their frustrations on perfectly innocent people with whom they have phone contact in the mistaken belief that if you are not really in a person's presence, rude behavior is somehow excusable—or that you will never be called to account for it to a stranger on the telephone whom you will probably never meet. I must stress that this is an immature and unkind attitude. Telling someone "off" on the phone can never be justified and we should all be on guard about being rude on the telephone because "it doesn't matter," or "it's not important." It is always important.

32

Correspondence

To her I very much respect —Mrs. Margaret Clark. —Lovely, and oh¹ that I could write loving, Mrs. Margaret Clark, I pray you let affection excuse presumption. Having been so happy as to enjoy the sight of your sweet countenance and comely body sometimes, when I had occasion to buy treacle or liquorish powder at the apothecary's shop, I am so enamored with you, that I can no more keep close my flaming desire to become your servant. And I am the more bold now to write to your sweet self, because I am now my own man, and may match where I please, for my father is taken away, and now I am come into my living, which is ten yard land and a house, and there is never a yard of land in our field but is as well worth ten pounds a year as a thief is worth a halter, and all my brothers and sisters are provided for. Besides I have good household stuff, though I say it, both brass and pewter, and though my house be thatched, yet if you and I match it shall go hard but I will have one half of it slated. If you think well of this notion I shall wait upon you as soon as my new clothes is made and hay harvest is in. I could, though I say it, have good matches amongst my neighbors. Your loving servant till death,

Mr. Gabriel Bullock

THIS ELEGANT EXAMPLE OF EPISTOLOGRAPHY WILL PROBably sound comic to the modern ear or even seem a warning on how not to write a love letter. But in point of fact it is cited in the volume where it appears* as a model of correct usage. If we are to believe the editor of the work published in Philadelphia in 1875 and probably imported from England, the letter "conveys a simplicity of affection preferable to the studied effusions of vanity."

This is not so ridiculous as it sounds. Disregarding its curious formality of language of a hundred years ago, the letter is perfect in a number of ways. It does not mention the weather, it does not describe the state of Mr. Bullock's health; and it tells Mrs. Clark, as every good letter should, the compelling reason why it was written. Mr. Bullock desires Mrs. Clark ardently, his proposal is honorable; he is a man of substance And best of all, it is not a "studied effusion." Mr. Bullock's lines fairly glow with the ardor of his passion. I would like to know what Mrs. Clark replied. I hope that it was the answer Mr. Bullock wanted and that after twenty years of marriage he still loved the one whom he had called "her whom I very much respect."

Though the complicated title of *Etiquette Letter Writer* points out that the preferred style is "plain and elegant," most of the letters in the book place their emphasis on "elegance." In the nineteenth century the plain and rugged speech and writing of the seventeenth and eighteenth centuries had gradually been supplanted by a tendency to flowery ornamentation of language. Americans were beginning to fear the charge of ignorance and uncouthness more than that of affectation.

A few quotations from the Preface and Introduction to the *Etiquette Letter Writer* illustrate the tendency:

For the express purpose of instructing the youthful and uninformed mind in the art of easy correspondence, we have added a few brief and indispensable rules, which if attended to, will place the epistolary writer in a respectable view.

---

* *Etiquette Letter Writer; Being the Complete Art of Fashionable Correspondence. Composed in a Plain and Elegant Style. Containing Business Letters, Juvenile and Parental Letters, Youth to Maturity, Love, Courtship and Marriage, Friendship, and Consolation, Relationship, Etc. Etc. With All Other Matter Befitting Such a Useful Work.* Anonymous. Philadelphia, J B. Lippincott and Co , 1875

To give weight and respectability to our epistolary production four things are indispensably necessary, viz. Orthography, Grammar, Style, and Punctuation.

False grammar, either in writing or speaking, throws a strong sarcasm on the education of the defaulter.

Vulgarism in language or writing is a certain characteristic of bad company, a bad education, or being little read in good authors. . . . An attentive writer would not say, "It was all through you it happened," but "It happened from your inattention!"

In short, to acquire a genteel style, little more is necessary than to follow nature and ease, to use the most polished and best turned sentiments the subject admits of, to avoid pedantry, affectation, and the adoption of phrases in common use with the *beau monde,* on the one hand, and vulgarity, cant words, and want of orthographical or grammatical accuracy, on the other.

Though that was good advice then and is good advice now, the sentences quoted above and many others in *Etiquette Letter Writer* could well be given to a student of English today with the request that he rewrite them in plain English with an economical use of words, as an exercise in composition. Every teacher would agree with the necessity (though a good teacher would not call anything "indispensably necessary") of "orthographical and grammatical accuracy," though he would probably call it "correct spelling and grammar." "Epistolary production" would be called "letter writing," and instead of urging his students to acquire a "genteel style" he would try to show them how to develop a "good style."

Even today, when "elegance and gentility" are little stressed and when, quite rightly, we use letters as a means of communication in order to say something more intimate or more permanent than can be said by speech or telegram, many of us tend to consider the proper forms of address, the shape, color, and quality of the paper we use, and the width of margins as more important than they really are.

Etiquette Letter Writer cautions: "The straightness of your lines ought to be strictly attended to, and if you rule lines with a lead pencil take care to efface them before your letter is sent away." Today no one, except perhaps a child, would think of ruling lines on his note paper before writing a letter. But perhaps what more of us, who write our letters in longhand, should think of is the legibility of our handwriting Fortunately for many of us there is a way out in the typewriter (discussed on p. 530).

During the three-quarters of a century since *Etiquette Letter*

Writer was published, emphasis has shifted from form to content. There are still conventions as to physical form which, if followed, add grace and dignity to both personal and business correspondence. But they are more flexible than they once were and of less importance than what a letter says and how it says it.

INFORMAL PERSONAL LETTERS

In a man's letters, you know Madam, [wrote the great Doctor Johnson] his soul lies naked, his letters are only the mirror of his heart. Whatever passes within him is shown undisguised in its natural process nothing is inverted, nothing distorted you see systems in their elements you discover actions in their motives.

Of this great truth, sounded by the knowing to the ignorant, so echoed by the ignorant to the knowing, what evidence have you now before you? Is not my soul laid open in these veracious pages? Do you not see me reduced to my first principles? Is not this the pleasure of corresponding to a friend, where doubt and distrust have no place, and everything is said as it is thought?*

Doctor Johnson was commenting here on correspondence at its best. The kind of letter which he had in mind would be read avidly by the friend to whom it was addressed even if written in pencil on wrapping paper, with uneven margins, and with afterthoughts scribbled along the edges and between the lines. The graces prescribed by convention, here missing, would be of only minor importance. A letter which showed that the writer had followed meticulously all the formal rules of etiquette, but had little or nothing to say, would receive a cool welcome by comparison.

A letter, written and read, is at its best a meeting of two personalities. Even more than a telephone conversation (in which the voice supplements the message) letters depend entirely on words, their proper use, their simplicity and clarity, and their grace. Plain talk, the mark of good conversation, is even more highly desirable in letter writing than in speech, for when one talks with another the listener's questions, in words or looks, may bring about clarification and understanding, in a letter the words remain as written, and if unclear can be explained (if ever) only by further correspondence.

* Samuel Johnson to Mrs Thrale, October 27, 1777 Cited in *A Treasury of the World's Great Letters*, selected and edited by M Lincoln Schuster. New York, Simon and Schuster, 1940. Paper-covered ed., 1960

How many hours of human life have been wasted by such a sequence as this A has written a letter which offends B. B writes back angrily, or humbly apologetic. A replies, "When I wrote such and such I did not mean . . . but intended to say . . . ." If only he had said it in the first place, and said it so lucidly that there could have been no misunderstanding! And then perhaps it is necessary for B to write again, explaining certain obscurities in his first letter that have caused A to take it too seriously!

The ideal letter reflects the personality of the writer; it is, if you like, a gift of that personality to the one to whom it is written, with restraint or unreservedly as the relationship warrants. It may or may not contain news in the ordinary sense, but if it does, what the writer has to say is colored and made vital by his mind and emotions, and so adds revelation and a warm sense of companionship to what might be mere fact-giving.

We hear often today of the "lost" art of letter writing It is true that the accelerated tempo of contemporary life, the almost universal spread of news by the daily and weekly press, the radio, television, the convenience of the telephone and telegraph have all tended to make personal letters less frequent, less contemplative, and shorter than they once were. Yet among thoughtful, articulate people who love the potential beauties of the written word, letters still achieve a unique and permanent quality that makes their receiver treasure them.

Here are four examples that illustrate my meaning. Two of them are imaginary paraphrases, two are extracts from actual letters

The first, had it been written merely as factual narration, might have said

"The temperature was so pleasant and the moonlight so bright that I took a walk in the woods and spent most of the night there, thinking of how wholesome the people around here are, especially Pauline, and of you and the children, and Harry, and the lectures which I am to give at Edinburgh It was one of the most lonesome nights I have ever known, but a happy one, and I am sure that the lectures I am planning will benefit from it."

Here is what was actually written:

The temperature was perfect either inside or outside the cabin, the moon rose and hung above the scene before midnight, leaving only a few of the larger stars visible, and I got into a state of spiritual alertness of the most vital description. The influences of nature, the wholesomeness of

the people round me, especially the good Pauline, the thought of you
and the children, dear Harry on the wave, the problem of the Edinburgh
lectures, all fermented within me till it became a regular Walpurgis
Nacht. I spent a good deal of it in the woods, where the streaming moonlight lit up things in a magical checkered play, and it seemed as if the
gods of all the nature-mythologies were holding an indescribable meeting
in my breast with the moral gods of the inner life. The two kinds of gods
have nothing in common—the Edinburgh lectures made quite a hitch
ahead The intense significance of some sort, of the whole scene, if only
one could *tell* the significance, the intense inhuman remoteness of its
inner life, and yet the intense *appeal* of it; its everlasting freshness and its
immemorial antiquity and decay, its utter Americanism, and every sort of
patriotic suggestiveness, and you, and my relation to you part and parcel
of it all, and beaten up with it, so that memory and sensation all whirled
inexplicably together, it was indeed worth coming for, and worth repeating year by year, if repetition could only procure what in its nature I
suppose must all be unplanned for and unexpected. It was one of the
happiest lonesome nights of my existence, and I understand now what
a poet is He is a person who can feel the immense complexity of influences that I felt, and made partial tracks in them for verbal statement
In point of fact I can't find a single word for all that significance, and
don't know what it was significant of, so there it remains, a mere boulder
of *impression*. Doubtless in more ways than one, though, things in the
Edinburgh lectures will be traceable to it.

Here is an extract from another letter, also about a walk. First
a paraphrase of how it might have been written so as to tell the
mere objective facts which the writer wanted to convey:

"Today all three of us went for a walk in the country. It was a
windy fall day. After we had crossed a wide field we saw the cleared
expanse of a part of the prairie which is to be the site of the largest
artificial lake in the country. For three hours we walked toward a
little mountain we could barely see, a bit of the Appalachians. A dog
joined us and stayed with us all afternoon. There was a fine sunset
We stopped at a grocery and bought Mint Colas for ourselves and
a can of sausages for the dog, then walked home at night."

This is what was actually written.

Today all three of us went, and discovered something wondrous. It
is early fall weather here, and the cold was all day blowing in—the sort
of wind you imagine the earth *should* make whirling through space was
blowing in big waves and sheets all through us, and we stumbled through
what seemed to be just a wide field, only to see a tremendous stretch of
rolling horizon—the prairie, I swear to God, the whole searingly vast

prairie seemed to be there. It is actually the cleared and blasted land for what's going to be the largest artificial lake in the country, and it goes on and on like Scottish moorlands, with sometimes little hillocks and pine groves and fields,—way off is an out-of-the-way little ghost of a mountain that we could barely see—the toe of the foothills of the Appalachians, and we walked west toward it for three hours, with a new friend—a hound from some shack we'd been past, a nervously hungry, meltingly friendly old pooch, dirty and gray and white-spotted, with brown ears, and cracked old collar, thin and silent, licking our hands and following us all afternoon, until I finally had to leave him whimpering at the door of the dorms a few hours ago. We just kept walking, sometimes the land would rise up razor-sharp and seemingly naked to cut into the sky and I could feel what it was that made men move over continents. It was a great fall sunset, seen over the hills toward the mountains you can look toward and sense without really seeing—the red-orange hole in the sky through which you imagine you can see the furnace that runs the universe and its fiery bowels. We stopped at a grocery where the machines have all the weird and delightful soft-drink flavors the city stores never touch and I had a Mint Cola—first one in my whole life It was good. And we bought a can of Vienna sausages for the pooch, which he ate starvingly and licked the juice up and cried for more. Then walked home at night, two miles on the country highway to the college, and contemplated another small walk for a beer, but everyone was sated of walking by then. It was great.

The first letter is from William James to his wife written on July 9, 1898 and published in *The Letters of William James,* edited by his son, Henry James (Boston, Atlantic Monthly Press, 1920). "The Edinburgh Lectures" became that magnificent book, *The Varieties of Religious Experience.* The second is part of an unpublished letter from William R. Trotter to Robert O. Ballou, October 21, 1961.

The first letter was written over sixty years ago by a scholarly philosopher then in his fifty-seventh year, the second in 1961 by an eighteen-year-old college student. Yet it would not be at all difficult to imagine that both had been written by the same hand, for both communicate not merely the bare facts which I have included honestly in my paraphrases, but the exaltation stimulated by the facts. Each is an outpouring of the spirit of the writer to (in the case of James to his wife) a friend—one of the most precious gifts possible from one human being to another.

To be sure these letters are from two exceptionally articulate human beings. Most of us cannot write as well as this. But the element that gives their letters life, that raises them above mere reporting of the facts and belies the statement that "the art of letter writing has been lost" is the ability and willingness of each to give of himself, to reveal his inner life to another, rather than the literary ability both display.

This we can all do in a measure—not by merely writing about ourselves and our news, but by putting ourselves into our letters. None of the new means of communication, not even the telephone, could deliver to the receivers of these letters as they do the gift of a whole personality wrapped up in four sheets of plain note paper.

Typewriter or Pen?

Not very many years ago, when a typewritten letter was evidence that it had been dictated to a stenographer, the use of a typewriter for personal correspondence was considered bad form. Today with the number of amateur typists increasing and the legibility of handwriting accordingly decreasing, the typewritten letter not merely is accepted in personal correspondence, but is preferred to a handwritten one that is difficult to read, especially if it is long.

There are a few exceptions to this rule. Generally speaking, it is not considered good form to typewrite an invitation, an acceptance or regret, a letter of condolence, or a formal social note, but whether you observe these exceptions rigidly will depend somewhat upon your relationship to your correspondent, and what you have to say. Certainly there can be no possible offense today in typing a note to your good friend Mary, asking her and her husband John to have dinner with you and your husband, or in answering a similar invitation from Mary and John, or in typing a letter of sympathy and comfort to a dear friend who has lost a loved one. In the latter case especially, what you say and the sincerity of your words are far more important than the instrument which you use to get them onto paper.

There is one thing to remember, however, if you use a typewriter in personal correspondence. (It is equally important of course in business usage.) You would not send a friend a handwritten letter covered with blots and spatters of ink No more would you send him a typewritten one transcribed on a machine so dirty that the spaces in the letters were filled, and marks along the margins showed where the dirty rubber rollers which hold the paper against the platen have passed over them. Keep your typewriter clean. Type as carefully as you can. A good clean erasure is better than x-ing out misspelled words and errors. But your friends do not expect you to be an expert typist (unless in fact they know that you are) and either method of obliterating mistakes is no grievous social sin. What you say and how you say it, rather than slight physical imperfections such as these will be the measure of your success as a letter writer.

How to Begin a Letter

The forms with which you may properly open a letter vary in accordance with your relationship to the one to whom you are writing.

If your correspondent is one whom you have never met, to whom you have never written, and who has never written to you, you will avoid the familiar forms of address that are reserved for old friends or those with whom you have an even closer relationship.

You may begin, if you like, with his name (and title if he has one) and his address in the upper left-hand corner, a line below the level on which the date is written at the upper right-hand corner, thus:

September 16, 1961

Mr. James G. Mason, President
Scholars University
417 Millahasee Street
Estaban
Nevada

Some correspondents stagger these lines, indenting each one a space to the right from the one preceding it, but it seems to me that keeping the left margin flush makes a better appearance. Still, in this, you may follow your own taste.

Or you may put his name and address at the end of the letter, just below the line of the signature, and at the extreme left. This, which is perhaps a little less formal, seems to me the better practice, since here it does not erect a barrier to the warmth or respect of your opening salutation. Or you may omit them entirely.

For intimate personal correspondence the name and address are always omitted. Your letter should begin with the salutation and end with your signature.

Your letter would then begin "My dear President Mason," (with a comma, a semicolon, or a colon following the name, in personal correspondence a comma is preferred). If Mr. Mason has no title you would begin "My dear Mr. Mason." "Dear Sir," or "My dear Sir," (or "Madam") are reserved for business letters, and even in them are more and more replaced by "My dear (or dear) Mr." and the name of the person to whom the letter is addressed.

If you are writing to someone you know slightly, or if you want to give an air of less formality and greater warmth when writing to a stranger, you may omit the "my" and write simply, "Dear President Mason" (Remember, however, that if your correspondent is English, living in England, and following English customs, the reverse is true. There "Dear Mr Mason" is the more formal address, and "My dear" the more intimate In fact, when writing to an Englishman called Mason whom you know intimately you would begin the letter, "My dear Mason ")

More intimate still is the letter that begins with no salutation, but inserts the name in the first sentence: "You are constantly in my thoughts, dear Mary, . . ."

Interestingly enough, in view of the outcome, this is the form that was used by both Robert Browning and Elizabeth Barrett in the first letters written in what has become one of the classic letter sequences of the English language. "I love your verses with all my heart, dear Miss Barrett,—and this is no off-hand complimentary letter that I shall write," Robert Browning wrote on January 10, 1845, in his first letter to the woman who later became his wife. And "I thank you, dear Mr. Browning, from the bottom of my heart," answered Miss Barrett, on the following day, in a letter that clearly invited further correspondence.

Then as if perhaps a little frightened by the revelation which seemed clear even in these first two letters, both reverted to more formal usage Browning's second letter begins, "Dear Miss Barrett," (not even "My dear Miss Barrett," which as I have explained, would have been the more intimate address in England) and her reply, "Dear Mr. Browning,". But on February 3, less than a month after the first letter, Elizabeth Barrett once more adopts the more intimate beginning "Why how could I hate to write to you, dear Mr. Browning?" But Browning responds "Dear Miss Barrett," and as if rebuked for her intimacy, her answer begins "Dear Mr Browning,". And then Browning capitulates and his next letter begins, "Real warm Spring, dear Miss Barrett, and the birds know it; and in Spring I shall see you, surely see you——"

By the time the spring arrived, even the "Miss Barrett" and "Mr. Browning" were usually omitted, as if too formal. Yet their relationship had not yet advanced to that intimacy which would make them feel free to use their given names, or terms of especial endearment, though Browning often ended his letters with some such sentiment as "God bless you, my dear friend," and sometimes "my dearest friend." And so for the most part they remained nameless in their correspondence, speaking fully and freely to each other without preliminaries, as they might never have done face to face (and perhaps in this fact is conveyed the special virtue of the letter).

This to me is the most interesting and significant fact about this famous correspondence that fills two volumes, though it continued for only a little less than two years. (After their marriage they were never separated and there were no more letters.) Though the letters increased in intimacy and in concern on the part of each for the personal welfare of the other, essentially from first to last their basic tone did not change. They were, from the beginning, and continued throughout, to be the meeting of two, vital, warm and sensitive personalities, each revealing itself to the other. This, even more than the love that increasingly is expressed in them, or the beauty of their style, is what has made them classic examples of letter writing and has preserved them as a part of our literary heritage.

The Opening Paragraph

There is an old saying, "Well begun is half done." It is as true of letter writing as it is of other occupations. The correspondent who sits for half an hour chewing the end of his pen, or staring blankly at the keys of his typewriter, trying to think what to say, or conversely, jots down at random the first thing that comes into his head should not be writing at all, for if he does, the poor result will show. My advice to you is: if you can't find a beginning that interests you wait until you *can* find one.

Yet the technique of beginning a letter well is very simple. Don't try too hard, but on the other hand, before beginning, run over in your own mind the two or three things you really want to say. Then plunge into your letter as you would into a conversation over the lunch table or on the train, and as you would on these occasions, keep what you write within the interests of your correspondent. There is this difference, however, between a letter and a conversation if your conversation bores your friend, you can turn to another subject. Unless you tear up your letter and begin again, what you have written cannot be erased.

Above all, don't begin a letter to a friend to whom you have not written for some weeks, "I am ashamed of not having written you for so long, but many things have interfered. Johnnie has had the measles, and I have had to take care of him. Then Helen got into difficulties with her intermediate algebra, and I have spent long hours coaching her, trying to make it possible for her to catch up with her class. Life has been a veritable rat race."

Your letter begins with an apology and a tone of self-pity, neither of which is attractive. (Actually I feel that any apology for not writing over a period of time, unless you have neglected to answer a letter that clearly called for an answer, is out of place. Personal correspondence should be a spontaneous, natural expression of friendship, not a matter of obligation. When you apologize for not having written, you seem to imply that you write only because it is your obligation to do so.)

Instead of wording the opening of your letter as I have done above, you might say the same things like this: "You may have thought that I have completely forgotten you, but you have been very much in my mind through the weeks when I have not found the time to write you. While I was taking care of Johnnie during his illness, I remembered the long siege you had gone through with Bill's influenza and pneumonia and realized how lucky I was that Johnnie had only a fairly simple measles. During the long evenings in which I have been coaching Helen in her intermediate algebra (so that she could catch up with her class), I kept thinking of things I wanted to say to you, and remembered what fun we used to have doing our algebra together when we were kids. And one day when the rat race seemed to me to be so intense that I could scream, I suddenly heard you saying, as you did to me once, 'It's better to have too much to do than too little.' "

I hold no particular brief for this opening paragraph: it is neither William James nor Doctor Johnson, but it has one virtue. It puts your correspondent and his or her interests directly into the letter from the very start. It immediately transmits your personality, and your interest in the one to whom you are writing, rather than cataloguing a list of not particularly interesting facts. The circumstances which I have presupposed here would probably not be your circumstances, but the principle which I have suggested may be applied to almost any personal correspondence, and to many business letters as well.

Often you may impart the right tone to a letter by beginning at once with news which you know will be of special interest to the receiver. If (as an example) he has advanced ideas on education "What would you think, I wonder, of a teacher who disciplines her pupils by making them commit to memory the first two chapters of Genesis, as Johnnie's teacher did last week?" Or, "You once told me that I was a good housekeeper, and I think with longing of the neatness and orderliness of your own house. I'm glad that you cannot see me now as I sit down to write to you surrounded by the confusion which the painters have left behind them———"

In these approaches you would be bringing your correspondent into the orbit of your letter at once, and creating a warm and companionable atmosphere for the letter you are about to write; your personality and his would be coming into contact with each other.

Generally speaking "you" is a better word to open a letter than "I." It is not always possible to begin a letter thus without awkwardness, and an "I" is better than an awkward, stilted sentence. But often the question can be avoided by beginning the letter without them, and bringing the correspondent into the first sentence. "The day you were here you told me———," "When Jim phoned this morning and I told him I was going to write you he asked me to tell you———," etc.

Content of the Letter

What can one say about the contents of the letters you write? They will vary widely depending upon your relationship with your correspondent, the things you will want to say, and the reason for your writing. But here are some general suggestions·

As in the opening, keep the general tone of your letter within the sphere of your correspondent's interest. All letters, even love letters, have the primary function of being news. Therefore never completely avoid writing of yourself and of your affairs A friend is always interested in what is happening to you. This does not mean that you should fill your letter with endless details about *yourself*, about your daily life, with complaints and self-pity, or the reverse. If your friend is not a golfer, don't take two pages to tell him how you broke

80. On the other hand if both you and he are weekend painters, tell him of the problems involved in your latest landscape. And above all learn the habit of writing to him as you would talk. Don't try to be brilliant. You are not writing a book, and you will end up by being self-conscious or worse.

I cannot repeat too often the principle that the good letter conveys the personality of the one who writes it to the one who receives it. Someone once said, "A good letter writer crawls into the envelope with the letter itself."

Closing the Letter

As in choosing the opening, your choice of a proper close will depend upon your relationship to your correspondent.

Perhaps the least intimate of all closings for personal letters is "Sincerely yours." Perhaps a little less formal is "Sincerely." "As ever," "Ever sincerely," "Affectionately," "With love," or merely "Love" are all appropriate in personal correspondence. Use the one that best expresses your feeling for your correspondent. And if you are writing a love letter, of course say simply what is in your heart to say. But in any case write it clearly. I remember looking at the ending of a letter a young woman had written to a young man, which the latter had shown me in order to ask what I thought she had meant. The letter ended with "your" and a little squiggle that might or might not have been an "s" and the signature "Jane." The young man who was rapidly falling under the spell of the girl's charm could not be sure whether she had signed, "Yours, Jane," or "Your Jane." The "s" or its absence would make all the difference between a friendly closing and a declaration of love. I told him that I thought Jane had been very naughty (for I was quite sure she had been intentionally ambiguous) and that the thing for him to do was to write her, telling her exactly how he felt about her (if he was ready to do so) and asking her what her signature had meant.

"Duty" Letters

Generally speaking, letters written to a friend because you "owe" them are better left unwritten. There are some occasions, however, when if you do not write you will be guilty of bad manners.

If you have spent a night or a weekend in the house of a friend, write within a day or two after you have returned home to say thank you and tell what a good time you had. If you can mention some circumstance during your stay which you especially enjoyed, do so.

If you have received a gift by mail or congratulations on your engagement or a business promotion or your graduation from college, acknowledge it and say "thank you" by mail, though if it is from a close friend, a phone call will do almost as well.

Letters of condolence should be written only if they can be spontaneous and sincere. Indeed, unless you know the bereaved well and can write with a genuine sense of your own personal loss, your letter may be an intrusion at a time when intrusions are inexcusably rude. But there can be no argument about your obligation if you have received a letter of condolence from someone else You must acknowledge it and thank the sender. Your acknowledgment need not be long or intimate unless you wish to make it so, but to send no acknowledgment at all is to be rude. Such a letter even today is better written by hand than on a typewriter, but if it is to a close friend, it does not really matter greatly. A printed or engraved form ought never to be used unless the one who has died was so prominent that the flood of condolences would make their personal acknowledgment by letter an almost impossible task. In that case you can modify some of its coldness by writing a personal message on it for your closest friends.

When to Stay Away from the Mailbox

All of us at one time or another have written letters under the stress of anger or other powerful emotion, and later regretted having mailed them. To be sure there are times when anger is justified, and its expression a good thing. In any case putting your emotion into words on paper is often a good way to find release from it. Yet often when you have written it out, if you stop to reconsider the whole thing you often find that you have overstated the case or that the mere writing it out has made you feel quite differently.

So when you have written an angry letter, don't rush off to the nearest mailbox. Regardless of how sure you are at the moment that you have written well and said something that needed to be said, put the letter aside with the envelope unsealed until the next day. Then after you have had a good night's sleep, read it over again. Often you will find that you want to tear it up, and do so, glad that it has not been posted beyond recall.

Paper and Envelopes

When you are writing to your most intimate friends your
choice of paper and envelope is far less important than the tone and
content of your letter. No friend worth the name would be offended
by receiving from you a letter typed on the wood-pulp paper which
newspaper reporters use for copy, and mailed in a government
stamped envelope.

But when you correspond with someone whom you know only
slightly or not at all, when you issue, accept, or decline social invitations, formal or semiformal, or when you merely want to be sure
that you are following the conventional social usage in correspondence, you should take care to use stationery that has been selected
with the conventions in mind.

These are not complicated or difficult to observe. At their best
they are simply expressions of good taste.

The letter paper and envelopes used by a woman and by a man
may, but need not, differ. A woman may, if she likes, express her
feminine personality with dignity and taste by using paper, white,
or tinted in any delicate shade, that is slightly smaller and perhaps
thinner than that her husband uses, and an envelope of thin paper
to match, but lined with a darker, preferably unpatterned paper to
make it opaque. The paper will usually fold twice to fit into the
envelope, though for ordinary correspondence a paper that folds
only once is quite proper. She may have her name and address
printed or engraved at the center of the top of the page (the first
page only, if it is a two-fold paper) and on the envelope. Or she
may have a monogram printed or engraved on the paper, and her
address on the envelope.

Social custom dictates that if the name and address are printed
on the envelope they shall be on the back flap, but the post office, for
obvious reasons, prefers to have them in the upper left-hand corner
of the front. This is a case where I think that the rule of kindness to
the hard-working postal clerks should supersede that of formal etiquette. If you like you may simply write the return address in the
upper left-hand corner instead of having it printed or engraved there.

The envelope, which of course is made to fit the folded letter,
should be more nearly square in shape than that used for business
correspondence and should have a plain flap, either pointed or with
a straight elongated edge; but if the former, the point should not be

exaggerated nor yet too stubby, and if the latter, the edge should pass horizontally across the back of the envelope, and not ascend from bottom to top at an angle

Whether you have your stationery printed or engraved is a matter of choice. It is pleasant to have some engraved stationery for special use; but it is expensive and for ordinary use may seem somewhat ostentatious. Plain good printing is perfectly good form.

A man would not use stationery such as this, which suggests a feminine personality. If he wishes to seem very masculine he will choose a paper somewhat larger and probably heavier than that used by his wife, in plain white or possibly a light gray or cream tint. He will not have a monogram printed or engraved on it, but may use his initials, or his name and address. His envelopes will be of paper thick enough to make lining unnecessary, a lined envelope always suggests a letter from a woman. He may or may not have his address (with or without his name, if the address is sufficient) printed on the envelope—on the back flap if he wishes to follow the time-honored social convention, or in the upper left-hand corner of the front, or he may leave the envelope blank and write his name and address in ink, or type it, or even, without impropriety, use a sticker with his name and address printed on it.

This highly personalized, masculine stationery is not likely to be pleasing to a wife, though strangely enough if she uses her husband's stationery it will be less unsuitable than if he used her very feminine paper and envelopes.

But there is a very simple solution for the couple who do not wish to go to the bother of having two sets of stationery in the house, and that is the common supply, selected and imprinted with taste and dignity that makes it suitable for the use of both

A supply of paper and envelopes that will serve for all ordinary uses should include the following

Plain note paper, about 5" x 7¾", with one fold before use, and to be folded again before insertion in the envelope, on which to issue or answer invitations when formality is called for or for thank-you notes, or other short, slightly formal letters. If these are plain white, or light gray or cream, they will be suitable for husband or wife. They may be imprinted on the first page, if you like, with your address, but since you are both going to use them, do not make the matter complicated by using both your names. Simply leave the name off If you live in an apartment, be sure to include the apartment number If you live in a country house to which you have given a name, the name may be used.

A box of letter paper for longer personal letters, to be written by typewriter or in longhand For this you may select a good quality bond paper of the regular business paper size, 8½" x 11", though a slightly smaller sheet, say 7¼" x 10¾", is more intimate and equally appropriate for husband or wife. The address (with apartment number or with the name of your country place) and, if you like, your phone number (this is more commonly used on country than on city stationery) may be printed in the center or at the left of the top of the sheet.

To these two kinds of stationery for common use a wife may wish to add a more personal double card (fold at top) with her name engraved on the first page and the two inner pages left blank for short notes, invitations, acceptances, regrets, and thank you's—in short for the uses to which both she and her husband may put the small plain note paper I have mentioned earlier. But she does not really need them, for the note paper which her husband uses will serve the same purposes.

BUSINESS CORRESPONDENCE

Business Stationery

The standard size for a business letterhead is 8½" x 11". Some organizations also use a half-size sheet, 5½" x 8½" for short letters

Two sizes of envelopes are desirable, the small one into which an 8½" x 11" sheet will fit when folded once from top to bottom, and twice in the other direction, or the 5½" x 8½" sheet when folded in thirds, and a larger one (for letters of many pages, reports, etc.) into which an 8½" x 11" sheet will fit when folded twice from top to bottom. The letter paper and envelopes should be of good quality, and if (as is usually the case) imprinted with the name of the organization, the type or lettering selected should be conservative in size, not too large, and dignified rather than flamboyant in style.

The letterhead commonly consists of the name of the organization, the address (number, street, zone, city and state), and the telephone number. If the firm has a cable address it should be included. The business trademark may be used as an attractive part of the design, or omitted. Sometimes the nature of the business is stated, if the name does not make it clear, and the names of the officers may or may not be included.

In large organizations various officers may have special letter-heads, marked "Office of the President," "Office of the Treasurer," etc.

"Business English"

Business colleges still teach courses in "business English." I think that our business letters would improve in dignity and clarity if teachers and others firmly adopted the principle that English, good or bad, is English, whether it is used in business or personal letters or other forms of writing or speech. I believe that this is the actual trend in business schools today, and I am sure that it is in the best type of business correspondence.

There are, without question, some differences between the good personal letter and the good business letter. Yet in a sense a business letter is a personal letter too, for it is written from one person to another, even though it may be addressed to an impersonal organization. The best and most effective business letters, like the best personal letters, reveal the warmth of a human personality and the keenness of a good mind, and are written with an appreciation of our language when it is properly and skillfully used.

In addition, an important business letter has a specific reason for being written. You may be pointing out an error in the quoted terms of a sale, you may be suggesting the alteration of a clause in a contract, whatever it is, if what you have to say is not clearly stated, if there is the slightest possibility that your correspondent can misunderstand the various points which you wish to make, then your letter is a failure.

The good business letter will of course not contain the intimacy of a letter to a close friend. But it should carry personality and dignity. The language, however, should be informal and completely devoid of the old-fashioned awkward clichés that at one time were thought to be the hallmark of business dignity. "Yours of the 13th inst. received, and in reply would say," "We have your esteemed favor of the 30th, ult.," "This is to acknowledge receipt of your valued order"—all such expressions have been wisely abandoned by progressive business houses. No longer do they "beg to announce," they simply "announce." Such teeth-grating mouthfuls as "Replying to your letter of the 5th inst. wish to say we have noted its contents" have become "Thank you for your letter of the fifth." That the contents have been noted may be assumed by the fact that the letter is being answered.

Let your English be simple, clear, and according to good usage, your use of words economical, keep your letter to the subject about which you are writing, forget that anyone ever propounded the idea that business English should be different from any other English. Remember too that you are writing to a human being, and that on the character of what you write may depend a successful and long-continuing association. If you follow these rules you will write business letters that will be read with pleasure and result in profit.

The Form of the Business Letter

The date on which the letter is written is typed under the letterhead, and customarily at the extreme right, so that the end of the date is approximately at the beginning of the right-hand margin. It is usually written in one line, though it may be written with the month and date of the month on one line, and the year underneath it, or even with the month, the date of the month, and the year each on a separate line. It also may be placed in the center of the page directly under the letterhead.

The name and address of the person or organization to whom the letter is written are typed at the extreme left, so that the beginning of the first line (or all lines if it is typed in block style) is flush with the left-hand margin, and a little below the line on which the date is written at the right.

This may be written in block style, thus:

> Mr. John Henry Clay
> 2239 Lexington Avenue
> Washita, Virginia

or with the second and third lines indented, thus:

> Mr. John Henry Clay
> 2239 Lexington Avenue
> Washita, Virginia

The block style is preferred by most business houses, and in my opinion looks better.

Also you may put commas after the first and second line, and a period after the third, but it is more usual not to punctuate, save with a comma between the name of the city and state, written on the same line.

The name and address may be put at the end of the letter, to the left, below the line of the signature, if you wish to make the letter seem slightly less forbidding, though in strict usage this practice is reserved for letters written to government officials.

If the letter is written to any member of the staff of another business, the name of his firm is customarily inserted between his name and the address. If he is an officer in the firm, his title follows, never precedes, his name.

If you know the last name of the man to whom you are writing, but not his first name, you may properly include only the name of his firm in the interior name and address, and under it, with space intervening, and often in the middle of the page, write "Attention of Mr. Brown."

The old-fashioned "Messrs." is seldom used today, but if you do use it, use it properly. It is never used before an impersonal company name such as "The Anaconda Company," but only in addressing professional partnerships You may, if you like, write "Messrs. Brown and Robertson," especially if they constitute a professional partnership, but you will possibly be charged with affectation. "Brown and Robertson" is the simpler and better form.

If you are writing to a close friend, even though it is on a business matter and the letter dictated and typed on your business letterhead, it is considered better form to omit opening it with his name and address, as it would be if you were writing him on your personal stationery.

The Salutation

If you are writing to an individual whose name you have included in the address, or in the line "Attention of ———," the proper beginning for your letter is "Dear Mr. (or Mrs.) Jones.". The slightly more formal "My dear" may be used in business letters as it is in personal communications, but is less usual now than it once was, and denotes an especial desire for formality rather than, as in a personal letter, an indication that you are not assuming a close personal relationship. If you are writing to a business organization rather than to an individual in the organization, your letter will begin

"Gentlemen·" or "Dear Sirs:", preferably the former. If you are writing to an officer of the company, but do not know his name, the interior name and address should include his title, and the letter should begin "Dear Sir " or "Dear Madam.".

If you are writing to a woman whose name you know, the salutation is either "Dear Mrs. (or Miss) Heywood." or "Dear Madam ", never "Dear Miss ". If you are addressing a women's organization and not an individual in that organization the salutation is awkward, but unavoidable. It is either "Mesdames " or "Ladies ".

Forms for salutations in letters to various dignitaries will be found in Chapter 26.

The Body of the Letter

The letter itself may be single-spaced or double-spaced, depending upon its length. Today most letters are customarily double-spaced and the beginning of each paragraph indented, but very long letters may be single-spaced, the paragraphs starting flush with the left-hand margin, and a blank space left between every two paragraphs. The side and bottom margins should be approximately an inch wide; avoid a crowded appearance.

If the letter is more than a page in length the second and succeeding pages are written on plain paper without letterhead, or with an abbreviated letterhead. The name or initials of the person to whom the letter is written should appear at the top left of every succeeding page, the number of the page at the top center, and the date at the top right. Or the positions may be varied. The page number, initials, and date may be typed together at the top left, or the page number at the top left, and the initials or name of the addressee and the date at the top right

The Close and Signature

Avoid ending your business letters with platitudes such as "Trusting to hear from you soon," or "Assuring you of our appreciation of your valued business." When you have said what you have to say, stop. You have your choice of several phrases for the actual close. If you have especial reason to honor the one to whom you have written or wish to soften slightly the critical tone of a letter, you may end it with "Respectfully yours." The least personal of all endings are "Yours truly," "Yours very truly," and "Very truly yours." No one today uses them unless he especially wishes to be extremely formal and impersonal. Because they are warmer and more familiar, usually one of these closings is used "Sincerely yours," "Faithfully yours," "Ever sincerely," "Ever faithfully," "Cordially yours," "Cordially," or even "Ever yours."

The firm name is typed below this complimentary line, two or three spaces are left blank for the written signature, the individual's name is then typed, and below that the name of the department of which he is a part, or his title if he is an officer.

IX

SHOWING

YOUR COLORS

33

Patriotism, the Flag, and the National Anthem

N O BOOK OF ETIQUETTE WOULD BE COMPLETE WITHOUT
a discussion of patriotism and its most familiar symbols
—the flag and the national anthem. Each of these symbols requires
us to behave towards them in a specified manner. Every American
should be familiar with these acts of respect because, while they may
superficially signify that we *know* how to behave, they also mark our
way of showing respect for our country and the ideals for which free
men have lived and worked and died for generations.

During the past forty or more years of world tension and trouble,
we have often heard the words: "One hundred per cent American,"
and "The American Way of Life." These expressions are so general
and vague that they probably mean many different things to different people. I have found that with some people they are used
with a considerable sense of smugness and superiority coupled with
an intolerance of people of other nations. All of us, and these people
in particular, should remember that no amount of flag-waving,

pledging allegiance, or fervent singing of the national anthem is evidence that we are patriotic in the real sense of the word.

We should also remember that the converse is equally true. If you accuse someone of being unpatriotic simply because he does not indulge frequently in the outward gestures of patriotism, you may very well be accusing him quite unfairly. Outward behavior, while important, is not the real measure of a man's patriotism.

One of the wisest of the great eighteenth century libertarians was Richard Price, a British Unitarian minister whose pamphlets on religious, social, political, and economic matters deeply influenced the thought of his time. In 1789 he delivered an address which states beautifully, I think, certain principles which all twentieth century Americans, indeed the people of all countries, would do well to keep in mind. He said:

In pursuing particularly the interest of our country we ought to carry our views beyond it. We should love it ardently, but not exclusively. We ought to seek its good by all the means that our different circumstances and abilities will allow, but at the same time we ought to consider ourselves as citizens of the world, and take care to maintain a just regard to the rights of other countries. . . .

You love your country and desire its happiness, and without doubt you have the greatest reason for loving it. . . . Do you practise virtue yourselves and study to promote it in others? Do you obey the laws of your country and aim at doing your part towards maintaining and perpetuating its privileges? Do you always give your vote on the side of public liberty, and are you ready to pour out your blood in its defence? Do you look up to God for the continuance of his favor to your country, and pray for its prosperity, preserving at the same time a strict regard to the rights of other countries, and always considering yourselves more as citizens of the world than as members of any particular community? If this is your temper and conduct you are blessings to your country, and were all like you, this world would soon be heaven.

True patriotism springs from a belief in the dignity of the individual, freedom and equality not only for Americans but for all people on earth, universal brotherhood and good will, and a constant and earnest striving toward the principles and ideals on which this country was founded. When you salute the flag of the United States of America, or stand at attention and sing our national anthem, it is these ideals to which you are subscribing. Otherwise, your claim to patriotism and all your demonstrations of it are empty and meaningless.

THE FLAG

The Flag in a Parade

If you are a male civilian watching a parade in which the American flag is carried, bare your head as it approaches and stand at attention, holding your hat in your right hand over your heart until the flag has passed several paces beyond where you are standing. If you are a member of the Armed Forces and in uniform, stand at attention, salute the flag as it approaches, and hold the salute until the flag has passed. A woman should also stand at attention when the flag passes and, to be strictly correct, should place her right hand over her heart If there are several sections to the parade, each with a flag, this same gesture of respect should be repeated as each passes.

In the United States, if you witness a parade in which the flags of other nations appear, you should merely stand in a respectful position of attention while they pass. There is no need to salute if you are in uniform When abroad, you should respect your own country's flag or that of another nation as you would at home.

If you are involved in any parade or procession in which the flag is displayed, remember these rules

The flag must be at the top of a staff and allowed to wave freely whether carried by someone marching or as part of a float. It should not be carried horizontally or draped over the back of an automobile.

Flags carried in a funeral procession are never flown at half-mast. If the procession is in honor of someone for whom the President has proclaimed a national day of mourning, a crepe bow, with or without streamers, may be fastened to the staff. But this must not be done for private funerals.

If regimental flags, lodge flags, state flags, flags of any other country, or any other banners or insignia are also carried in a procession, the flag of the United States must be flown above them, precede them, or be at their right.

Displaying a Stationary Flag

A flag displayed *on a flagstaff* at home, in a school yard, before a business office, or anywhere else, should be hung at the top of the staff with the field of stars at the top and next to the staff.

Any other flag flown from the same staff must be below. Nothing should ever be placed above the flag, except an American Eagle which may decorate the top of the staff. (There is one exception to this rule. On ships, the flag of the United States is flown from the aft deck and the signal and officers' flags are flown from the mast, which is considerably higher.)

If flags of other nations are displayed along with that of the United States, they should be flown on separate staffs. They should be the same size as our flag and flown at the same height. In time of peace, if there are several flags of other countries to be displayed, the flag of the United States is given central position. In time of war, no other flag, not even that of an ally, is flown to our own flag's right

Flying the Flag

The flag may be raised at sunrise or later and must always be lowered at sunset, except that when it rains it must be lowered at once In raising or lowering the flag, care must be taken to see that it never touches the ground. If other flags are being flown with it, the United States flag is the first to be raised and the last to be lowered, except when it is lowered because of rain. In this case, the United States flag is the first lowered.

The flag is never flown upside down except as a distress signal.

A flag is flown at half-staff only by Federal, State, or City order It is never so flown to indicate the death of a member of the family unless there is an official proclamation of mourning. When flying the flag at half-mast, it should first be raised to the top of the staff, then lowered to a point midway on the staff. When taken down, it should first be raised to the top of the staff and then lowered.

On Memorial Day, the flag is ordinarily flown at half-mast from sunrise until noon, then hoisted to the top of the staff.

When the flag is displayed on a staff on a speaker's platform, it is placed at the speaker's right, the place of honor.

In a church, the flag displayed on a staff should be at the right of the congregation unless it is on the platform. Then it should be on the clergyman's right, the congregation's left.

The flag must never be draped over a table, desk, or platform and care should always be taken to see that it does not touch the floor.

Displaying the Flag

When displayed against a wall, the flag must be flat with the field of stars (the Union) uppermost and to the flag's right

If hung from a window or against the outside of a house, the field of stars should be to the left of the observer from the street. Displayed on the wall of a speaker's platform, the flag should be behind and above the speaker with the field of stars to the flag's right, the left of the audience Above a street, the flag should hang vertically with the field of stars to the north on an east-west street and to the east on a north-south street.

A Few Don't's

The flag must never be used as a decoration on paper napkins, clothing, draperies, tablecloths, boxes, or on personal or business stationery It must never be used in advertising save by the Federal Government. No advertising may be placed on the staff from which the flag is flown nor advertising pennants flown from it while the flag is displayed. No lettering of any kind may ever be placed on the flag or on pictorial reproductions of it.

Do not use the flag to veil a monument or statue, even if it is a patriotic one, though it may be used in unveiling ceremonies.

There is one exception to the rule against using the flag as a draping. This is in the case of a funeral for a member of the Armed Forces, cabinet officers of the Federal and State governments, or any others for whom the President has proclaimed national mourning. In this case the flag may be used to cover the casket, but it is removed before the casket is lowered into the ground, with care taken so that the flag itself does not touch the ground.

Retiring the Flag

When a flag has become so tattered that it is no longer serviceable, it may be retired by burning. It should never be cut up. The fabric may not be used for other purposes, nor thrown away heedlessly It is still permissible and perfectly proper to fly a flag that predates the entrance of our two most recently admitted states, Alaska and Hawaii. The forty-eight star flag or even a flag with fewer stars may be flown as long as it is in proper condition.

One Last Word

Always respect the flag of the United States. Do not handle it carelessly or use it frivolously To do so is an offense to the good taste of everyone and a disservice to your country. Always raise the flag briskly and lower it slowly and in a respectful manner. Treat the flag at all times with respect and remember that it is a symbol of freedom for men all over the world.

THE NATIONAL ANTHEM

⟨✦⟩ The national anthem, like our flag, calls for specific marks of respect. In a public place, men, women, and children rise and stand at attention when it is played. If outdoors, men should remove their hats and place them over their hearts. A woman should stand at attention and, if she wishes to be completely correct, place her right hand over her heart If the occasion is one at which the words may be sung, everyone should sing them The *Star-Spangled Banner* has a melody that many people find difficult to sing. Try to manage as best you can. Your enthusiasm for singing your national anthem will make up for any lack of musical ability. Usually only the first and last verses are sung, but we should all know the words of the song:

Oh, say can you see by the dawn's early light
    What so proudly we hailed at the twilight's last gleaming?
Whose broad stripes and bright stars, thro' the perilous fight,
    O'er the ramparts we watched were so gallantly streaming?
And the rockets' red glare, the bombs bursting in air,
    Gave proof through the night that our flag was still there.
Oh, say does that star-spangled banner yet wave
    O'er the land of the free and the home of the brave?

On the shore, dimly seen through the mists of the deep,
    Where the foe's haughty host in dread silence reposes,
What is that which the breeze, o'er the towering steep,
    As it fitfully blows, now conceals, now discloses?
Now it catches the gleam of the morning's first beam, ·
    In full glory reflected now shines on the stream.
'Tis the star-spangled banner! O long may it wave
    O'er the land of the free and the home of the brave!

And where is that band who so vauntingly swore
    That the havoc of war and the battle's confusion,
A home and a country should leave us no more!
    Their blood has washed out their foul footsteps' pollution.
No refuge could save the hireling and slave

From the terror of flight, or the gloom of the grave
And the star-spangled banner in triumph doth wave
    O'er the land of the free and the home of the brave!

Oh! Thus be it ever when freemen shall stand
    Between their loved homes and the war's desolation!
Blest with victory and peace, may the heav'n rescued land
    Praise the Power that hath made and preserved us a nation.
Then conquer we must, when our cause it is just,
    And this be our motto "In God is our trust."
And the star-spangled banner in triumph shall wave
    O'er the land of the free and the home of the brave.

If you enter a meeting or gathering of any kind while the national anthem is being played, stop and stand at attention until it has finished and then continue to your seat

It is not considered a mark of disrespect to remain seated in a private home while the national anthem is played over radio or television If the music is "live," however, you are expected to rise when the national anthem is begun.

The same marks of respect should be shown by all Americans for the national anthems of other countries, whether played here or abroad.

There is one other piece of music which calls for a special word and that is *Hail to the Chief*. Every public appearance of the President of the United States is marked by playing it before the playing of the national anthem. At the first notes of *Hail to the Chief* everyone in the group rises and stands at attention.

In all of the preceding circumstances you are paying tribute not to a piece of cloth which is the flag, not to a song nor even to a man as a personality, but to your country and the ideals for which it stands.

BOOKLIST

THIS is not a bibliography of etiquette books, but rather a list of publications that have been found helpful in the writing of *Eleanor Roosevelt's Book of Common Sense Etiquette,* and which may be of interest to its readers.

COMMUNICATION

The Art of Making Sense, by Lionel Ruby. New York: J. B. Lippincott Co., 1954.

The Art of Plain Talk, by Rudolf Flesch. New York: Harper & Bros., 1946.

The Elements of Style, by William Strunk, Jr., with revisions and introduction and a New Chapter on Writing by E. B. White. New York: The Macmillan Company, 1959.

How to Build a Better Vocabulary, by Maxwell Nurnberg and Morris Rosenblum. New York: Prentice-Hall, 1945. Also Popular Library, 1961.

The Letters of Robert Browning and Elizabeth Barrett. 2 vols. New York Harper & Bros., 1898.

The Letters of William James, ed. by his son Henry James. Boston: Atlantic Monthly Press, 1920.

The Secretary's Handbook, 8th ed , by Augusta Taintor and Kate M. Monro. New York. The Macmillan Company, 1958.

The Story of Language, by Mario Pei. New York. J. B. Lippincott Co., 1949. Also Mentor Books, 1960.

A Treasury of the World's Great Letters, selected and edited by M. Lincoln Schuster. New York: Simon and Schuster, 1940. Paper-covered edition, 1960.

Watch Your Language, by Theodore M. Bernstein. Great Neck: The Channel Press, 1958.

COMPANY MANNERS [Office Etiquette]

News Front, July, 1959.

Profits from Courtesy, by Mary Alden Hopkins. Garden City: Doubleday-Doran, 1937.

Several interoffice publications of the New York Telephone Co., Trans-World Airlines, and United Airlines.

DEBUTS

The Private World of High Society, by Lucy Kavaler. New York: David McKay Co., 1960.

THE HANDICAPPED

"Concept of Acceptance in Physical Rehabilitation," by Morris Grayson, M.D. *Journal of the American Medical Association,* March 24, 1951.

"The Emotional, Social, and Occupational Aspects of Disablement," by E. D. Witkower. Address at the Third Annual Meeting of the Canadian Association of Physical Medicine and Rehabilitation, Montreal, June 25, 1955.

"Psychiatric Aspects of Rehabilitation of the Physically Handicapped," by Camille K. Cayley, M.D. *American Journal of Psychotherapy,* July, 1954.

ALCOHOLISM

"The Alcoholic, His Family, and His Nurse," by Grace M. Colder. *Nursing Outlook*, October, 1955. Reprinted and distributed by Publications Division, The Yale Center for Alcoholic Studies, New Haven, Conn.

"The Alcoholic Husband." Alcoholics Anonymous Publishing Co.

"Do's and Dont's for the Wives of Alcoholics." National Council on Alcoholism.

"The Role of the Nurse in the Treatment of Alcoholism," *Connecticut Review on Alcoholism*, March, 1954. Reprinted and distributed by The Yale Center for Alcoholic Studies, New Haven, Conn.

"Social Workers Can Help Alcoholics." National Council on Alcoholism.

"Thirteen Steps to Alcoholism." National Council on Alcoholism.

BLINDNESS

The Adjustment of the Blind, by Hector Chevigny and Sydell Braverman. New Haven Yale University Press, 1950.

Blindness—Ability, Not Disability, by Maxine Wood. The Lighthouse of the New York Association for the Blind, 1960.

Evaluation of Adjustment to Blindness, by Edward A. Fitting. American Foundation for the Blind, 1954.

Hobbies of Blind Adults, by Charles G. Ritter. American Foundation for the Blind, 1960.

Methods of Communication with Deaf-Blind People, rev. ed., by Annette B. Dinsmore. American Foundation for the Blind, 1954.

Training and Employment of Blind-Deaf Adults, report of a workshop held in New York, February, 1956. American Foundation for the Blind, 1956.

When You Meet a Blind Person. American Foundation for the Blind.

DEAFNESS

Ears and the Man, by Annetta W. Peck, Estelle E. Samuelson, and Ann Lehman. F. A. Davis Co., 1926.

Hearing Loss a Community Loss. The American Hearing Society, 1958.

Hearing Loss and the Family Doctor, by Aram Glorig, M.D. Zenith Radio Corporation.

How to Help the Hard of Hearing in Your Classroom. New York League for the Hard of Hearing.

KEEP TO THE RIGHT [The Etiquette of Driving]

Car Driving as an Art, by S. C. H. David. London · Iliffe and Sons, Ltd , 1957.

Driving Tips from the Pros (pamphlet). Chicago. National Safety Council.

Touring with Touser (pamphlet). New York: Gaines Dog Research Center.

MANNERS OF OTHER DAYS

The American Woman's Home, a Guide to the Formation and Maintenance of Economical and Christian Homes, by Catherine E. Beecher and Harriet Beecher Stowe. New York J. B. Ford and Co., 1869.

Essays, First and Second Series, by Ralph Waldo Emerson. New York: E. P. Dutton, 1910.

Learning How to Behave: A Historical Study of American Etiquette Books, by Arthur M. Schlesinger. New York: The Macmillan Company, 1947.

PATRIOTISM

"A Discourse on Love of Your Country," by Richard Price. In *Tracts and Pamphlets,* ed by A. C. Ward. London · Oxford University Press, 1927

THIRTEEN TO NINETEEN [Teenage Behavior]

The Art of Dating, by Evelyn Millis Duvall and Joy D Johnson. New York: Permabooks, 1960.

The Cheshire Academy Manual. Cheshire Academy, Cheshire, Conn.

The Correct Thing, a Guide Book of Etiquette for Young Men, by William O. Stevens. New York: Dodd, Mead and Co., 1939.

Premarital Dating Behavior, by Winston Ehrmann. New York. Bantam Books, 1960.

Talks to Teachers on Psychology, and to Students on Some of Life's Ideals, by William James. New York. Henry Holt and Co , 1916.

Your Adolescent at Home and in School, by Lawrence K. Frank and Mary Frank. New York The Viking Press, 1956.

Your Happiest Years, by Dick Clark. New York, Cardinal Editions, 1959.

V. I P.'s [Protocol]

Etiquette and Protocol, a Handbook of Conduct in American and International Circles, by I. Monte Radlovic. New York. Harcourt, Brace and Co , 1956.

WELCOMING THE NEW ARRIVAL [Christenings]

A Handbook of the Catholic Faith, ed. by the Rev. John Greenwood. Garden City. Doubleday, 1961.

Judaism, a Historical Presentation, by Isidore Epstein. Baltimore. Penguin Books, 1961.

The Origins of Christian Supernaturalism, by Shirley Jackson Case. Chicago University of Chicago Press, 1946

The Oxford Dictionary of the Christian Church. New York. Oxford University Press, 1957.

The Protestant Era, by Paul Tillich. Chicago. University of Chicago Press, 1957.

This Is My God, by Herman Wouk. Garden City: Doubleday, 1961.

WHEN IN ROME DO AS ROME DOES [Travel Abroad]

American into English, by G. V. Carey. London William Heinemann, Ltd., 1953

Newman's Travel Guide. New York Harper & Bros , 1959.

The Silent Language, by Edward T. Hall. New York Doubleday, 1959.

Some of the stories of my experiences in the East have been previously told in *India and the Awakening East.* New York Harper & Bros., 1953.

INDEX

INDEX

CPSIA information can be obtained at www.ICGtesting.com
Printed in the USA
LVOW100312260313

326035LV00006B/127/P